# The Unified
# Software Development
# Process

# The Addison-Wesley Object Technology Series

Grady Booch, Ivar Jacobson, and James Rumbaugh, Series Editors

For more information check out the series web site [http://www.awl.com /cseng/otseries/] as well as the pages on each book [http://www.awl.com/cseng/I-S-B-N/] (I-S-B-N represents the actual ISBN, including dashes).

David Bellin and Susan Suchman Simone, *The CRC Card Book*
ISBN 0-201-89535-8

Grady Booch, *Object Solutions: Managing the Object-Oriented Project*
ISBN 0-8053-0594-7

Grady Booch, *Object-Oriented Analysis and Design with Applications, Second Edition*
ISBN 0-8053-5340-2

Grady Booch, James Rumbaugh, and Ivar Jacobson, *The Unified Modeling Language User Guide*
ISBN 0-201-57168-4

Don Box, *Essential COM*
ISBN 0-201-63446-5

Don Box, Keith Brown, Tim Ewald, and Chris Sells, *Effective COM: 50 Ways to Improve Your COM and MTS-based Applications*
ISBN 0-201-37968-6

Alistair Cockburn, *Surviving Object-Oriented Projects: A Manager's Guide*
ISBN 0-201-49834-0

Dave Collins, *Designing Object-Oriented User Interfaces*
ISBN 0-8053-5350-X

Bruce Powel Douglass, *Doing Hard Time: Designing and Implementing Embedded Systems with UML*
ISBN 0-201-49837-5

Bruce Powel Douglass, *Real-Time UML: Developing Efficient Objects for Embedded Systems*
ISBN 0-201-32579-9

Desmond F. D'Souza and Alan Cameron Wills, *Objects, Components, and Frameworks with UML: The Catalysis Approach*
ISBN 0-201-31012-0

Martin Fowler, *Analysis Patterns: Reusable Object Models*
ISBN 0-201-89542-0

Martin Fowler with Kendall Scott, *UML Distilled: Applying the Standard Object Modeling Language*
ISBN 0-201-32563-2

Peter Heinckiens, *Building Scalable Database Applications: Object-Oriented Design, Architectures, and Implementations*
ISBN 0-201-31013-9

Ivar Jacobson, Grady Booch, and James Rumbaugh, *The Unified Software Development Process*
ISBN 0-201-57169-2

Ivar Jacobson, Magnus Christerson, Patrik Jonsson, and Gunnar Overgaard, *Object-Oriented Software Engineering: A Use Case Driven Approach*
ISBN 0-201-54435-0

Ivar Jacobson, Maria Ericsson, and Agneta Jacobson, *The Object Advantage: Business Process Reengineering with Object Technology*
ISBN 0-201-42289-1

Ivar Jacobson, Martin Griss, and Patrik Jonsson, *Software Reuse: Architecture, Process and Organization for Business Success*
ISBN 0-201-92476-5

David Jordan, *C++ Object Databases: Programming with the ODMG Standard*
ISBN 0-201-63488-0

Philippe Kruchten, *The Rational Unified Process: An Introduction*
ISBN 0-201-60459-0

Wilf LaLonde, *Discovering Smalltalk*
ISBN 0-8053-2720-7

Lockheed Martin Advanced Concepts Center and Rational Software Corporation, *Succeeding with the Booch and OMT Methods: A Practical Approach*
ISBN 0-8053-2279-5

Thomas Mowbray and William Ruh, *Inside CORBA: Distributed Object Standards and Applications*
ISBN 0-201-89540-4

Ira Pohl, *Object-Oriented Programming Using C++, Second Edition*
ISBN 0-201-89550-1

Rob Pooley and Perdita Stevens, *Using UML: Software Engineering with Objects and Components*
ISBN 0-201-36067-5

Terry Quatrani, *Visual Modeling with Rational Rose and UML*
ISBN 0-201-31016-3

Brent E. Rector and Chris Sells, *ATL Internals*
ISBN 0-201-69589-8

Doug Rosenberg with Kendall Scott, *Use Case Driven Object Modeling with UML: A Practical Approach*
ISBN 0-201-43289-7

Walker Royce, *Software Project Management: A Unified Framework*
ISBN 0-201-30958-0

William Ruh, Thomas Herron, and Paul Klinker, *IIOP Complete: Middleware Interoperability and Distributed Object Standards*
ISBN 0-201-37925-2

James Rumbaugh, Ivar Jacobson, and Grady Booch, *The Unified Modeling Language Reference Manual*
ISBN 0-201-30998-X

Geri Schneider and Jason P. Winters, *Applying Use Cases: A Practical Guide*
ISBN 0-201-30981-5

Yen-Ping Shan and Ralph H. Earle, *Enterprise Computing with Objects: From Client/Server Environments to the Internet*
ISBN 0-201-32566-7

David N. Smith, *IBM Smalltalk: The Language*
ISBN 0-8053-0908-X

Daniel Tkach, Walter Fang, and Andrew So, *Visual Modeling Technique: Object Technology Using Visual Programming*
ISBN 0-8053-2574-3

Daniel Tkach and Richard Puttick, *Object Technology in Application Development, Second Edition*
ISBN 0-201-49833-2

Jos Warmer and Anneke Kleppe, *The Object Constraint Language: Precise Modeling with UML*
ISBN 0-201-37940-6

# The Unified Software Development Process

Ivar Jacobson
Grady Booch
James Rumbaugh

*Rational Software Corporation*

**ADDISON–WESLEY**

**An Imprint of Addison Wesley Longman, Inc.**

Reading, Massachusetts • Harlow, England • Menlo Park, California
Berkeley, California • Don Mills, Ontario • Sydney
Bonn • Amsterdam • Tokyo • Mexico City

Many of the designations used by manufacturers and sellers to distinguish their products are claimed as trademarks. Where those designations appear in this book, and Addison Wesley Longman, Inc. was aware of a trademark claim, the designations have been printed in initial capital letters or in all capitals.

The authors and publisher have taken care in the preparation of this book, but make no expressed or implied warranty of any kind and assume no responsibility for errors or omissions. No liability is assumed for incidental or consequential damages in connection with or arising out of the use of the information or programs contained herein.

The publisher offers discounts on this book when ordered in quantity for special sales. For more information, please contact:

AWL Direct Sales
Addison Wesley Longman, Inc.
One Jacob Way
Reading, Massachusetts 01867
(781) 944-3700
Visit AW on the Web: www.awl.com/cseng/

*Library of Congress Cataloging-in-Publication Data*

Jacobson, Ivar.
    The unified software development process / Ivar Jacobson, Grady
Booch, James Rumbaugh.
        p.   cm.
    Includes bibliographical references (p.    ) and index.
    ISBN 0-201-57169-2
    1. Computer software—Development.  2. UML (Computer science)
I. Booch, Grady.  II. Rumbaugh, James.  III. Title.
QA76.76.D47J35    1998
005.1—dc21                                              98–37256
                                                           CIP

Executive Editor: J. Carter Shanklin          Project Editor: Krysia Bebick
Production Manager: John Fuller               Production Coordinator: Jacquelyn Young
Cover Designer: Simone R. Payment             Compositor: Stratford Publishing Services

ISBN 0-201-57169-2
Text printed on recycled paper
1 2 3 4 5 6 7 8 9 10—MA—0302010099
First printing, January 1999

# Contents

# Preface

There is a belief held by some that professional enterprises should be organized around the skills of highly trained individuals. They know the work to be done and just do it! They hardly need guidance in policy and procedure from the organization for which they work.

This belief is mistaken in most cases, and badly mistaken in the case of software development. Certainly, software developers are highly trained, but the profession is still young. Consequently, developers need organizational guidance, which, in this book, we refer to as the "software development process." Moreover, because the process we set forth in this book represents the bringing together of previously separate methodologies, we feel justified in calling it the "Unified Process." It not only unifies the work of the three authors but incorporates the numerous contributions of other individuals and companies that contributed to the UML, as well as a significant number of key contributors at Rational Software Corporation. It draws significantly from the on-the-spot experience of hundreds of user organizations working with early versions of the process at customer sites.

A symphony orchestra conductor, for example, does little more during a performance than tell the players when to start and help them stay together. He or she can do so little because the conductor has guided the orchestra during rehearsals and preparation of the score, and because each musician is highly skilled on his own instrument and actually plays it independently of the other orchestra members. More importantly for our purpose, each musician follows a "process" laid out long ago by the composer. It is the musical score that provides the bulk of the "policy and procedure" that guides the performance. In contrast, software developers do not play independently. They interact with each other and the users. They have no score to follow—until they have a *process.*

The need for process promises to become more critical, particularly in companies or organizations in which the software systems are "mission-critical," such as financial, air traffic control, defense, and telecommunications systems. By this we mean that the successful conduct of the business or execution of the public mission depends upon the software that supports it. These software systems are becoming more complex, their time to market needs to shrink, and their development, in turn, is becoming more difficult. For reasons such as these, the software industry needs a process to guide developers, just as an orchestra needs a composer's score to guide a performance.

## What Is a Software Development Process?

A process defines *who* is doing *what when* and *how* to reach a certain goal. In software engineering the goal is to build a software product or to enhance an existing one. An effective process provides guidelines for the efficient development of quality software. It captures and presents the best practices that the current state of the art permits. In consequence, it reduces risk and increases predictability. The overall effect is to promote a common vision and culture.

We need such a process to serve as a guide for all the participants—customers, users, developers, and executive managers. Any old process will not do; we need one that will be the *best* process the industry is capable of putting together at this point in its history. Finally, we need a process that will be widely available so that all the stakeholders can understand its role in the development under consideration.

A software development process should also be capable of evolving over many years. During this evolution it should limit its reach at any given point in time to the realities that technologies, tools, people, and organizational patterns permit.

- *Technologies.* Process must be built on technologies—programming languages, operating systems, computer systems, network capabilities, development environments, and so on—that are usable at the time the process is to be used. For example, twenty years ago visual modeling was not really mainstream. It was too expensive. At that time, a process builder almost had to assume that hand-drawn diagrams would be used. That assumption greatly limited the degree to which a process originator could build modeling into the process.

- *Tools.* Process and tools must develop in parallel. Tools are integral to process. To put it another way, a widely used process can support the investment that creates the tools that support it.

- *People.* A process builder must limit the skill set needed to operate the process to the skills that current developers possess or target ones that developers can be quickly trained to use. In many areas it is now possible to embed techniques that once required extensive skill, such as checking model drawings for consistency, in computer-based tools.

- *Organizational patterns.* While software developers may not be as independently expert as symphony musicians, they are far from the automaton workers on whom Frederick W. Taylor based "scientific management" one hundred years ago. The process builder has to adapt the process to today's realities—the facts of virtual organization; working at a distance through high-speed lines; the mix of partial owners (in small start-ups), salaried employees, contract workers, and outsourcing subcontractors; and the continuing shortage of software developers.

Process engineers need to balance these four sets of circumstances. Moreover, the balance must exist not just now but into the future. The process builder must design the process so it can evolve, just as a software developer tries to develop a system that not only works this year but evolves successfully for years to come. A process needs to mature for several years before it achieves the level of stability and maturity that will enable it to stand up to the rigors of commercial product development while holding the risk of its use to a reasonable level. Developing a new product is risky enough by itself without adding to it the risk of a process insufficiently tested by actual experience. Under these circumstances, a process can be stable. Without this balance of technologies, tools, people, and organization, using the process would be quite risky.

## Goals of the Book

This book presents the software process that was constantly on our minds when we developed the Unified Modeling Language. While UML gives us a standard way to visualize, specify, construct, document, and communicate the artifacts of a software-intensive system, we of course recognize that such a language must be used within the context of an end-to-end software process. UML is a means, not an end. The ultimate end is a robust, resilient, scaleable software application. It takes both a process and a language to get there, and illustrating the process portion is the goal of this book. While we provide a brief appendix on the UML, it is not intended to be comprehensive or detailed. For a detailed UML tutorial refer to *The Unified Modeling Language User Guide* [11]. For a comprehensive UML reference refer to *The Unified Modeling Language Reference Manual* [12].

## Audience

The Unified Software Development Process can be used by anyone involved in the development of software. It is primarily addressed to members of the development team who deal with the life-cycle activities requirements, analysis, design, implementation, and testing—that is, in work that results in UML models. Thus, for instance, this book is relevant to analysts and end users (who specify the required structure and behavior of a system), application developers (who design systems that satisfy those requirements), programmers (who turn those designs into executable code), testers (who verify and validate the system's structure and behavior), component developers (who create and catalogue components), and project and product managers.

This book assumes a basic grasp of object-oriented concepts. Experience in software development and in an object-oriented programming language is also helpful, but not required.

## Approach of the Book

We give the most space in this book to those activities—requirements, analysis, and design—on which UML places primary emphasis. It is in these fields of emphasis that the process develops the *architecture* of complex software systems. We do, however, treat the entire process, although in less detail. Still, it is the executable program that finally runs. To get there, a project depends on the efforts of every member of its team as well as the support of the stakeholders. As you will see, the process rests on a tremendous variety of activities. Many artifacts must be produced and kept track of. All the activities must be managed.

A complete account of a comprehensive, full life-cycle process is beyond the scope of any one book. Such a book would have to cover design guidelines, templates for artifacts, quality indicators, project management, configuration management, metrics, and more—much more! With the development of on-line access, that "more" is now available, and it can be updated as new developments dictate. For this, we refer you to the Rational Unified Process, a new Web-enabled software product that guides software development teams to more effective software development practices. (See http://www.rational.com for more information.) In covering the full software life cycle, the Rational Unified Process extends the Unified Process beyond areas described in this book and provides additional workflows that are not covered in this book or are mentioned only in passing, such as business modeling, project management, and configuration management.

## History of the Unified Process

The Unified Process is balanced because it is the end product of three decades of development and practical use. Its development as a product follows a path (see Figure P.1) from the Objectory Process (first released in 1987) via the Rational Objectory Process (released in 1997) to the Rational Unified Process (released in 1998). Its development has been influenced by many sources. We don't intend to try to identify them all (we actually don't know what they all are) and leave that for software archeologists to research. However, we will describe the impact of the Ericsson and Rational approaches to the product as well as several other sources.

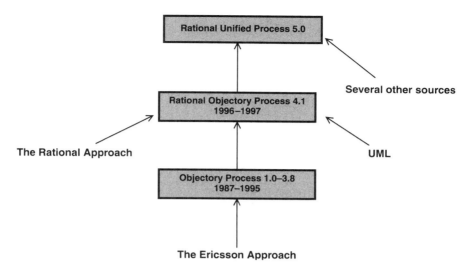

**Figure P.1** The development of the Unified Process. (Versions of the product are denoted in gray rectangles.)

## The Ericsson Approach

The Unified Process has deep roots. To employ the language of Peter F. Drucker, it is a "knowledge-based innovation." "There is a protracted span between the emergence of new knowledge and its distillation into usable technology," he advises us. "Then there is another long period before this new technology appears in the marketplace in products, processes, or services." [1]

One reason for this long lead-time is that knowledge-based innovation is grounded on the bringing together of many kinds of knowledge, and this takes time. Another reason is that the people who have to make the new idea effective need time to digest it and spread it to others.

As a first step toward illuminating the development of the Unified Process, let us go back to 1967 and outline more specifically what Ericsson achieved [14], [15], [16]. Ericsson modeled the whole system as a set of interconnected blocks (in UML these are known as "subsystems" and implemented as "components"). They assembled the lowest-level blocks into higher-level subsystems to make the system more manageable. They found the blocks by working through the previously specified traffic cases—now called "use cases." For each use case, they identified the blocks that cooperate to realize it. Knowing the responsibilities of each block, they prepared a specification for it. Their design activities resulted in a set of static block diagrams with their interfaces, and groupings into subsystems. These block diagrams correspond directly to a simplified version of UML class or package diagrams—simplified in that it only showed associations used for communications.

The first work product in the design activities was a software *architecture description*. It was based on understanding the most critical requirements. It described briefly each block and their groupings into subsystems. A set of block diagrams described the blocks and their interconnections. Over the interconnections, signals, that is, a kind of message, were communicated. All messages were described one by one in a message library. The software architecture description and the message library were key documents that guided the development work, but they were also used to present the system to customers. At that time (1968) customers were not used to having software products presented to them by means similar to engineering blueprints.

For each use case, the engineers prepared either a sequence diagram or a collaboration diagram (now further developed in the UML). These diagrams showed how the blocks dynamically communicate to realize the use case. They prepared a specification in the form of a state graph (including states and transitions only) and a state-transition graph (a simplified version of the UML activity diagrams). This approach, designing with blocks with well-defined interfaces, was key to the success. Now a new configuration of the system could be created—for instance, for a new customer—by exchanging a block with another one that provided the same interfaces.

Now, the blocks were not just subsystems and source-code components; they were compiled into executable blocks, they were installed in the target machine one by one, and it was established that they worked with all the rest of the executable blocks. Beyond that, they must be able to install each new or changed executable block in the field in a running system while it was executing calls for telephone systems operating 100% of the time. One does not shut down such a system just to make changes. It is like changing tires while a car is moving 60 miles an hour.

In essence, the approach used was what we today call *component-based development*. Ivar Jacobson was the originator of this development method. He guided its evolution into a software development process over the many years of the pre-Objectory period.

## The Specification and Description Language

A significant development during this period was the issuance in 1976 by CCITT, the international body for standardization in the telecommunications field, of the *Specification and Description Language* (SDL) for the functional behavior of telecommunications systems. This standard, significantly influenced by the Ericsson approach, specified a system as a set of interconnected blocks that communicated with each other solely through messages (called "signals" in the standard). Each block owned a set of "processes," which was the SDL term for active classes. A process had instances much as classes do in object-oriented terms. Process instances interacted by messages. It recommended diagrams that were specializations of what UML now calls class diagrams, activity diagrams, collaboration diagrams, and sequence diagrams.

Thus, SDL was a specialized object-modeling standard. Periodically updated, it is still in use by more than 10,000 developers and supported by several tool vendors.

Developed originally more than 20 years ago, it was far ahead of its time. However, it was developed at a time when object modeling had not matured. SDL will likely be supplanted by the Unified Modeling Language, which was standardized in November 1997.

## Objectory

In 1987 Ivar Jacobson left Ericsson and established Objectory AB in Stockholm. During the next eight years he and his associates developed a process product called Objectory ("Objectory" is an abbreviation of "Object Factory."). They extended it to industries outside of telecommunications and to countries beyond Sweden.

Although the concept of the *use case* had been present in the work at Ericsson, it now had a name (which was introduced at the OOPSLA conference in 1987), a diagramming technique was developed, and the idea was extended to embrace a variety of applications. That it is use cases that drive development became more clear. That it is architecture that guides the developers and informs the stakeholders came to the fore.

The successive workflows were represented in a series of models: requirements-use cases, analysis, design, implementation, and test. A model is a perspective of a system. The relationships between the models in this series were important to developers as a way of following a feature from one end of the model series to the other end. In fact, traceability became a prerequisite of use-case-driven development. Developers could trace a use case through the model sequence to the source code or, when problems arose, back again.

Development of the Objectory process proceeded in a series of releases, from Objectory 1.0 in 1988 to the first on-line version, Objectory 3.8, in 1995 (an overview of Objectory is presented in [2]).

It is important to note that the Objectory product itself came to be viewed as a system. This way of describing the process—as a system product—provided a better way to develop a new version of Objectory from an earlier one. This way of designing Objectory made it easier to tailor it to meet the particular needs of different development organizations. The fact that the Objectory software development process itself was engineered was a unique feature.

The experience in developing Objectory also provided insights into how to engineer the processes on which a business in general operates. The same principles were applicable and were incorporated in a 1995 book [3].

## The Rational Approach

Rational Software Corporation acquired Objectory AB in the fall of 1995 and the task of unifying the basic principles underlying the existing software development processes gained new urgency. Rational had developed a number of software development practices, many of which were complementary to those embodied in Objectory.

For example, "In 1981, Rational set out to produce an interactive environment that would improve productivity for the development of large software systems,"

James E. Archer Jr. and Michael T. Devlin recalled in 1986 [4]. In this effort, object-oriented design, abstraction, information hiding, reusability, and prototyping were important, they went on to say.

Scores of books, papers, and internal documents detail Rational developments since 1981, but perhaps the two most important contributions to *process* were the emphases on architecture and iterative development. For instance, in 1990 Mike Devlin wrote a vision paper on an architecture-driven iterative development process. Philippe Kruchten, in charge of the Architecture Practice within Rational, authored papers on iteration and architecture.

We cite one, an article on an architectural representation in four views: the logical view; the process view; the physical view; and the development view, plus an additional view that illustrates the first four views with uses cases or scenarios [6]. The value of having a set of views, rather than trying to cram everything into one type of diagram, grew out of Kruchten's experience on several large projects. Multiple views enabled both stakeholders and developers to find what they needed for their diverse purposes in the appropriate view.

Some have perceived iterative development as somewhat chaotic or anarchic. The four-phase approach (inception, elaboration, construction, and transition) was devised to better structure and control progress while iterating. The phases impose order on the iterations. The detailed planning of the phases and ordering of the iterations within phases was a team effort with Walker Royce and Rich Reitman, as well as the continuing participation of Grady Booch and Philippe Kruchten.

Booch was on the scene from the very beginning of Rational, and in 1996 in one of his books he cited two "first principles" that bear upon architecture and iteration:

- "An architecture-driven style of development is usually the best approach for the creation of most complex software-intensive projects."
- "A successful object-oriented project must apply an incremental and iterative process." [7]

## Rational Objectory Process: 1995–1997

At the time of the merger, Objectory 3.8 had shown how a software development process as a product could be developed and modeled. It had designed the original architecture of a software development process. It had identified a set of models that recorded the outcome of the process. In areas such as use-case modeling, analysis, and design, it was well developed. In other areas—requirements management other than use cases, implementation, and test—it was less well developed. Moreover, it contained little on project management, configuration management, deployment, and the preparation of the development environment (tools and process procurement).

Now Rational's experience and practices were added to form the Rational Objectory Process 4.1. The phases and the *controlled* iterative approach, in particular, were added. Architecture was made explicit in the form of an architecture description—the "bible" of the software development organization. A precise definition of architecture was developed. It treated architecture as being the significant parts of the organization of the system. It depicted the architecture as architectural views of the models. Iterative development was advanced from a relatively general concept to a risk-driven approach that put architecture first.

At this time UML was in development and was used as the modeling language of the Rational Objectory Process (ROP). The authors of this book contributed as the original developers of UML. The process development team, headed by Philippe Kruchten, alleviated some of the weaknesses in ROP by strengthening project management, for instance, based on contributions from Royce [8].

## Unified Modeling Language

The need for a uniform and consistent visual language in which to express the results of the rather numerous object-oriented methodologies extant in the early 1990s had been evident for some time.

During this period Grady Booch, for example, was the author of the Booch method [9]. James Rumbaugh was the principal developer at the General Electric Research and Development Center of OMT (Object Modeling Technique) [10] When he joined Rational in October 1994, the two began an effort, in concert with many of Rational's customers, to unify their methods. They released version 0.8 of the Unified Method in October 1995, about the same time that Ivar Jacobson joined Rational.

The three, working together, released Unified Modeling Language 0.9. The effort was expanded to include other methodologists and a variety of companies, including IBM, HP, and Microsoft, each of which contributed to the evolving standard. In November 1997 after going through the standardization process, the Unified Modeling Language version 1.1, was promulgated as a standard by the Object Management Group. For detailed information refer to the *User Guide* [11] and the *Reference Manual* [12].

UML was used for all models in the Rational Objectory Process.

## Rational Unified Process

During this period Rational acquired or merged with other software tool companies. Each brought to the mix expertise in process areas that further expanded the Rational Objectory process:

- Requisite Inc. brought experience in requirements management.
- SQA Inc. had developed a test process to go with its test product, adding to Rational's long experience in this field.
- Pure-Atria added its experience in configuration management to that of Rational.
- Performance Awareness added performance testing and load testing
- Vigortech added expertise in data engineering.

The process was also expanded with a new workflow for business modeling, based on [3], that is used to derive requirements from the business processes the software was to serve. It also was extended to design user interfaces driven by use cases (based on work done at Objectory AB).

By mid-1998 the Rational Objectory Process had become a full-fledged process able to support the entire software development life cycle. In so doing, it unified a wide variety of contributions, not only by the three present authors but by the many sources from which Rational and the UML were able to draw upon. In June, Rational released a new version of the product, the Rational Unified Process 5.0 [13]. Many elements of this proprietary process now become available to the general public for this first time in the form of this book.

The name change reflects the fact that unification had taken place in many dimensions: unification of development approaches, using the Unified Modeling Language, and unification of the work of many methodologists—not just at Rational but also at the hundreds of customer sites that had been using the process over many years.

## Acknowledgments

A project of this magnitude is the work of many people, and we would like to acknowledge as many as is practical by name.

### For Contributions to This Book

Birgitte Lønvig prepared the Interbank system example and worked it through all models. This is the primary example used throughout the book.

Patrik Jonsson extracted material from the Rational Objectory Process documentation and arranged it in the order of the proposed chapters. He also assisted in the preparation of the examples. In doing so, he contributed many ideas on how best to present the Unified Process.

Ware Myers participated in the development of this book from the initial outlines forward. He took first drafts prepared by the lead author and turned them into more readable English prose.

Of the reviewers we particularly thank Kurt Bittner, Cris Kobryn, and Earl Ecklund, Jr. In addition, we are most appreciative of the reviews by Walker Royce, Philippe Kruchten, Dean Leffingwell, Martin Griss, Maria Ericsson, and Bruce Katz. The reviewers also include Pete McBreen, Glenn Jones, Johan Galle, N. Venu Gopal, David Rine, Mary Loomis, Marie Lenzi, Janet Gardner, and some anonymous reviewers, all of whom we want to thank.

Terry Quatrani of Rational improved the English in Chapters 1-5. Karen Tongish copyedited the whole book. We thank both of them.

In particular, we want to thank Stefan Bylund who reviewed the drafts extensively and suggested improvements in detail, many of which we incorporated. His contributions have substantially increased the quality of the book.

## Over The Years

We also want to thank several people who have over the years helped us to "get the process right" and supported the work in its various forms. Specifically, we would like to thank the following individuals: Stefan Ahlquist, Ali Ali, Gunilla Andersson, Kjell S. Andersson, Sten-Erik Bergner, Dave Bernstein, Kurt Bittner, Per Bjork, Hans Brandtberg, Mark Broms, Stefan Bylund, Ann Carlbrand, Ingemar Carlsson, Margaret Chan, Magnus Christerson, Geoff Clemm, Catherine Connor, Hakan Dahl, Stephane Desjardins, Mike Devlin, Hakan Dyrhage, Susanne Dyrhage, Staffan Ehnebom, Christian Ehrenborg, Maria Ericsson, Gunnar M. Eriksson, Iain Gavin, Carlo Goti, Sam Guckenheimer, Bjorn Gullbrand, Sunny Gupta, Marten Gustafsson, Bjorn Gustafsson, Lars Hallmarken, David Hanslip, Per Hedfors, Barbara Hedlund, Jorgen Hellberg, Joachim Herzog, Kelli Houston, Agneta Jacobson, Sten Jacobson, Paer Jansson, Hakan Jansson, Christer Johansson, Ingemar Johnsson, Patrik Jonsson, Dan Jonsson, Bruce Katz, Kurt Katzeff, Kevin Kelly, Anthony Kesterton, Per Kilgren, Rudi Koster, Per Kroll, Ron Krubeck, Mikael Larsson, Bud Lawson, Dean Leffingwell, Rolf Leidhammar, Hakan Lidstrom, Lars Lindroos, Fredrik Lindstrom, Chris Littlejohns, Andrew Lyons, Jas Madhur, Bruce Malasky, Chris McClenaghan, Christian Meck, Sue Mickel, Jorma Mobrin, Christer Nilsson, Rune Nilsson, Anders Nordin, Jan-Erik Nordin, Roger Oberg, Benny Odenteg, Erik Ornulf, Gunnar Overgaard, Karin Palmkvist, Fabio Peruzzi, Janne Pettersson, Gary Pollice, Tonya Prince, Leslee Probasco, Terry Quatrani, Anders Rockstrom, Walker Royce, Goran Schefte, Jeff Schuster, John Smith, John Smith, Kjell Sorme, Ian Spence, Birgitta Spiridon, Fredrik Stromberg, Goran Sundelof, Per Sundquist, Per-Olof Thysselius, Mike Tudball, Karin Villers, Ctirad Vrana, Stefan Wallin, Roland Wester, Lars Wetterborg, Brian White, Lars Wiktorin, Charlotte Wranne, and Jan Wunsche..

In addition, the following people have given the lead author personal support over the years, for which he is highly appreciative: Dines Bjorner, Tore Bingefors, Dave Bulman, Larry Constantine, Goran Hemdal, Bo Hedfors, Tom Love, Nils Lennmarker, Lars-Olof Noren, Dave Thomas, and Lars-Erik Thorelli.

## Finally, We Would Like to Thank in Particular

Mike Devlin, president of Rational Software Corporation, for his belief in the Objectory process as a product to help those developing software worldwide, and for his continued support in using effective software process as a driver for the development of software tools.

And lastly, we would like to thank Philippe Kruchten, director of the Rational Unified Process, and all the members of the Rational process team for integrating the best of Objectory with Rational's best practices and the UML, while preserving the values of each. In addition, we could not have reached this objective without Philippe's personal commitment and perseverance to the task of building, quite simply, the best software process the world has ever seen.

## Process Breaks Through

Through this book and its related books, on-line versions, and tools, software development *process* comes of age. The Unified Process drew its inspiration from many sources. Already it is being widely used. It provides a common medium of process understanding from which management, developers, and stakeholders can draw.

Still, much work remains to be done. Developers have to learn unified ways of working. Stakeholders and management have to support them. For many software organizations, the breakthrough is only potential. You can make it actual.

*Ivar Jacobson*
*Palo Alto, California*
*December 1998*
*ivar@rational.com*

## References

[1]  Peter F. Drucker, "The Discipline of Innovation," *Harvard Business Review,* May-June, 1985; reprinted Nov.-Dec. 1998, pp. 149–157.

[2]  Ivar Jacobson, Magnus Christerson, Patrik Jonsson, and Gunnar Övergaard, *Object-Oriented Software Engineering: A Use-Case Driven Approach,* Reading, MA: Addison-Wesley, 1992.

[3]  Ivar Jacobson, Maria Ericsson, and Agneta Jacobson, *The Object Advantage: Business Process Reengineering with Object Technology,* Reading, MA: Addison-Wesley, 1995.

[4]  James E. Archer Jr. and Michael T. Devlin, "Rational's Experience Using Ada for Very Large Systems," *Proceedings of the First International Conference on Ada Programming Language Applications for the NASA Space Station,* June, 1986.

[6]  Philippe B. Kruchten, "The 4 + 1 View Model of Architecture," *IEEE Software,* November 1995, pp. 42–50.

[7]  Grady Booch, *Object Solutions: Managing the Object-Oriented Project,* Reading, MA: Addison-Wesley, 1996.

[8]  Walker Royce, *Software Project Management: A Unified Framework,* Reading, MA: Addison-Wesley, 1998.

[9]  Grady Booch, *Object-Oriented Analysis and Design with Applications,* Redwood City, CA: Benjamin/Cummings, 1994.

[10]  James Rumbaugh, Michael Blaha, William Premerlani, Frederick Eddy, and William Lorensen, *Object-Oriented Modeling and Design,* Englewood Cliffs, NJ: Prentice Hall, 1991.

[11]  Grady Booch, James Rumbaugh, and Ivar Jacobson, *The Unified Modeling Language User Guide,* Reading, MA: Addison-Wesley, 1998.

[12] James Rumbaugh, Ivar Jacobson, and Grady Booch, *The Unified Modeling Language Reference Manual,* Reading, MA: Addison-Wesley, 1998.

[13] Philippe Kruchten, *The Rational Unified Process: An Introduction,* Reading, MA: Addison-Wesley, 1998.

[14] Ivar Jacobson, *Concepts for Modeling Large Real Time Systems,* Chapter 2, Dissertation, Department of Computer Systems, The Royal Institute of Technology, Stockholm, Sept. 1985.

[15] Ivar Jacobson, "Object-Orientation as a Competitive Advantage," *American Programmer,* Oct. 1992.

[16] Ivar Jacobson, "A Large Commercial Success Story with Objects, Succeeding with Objects," *Object Magazine,* May 1996.

# BUSINESS REPLY MAIL

FIRST CLASS MAIL   PERMIT NO. 1011   SANTA CLARA,CA

POSTAGE WILL BE PAID BY ADDRESSEE

**RATIONAL SOFTWARE CORPORATION**
**2800 SAN TOMAS EXPY**
**SANTA CLARA CA  95051-9813**

"We hope that you have found this book to be useful, and we encourage you to learn more about visual modeling and the UML. Wherever you are in your exploration of object technology, from novice to expert, we are confident that Rational has the people, products, and knowledge to help you succeed."

| Grady Booch | Jim Rumbaugh | Ivar Jacobson |
|---|---|---|
| Chief Scientist | Rational Fellow | VP, Business Engineering |

Rational Software Corporation

**Why are organizations standardizing on the UML? How can you incorporate the UML into your software development process? Get the answers from *Inside the UML* – the powerful multimedia educational tool (featuring audio, video, and animation), that provides a comprehensive introduction to visual modeling with the Unified Modeling Language, plus your very own Rational Rose Evaluation software! To receive your FREE CD-ROM of *Inside the UML* please complete the form below and fax to (781) 229-3537 or visit *www.rational.com/umlcd/*.**

Rational Rose, the world's leading visual modeling tool, allows developers to define and communicate a software architecture, resulting in:

- Accelerated development, by improved communication among various team members
- Improved quality, by mapping business processes to software architecture, and
- Increased visibility and predictability, by making critical design decisions explicit visually

Try Rational Rose for FREE! It's on the Inside the UML CD. Get your copy today!

Name _____

Company _____

Address _____

City _____ State/province _____ Zip/postal code _____

Country _____ Telephone _____ Fax _____

**For more information about Rational Rose, visit our Web site at**

**www.rational.com/rose/**

RATIONAL
SOFTWARE

Australia +61-2-9419-0100; Belgium +32-16-46-24-11; Brazil +55-11-829-7585; Canada 613-599-8581; Finland +358-9-6969-2616; France +33-1-30-12-09-50; Germany +49-89-628-38-0; India +91-80-553 8082/9864; Japan +81-3-5423-3611; Korea +82-2-556-9420; The Netherlands +31-23-569-4300; New Zealand +64-4-568-9591; South Africa +27-12-663-5677; Sweden +46-8-566-282-00; Switzerland +41-1-445-36-00; Taiwan +886-2-720-1938; UK +44-1344-462-500

0-201-96545-3

# Part I

## The Unified Software Development Process

In Part I we introduce key ideas.

Chapter 1 describes the Unified Software Development Process in a nutshell, emphasizing that it is use-case driven, architecture-centric, iterative, and incremental. The process uses the Unified Modeling Language (UML), a language that produces drawings comparable in their intent to the blueprints long used in other technical disciplines. The process makes it practical to base much of a development project upon reusable components, that is, a piece of software with a well-defined interface.

Chapter 2 introduces the four *P*s: people, project, product, and process, and describes their relationships, which are critical to understanding the whole book. *Artifact*, *model*, *worker*, and *workflow* are the key concepts necessary to understand the process covered here.

Chapter 3 discusses the concept of use-case driven development in further detail. Use cases are a means of finding the right requirements and using them to drive the development process.

Chapter 4 describes the role of architecture in the Unified Process. Architecture establishes what is to be done; it lays out the significant levels of the organization of the software and focuses on the skeleton of the system.

Chapter 5 emphasizes the importance of taking an *iterative and incremental* approach to software development. In practice, this means trying out the risk-laden parts of a system first, finding a stable architecture early, and then filling in the more routine parts in successive iterations, each of which leads to an increment of progress toward the final release.

In Part II we go deeper. A chapter is devoted to each core workflow: requirements, analysis, design, implementation, and test. These workflows will be used later in Part III as the substantive activities in the different kinds of iterations in the four phases into which we divide the process.

In Part III we describe concretely how work is performed in each phase: in inception to make a business case, in elaboration to create the architecture and make a plan, in construction to grow the architecture into a deliverable system, and in transition to assure that the system operates correctly in the users' environment. In this part we reuse the core workflows and combine them in a way that is tailored to each phase so that we will be able to achieve the desired results.

An organization's underlying purpose, however, is not to own good software, but to operate its business processes, or embedded systems, in a fashion that enables the rapid production of high quality goods and services at a reasonable cost in response to market demands. Software is the strategic weapon with which businesses or governments can achieve enormous reductions in cost and production time for both goods and services. Reacting quickly to market dynamics is not possible without good organizational processes in place. In a global economy that operates twenty-four hours a day, seven days a week, many of these processes would not function without software. A good software development process thus becomes a critical element in any organization's success.

*Chapter 1*

# The Unified Process: Use-Case Driven, Architecture-Centric, Iterative, and Incremental

Today, the trend in software is toward bigger, more complex systems. This is due in part to the fact that computers become more powerful every year, leading users to expect more from them. This trend has also been influenced by the expanding use of the Internet for exchanging all kinds of information—from plain text to formatted text to pictures to diagrams to multimedia. Our appetite for ever-more sophisticated software grows as we learn from one product release to the next how the product could be improved. We want software that is better adapted to our needs, but that, in turn, merely makes the software more complex. In short, we want more.

We also want it faster. Time to market is another important driver.

Getting there, however, is difficult. Our demands for powerful, complex software have not been matched with how software is developed. Today, most people develop software using the same methods that were used as long as 25 years ago. This is a problem. Unless we update our methods, we will not be able to accomplish our goal of developing the complex software needed today.

The software problem boils down to the difficulty developers face in pulling together the many strands of a large software undertaking. The software development community needs a controlled way of working. It needs a process that integrates the many facets of software development. It needs a common approach, a process that

- Provides guidance to the order of a team's activities.
- Directs the tasks of individual developers and the team as a whole.
- Specifies what artifacts should be developed.
- Offers criteria for monitoring and measuring a project's products and activities.

The presence of a well-defined and well-managed process is a key discriminator between hyperproductive projects and unsuccessful ones. (See Section 2.4.4 for more reasons why you need a process.) The Unified Software Development Process—the outcome of more than 30 years of experience—is a solution to the software problem. This chapter provides an overview of the entire Unified Process. Later chapters examine each element of the process in detail.

## 1.1  The Unified Process in a Nutshell

First and foremost the Unified Process is a software development process. A software development *process* is the set of activities needed to transform a user's requirements into a software system (see Figure 1.1). However, the Unified Process is more than a single process; it is a generic process framework that can be specialized for a very large class of software systems, for different application areas, different types of organizations, different competence levels, and different project sizes.

The Unified Process is *component-based,* which means that the software system being built is made up of software **components** (Appendix A) interconnected via well-defined **interfaces** (Appendix A).

The Unified Process uses the *Unified Modeling Language* (UML) when preparing all blueprints of the software system. In fact, UML is an integral part of the Unified Process—they were developed hand in hand.

However, the real distinguishing aspects of the Unified Process are captured in the three key words—use-case driven, architecture-centric, and iterative and incremental. This is what makes the Unified Process unique.

In the next three sections we will describe these three key words. Then, in the rest of the chapter, we will give a brief overview of the process: its lifecycle, phases, releases, iterations, workflows, and artifacts. The whole intention with this chapter is to introduce the most important ideas and to get a helicopter perspective of the whole process. After reading this chapter you should know, but not necessarily fully understand, what the Unified Process is all about. The rest of the book will flesh out the details. In Chapter 2 we will put into context the four *P*s of software development:

**FIGURE 1.1**  A software development process.

people, project, product, and process. Then we devote a chapter each to the three key ideas. All this will be in the first part of the book. Parts II and III—the core of the book—will describe the various workflows of the process in detail.

## 1.2  The Unified Process Is Use-Case Driven

A software system is brought into existence to serve its users. Therefore, to build a successful system we must know what its prospective users want and need.

The term *user* refers not only to human users but to other systems. In this sense, the term *user* represents someone or something (such as another system outside the proposed system) that interacts with the system being developed. An example of an interaction is a human who uses an automatic teller machine. He (or she) inserts the plastic card, replies to questions called up by the machine on its viewing screen, and receives a sum of cash. In response to the user's card and answers, the system performs a sequence of **actions** (Appendix A) that provide the user with a result of value, namely the cash withdrawal.

An interaction of this sort is a **use case** (Appendix A; see also Chapter 3). A use case is a piece of functionality in the system that gives a user a result of value. Use cases capture functional requirements. All the use cases together make up the **use-case model** (Appendix B; see also Section 2.3) which describes the complete functionality of the system. This model replaces the traditional functional specification of the system. A functional specification can be said to answer the question, What is the system supposed to do? The use case strategy can be characterized by adding three words to the end of this question: *for each user?* These three words have a very important implication. They force us to think in terms of value to users and not just in terms of functions that might be good to have. However, use cases are not just a tool for specifying the requirements of a system. They also drive its design, implementation, and test; that is, *they drive the development process.* Based on the use-case model, developers create a series of design and implementation models that realize the use cases. The developers review each successive model for conformance to the use-case model. The testers test the implementation to ensure that the components of the implementation model correctly implement the use cases. In this way, the use cases not only initiate the development process but bind it together. *Use-case driven* means that the development process follows a flow—it proceeds through a series of workflows that derive from the use cases. Use cases are specified, use cases are designed, and at the end use cases are the source from which the testers construct the test cases.

While it is true that use cases drive the process, they are not selected in isolation. They are developed in tandem with the system architecture. That is, the use cases drive the system architecture and the system architecture influences the selection of the use cases. Therefore, both the system architecture and the use cases mature as the life cycle continues.

## 1.3 The Unified Process Is Architecture-Centric

The role of software architecture is similar in nature to the role architecture plays in building construction. The building is looked at from various viewpoints: structure, services, heat conduction, plumbing, electricity, and so on. This allows a builder to see a complete picture before construction begins. Similarly, architecture in a software system is described as different views of the system being built.

The software architecture concept embodies the most significant static and dynamic aspects of the system. The architecture grows out of the needs of the enterprise, as sensed by users and other stakeholders, and as reflected in the use cases. However, it is also influenced by many other factors, such as the platform the software is to run on (e.g., computer architecture, operating system, database management system, protocols for network communication), the reusable building blocks available (e.g., a **framework** (Appendix C) for graphical user interfaces), deployment considerations, legacy systems, and nonfunctional requirements (e.g., performance, reliability). Architecture is a view of the whole design with the important characteristics made more visible by leaving details aside. Since what is significant depends in part on judgment, which, in turn, comes with experience, the value of the architecture depends on the people assigned to the task. However, process helps the architect to focus on the right goals, such as understandability, resilience to future changes, and reuse.

How are use cases and architecture related? Every product has both function and form. One or the other is not enough. These two forces must be balanced to get a successful product. In this case function corresponds to use cases and form to architecture. There needs to be interplay between use cases and architecture. It is a "chicken and egg" problem. On the one hand, the use cases must, when realized, fit in the architecture. On the other hand, the architecture must allow room for realizations of all the required use cases, now and in the future. In reality, both the architecture and the use cases must evolve in parallel.

Thus the architects cast the system in a *form*. It is that form, the architecture, that must be designed so as to allow the system to evolve, not only through its initial development but through future generations. To find such a form, the architects must work from a general understanding of the key functions, that is, the key use cases, of the system. These key use cases may amount to only 5% to 10% of all the use cases, but they are the significant ones, the ones that constitute the core system functions. In simplified terms, the architect:

- Creates a rough outline of the architecture, starting with the part of the architecture that is not specific to the use cases (e.g., platform). Although this part of the architecture is use-case independent, the architect must have a general understanding of the use cases prior to the creation of the architectural outline.
- Next, the architect works with a subset of the identified use cases, the ones that represent the key functions of the system under development. Each selected use case is specified in detail and realized in terms of **subsystems**

(Appendix A; see also Section 3.4.4), **classes** (Appendix A), and components (Appendix A).

■ As the use cases are specified and they mature, more of the architecture is discovered. This, in turn, leads to the maturation of more use cases.

This process continues until the architecture is deemed stable.

## 1.4  The Unified Process Is Iterative and Incremental

Developing a commercial software product is a large undertaking that may continue over several months to possibly a year or more. It is practical to divide the work into smaller slices or mini-projects. Each miniproject is an iteration that results in an increment. Iterations refer to steps in the workflow, and increments, to growth in the product. To be most effective, the iterations must be *controlled;* that is they must be selected and carried out in a planned way. This is why they are mini-*projects.*

Developers base the selection of what is to be implemented in an iteration upon two factors. First, the iteration deals with a group of use cases that together extend the usability of the product as developed so far. Second, the iteration deals with the most important risks. Successive iterations build on the development artifacts from the state at which they were left at the end of the previous iteration. It is a miniproject, so from the use cases it continues through the consequent development work—analysis, design, implementation, and test—that realizes in the form of executable code the use cases being developed in the iteration. Of course, an increment is not necessarily additive. Especially in the early phases of the life cycle, developers may be replacing a superficial design with a more detailed or sophisticated one. In later phases increments are typically additive.

In every iteration, the developers identify and specify the relevant use cases, create a design using the chosen architecture as a guide, implement the design in components, and verify that the components satisfy the use cases. If an iteration meets its goals—and it usually does—development proceeds with the next iteration. When an iteration does not meet its goals, the developers must revisit their previous decisions and try a new approach.

To achieve the greatest economy in development, a project team will try to select only the iterations required to reach the project goal. It will try to sequence the iterations in a logical order. A successful project will proceed along a straight course with only small deviations from the course the developers initially planned. Of course, to the extent that unforeseen problems add iterations or alter the sequence of iterations, the development process will take more effort and time. Minimizing unforeseen problems is one of the goals of risk reduction.

There are many benefits to a controlled iterative process:

■ Controlled iteration reduces the cost risk to the expenditures on a single increment. If the developers need to repeat the iteration, the organization loses only the misdirected effort of one iteration, not the value of the entire product.

- Controlled iteration reduces the risk of not getting the product to market on the planned schedule. By identifying risks early in development, the time spent resolving them occurs early in the schedule when people are less rushed than they are late in the schedule. In the "traditional" approach, where difficult problems are first revealed by system test, the time required to resolve them usually exceeds the time remaining in the schedule and nearly always forces a delay of delivery.
- Controlled iteration speeds up the tempo of the whole development effort because developers work more efficiently toward results in clear, short focus rather than in a long, ever-sliding schedule.
- Controlled iteration acknowledges a reality often ignored—that user needs and the corresponding requirements cannot be fully defined up front. They are typically refined in successive iterations. This mode of operation makes it easier to adapt to changing requirements.

These concepts—use-case driven, architecture-centric, and iterative and incremental development—are equally important. Architecture provides the structure in which to guide the work in the iterations, whereas use cases define the goals and drives the work of each iteration. Removing one of the three key ideas would severely reduce the value of the Unified Process. It is like a three-legged stool. Without one of its legs, the stool will fall over.

Now that we have introduced the three key concepts, it is time to take a look at the whole process, its life cycle, artifacts, workflows, phases, and iterations.

## 1.5  The Life of the Unified Process

The Unified Process repeats over a series of cycles making up the life of a system, as depicted in Figure 1.2. Each cycle concludes with a product **release** (Appendix C; see also Chapter 5) to customers.

Each cycle consists of four phases: inception, elaboration, construction, and transition. Each **phase** (Appendix C) is further subdivided into iterations, as discussed earlier. See Figure 1.3.

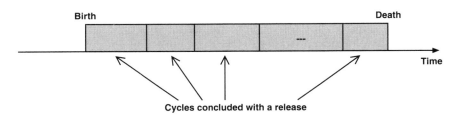

**FIGURE 1.2** The life of a process consists of cycles from its birth to its death.

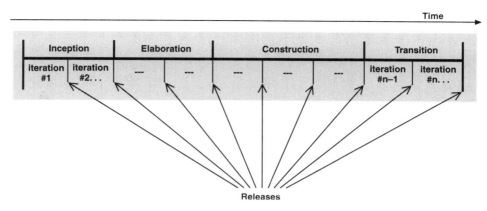

**FIGURE 1.3**  A cycle with its phases and its iterations.

### 1.5.1  The Product

Each cycle results in a new release of the system, and each release is a product ready for delivery. It consists of a body of source code embodied in components that can be compiled and executed, plus manuals and associated deliverables. However, the finished product also has to accommodate the needs, not just of the users, but of all the stakeholders, that is, all the people who will work with the product. The software product ought to be more than the machine code that executes.

The finished product includes the requirements, use cases, nonfunctional specifications, and test cases. It includes the architecture and the visual models—artifacts modeled by the Unified Modeling Language. In fact, it includes all the elements we have been talking about in this chapter, because it is these things that enable the stakeholders—customers, users, analysts, designers, implementers, testers, and management—to specify, design, implement, test, and use a system. Moreover, it is these things that enable the stakeholders to use and modify the system from generation to generation.

Even if executable components are the most important artifacts from the users' perspective, they alone are not enough. This is because the environment mutates. Operating systems, database systems, and the underlying machines advance. As the mission becomes better understood, the requirements themselves may change. In fact, it is one of the constants of software development that the requirements change. Eventually developers must undertake a new cycle, and managers must finance it. To carry out the next cycle efficiently, the developers need all the representations of the software product (Figure 1.4):

- A use case model with all the use cases and their relationships to users.
- An analysis model, which has two purposes: to refine the use cases in more detail and to make an initial allocation of the behavior of the system to a set of objects that provides the behavior.

■ A design model that defines (a) the static structure of the system as subsystems, classes, and interfaces and (b) the use cases realized as **collaborations** (Appendix A; see also Section 3.1) among the subsystems, classes, and interfaces.

■ An implementation model, which includes components (representing source code) and the mapping of the classes to components.

■ A deployment model, which defines the physical nodes of computers and the mapping of the components to those nodes.

■ A test model, which describes the test cases that verify the use cases.

■ And, of course, a representation of the architecture.

The system may also have a domain model or a business model that describes the business context of the system.

All these models are related. Together, they represent the system as a whole. Elements in one model have **trace** (Appendix A; see also Section 2.3.7) dependencies backwards and forwards with the help of links to other models. For instance, a use case (in the use-case model) can be traced to a use-case realization (in the design model) to a test case (in the test model). Traceability facilitates understanding and change.

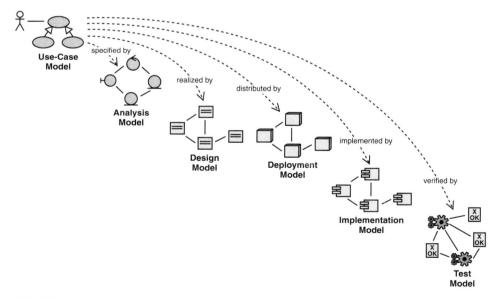

**FIGURE 1.4** Models of the Unified Process. There are dependencies between many of the models. As an example, the dependencies between the use-case model and the other models are indicated.

## 1.5.2 Phases within a Cycle

Each cycle takes place over time. This time, in turn, is divided into four phases, as shown in Figure 1.5. Through a sequence of models, stakeholders visualize what goes on in these phases. Within each phase managers or developers may break the work down still further—into iterations and the ensuing increments. Each phase terminates in a **milestone** (Appendix C; see also Chapter 5). We define each milestone by the availability of a set of artifacts; that is, certain models or documents have been brought to a prescribed state.

The milestones serve many purposes. The most critical is that managers have to make certain crucial decisions before work can proceed to the next phase. Milestones also enable management, as well as the developers themselves, to monitor the progress of the work as it passes these four key points. Finally, by keeping track of the time and effort spent on each phase, we develop a body of data. This data is useful in estimating time and staff requirements for other projects, projecting staff needs over project time, and controlling progress against these projections.

Figure 1.5 lists the workflows—requirements, analysis, design, implementation, and test—in the left-hand column. The curves approximate (they should not be taken too literally) the extent to which the workflows are carried out in each phase. Recall that each phase usually is subdivided into iterations, or mini-projects. A typical iteration goes through all the five workflows as shown for an iteration in the elaboration phase in Figure 1.5.

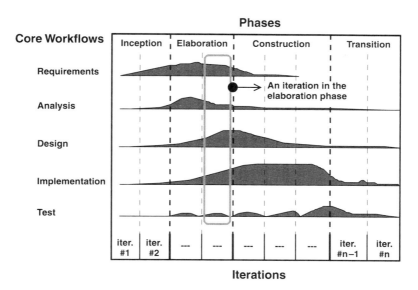

**FIGURE 1.5** The five workflows—requirements, analysis, design, implementation, and test—take place over the four phases: inception, elaboration, construction, and transition.

During the *inception phase,* a good idea is developed into a vision of the end product and the business case for the product is presented. Essentially, this phase answers the following questions:

- What is the system primarily going to do for each of its major users?
- What could an architecture for that system look like?
- What is the plan and what will it cost to develop the product?

A simplified use-case model that contains the most critical use cases answers the first question. At this stage the architecture is tentative. It is typically just an outline containing the most crucial subsystems. In this phase, the most important risks are identified and prioritized, the elaboration phase is planned in detail, and the whole project is roughly estimated.

During the *elaboration phase,* most of the product's use cases are specified in detail and the system architecture is designed. The relationship between the architecture of a system and the system itself is paramount. A simple way to put it is that the architecture is analogous to a skeleton covered with skin but with very little muscle (the software) between the bone and the skin—just enough muscle to allow the skeleton to make basic movements. The system is the whole body with skeleton, skin, and muscle.

Therefore, the architecture is expressed as views of all the models of the system, which together represent the whole system. This implies that there are architectural views of the use-case model, the analysis model, the design model, the implementation model, and the deployment model. The view of the implementation model includes components to prove that the architecture is executable. During this phase of development the most critical use cases identified during the elaboration phase are realized. The result of this phase is an architecture **baseline** (Appendix C; see also Section 4.4).

At the end of the elaboration phase, the project manager is in a position to plan the activities and estimate the resources required to complete the project. Here the key question is, Are the use cases, architecture, and plans stable enough, and are the risks under sufficient control to be able to commit to the whole development work in a contract?

During the *construction phase* the product is built—muscle (completed software) is added to the skeleton (architecture). In this phase, the architecture baseline grows to become the full-fledged system. The vision evolves into a product ready for transfer to the user community. During this phase of development, the bulk of the required resources is expended. The architecture of the system is stable, however, because the developers may discover better ways of structuring the system, they may suggest minor architectural changes to the architects. At the end of this phase, the product contains all the use cases that management and the customer agreed to develop for this release. It may not be entirely free of defects, however. More defects will be discovered and fixed during the transition phase. The milestone question is, Does the product meet users' needs sufficiently for some customers to take early delivery?

The *transition phase* covers the period during which the product moves into beta release. In the beta release a small number of experienced users tries the product and reports defects and deficiencies. Developers then correct the reported problems and incorporate some of the suggested improvements into a general release for the larger user community. The transition phase involves activities such as manufacturing, training customer personnel, providing help-line assistance, and correcting defects found after delivery. The maintenance team often divides these defects into two categories: those with sufficient effect on operations to justify an immediate delta release and those that can be corrected in the next regular release.

## 1.6  An Integrated Process

The Unified Process is component based. It uses the new visual modeling standard, the Unifed Modeling Language (UML), and relies on three key ideas—use cases, architecture, and iterative and incremental development. To make these ideas work, a multifaceted process is required, one that takes into consideration cycles, phases, workflows, risk mitigation, quality control, project management, and configuration control. The Unified Process has established a framework that integrates all those different facets. This framework also works as an umbrella under which tool vendors and developers can build tools to support the automation of the process, to support the individual workflows, to build all the different models, and to integrate the work across the life cycle and across all models.

The purpose of this book is to describe the Unified Process with a particular focus on the engineering facets, on the three key ideas (i.e., use cases, architecture, and iterative and incremental development), and on component-based design and the use of UML. We will describe the four phases and the different workflows, but we will not cover management issues, such as project planning, resource planning, risk mitigation, configuration control, metrics capturing, and quality control, in great detail, and we will only briefly discuss the automation of the process.

*Chapter 2*

# The Four *P*s: People, Project, Product, and Process in Software Development

The end result of a software **project** (Appendix C) is a product that is shaped by many different types of people as it is developed. Guiding the efforts of the people involved in the project is a software development process, a template that explains the steps needed to complete the project. Typically, the process is automated by a tool or set of tools. See Figure 2.1.

Throughout this book we will use the terms *people, project, product,* **process** (Appendix C), and *tools,* which we define as follows:

- *People:* The architects, developers, testers, and their supporting management, plus users, customers, and other stakeholders are the prime movers in a software project. People are actual human beings, as opposed to the abstract construct of *workers,* which we will introduce later on.
- *Project:* The organizational element through which software development is managed. The outcome of a project is a released product.
- *Product:* Artifacts that are created during the life of the project, such as **models** (Appendix A), source code, executables, and documentation.
- *Process:* A software engineering process is a definition of the complete set of activities needed to transform users' requirements into a product. A process is a template for creating projects.
- *Tools:* Software that is used to automate the activities defined in the process.

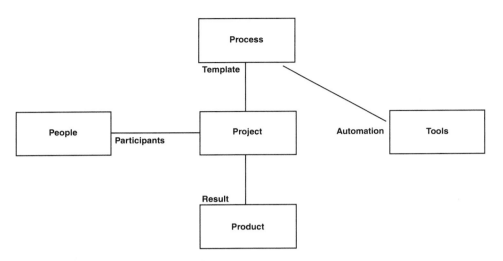

**FIGURE 2.1**  The 4 *P*s in software development.

## 2.1  People Are Crucial

People are involved in the development of a software product throughout its entire life cycle. They finance the product, schedule it, develop it, manage it, test it, use it, and benefit from it. Therefore, the process that guides this development must be people oriented, that is, one that works well for the people using it.

### 2.1.1  Development Processes Affect People

The way in which a software project is organized and managed profoundly affects the people involved in the project. Concepts such as feasibility, risk management, team organization, project scheduling, and project understandability all play important roles:

- *Project feasibility:* Most people do not enjoy working on projects that are deemed infeasible—nobody wants to go down with the ship. As we saw in Chapter 1, an iterative approach to development allows the feasibility of a project to be assessed early on. Infeasible projects can then be terminated at an early stage, thus alleviating morale problems.
- *Risk management:* Similarly, when people sense that risks have not been analyzed and reduced, they become uneasy. The exploration of significant risks in the early phases mitigates this problem.
- *Team structure:* People work most effectively in small groups of six to eight members. A process that yields meaningful work for small groups, such as assessing a particular risk, developing a subsystem (Appendix A), or perform-

ing an iteration, provides this opportunity. A good architecture with well-defined interfaces (Appendix A; see also Chapter 9) between subsystems and components (Appendix A; see also Chapter 10) makes such a division of effort possible.

■ *Project schedule:* When people believe that a schedule is unrealistic, morale will plummet—people don't like to go to work knowing that no matter how hard they try, they will never be able to produce the expected results. The techniques used in the inception and elaboration phases allow developers to get a good idea of what the end result of the project should be—that is what the released product should do. Since there is a good feeling of what the product should do, a realistic project plan for the effort involved as well as the time needed to accomplish the goals may be created, thus alleviating the "we'll never finish" people problem.

■ *Project understandability:* People like to know what they are doing; they want to understand the whole picture. The architecture description provides an overview for everyone involved in a project.

■ *Sense of accomplishment:* In an iterative life cycle, people receive frequent feedback, which in turn, provides closure. Frequent feedback and the resulting closure increases the work tempo. A fast work pace combined with frequent closure heightens people's sense of accomplishment.

### 2.1.2 Roles Will Change

Since the key activities of software development are executed by people, there is a need for a uniform development process that is supported by tools and a Unified Modeling Language (now available in UML) (Appendix C) to enable people to be more effective. Such a process will enable developers to build better software in terms of time-to-market, quality, and cost. It enables them to specify requirements that better meet users' needs. It enables them to select an architecture that allows systems to be built in a cost-effective, timely manner. A good software process has another advantage: It helps us build more complex systems. We noted in Chapter 1 that as the real world becomes more complex, so customers will require more complex software systems. Business processes and the corresponding software will have a longer life. Because changes in the real world will continue to occur throughout these life cycles, software systems will have to be designed in such a way as to enable them to grow over longer periods of time.

To understand and support these more complex business processes and to implement them in software, developers will find themselves working with many other developers. To work effectively in larger and larger teams, a process is needed to provide guidance. This guidance will result in developers "working smarter," that is, to restrict one's effort to that which adds value to the customer. One step in this direction is use-case modeling, which focuses effort on what the user needs to do. Another step is an architecture that will permit systems to continue to evolve for years to come. A third step is to buy or reuse as much software as possible. That, in turn, can be accomplished only if there is a consistent way of integrating reusable components with newly developed elements.

In the coming years, most software people will begin to work closer to the mission they support, and they will be able to develop more complex software thanks to an automated process and reusable components. People will be crucial to software development for the foreseeable future. In the end, it is having the right people that makes us succeed. The issue comes down to making them effective and allowing them to do what only humans can—to be creative, to find new opportunities, to use judgment, to communicate with customers and users, and to understand a rapidly changing world.

### 2.1.3 Turning "Resources" into "Workers"

People fill many different positions in a software development organization. Preparing them for these positions takes education and pin-pointed training followed by careful assignment supported by mentoring and helpful supervision. An organization faces a substantial task when it moves a person from a latent "resource" to a particular position as a "worker."

We have selected the word **worker** (Appendix C) to stand for the positions to which people may be assigned and which they accept [4]. A *worker type* is a role that an individual may play in software development, such as use-case specifier, architect, component engineer, and integration tester. We do not use the term *role* (instead of *worker*) for primarily two reasons: it has a precise and different meaning in UML, and the concept of a worker needs to be very concrete; we need to think in terms of individual workers as the positions taken by individuals. We also need to use the term *role* to talk about roles of a worker. A worker may play roles in relation to other workers in different workflows. For instance, the worker component engineer may participate in several workflows and in each workflow he plays a particular role.

Each worker (i.e., a worker instance) is responsible for a whole set of activities, such as the activities involved in the design of a subsystem. To work effectively, workers need the information that is required to carry out those activities. They need to understand what their roles are relative to those of other workers. At the same time, if they are to do their work, the tools they employ must be adequate. The tools must not only help workers carry out their own activities but shield them from information that is not relevant. To accomplish these objectives, the Unified Process formally describes the positions—that is, the workers—that people can take in the process.

Figure 2.2 illustrates how individual people may be different workers in a project.

A worker may also be realized as a set of individuals working together. For example, an architect worker may be realized as an architectural board.

Each worker has a set of responsibilities and performs a set of activities in developing software.

When allocating resources to workers in a project, the project manager needs to identify the competencies of individuals and match them with the required competen-

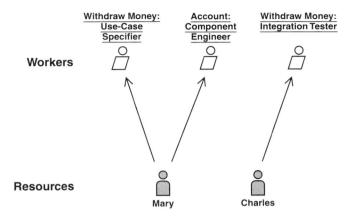

**FIGURE 2.2**  Workers and resources that realize them.

cies of the workers. This is not an easy task, especially the first time the Unified Process is used. The skills of the resources (i.e., real people) must be matched against the competencies specified by the various workers needed by the project. The competencies needed by some workers may be achieved through training, while the competencies needed by other workers may be gained only through experience. For example, the skills needed to be a use-case specifier may be learned through training, but those of an architect are typically acquired through experience.

One individual may be many workers during the life of a project. For example, Mary may start as a use-case specifier and later become a component engineer.

When allocating resources, the project manager should minimize the handoff of artifacts from one resource to another in a way that makes the flow of the process as seamless as possible. For example, the use-case engineer of the Withdraw Money use case (Appendix A; see also Chapter 7) will acquire a lot of knowledge about the responsibilities of the class Account (Appendix A), so he or she would be a logical choice to be the component engineer of the Account class. The alternative would be to train a new person to take on this work, which could be done, but it would be less efficient because of the loss of information, risk of misunderstandings, and so on.

## 2.2  Projects Make the Product

A development project results in a new release of a product. The first project in the life cycle (i.e., the first development cycle, sometimes called the "green-field project") develops and releases the initial system, or product. Successive project cycles extend the life of the system over many releases. See [9] and [10] for more complete presentation of project management.

Throughout its life cycle, a project team has to be concerned with change, iterations, and the organizational pattern within which the project is conducted:

- *A sequence of change:* System development projects result in products, but the course along the way is a series of changes. This fact of project life has to be borne in mind as workers proceed through phases and iterations. Every cycle, every phase, and, yes, every iteration changes the system from one thing to something else. The first development cycle is a special case that changes the system from nothing into something. Each cycle leads to a *release,* and beyond a sequence of cycles, change continues for *generations.*
- *A series of iterations:* Within each phase of a cycle, workers carry out the activities of the phase through a series of iterations. Each iteration implements a set of related use cases or mitigates some risks. In an iteration developers proceed through a series of workflows: requirements, design, implementation, and test. Since each iteration goes through each of these workflows, we can think of an iteration as a *miniproject.*
- *An organizational pattern:* A *project* involves a team of people assigned to accomplish a result within business constraints, that is, time, cost, and quality. The people work as different workers. The idea of "process" is to provide a pattern within which people as workers execute a project. This pattern or template indicates the types of workers the project needs and the artifacts with which it is to work. The process also offers a lot of guidelines, heuristics, and documentation practices that help the assigned people do their job.

## 2.3  Product Is More Than Code

In the context of the Unified Process, the product developed is a software system. The term *product* here refers not just to the code that is delivered but to the whole system.

### 2.3.1  What Is a Software System?

Is a software system the machine code, the executables? It is that, of course, but what is machine code? It is a description! It is a description in binary form that can be "read" and "understood" by a computer.

Is a software system the source code? That is, is it a *description* that is written by programmers that can be read and understood by a compiler? Yes, that may be the answer.

We can continue in this manner to ask similar questions about the design of a software system in terms of subsystems, classes, **interaction diagrams** (Appendix A), **statechart diagrams** (Appendix A), and other artifacts. Are they the system? Yes, they are part of it. What about requirements, testing, sales, production, installation, and operation? Are they the system? Yes, they are also part of the system.

A system is all the artifacts that it takes to represent it in machine or human readable form to the machines, the workers, and the stakeholders. The machines are tools, compilers, or target computers. Workers include management, architects, developers, testers, marketers, administrators, and others. Stakeholders are the funding authorities, users, salespeople, project managers, line managers, production people, regulatory agencies, and so on. In this book, we will use the term *worker* for these three categories collectively, unless we explicitly note otherwise.

### 2.3.2 Artifacts

**Artifact** (Appendix C) is a general term for any kind of information created, produced, changed, or used by workers in developing the system. Some sample artifacts are UML diagrams and their associated text, user-interface sketches and **prototypes** (Appendix C; see also Chapters 7 and 13), components, test plans (see Chapter 11), and test procedures (see Chapter 11).

Basically, there are two kinds of artifacts: engineering artifacts and management artifacts. This book focuses on the engineering artifacts created during the various phases of the process (i.e., requirements, analysis, design, implementation, and test).

However, software development also requires management artifacts. Several management artifacts have a short lifetime—they live only during the life of a project. To this set belong artifacts such as the business case, the development plan (including release and iteration plans), a plan for the allocation of individual people to workers (i.e., to the different positions, or responsibilities, in the project), and laying out the worker activities in the plan. These artifacts are described in text or diagrams, using any kind of visualization needed to specify the commitment made by the project team to the funding stakeholders. Management artifacts also include the specifications of the development environment—process automation software as well as the hardware platform required for developers and as a repository for the engineering artifacts.

### 2.3.3  A System Has a Collection of Models

The most interesting type of artifact employed in the Unified Process is the model. Every worker needs a unique perspective of the system (see Figure 2.3). When designing the Unified Process, we identified all the workers and every perspective that the workers could possibly need. The collected perspectives of all the workers are structured into larger quanta, that is, models, in such a way that a worker can retrieve any particular perspective from the set of models.

Building a system is thus a process of model building using different models to describe all the different perspectives of the system. Selecting the models for a system is one of the most important decisions the development team makes.

In Chapter 1 we introduced the primary models of the Unified Process (see Figure 2.4).

The Unified Process provides a carefully selected set of models with which to start. This set of models illuminates the system for all the workers, including customers, users, and project managers. It is selected so as to satisfy those workers' need for information.

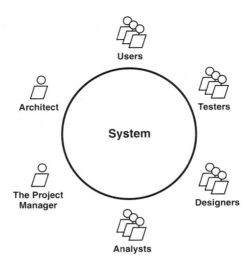

**FIGURE 2.3** Workers participating in software development. (Some are singleton workers; others are multitypes and multiobjects.)

### 2.3.4 What Is a Model?

A model is an abstraction of a system, specifying the modeled system from a certain viewpoint and at a certain level of abstraction [1]. A viewpoint is, for instance, a specification view or a design view of the system.

Models are abstractions of the system that the architects and developers build. For instance, the workers modeling the functional requirements think of the system as having users outside the system and having use cases inside the system. They don't care about what the system looks like from the inside, only what it can do for its users. The workers making up the design think about structural elements such as subsystems and classes; they think in terms of how these elements work in a given context and how they collaborate to provide the use cases. They understand how these abstract things work, and they have a particular interpretation in their minds.

### 2.3.5 Each Model Is a Self-Contained View of the System

A model is a semantically closed abstraction of the system. It is a self-contained view in the sense that a model user doesn't need other information (e.g., from other models) to interpret it.

The idea of self-containment means that the developers intended there to be only one interpretation of what will happen in a system when an event described by the model is triggered. In addition to the system under consideration, a model also has to describe interactions between the system and its surroundings. Thus, apart from the system being modeled, the model also has to contain elements that describe relevant parts of its environment, that is, its **actors** (Appendix A; see also Chapter 7).

**FIGURE 2.4** The primary model set of the Unified Process[1].

Most engineering models are defined by a carefully selected subset of the UML. For example, the use-case model consists of the use cases and the actors. That is basically all a viewer needs to understand it. The design model describes the subsystems and classes of the system and how they interact to realize the use cases. Both the use-case model and the design model describe two different but mutually consistent interpretations of what the system will do given a set of external stimuli from the actors. They are different because they are intended to be used by different workers with different tasks and missions. The use-case model is an outside view of the system, the design model is an inside view. The use-case model captures the uses of the system, whereas the design model represents the building of the system.

### 2.3.6  Inside a Model

A model always identifies the system being modeled. This system element is then the container of other elements. The **top-level subsystem** (Appendix B) represents the system being built. In the use-case model, the system contains use cases; in the design model, it contains subsystems, interfaces, and classes. It also contains collaborations (Appendix A) that identify all participating subsystems or classes, and it may contain more, such as statechart diagrams or interaction diagrams. In the design model every subsystem can itself be a container of similar constructs. This implies that there is a hierarchy of elements in this model.

### 2.3.7  Relationships between Models

A system contains all the **relationships** (Appendix A) and constraints between model elements contained in different models [1]. Thus a system is not just the collection of its models but the relationships between them as well.

For instance, every use case in the use-case model has a relationship with a collaboration in the analysis model (and vice versa). Such a relationship is in UML called a trace dependency, or simply a trace (Appendix A). See Figure 2.5, in which traces in only one direction are indicated.

There are also traces between, for instance, collaborations in the design model and collaborations in the analysis model, and between components in the

---

1. In UML terms, these "packages" represent «business entities» (or «work units») in the Unified Process and not model elements to model a particular system. See also the explanation in the sidebar in Section 7.1.

**FIGURE 2.5** Models are tightly linked to one another through traces.

implementation model and subsystems in the design model. Thus we can connect elements in one model to elements in another model using traces.

The fact that the elements in two models are connected does not change what they do inside the models to which they belong. Trace relationships between elements in different models add no semantic information to help understand the related models themselves; they just connect the models. The ability to trace is very important in software development for reasons such as understandability and change propagation.

## 2.4  Process Directs Projects

The word *process* is an overused term. It is used in many different contexts, such as business process, development process, and software process, with many different meanings. In the context of the Unified Process, we mean the key "business" process in a software development business, that is, an organization that develops and supports software (on designing a software development business, see [2]). In this business there are other processes as well, such as the support process, which interacts with users of the products, and a sales process, which starts with an order and delivers a product. However, our focus in this book is the development process [3].

### 2.4.1  Process: A Template

In the Unified Process, *process* refers to a concept that works as a template that can be reused by creating instances of it. It is comparable to a class form, which you can use to create objects in the object-oriented paradigm. *Process instance* is a synonym for *project*.

In this book, a *software development process* is a definition of the complete set of activities needed to transform users' requirements into a consistent set of artifacts that represents a software product and, later, to transform changes in those requirements into a new, consistent set of artifacts.

The word *requirement* is used in a general sense, meaning "needs." At the outset, these needs are not necessarily understood in their entirety. To capture these requirements, or needs, more completely, we may have to understand the business of the customers and the environment in which their users work more fully.

The value-added result of the process is a consistent set of artifacts, a baseline that represents one application system or a family of such systems that comprise a software product.

A process is a definition of a set of activities, not their execution.

Finally, a process covers not just the first development cycle (the first release) but the most common later cycles. In later releases, an instance of the process takes incremental changes in the requirements and produces incremental changes to the artifact set.

## 2.4.2 Related Activities Make Up Workflows

The way we describe a process is in terms of workflows, where a workflow is a set of activities. What is the source of these workflows? We don't get them by splitting the process into a number of smaller interacting subprocesses. We don't use traditional flowcharts to describe how we decompose the process into smaller chunks. Those are not efficient ways to devise the workflow structure.

Instead, first we identify the different kinds of workers that participate in the process. Then we identify the artifacts that we need to create during the process for each type of worker. This identification, of course, is not something you can do in a blink. The Unified Process relies on a lot of experience in finding the feasible set of artifacts and workers. Once we have identified this set, we can describe how the process flows through the different workers and how they create, produce, and use each other's artifacts. In Figure 2.6 we show an **activity diagram** (Appendix A) that describes the workflow in use-case modeling. Note the **"swim lanes"** (Appendix A)— there is one for each worker—how the work flows from one worker to another, and how activities (represented by cogwheels) are performed in this flow by the workers.

Now we can easily find activities that these workers need to execute when they are activated. These worker-activities are meaningful work for one person acting as a worker. Moreover, from these descriptions we can immediately see if any individual worker needs to be involved more than once in the workflow.

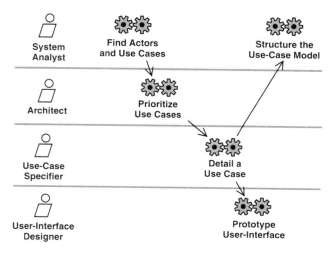

**FIGURE 2.6** A workflow with workers and activities in "swim lanes."

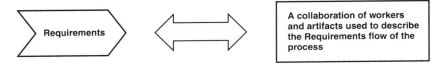

**FIGURE 2.7** The "fish" notation is a shorthand for a workflow.

In other words, we describe the whole process in pieces called **workflows** (Appendix C). In UML terms, a workflow is a **stereotype** (Appendix A) of collaboration, in which workers and artifacts are participants. Thus the workers and artifacts that participate in one workflow may (and usually do) participate in other workflows as well. We will use the notation given in Figure 2.7 for workflows.

An example of a workflow is the requirements workflow. It includes the following workers: system analyst, architect, use-case specifier, and user-interface designer. It includes these artifacts: use-case model, use cases, and others. Other examples of workers are component engineers and integration testers. Other examples of artifacts are **use-case realizations** (Appendix B; see also Chapters 8 and 9), classes, subsystems, and interfaces.

### 2.4.3 Specializing Process

No single software development process can be applied everywhere! Processes vary because they exist in different contexts, develop different types of systems, and meet different kinds of business constraints (e.g., schedule, cost, quality, and reliability). Consequently, a real-world software development process must be adaptable and configurable to meet the actual needs of a specific project and/or organization. The Unified Process is designed to be specialized (on designing a process, see [6]). It is a generic process, that is, a process framework. Every organization that uses the Unified Process will eventually specialize it so that it fits its situation (i.e., its kind of application, its platform, etc.) (on specializing a process, see [8]).

The Unified Process may be specialized to fit different application and organizational needs. At the same time, it is desirable that within an organization, at least, the process be fairly consistent. This consistency will allow components to be used interchangeably, people and managers to transfer between projects readily, and accomplishment metrics to be comparable.

The main factors that influence how the process will differ are

- *Organizational factors:* Organizational structure, organizational culture, project organization and management, competence and skills available, previous experience, and existing software systems.
- *Domain factors:* Application domain, business process to support, user community, and offerings available from competitors.
- *Life cycle factors:* Time to market, expected life span of the software, the technology and the people expertise in developing the software, and planned future releases.

- *Technical factors:* Programming language, development tools, database, frameworks and underlying "standard" architectures, communication, and distribution.

These are the causes. What effect will they have? Well, you may decide to remove workers and artifacts from the Unified Process to better fit less mature development organizations. It may also happen that you will extend the process with new—not yet specified—workers or artifacts because these extensions would make the process more efficient for your project. You may also change the way you think a particular artifact should be described; you might impose a different structure on its description. Our experience is that people in the first projects pretty much use what the Unified Process suggests. As time goes by and they gain more experience, they develop their own minor extensions.

What is it in the design of the Unified Process that permits it to be specialized [6]? The answer is simple but not easy to understand at first. Objectory is itself designed using what are, in effect, objects: use cases, collaborations, and classes. The classes here, of course, are not software, but business objects, that is, workers and artifacts. They can be specialized or exchanged with others without changing the design of the process. In later chapters when we describe the workflows, you will see that we use objects to describe them. Those objects are workers and artifacts.

### 2.4.4  Merits of Process

A common process within and across development teams provides many benefits:

- Everyone on the development team can understand what he or she has to do to develop the product.
- Developers can better understand what other developers are doing—at earlier or later stages of the same project, in similar projects in the same enterprise, at different geographic locations, and even in projects in other companies.
- Supervisors and managers, even those who cannot read code, can, thanks to architectural drawings, understand what developers are doing.
- Developers, supervisors, and managers can transfer between projects or divisions without having to learn a new process.
- Training can be standardized within a company. Training can be obtained from colleges and shortcourses.
- The course of software development is repeatable, meaning that it can be scheduled and cost estimated with sufficient accuracy to meet expectations.

Despite these advantages of a common process, some still insist that a common process does not solve the "really hard problems." To that we answer simply: "of course not." People still solve problems. But a good process helps people to excel as a team. Compare this to the organization of a military operation. Waging battle always boils down to individuals that do things, but the outcome is also decided by the effectiveness of their organization.

## 2.5  Tools Are Integral to Process

Tools support modern software development processes. Today, it is unthinkable to develop software without using a tool-supported process. The process and the tools come as a suite: the tools are integral to the process [5], [7].

### 2.5.1  Tools Impact Process

Process is strongly influenced by tool support. Tools are good at automating repetitive tasks, keeping things structured, managing large amounts of information, and guiding you along a particular development path.

With little tool support, a process would have to rely on a lot of manual work and would therefore be less formal. In practice, most of the formal work has to be postponed to the implementation activities. Without tool support that automates consistency across the life cycle, it would be hard to keep models and implementation up-to-date. Iterative and incremental development would be more difficult. Either they would end up inconsistent, or they would require a lot of manual work to update documents in order to maintain consistency. The latter would decrease the productivity of the team significantly. The team would have to do all the consistency checks manually. That is very hard, if not impossible, so there would be numerous flaws in the developed artifacts. And doing it that way would require more lead time.

Tools are developed to automate activities, fully or partially, to increase productivity and quality, and to shorten lead time. As we introduce tool support, we get a different, more formal process. We can introduce new activities that would be impractical to carry out without tools. We can work more precisely during the whole life cycle: We can use a formal modeling language like UML to ensure that each model is consistent within itself and with other models. We can use one model and from it generate parts of another model (e.g., design to implementation and vice versa).

### 2.5.2  Process Drives Tools

Process, whether explicitly or implicitly defined, specifies the tool functionality, that is, the use cases of the tools. The fact of "process" is, of course, the only reason we need any tools. The tools are there to automate as much of the process as possible.

The ability to automate a process depends on having a clear picture of which use cases each worker needs and which artifacts he or she needs to manage. An automated process provides an efficient means of allowing the whole set of workers to work concurrently, and it provides a means of checking consistency over all the artifacts.

The tools that implement an automated process should be *easy to use*. To make them highly usable means that tool developers need to give thoughtful consideration to the way in which software development is carried out. For instance, how will a worker approach a certain task? How will he become aware of what the tool can help him with? What tasks will be recurring and, hence, worth automating? What tasks will be rare and perhaps not worth embodying in a tool? How can a tool guide a worker into spending time on important tasks that only he can do, leaving repetitive tasks that the tool can do better to the tool? To answer questions like these, the tool must be easy for workers to understand and use. Moreover, to be worth the time it takes to learn, it must provide a substantial productivity boost.

There are special reasons for the ease-of-use goal. Workers should be able to try out different alternatives, and they should easily be able to massage the candidate designs for each alternative. They should be able to select one approach and try it out. If it turns out to be infeasible, they should be able to move easily from that approach to another one. Tools should enable workers to reuse as much as possible; they should not have to start all over again for each approach tried. In sum, it is essential that tools should both support the automation of repetitive activities and the management of the information represented by the series of models and artifacts and encourage and support the creative activities that are the crucial core of significant development.

### 2.5.3  Balance Process and Tools

Thus to develop a process without thinking about how it will be automated is academic. To develop tools without knowing what process (framework) they are to support may be fruitless experimentation. There has to be a balance between process and tools.

On the one hand, process drives tool development. On the other hand, tools guide process development. The development of process and its tool support must take place concurrently. At every release of process there must also be a release of tools. At every release there must be this balance. To get balance closer to the ideal will take several iterations, and the successive iterations must be guided by user feedback in between the releases.

This process-tool relationship is another chicken-and-egg problem. Which one comes first? In the case of tools, many of them in recent decades have come first. Process was not yet well developed. As a result, the tools did not work as well as expected in the rather hit-or-miss processes to which users tried to apply them. Many of us had our faith in tools shaken. Software development continued to be a none-too-efficient handicraft. In other words, process must learn from tools and tools must support a well-thought-out process.

We want to spell this point out with utmost clarity: Successful development of process automation (tools) cannot be achieved without the parallel development of the process framework in which the tools are to function. This point must be obvious to everyone. If a shadow of doubt still lurks in your mind, ask yourself whether it would be possible to develop IT support for the business processes at a bank without knowing what those processes were.

### 2.5.4  Visual Modeling Supports UML

We have just established that tools are important in carrying out the purpose of process.

Let us look at a significant example of such a tool in the context of the support environment for the Unified Process. Our example is the modeling tool for UML.

The UML is a visual language. As such, it is expected to have features common in many drawing packages, such as in-line editing, formatting, zooming, printing, color, and automatic layout. In addition to these features, UML defines syntactic rules that specify how elements of the language might be used together. So the tool has to be capable of assuring that these syntactic rules are followed. This capability is beyond that possessed by common drawing packages, where no rules are enforced.

Unfortunately, enforcing syntactic rules of this sort without exception would make the tool unusable. For instance, during model editing, the model will frequently be syntactically incorrect, and the tool needs to be able to allow for syntactical incorrectness in this mode. For example, a message in a **sequence diagram** (Appendix A; see also Chapter 9) might be allowed before any operations are defined for the class.

UML includes a number of semantic rules that also need to be supported. These rules can be incorporated in the modeling tool, as either instant enforcement or on-demand routines that traverse a model and check for common mistakes or look for semantic or syntactic incompleteness. In summary, the modeling tool needs to incorporate more than knowledge of UML; it needs to allow developers to work creatively with UML.

Using UML as the standard language, the market will experience much better tool support than any modeling language has ever had. This opportunity for better support is due in part to the precise definition of UML. It is also attributable to the fact that UML is now a widely adopted formal industry standard. Instead of tool vendors competing to support many different modeling languages, the game has now become one of finding who best supports UML. This new game is better for users and customers of software.

UML is only the modeling language. It does not define a process of how to use UML to develop software systems. The modeling tool does not have to enforce a process, but if the user uses a process, the tool can support it.

### 2.5.5  Tools Support the Whole Life Cycle

There are tools to support every aspect of the **software life cycle** (Appendix C):

- *Requirements management:* Used to store, browse, review, track, and navigate the various requirements of a software project. A requirement might have a status attached to it, and the tool might permit a requirement to be traced to other artifacts in the life cycle, such as a use case or a test case (see Chapter 11).
- *Visual modeling:* Used to automate the use of UML, that is, to model and assemble an application visually. With this tool we integrate with programming environments and ensure that the model and implementation are always consistent with each other.
- *Programming tools:* Used to provide a range of tools, including editors, compilers, debuggers, error detectors, and performance analyzers.
- *Quality assurance:* Used to test applications and components, that is, to record and execute test cases that drive testing of a GUI and an interface of a compo-

nent. In an iterative life cycle, regression testing is even more essential than it is in conventional development. Automating test cases is essential to allow for high productivity. In addition, many applications also need to be exposed to stress and load testing. How will this application's architecture stand up to the use of 10,000 concurrent users? You want to know the answer to this question before you deploy to the 10,000th user.

In addition to these functionally oriented tools, there are other tools that are cross–life cycle. These tools include version control, configuration management, defect tracking, documentation, project management, and process automation.

## 2.6 References

[1]   OMG Unified Modeling Language Specification. Object Management Group, Framingham, MA, 1998. Internet: www.omg.org.

[2]   Ivar Jacobson, Martin Griss, and Patrik Jonsson, *Software Reuse: Architecture, Process and Organization for Business Success,* Reading, MA: Addison-Wesley, 1997.

[3]   Watts S. Humphrey, *Managing the Software Process,* Reading, MA: Addison-Wesley, 1989.

[4]   Ivar Jacobson, Maria Ericsson, and Agneta Jacobson, *The Object Advantage: Business Process Reengineering with Object Technology,* Reading, MA: Addison-Wesley, 1995.

[5]   Ivar Jacobson and Sten Jacobson, "Beyond methods and CASE: The software engineering process with its integral support environment," *Object Magazine,* January 1995.

[6]   Ivar Jacobson and Sten Jacobson, "Designing a Software Engineering Process," *Object Magazine,* June 1995.

[7]   Ivar Jacobson and Sten Jacobson, "Designing an integrated SEPSE," *Object Magazine,* September 1995.

[8]   Ivar Jacobson and Sten Jacobson, "Building your own methodology by specializing a methodology framework," *Object Magazine,* November–December 1995.

[9]   Grady Booch, *Object Solutions: Managing the Object-Oriented Project,* Reading, MA: Addison-Wesley, 1996.

[10]  Walker Royce, *Software Project Management: A Unified Framework,* Reading, MA: Addison-Wesley, 1998.

# *Chapter 3*

# A Use-Case–Driven Process

The goal of the Unified Process is to guide developers in efficiently implementing and deploying systems that meet customer needs. Efficiency is measured in terms of cost, quality, and lead-time. The step from assessing customer needs to implementation is not trivial. First, customer needs are not easy to discern. This mandates that we have some way of capturing the users' needs so that they can be clearly communicated to everyone involved in the project. Then we need to be able to design a working implementation that meets those needs. Finally, we must verify that the customer needs have been fulfilled by testing the system. Due to its complexity, the process is described as a series of workflows that gradually build a working system.

As we said in Chapter 1, the Unified Process is use-case driven, architecture-centric, iterative and incremental. In this chapter we will explore the use-case–driven aspect of the Unified Process, first presented in [1] and further discussed in [2]. Its architecture-centric and iterative and incremental aspects are the focus of Chapters 4 and 5, respectively. By dividing the discussion, we hope to communicate the idea of use-case–driven development more simply and clearly. With the same goal, we also downplay how to prepare the deployment model, design high-integrity subsystems, develop good implementation components (see Section 10.3.2), and perform other kinds of tests. Those issues do not contribute to explaining use cases and how they drive the development work, and so an in-depth discussion of these topics is deferred until Part II.

Figure 3.1 depicts the series of workflows and models in the Unified Process. The developers begin by capturing customer requirements as use cases in the use-case model. Then they analyze and design the system to meet the use cases, thus creating first an analysis model, then a design and deployment model; and they implement the system in an implementation model, which includes all the code, that is, the components. Finally, the developers prepare a test model that enables them to verify that the system provides the functionality described in the use cases. All of the models are related to one another through trace dependencies. The implementation model is the most formal, while the use-case model is the least formal, in the sense that it is machine-interpretable, that is, parts of the implementation model can be compiled and linked into executables, whereas the use-case model primarily is described using natural language.

Use cases have been adopted almost universally for capturing the requirements of software systems in general but of component-based systems in particular [6], but use cases are much more than a tool for capturing requirements. They drive the whole development process. Use cases provide major input when finding and specifying classes, subsystems, and interfaces (Appendix A), when finding and specifying test

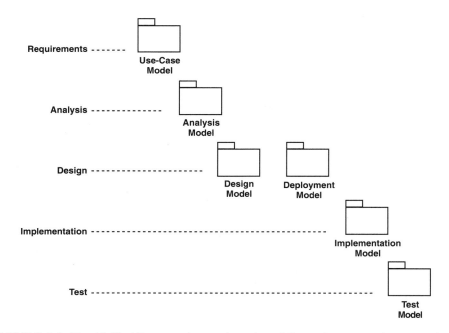

**FIGURE 3.1** The Unified Process is a series of workflows that range from requirements to test (left, from top to bottom). The workflows develop models, ranging from the use-case model to the test model.

cases, and when planning development iterations and system integration (see Chapter 10). For each iteration, they drive through the whole set of workflows from requirements capture, via analysis, design and implementation, to test and bind together these different workflows.

## 3.1  Use-Case–Driven Development in Brief

Requirements capture has two objectives: to find the true requirements (see Chapter 6) and to represent them in a suitable way for the users, customers, and developers. By "true requirements," we mean those requirements that when implemented will add the expected value to the users. By "represent them in a suitable way for the users, customers, developers" we mean in particular that the resulting description of the requirements must be understandable by users and customers. This is one of the major challenges of requirements workflow.

Normally, a system has many types of users. Each type of user is represented as an actor. Actors use the system as they interact with use cases. A use case is a sequence of actions that the system performs to offer some results of value to an actor. All the actors and the use cases of a system make up a use-case model [3], [4].

During analysis and design, the use-case model is then transformed into a design model via an analysis model. In brief, both an analysis model and a design model are structures made up of **classifiers** (Appendix A) and a set of use-case realizations (see Chapters 8 and 9) that describe how this structure realizes the use cases. Classifiers are, in general, "class-like" things. For example, they have **attributes** and **operations** (Appendix A), you may describe them with **statechart diagrams** (Appendix A), some of them can be instantiated, they can be participants in collaborations, and so on. UML has many kinds of classifiers. Subsystems, classes, and interfaces are examples of classifiers in this structure. Other classifiers are actors, use cases, components, and **nodes** (Appendix A; see also Section 9.3.7).

The analysis model is a detailed specification of the requirements and works as a first cut at a design model, although it is a model of its own. It is used by developers to understand more precisely the use cases as described in the requirements workflow by refining them as collaborations among conceptual classifiers (as opposed to design classifiers that will be implemented). The analysis model is also used to create a resilient, robust system (including an architecture) that employs considerable reuse of components. The analysis model is different from the design model in that it is a conceptual model rather than a blueprint of the implementation. The analysis model may be transient and survive only the first couple of iterations. In some cases, however, especially for large, complex systems, the analysis model will be maintained for the life of the system. In such cases, there is a seamless relation (via trace dependencies) between a use-case realization in the analysis model and the corresponding use-case realization in the design model. Every element in the analysis model is traceable from elements in the design model that realizes it. (The analysis model, its purpose, and its relation to the design model are discussed in length in Sections 8.1–8.3.)

The design model has the following characteristics:

- The design model is hierarchical, but it also contains relationships that transcend the hierarchy. The relationships are the usual ones in UML: **associations**, **generalizations**, and **dependencies** (Appendix A).
- The use case realizations are stereotypes of collaborations. A collaboration represents how classifiers participate and play roles in doing something useful, such as realizing a use case.
- The design model is also a blueprint of the implementation. There is a straightforward mapping between subsystems of the design model and components of the implementation model.

The developers create an analysis model that uses the use-case model as input [5]. Each use case in the use-case model will be realized as a use-case realization in the analysis model. The use case/use-case realization dualism supports seamless traceability between requirements and analysis. Working use case by use case, the developers can identify classes that participate in realizing the use cases. For example, the use case Withdraw Money can be realized by the analysis classes Withdrawal, Account, Dispenser, and several others that we don't need to identify to make the point. The developers allocate **responsibilities** (Appendix A) defined in the use case as responsibilities of the classes. In our example, the Account class would contain responsibilities such as "withdraw amount from account." In this way, we can ensure that we get a set of classes that together realize the use cases and are really needed by the users.

The developers then design the classes and use-case realizations to take better advantage of the products and technologies (e.g., object request brokers, GUI construction kits, and database management systems) used to implement the system. The design classes are grouped into subsystems, and interfaces may be defined between those subsystems. The developers also prepare the deployment model, where they define the physical organization of the system in computational nodes and verify that the use cases can be implemented as components that execute on those nodes.

Next, the developers implement the designed classes as a set of file components (source code) in the implementation model, from which the executables, such as DLLs, JavaBeans, and ActiveX components can be produced (i.e., compiled and linked). The use cases help the developers determine the order in which to implement and integrate the components.

Finally, during the test workflow the testers verify that the system indeed implements functionality described in the use cases and satisfies the system requirements. The test model consists of test cases (and other things to be discussed later in Chapter 11). A test case defines a collection of input, execution conditions, and results. Many test cases can be derived directly from the use cases and thus there is a trace dependency between the test case and the corresponding use case. This means that the testers will be verifying that the system can do what the users need it to do, that is, execute the use cases. Anyone who has tested software in the past has in fact tested use cases—even if the work was not described in such terms at the time [8]. What is new and different about the Unified Process is that testing can be planned early in the development cycle. As soon as the use cases have been captured, it is possible to specify the use-case tests ("black-box" tests) and to determine the order in which to realize, integrate, and test them. Later, as the use cases are realized during design, the use-case tests can be detailed ("white-box" tests). Each way to execute a use case—that is, every path through a use-case realization—is a candidate test case.

So far, we have presented the Unified Process as a sequence of steps, much like the old waterfall approach. But we have done this only to keep things simple at this point. In Chapter 5 we will see how these steps can be deployed in a much more interesting way using an iterative and incremental approach. Actually, what we have described here is one iteration. A whole development project will then be a series of iterations, in which each (but possibly the first) of the iterations consists of one pass through the requirements, analysis, design, implementation, and test workflows.

Let us take a closer look at the benefits of use cases before we study the different workflows in more detail.

## 3.2  Why Use Cases?

There are several reasons why use cases are good and have become popular and universally adopted [6]. The two major reasons are:

- They offer a systematic and intuitive means of capturing **functional requirements** (Appendix C; see also Chapters 6 and 7) with a focus on value added to the user.
- They drive the whole development process since most activities such as analysis, design, and test are performed starting from the use cases. Design and test can also be planned and coordinated in terms of use cases. This characteristic is even more obvious in the project when the architecture has stabilized after the first set of iterations.

### 3.2.1  To Capture the Value Adding Requirements

According to Karl Wieger, "the perspective provided by use cases reinforces the ultimate goal of software engineering: to create products that let customers do useful work." [9]. There are several reasons why this is true.

First, the use-case construct supports identifying software that meets user objectives. Use cases are the functions a system provides to add value to its users. By taking the perspective of each type of user, we can capture the use cases that they need to do their work. If, on the other hand, we start thinking up a set of good system functions without thinking of the use cases employed by the individual users, we will find it difficult to tell if these functions are important or even good. Whom do they help? What business needs do they satisfy? How much value do they add to the business?

The best use cases are those that add the most value to the business that deploys the system. A use case that adds negative value or allows the user to do things that he or she should not be able to do is not a use case. We could call it an "abuse case," because it specifies ways of using the system that must be prevented. An example of such a use case would be to allow a Bank Customer to move money from someone else's account to his own. Use cases that add little or no value will be used less often; they are superfluous "use-less cases."

As we mentioned in Chapter 1, many people have found that simply asking themselves what they want the system to do does not help them get the right answers. Instead, they get a list of system functions, which, at first glance may seem valuable, but upon closer scrutiny are not necessarily related to user needs. The use-case strategy of rephrasing the question by adding three words to the end—what do you want the system to do *for each user*?—may seem to be a small distinction, but it yields a very different result. It keeps us focused on understanding how the system needs to support each one of its users. It guides us in finding the functions that each user needs. It also helps us refrain from suggesting superfluous functions that none of the users needs.

Furthermore, use cases are intuitive. Users and customers do not have to learn complex notation. Instead, plain English (i.e., natural language) can be used most of the time, which makes it easier for to read use-case descriptions and to propose changes.

Capturing use cases involves the users, the customers, and the developers. Users and customers are the requirements experts. The developers' role is to facilitate the discussions and help the users and customers communicate their needs.

The use-case model is used to reach an agreement with the users and customers as to what the system should do for the users. We can think of the use-case model as a complete specification of all the possible ways of using the system (the use cases), This specification can be used as part of a contract with the customer. The use-case model helps us delimit the system by defining everything it must do for its users. An interesting approach to structuring use cases is presented in [12], and [11] provides a good general introduction to use cases.

### 3.2.2 To Drive the Process

As we said, to be use-case driven means that a development project proceeds through a series of workflows that are initiated from the use cases. The use cases help the developers to find the classes. The classes are harvested from the use case descriptions as the developers read them looking for classes that are suitable for realizing the use cases.[1] The use cases also help us develop user interfaces that make it easier for users to perform their tasks. Later, the use-case realizations are tested to verify that **instances** (Appendix A) of the classes can perform the use cases [8].

---

1. This is a simplification. In reality, each use case may hit several classes (subsystems, etc.) that have already been developed, so we will modify the use cases to fit these reusable building blocks. This will be discussed in Section 4.3.

**FIGURE 3.2** Use cases bind the core workflows together. The shaded ellipse in the background symbolizes how use cases bind together the workflows.

Use cases not only initiate a development process but bind it together as shown in Figure 3.2.

We also need to make sure that we capture the right use cases so that users will get the use cases they really need. The best way to address this issue is, of course, to do a good job during requirements. But that is usually not enough. An executing system allows us to validate further the use cases against real user needs.

The use cases help project managers plan, assign, and monitor many of the tasks that developers carry out. For every use case, a project manager can identify a number of tasks. Every use case to specify is a task, every use case to design is a task, and every use case to test is a task. The project manager can even estimate the effort and time that will be required for these tasks. The tasks identified based on the use cases help managers estimate project size and required resources. These tasks can then be assigned to individual developers, who are held accountable for them. A project manager might make an individual responsible for specifying five use cases during requirements, another individual responsible for designing three use cases, and a third developer responsible for specifying the test cases for two use cases.

Use cases are an important mechanism for supporting traceability through all the models. A use case in the requirements is traceable to its realization in analysis and design, to all the classes participating in realizing it, to components (indirectly), and finally, to the test cases that verify it. This traceability is an important aspect of managing a project. When a use case is changed, the corresponding realizations, classes, components, and test cases have to be checked for updating. Similarly, when a file component (source code) is changed, the corresponding classes, use cases, and test cases concerned also need to be checked, and so on (see [10]). The traceability between use cases and the other model elements makes it easier to maintain the integrity of the system and to keep the system as a whole up-to-date with changing requirements.

### 3.2.3 To Devise the Architecture and More...

Use cases help us carry out iterative development. Each iteration, apart from possibly the very first one in a project, is driven by the use cases through all the workflows, from requirements to design and testing, resulting in an **increment** (Appendix C). Each development increment is thus a working realization of a set of use cases. In other words, in each iteration a number of use cases is identified and implemented.

Use cases also help us devise the architecture. By selecting the right set of use cases—the architecturally significant use cases—to realize during the first few iterations, we can implement a system with a stable architecture, one that can be used for many subsequent development cycles. We will return to this in Chapter 4.

Use cases are also used as a starting point when writing the user manual. Since each use case describes one way of using the system, they are an ideal starting point for explaining how the user can interact with the system.

By estimating how often the different paths through the use cases are performed, it is possible to estimate which paths require the best performance. Such estimates can be used to dimension the processor capacity of the underlying hardware or to optimize a database schema for certain uses. Similar estimates can also be used to achieve good usability, that is, to select the most important paths to focus on when designing the user interface.

## 3.3 Capturing the Use Cases

Now we turn to an overview of how work proceeds through all the workflows. We will, as stated earlier, focus on the use-case–driven aspect. In the next section we will focus on capturing functional requirements as use cases, even when other types of requirements also need to be captured.

During the requirements workflow we identify user and customer needs as requirements. Functional requirements are expressed as use cases in a use-case model, other requirements are either "attached" to the use cases that they concern or kept in a separate list or described in some other way.

### 3.3.1 The Use-Case Model Represents the Functional Requirements

The use-case model helps the customer, users, and developers agree on how to use the system. Most systems have many types of users. Each type of user is represented as an *actor*. Actors use the system as they interact with use cases. All the actors and the use cases of a system make up a use-case model [2], [3]. A **use-case diagram** (Appendix A; see also Section 7.4.1) describes part of the use-case model and shows a set of use cases and actors with an association between each interacting pair of actor and use case (see Figure 3.3).

---

**Example**    A Use-Case Model of the ATM System

The Bank Customer actor uses an ATM system to withdraw and deposit money from and to accounts and to transfer money between accounts. This is represented by the three use cases shown in Figure 3.3 that have associations to the actor to indicate that they interact.

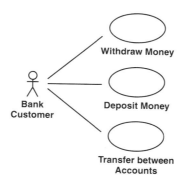

**FIGURE 3.3**  An example of a use-case diagram with an actor and three use cases.

### 3.3.2  Actors Are the Environment of the System

All actors need not represent humans. Actors can be other systems or external hardware that will interact with the system. Each actor takes a coherent set of roles when it interacts with the system. A physical user may act as one or several actors, playing the roles of those actors, as they interact with the system. Several individual users may act as different occurrences of one and the same actor. For example, there may be thousands of people who act as the Bank Customer actor.

Actors communicate with the system by sending **messages** (Appendix A) to and receiving messages from the system as it performs use cases. As we define what the actors do and what the use cases do, we make a clear separation between the responsibilities of the actors and those of the system. This separation helps us delimit the scope of the system.

We can find and specify all the actors by looking at which users will use the system and which other systems must interact with it. Each category of users or interacting systems are then represented as actors.

### 3.3.3  Use Cases Specify the System

Use cases are fashioned to meet the needs of the users as they use the system. The use-case model captures all the functional requirements of the system. We define a use case precisely as follows:

> *A use case specifies a sequence of actions, including variants, that the system can perform and that yields an observable result of value to a particular actor.*

We find the use cases by looking at how the users need to use the system to do their work (for a goal-based way to structure use cases, see [10]). Each such way of using the system that adds value to the user is a candidate use case. These candidates will then be elaborated on, changed, divided into smaller use cases, or integrated into more complete use cases. The use-case model is almost finished when it captures all functional requirements correctly in a way that the customer, users and developers can understand. The sequence of actions performed by a use case during operation (i.e., a use-case instance) is a specific path through the use case. Many paths are possible, and many may be very similar—they are variants of the performance of the sequence of actions specified in the use case. To make a use-case model understandable, we should group similar variant-path descriptions into one use case. When we say that we identify and describe a use case, we really mean that we identify and describe the various paths that are practical to define as one and the same use case.

---

**Example**    The Withdraw Money Use Case

The sequence of actions for a path through this use case is (very simplified here):

1. The Bank Customer identifies himself or herself.
2. The Bank Customer chooses from which account to withdraw money and specifies how much to withdraw.
3. The system deducts the amount from the account and dispenses the money.

---

Use cases are also used as "placeholders" for **nonfunctional requirements** (Appendix C; see also Chapter 6), such as performance, availability, accuracy, and security requirements that are specific to a use case. For example, the following requirement can be attached to the Withdraw Money use case: The response time for a Bank Customer measured from selecting the amount to withdraw to the delivery of the bills should be less than 30 seconds in 95% of all cases.

Summing up, all functional requirements are nailed down as use cases, and many of the nonfunctional requirements can be attached to the use cases. In fact, the use-case model is a vehicle for organizing the requirements in an easy-to-manage way. Customers and users can understand it and use it to communicate their needs in a consistent, nonredundant way. Developers can divide the requirements capture work among themselves, and then use the results (primarily use cases) as input when analyzing, designing, implementing, and testing the system.

## 3.4  Analysis, Design, and Implementation to Realize the Use Cases

During analysis and design, we transform the use-case model via an analysis model into a design model, that is, to a structure of classifiers and use-case realizations. The goal is to realize the use cases cost-effectively so that the system offers suitable performance and can evolve in the future.

In this section, we will now see how to go via analysis to develop a design to realize the use cases. In Chapters 4 and 5, we will look at how architecture and iterative and incremental development help us cost-effectively develop a system that can accommodate new requirements.

### 3.4.1 Creating the Analysis Model from the Use Cases

The analysis model grows incrementally as more and more use cases are analyzed. For each iteration, we select a set of use cases that we realize in the analysis model. We build the system as a structure of classifiers (analysis classes) and relationships between those classifiers. We also describe the collaborations that realize the use cases, i.e., the use-case realizations. Then, in the next iteration, we pick another set of use cases to realize, and these are then added to the previous iteration. In Sections 5.3 and 12.6, we discuss how to identify and select the most "important" sets of use cases for the first iterations to build a stable architecture early in the system life cycle.

A practical way of working is first to identify and describe the use cases for an iteration, then read through the description of each use case (as exemplified in Section 3.3.3), and suggest what classifiers and associations are needed to realize the use case. We do this for all use cases in an iteration as a coordinated effort. Depending on where we are in the life cycle and what type of iteration we are working with, an architecture may already be in place to guide us in finding new classifiers and reusing existing ones (see Section 4.3). Each classifier plays one or several roles in a use-case realization. Each classifier role specifies the responsibilities, attributes, and so on that the classifier must have to participate in realizing a use case. We can think of these roles as "embryos" of classifiers. In fact, in UML a role is also a classifier of its own. For example, we may think of a class's role as being a view of the class. Thus it includes what its class includes, that is, responsibilities, attributes, and so on—but only those that are of interest to its role in a use-case realization. Another way to describe a class role is to see it as what is left of the class when you put a filter over it, a filter that blocks all other roles of the class that do not have shared responsibilities. This role concept is briefly described in this chapter, although it is for simplicity not carried through in Part II of this book where all classifiers are discussed in detail.

---

**Example** | ## The Realization of a Use Case in the Analysis Model

In Figure 3.4 we describe how the Withdraw Money use case is realized by a collaboration (i.e., a use-case realization) with a «trace» dependency (trace is a stereotype of dependency that is indicated by the guillemets, « and ») between them, and that four classes participate and play roles in the use-case realization. As can be seen in the figure, the notation for a use-case realization or collaboration is an ellipse with a dashed line.

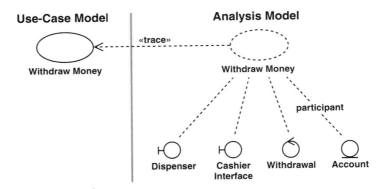

**FIGURE 3.4** The analysis classes that participate in a realization of the Withdraw Money. The Dispenser and the Cashier Interface are boundary classes, the Withdrawl is a control class, and the Account is an entity class.

We typically begin by looking at a few use cases, creating use-case realizations for them, and identifying classifier roles. Then we do the same for some more use cases and suggest new classifier roles. Some of these later roles can be specified as new or changed roles of already identified classifiers, while other roles require new classifiers. Then we once again look at the first few use cases, and so we alternate among the use cases and gradually build a stable analysis model. As a result, each classifier may participate and play roles in several use-case realizations.

## *Analysis Stereotypes*

In the analysis model, three different stereotypes on classes are used: «boundary class», «control class», and «entity class». The Dispenser and Cashier Interfaces are boundary classes that in general are used to model interaction between the system and its actors (i.e., users and external systems). The Withdrawal is a control class that is generally used to represent coordination, sequencing, transactions, and control of other objects—and it is often also used to encapsulate control related to a specific use case (in this case the Withdraw Money use case). The Account is an entity class that in general is used to model information that is long-lived and often persistent. Thus, each one of these class stereotypes encapsulates different types of behavior (or functionality, if you wish). As a result, the stereotypes help us build a robust system, something to which we will return and discuss in more detail in Chapter 8. It also help us find reusable assets, since entity classes are usually generic for many use cases and consequently for many different applications. The separation of analysis classes in these three stereotypes is described in more detail in [2]. It has been practiced for many years and is now in widespread use and adopted by UML [12].

| Example | A Class Participating in Several Use-Case Realizations in the Analysis Model |
|---|---|

On the left side of Figure 3.5 is a set of use cases for an ATM system (the same as in Figure 3.3), and on the right side is the corresponding system structure, in this case, the analysis classes that realize the use cases. The system structure is modeled in a **class diagram** (Appendix A). Class diagrams are generally used to show classes and their relationships, but they can also be used to show subsystems and interfaces (as we will see when we discuss design in Section 3.4.3). For simplicity, we have used different shadings to indicate which use-case realizations a class participates and plays roles in.

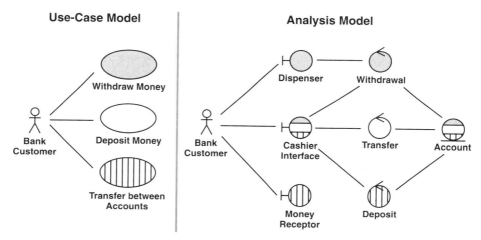

**FIGURE 3.5** The diagram shows how each use case (left) is realized as a structure of analysis classes (right). For example, the Cashier Interface, Withdrawal, Account, and Dispenser classes all participate in realizing the Withdraw Money use case. The Cashier Interface and Account classes are participating and playing roles in all three use-case realizations. The other classes participate in one use-case realization only, that is, they play only one role.

The class diagram for the ATM system (Figure 3.5) was found by going through the descriptions of the three use cases and then looking for ways to realize each one of them. We might have done something like the following:

- The realization of the three use cases, Withdraw Money, Transfer between Accounts, and Deposit Money involves the boundary class Cashier Interface and the entity class Account. The performance of each use case starts with an **object** (Appendix A) of the Cashier Interface. Then work is passed to a control object that coordinates most of the use case in question. The class of this object is unique for each use case. The Withdrawal class thus participates in the Withdraw Money use case and so on. The Withdrawal object asks the Dispenser to dispense money, and it asks the Account object to reduce the balance.

- The two Account objects involved in the use-case realization for Transfer between Accounts are asked by the Transfer object to update their balance.
- The Deposit object accepts money through the Money Receptor and asks the Account object to increase the balance.

So far we have been working to find a stable system structure for the current iteration. We have identified the responsibilities of the participating classifiers, and we have found relationships between the classifiers. However, we have not identified in detail the interaction that must take place in realizing the use cases. We have found the structure, but now we need to superimpose on that structure the different interaction patterns required by each use-case realization.

As we stated earlier, every use case is realized as a use-case realization, and every use-case realization has a set of participating classifiers, which play different roles. Understanding the interaction patterns means that we describe how a use-case realization is performed or executed (or instantiated). For example, what happens when an individual Bank Customer makes a withdrawal, that is, when he or she performs a Withdraw Money use case. We know that the classes Cashier Interface, Withdrawal, Dispenser, and Account will participate in realizing the use case. We also know what responsibilities they would have. However, we don't yet know how they—or more correctly, how objects of those classes—would interact to perform the use-case realization. This is what we need to find out next. We primarily use **collaboration diagrams** (Appendix A) to model interactions among objects in analysis. (UML also provides sequence diagrams to model interactions, to which we will turn our attention when we discuss design in Section 3.4.3.) A collaboration diagram resembles a class diagram, but it shows instances and **links** (Appendix A) instead of classes and associations. It shows how objects interact sequentially or in parallel by numbering the exchanged messages.

---

| **Example** | Using a Collaboration Diagram to Describe a Use-Case Realization in the Analysis Model |

In Figure 3.6 we use a collaboration diagram to describe how the Withdraw Money use-case realization is performed by a society of analysis objects.

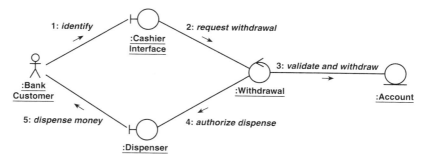

**FIGURE 3.6** A collaboration diagram for the Withdraw Money use-case realization in the analysis model.

The diagram shows how the focus moves from object to object as the use case is performed and the messages that are sent between the objects. A message sent from one object triggers the receiving object to take over focus and to carry out one of the responsibilities of its class.

The name of a message denotes the intent of the invoking object when interacting with the invoked object. Later, during design, these messages are refined into one or more operations provided by corresponding design classes (as we will see in Section 3.4.3).

As a complement to a collaboration diagram, developers may also use text to explain how the objects interact to perform the flow of events of the use case. There are many other ways to describe a realization, such as using structured text or pseudocode.

**Example** **Flow of Events Description of a Use-Case Realization**

We now describe the realization of the Withdraw Money use case in terms of interacting objects and actors, shown in Figure 3.6.

A Bank Customer chooses to withdraw money and activates the Cashier Interface object. The Bank Customer identifies himself or herself and specifies how much to withdraw and from which account (1). The Cashier Interface verifies the Bank Customer's identity and asks a Withdrawal object to perform the transaction (2).

If the Bank Customer's identity is valid, the Withdrawal object is asked to confirm that the bank customer has the right to withdraw the specified amount from the Account. The Withdrawal object confirms this by asking the Account object to validate the request and, if the request is valid, withdraw the amount (3).

Then the Withdrawal object authorizes the Dispenser to dispense the amount that the Bank Customer requested (4). The Bank Customer then receives the requested amount of money (5).

Note that this simple example shows only one path through the use-case realization, when everything runs without any complications. A complication would occur, for example, if the balance on the Account is too low to allow a withdrawal.

At this point, we will have analyzed each use case and thus identified all class roles participating in each use-case realization. Now we turn the discussion to how we analyze each class.

### 3.4.2 Each Class Must Fulfill All Its Collaboration Roles

The responsibilities of a class are simply a compilation of all the roles it plays in all of the use-case realizations. Taken together and removing overlap between the roles, we will get a specification of all the responsibilities and attributes of the class.

The developers responsible for analyzing and realizing the use cases are responsible for specifying class roles. A developer who is responsible for a class collects all the roles of the class into a complete set of responsibilities for the class and then integrates these into a consistent set of responsibilities.

The developers responsible for analyzing use cases must ensure that the classes realize the use cases with appropriate quality. If a class is changed, the developer of the class must verify that the class still can fulfill its roles in use-case realizations. If a role in a use-case realization is changed, the use-case developer must convey the change to the class developer. The roles thus help both the developers of classes, and the developers of use cases, to maintain the integrity of the analysis.

### 3.4.3 Creating the Design Model from the Analysis Model

The design model is created using the analysis model as the primary input, but is adapted to the selected implementation environment, such as to an object request broker, a GUI construction kit, or a database management system. It may also be adapted to reuse **legacy systems** (Appendix C) or other frameworks developed for the project. Thus, whereas the analysis model works as a first initial cut on the design model, the design model works as a blueprint for the implementation.

Similar to the analysis model, the design model also defines classifiers (classes, subsystems, and interfaces), relationships between those classifiers, and collaborations that realize the use cases (i.e., the use-case realizations). However, the elements defined in the design model are the "design counterparts" of the more conceptual elements defined in the analysis model in the sense that the former (design) elements are adapted to the implementation environment whereas the latter (analysis) elements are not. In other words, the design model is more "physical" in nature, whereas the analysis model is more "conceptual."

A use-case realization in the analysis model can be traced from a use-case real-ization in the design model.

**Example**  Use-Case Realizations
in the Analysis and Design Models

In Figure 3.7 we describe how the Withdraw Money use case is realized by a use-case realization both in the analysis model and in the design model.

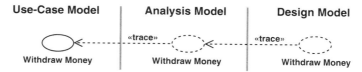

**FIGURE 3.7**  Use-case realizations in different models.

The use-case realizations in the different models serve different purposes. Recall from Section 3.4.1 (Figure 3.4) that the analysis classes Cashier Interface, With-drawal, Account, and Dispenser all participate in realizing the Withdraw Money use case in the analysis model. However, when these analysis classes are designed, they all specify and give rise to more refined design classes that are adapted to the implementation environment, as exemplified in Figure 3.8.

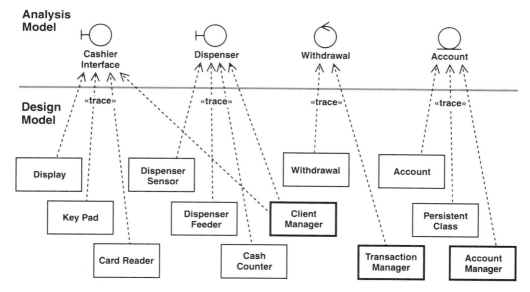

**FIGURE 3.8**  Design classes in the design model tracing to analysis classes in the analysis model.

For example, the analysis class named Cashier Interface is designed by four design classes: Display, Key Pad, Card Reader, and Client Manager (which is an active class and is therefore depicted with a thick border; see Appendix A).

Note that in Figure 3.8 most design classes usually trace to only one analysis class. This is normal for design classes that are application specific, designed to support an application or a suite of applications. Therefore, the structure of the system defined by the analysis model is naturally preserved during design, although some compromises may be needed (such as when the Client Manager participates in the design of both the Cashier Interface and Dispenser classes). Moreover, the active classes (Client Manager, Transaction Manager, and Account Manager) represent processes that organize the work of the other (nonactive) classes when the system is distributed (we return to this issue in Section 4.5.3).

As a consequence, the realization of the Withdraw Money use case in the design model needs to describe how the use case is realized in terms of the corresponding design classes. Figure 3.9 depicts a class diagram that is part of the use-case realization.

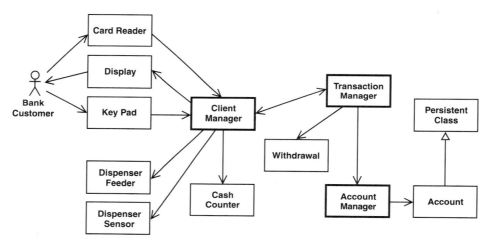

**FIGURE 3.9**  A class diagram that is part of a realization of the Withdraw Money use case in the design model. Each design class participates and plays roles in the use-case realization.

It is obvious that this class diagram introduces more detail than the class diagram in the analysis model (Figure 3.5) does. This detail is needed due to the adaptation of the design model to the implementation environment.

Similarly as in analysis (Figure 3.6), we must identify in detail the interaction among design objects that takes place when the use case is realized in the design model. We primarily use sequence diagrams to model interactions among objects in design, as depicted in Figure 3.10.

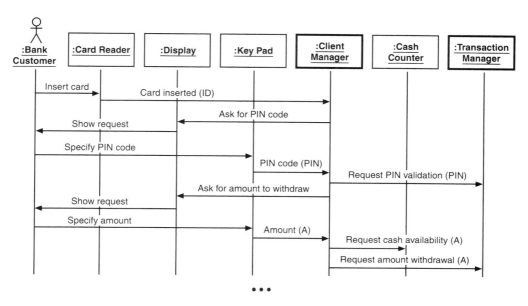

**FIGURE 3.10** A sequence diagram that is part of a realization of the Withdraw Money use case in the design model.

The sequence diagram shows how the focus—starting at the upper left corner—moves from object to object as the use case is performed and messages are sent between objects. A message sent from one object triggers the receiving object to take over focus and to carry out one of the operations of its class.

It is an interesting exercise to compare this sequence diagram with the "analysis counterpart"—that is, the collaboration diagram—in Figure 3.6. As a matter of fact, the first two messages in the collaboration diagram ("1: identify" and "2: request withdrawal") are designed by all messages in the sequence diagram of Figure 3.10. This gives us a hint of the complexity and the amount of detail that is introduced in the design model as compared to the analysis model.

As in collaboration diagrams, developers may also use text to complement the sequence diagrams—explaining how the design objects interact to perform the flow of events of the use case.

As can be noted from this example, the design model is likely to contain many classes. Thus, we need a way to organize the classes. This is done in terms of subsystems, to which we turn our attention in the next section.

### 3.4.4  Subsystems Group Classes

For a large system with hundreds or thousands of classes, using only classes to realize use cases would not be possible: The system is too large to grasp without a higher-order grouping. The classes are grouped in subsystems. A subsystem is a semantically useful grouping of classes or other subsystems. A subsystem has a set of interfaces that it provides and uses. These interfaces define the context of the subsystem (actors and other subsystems and classes).

Low-level subsystems are called **service subsystems** (Appendix B; see also Chapter 9) because their classes realize a service (for a more elaborate description of the service concept, see Section 8.4.5.1). Service subsystems make up a manageable unit of optional (or potentially optional) functionality. It should be possible to install a subsystem in a customer system only in its entirety. Service subsystems are also used to model groups of classes that tend to change together.

Subsystems can be devised either bottom-up or top-down. When working bottom-up, developers suggest subsystems based on the classes they have already found; they suggest subsystems that package the classes into units of clearly defined functions. If developers choose to work top-down instead, the architect identifies the high-level subsystems and their interfaces before any of the classes are identified. Developers are then assigned to work with individual subsystems to find and design the classes within their subsystem. Subsystems were introduced in Chapter 1, and they will be discussed further in Chapters 4 and Chapter 9.

## Example     Subsystems Group Classes

The developers group the classes into the three subsystems shown in Figure 3.11. These subsystems are chosen so that all classes that provide the user interface are placed in one subsystem, all that have to do with accounts in one subsystem, and the use-case specific classes in one subsystem. The advantage of placing all user-interface classes in the ATM Interface subsystem is that this subsystem can then be replaced by another that offers the same functionality to the Transaction Management subsystem. An alternative ATM Interface subsystem may have a very different UI implementation, perhaps designed to receive and deliver coins instead of bills.

The use-case–specific classes, such as the Withdrawal class, in the Transaction Management subsystem each end up in a separate service subsystem. Each such service subsystem would in reality hold more than one class, but that has not been shown in our simple example.

Figure 3.11 also shows the interfaces between the subsystems. A circle represents an interface. The solid line from a class to an interface means that the class provides the interface. A dashed arrow from a class to an interface means that the class uses the interface. For simplicity we don't show interfaces provided or used by the actor; we use ordinary associations here.

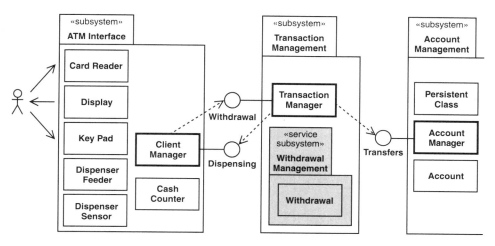

**FIGURE 3.11** Three subsystems and a service subsystem (gray within the Transaction Management subsystem) of our simple ATM example.

The Transfers interface defines operations for moving money between accounts, withdrawing money, and depositing money into accounts. The Withdrawal interface defines operations for requesting withdrawals from an account. The Dispensing interface defines operations to be used by other subsystems for delivering money to the bank customer, such as by the Transaction Management subsystem.

## 3.4.5 Creating the Implementation Model from the Design Model

During the implementation workflow we develop everything needed to produce an executable system: the executable components, file components (source code, shell scripts, etc), table components (database elements), and so on. A component is a physical and replaceable part of a system that conforms to and provides the realization of a set of interfaces. The implementation model is made up of components, which include all **executables** (Appendix A; see also Chapter 10) such as ActiveX components and JavaBeans, as well as all other kinds of components.

---

| **Example** | Components in the Implementation Model |

In Figure 3.12 we depict components implementing design classes from the design model (as presented in Section 3.4.3).

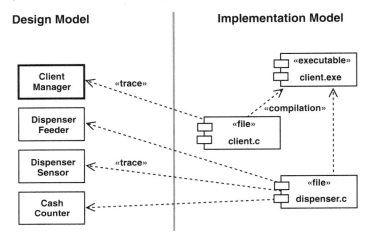

**FIGURE 3.12** Components implementing design classes.

For example, the dispenser.c file component contains the source code (and thus implements) the three classes, Dispenser Feeder, Dispenser Sensor, and Cash Counter. This file component is then compiled and linked together with the client.c file component into the client.exe component, which is executable.

---

A component assumes an architectural context defined by its interfaces. It is also replaceable, meaning that developers can replace one component with another, maybe better, one, as long as the new one provides and requests the same interfaces. There is usually a straightforward way to implement a service subsystem from the design model to components that can be allocated to nodes in the deployment model. Each service subsystem is implemented by one component if it is always allocated to one type of node in the deployment model. If it is allocated to more than one node, the service subsystem may be divided—usually by dividing some classes—into as many parts as there are types of nodes. Each part of the service subsystem will in this case be implemented as a component.

---

**Example**    A Service Subsystem Implemented as Components

Suppose we have chosen a **client/server** (see Section 9.5.1.1) solution for our ATM example. We could then have part of the Withdrawal Management service subsystem (Figure 3.11) that contains the Withdrawal class deployed on both the client and the server. The Withdrawal Management service subsystem would then be implemented as two components: "Withdrawal on Client" and "Withdrawal on Server."

---

If the components are implemented with an object-oriented programming language, the implementation of the classes is also straightforward. Each design class corresponds to a class in the implementation, such as a C++ or a Java class. Each file component may implement several such classes, depending on the conventions of the programming language.

But there is more to implementation than developing the code to create an executable system. The developers who are responsible for implementing a component are also responsible for unit testing it before handing it off to integration and system tests.

## 3.5  Testing the Use Cases

During test, we verify that the system correctly implements its specification. We develop a test model that consists of **test cases** and **test procedures** (Appendix C; see also Chapter 11) and then execute the test procedures to make sure that the system works as expected. A test case is a set of test inputs, execution conditions, and expected results developed for a particular objective, such as to exercise a particular path through a use case or to verify compliance with a specific requirement. A test procedure is a specification of how to perform the setup, execution, and evaluation of results for a particular test case. Test procedures can be derived from use cases as well. Defects found are analyzed to locate the problem. These problems are then prioritized and corrected in order of importance.

In Section 3.3, we started to capture the use cases, and then in Section 3.4 we analyzed, designed, and implemented a system that realized the use cases. Now, we will describe how to test that the use cases are implemented correctly. In a way, this is nothing new. Developers have always tested use cases, even before the term *use case* was coined. Testing that the system can be used in a way that makes sense to users has been the practical way to test the functions of a system. However, in another way, this is a new approach. It is new in that we identify the test cases (as use cases during the requirements workflow) before we even begin to design the system, and then we make sure that our design really implements the use cases.

| **Example** | Identifying a Test Case from a Use Case |
|---|---|

In Figure 3.13 we depict a test case, Withdraw Money—Basic Flow, that specifies how to test the basic flow of the Withdraw Money use case.

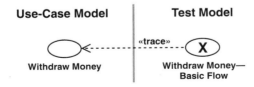

**FIGURE 3.13** A test case in the test model specifying how to test a use case (Withdraw Money) in the use-case model.

Note that we introduce a new stereotype for test cases here, that is, a use-case symbol with a cross within it. This is done to make it possible to depict test cases in diagrams (see Chapter 11).

The test case specifies the input, expected result, and other conditions relevant for verifying the basic flow of the Withdraw Money use case:

*Input:*

■ The Bank Customer's account 12-121-1211 has a balance of $350.
■ The Bank Customer identifies himself correctly.
■ The Bank Customer request to withdraw $200 from account 12-121-1211.
■ There is enough money (at least $200) in the ATM.

*Result:*

■ The balance of the Bank Customer's account 12-121-1211 decreases to $150.
■ The Bank Customer receives $200 from the ATM.

*Conditions:*

No other use cases (instances) are allowed to access the account 12-121-1211 during this test case.

Note that this test case is based on the description of the Withdraw Money use case as exemplified in Section 3.3.3. By identifying the use cases early, we can start planning the test activities early, and we can suggest useful test cases early. These test cases can then become more elaborate during design, when we learn more about how the system will perform the use cases. Some tools actually generate test cases from a design model—all that must be entered manually is the test data needed to run the tests.

Use case tests can be performed either from the point of view of an actor that treats the system as a black box, or from a design perspective, where the test case is constructed to verify that instances of the participating classes in the use-case realization do what they should. Black-box tests can be identified, specified, and planned as soon as the requirements are somewhat stable.

There are also other types of tests, such as system tests, acceptance tests, and tests of user documentation. We will say more about testing in Chapter 11.

## 3.6 Summing Up

Use cases drive the process. During the requirements workflow, developers can represent requirements as use cases. Project managers can then plan the project in terms of the use cases that developers work with. During analysis and design, developers create use-case realizations in terms of classes or subsystems. Developers then implement components. Components are integrated into increments that each realize a set of use cases. Finally, testers verify that the system implements the right use cases for the users. In other words, use cases bind together all development activities and drive the development process—this is perhaps the most important benefit of the use-case–driven approach.

Use cases provide a project with many benefits. However, they are not everything. In the next chapter we will talk about another very important aspect of the Unified Process—its being architecture-centric.

## 3.7 References

[1]    Ivar Jacobson, "Object-oriented development in an industrial environment," *Proceedings of OOPSLA'87,* Special issue of *SIGPLAN Notices* 22(12): 183–191, December 1987.

[2]    Ivar Jacobson, Magnus Christerson, Patrik Jonsson, and Gunnar Övergaard, *Object-Oriented Software Engineering: A Use-Case Driven Approach,* Reading, MA: Addison-Wesley, 1992 (Revised fourth printing, 1993).

[3]    Ivar Jacobson, "Basic use case modeling," *ROAD* 1(2), July–August 1994.

[4]    Ivar Jacobson, "Basic Use Case Modeling (continued)," *ROAD* 1 (3), September–October 1994.

[5]    Ivar Jacobson, "Use cases and objects," *ROAD* 1(4), November–December 1994.

[6]    Ivar Jacobson and Magnus Christerson, "A growing consensus on use cases," *Journal of Object-Oriented Programming,* March–April 1995.

[7]    Ivar Jacobson and Sten Jacobson, "Use-case engineering: Unlocking the power," *Object Magazine,* October 1996.

[8]    Karl Wieger, "Use cases: Listening to the customer's voice," *Software Development,* March 1997.

[9]    E. Ecklund, L. Delcambre, and M. Freiling, "Change cases: Use cases that identify future requirements," *Proceedings, Conference on Object-Oriented Programming Systems, Languages, & Applications (OOPSLA'96),* ACM, 1996, pp. 342–358.

[10]    Alistair Cockburn, "Structuring use cases with goals," *Report on Analysis & Design* (ROAD), 1997.

[11]    Geri Schneider and Jason Winters, *Applying Use Cases: A Practical Approach,* Reading, MA: Addison-Wesley, 1998.

[12]    OMG Unified Modeling Language Specification. Object Management Group, Framingham, MA, 1998. Internet: www.omg.org.

# Chapter 4

## An Architecture-Centric Process

In Chapter 3, we started with a simplification, saying that use cases alone would show the way through requirements, analysis, design, implementation, and test to produce a system. However, there is more to software development than going blindly through the workflows driven only by use cases.

Use cases alone are not enough. Something more is needed to achieve a working system. That "more" is architecture. We can think of the architecture of a system as the common vision that all the workers (i.e., developers and other stakeholders) must agree on or at least accept. The architecture gives us a clear perspective of the whole system, which is necessary to control its development.

We need an architecture that describes the model elements that are most important to us. How do we determine which elements are important? Their importance lies in the fact that they guide us in our work with the system, both in this cycle and throughout the entire life cycle. These architecturally significant model elements include some of the subsystems, dependencies, interfaces, collaborations, nodes, and **active classes** (Appendix A; see also Section 9.3.2). They describe the foundations of the system that we need as a base to understand, develop, and evolve it cost-effectively.

Let us compare a software project with the building of a one-car garage. First, the builder would consider how the user wants to use the garage. One use case would certainly be Shelter the Car, that is, to drive the car in, leave it there, and then take it out later. Does the user have any other uses in mind? Suppose he wants to be able to use it as a home workshop as well. That leads the builder to think about the need for light—some windows and an electric light. Many tools are electrically driven, so the builder also plans half a dozen electrical outlets and sufficient wattage to support them. In a sense, the builder is developing a simple architecture. He can do it in his head, because he has seen a garage before. He has seen a workbench before. He knows what a human being needs to work at a workbench. The builder's approach is not really blind because he is already familiar with the architecture typical of a small garage. He merely has to put the parts together to suit the way the garage will be used. Had the builder never seen a garage and blindly focused on the way it would be used, he might end up with a strange building indeed. So he needs to consider not only the function of the garage but its form.

Building a 10-room house, a cathedral, a shopping center, or a skyscraper is different. There are many ways to build large buildings such as these. Designing them requires a team of architects. The members of the team will have to keep each other informed of the progress of the architecture. That means they have to record their work in a form that is comprehensible to other team members. They also have to present it in a form accessible to laymen—the owner, the users, and the other stakeholders. Finally, they also have to communicate the architecture to the builders and the suppliers of materials through construction drawings.

Similarly, the development of most software systems—or of a software system and the hardware it runs on—takes forethought and the recording of those thoughts in a form usable not only by subsequent developers but by other stakeholders. Furthermore, these thoughts, this architecture, does not spring full-blown from the brow of Zeus: Architects develop it over several iterations during the inception and elaboration phase. In fact, the primary goal of the elaboration phase is to establish a sound architecture in the form of an executable **architectural baseline** (Appendix C). As a result, we enter the construction phase with a solid foundation for building the complete system.

## 4.1 Architecture in Brief

We need an architecture. Fine. But what do we really mean by "architecture of software systems"? As one searches the literature on software architecture, one is reminded of the parable of the blind men and the elephant. An elephant is what each of the blind men happened to encounter—a big snake (the trunk), a piece of cord (the tail), or a small tree (the leg). Similarly, the idea of architecture, at least when reduced to a single defining sentence, is what happened to be in the front of the author's mind at that point.

Let us again compare software architecture to the building of houses. A building is usually a single unit from the client's perspective. The building architect may therefore find it useful to make a scale model of the building, together with drawings of the building from several perspectives. These drawings are usually not very detailed but are comprehensible to the client.

However, building construction involves other kinds of workers during the construction phase, such as carpenters, laborers, bricklayers, roofers, plumbers, electricians, and so on. They all need more detailed and specialized construction drawings of the building, and all those drawings must be consistent with one another. The ventilation pipes and the water pipes, for instance, must not be positioned in the same physical space. The role of the architect is to create the most significant aspects of the overall design of the building. Thus, the architect makes a set of drawings of the building that describe most of the building blocks, such as the foundation in an excavation. A structural engineer determines the size of the beams to support the structure. The foundation supports walls, floors, and a roof. This structure contains systems for elevators, water, electrical, air conditioning, sanitation, and so on. However, these architectural drawings are not detailed enough for the builders to work from. Architectural draftsmen in many specialties prepare drawings and specifications that provide details about the choice of materials, ventilation subsystems, electrical subsystems, water subsystems, and so on. The architect has the overall responsibility for the project, but these other types of designers flesh out the details. In general, the architect is an expert in integrating every aspect of the building but not an expert in every aspect. When all the drawings are done, the architectural drawings cover only the most significant parts of the building. The architectural drawings are views of all the other drawings, but they are consistent with these other drawings.

During construction, various workers use the architectural drawings—the views of the detailed drawings—to get a good overall picture of the building, but they rely on the more detailed construction drawings to carry out their work.

Like a building, a software system is a single entity, but the software architect and the developers find it helpful to present the system from different perspectives to better understand its design. These perspectives are elucidated **views** (Appendixes A and C) of the models of the system. Together, the views present the architecture.

Software architecture encompasses the significant decisions about

- The organization of a software system.
- The structural elements and their interfaces that will comprise the system, together with their behavior as specified in the collaborations among those elements.
- The composition of the structural and behavioral elements into progressively larger subsystems.
- The **architectural style** (Appendix C) that guides this organization: the elements and their interfaces, their collaborations, and their composition.

However, software architecture is concerned not only with structure and behavior but with usage, functionality, performance, resilience, reuse, comprehensibility, economic and technological constraints and trade-offs, and aesthetics.

In Section 4.4, we will discuss the concept of software architecture in more concrete terms and describe how to represent it using the Unified Process. However, we will here hint at what an **architecture description** (Appendix C) looks like. We have already said that the architecture is represented as views of the models: a view of the use-case model, a view of the analysis model, a view of the design model, and so on. This set of views aligns well with the 4+1 views discussed in [3]. Since a view of a model is an extract, or a slice of it, a view of the use-case model, for instance, looks like a use-case model itself. It has actors and use cases but only those that are architecturally significant. In a similar way, the architectural view of the design model looks like a design model, but it contains only those design elements that realize the architecturally significant use cases (see Section 12.6.2).

There is nothing magic about an architecture description. It looks like a complete system description with all its models (there are some differences that we will come back to later), but it is smaller. How small is it? There is no absolute size for an architecture description, but in our experience for a large class of systems, it should be about 50 to 100 pages. That range applies to single-**application systems** (Appendix C); architecture descriptions for **application system suite**s (Appendix C) will be larger.

## 4.2  Why We Need Architecture

A large and complex software system requires an architect, so that the developers can progress toward a common vision. A software system is difficult to envision because it does not exist in our three-dimensional world. It is often unprecedented or unique in some respect. It often uses unproved technology or a novel mix of technologies. It often pushes existing technology to its very limits. Also, it must be built to accommodate a huge class of future changes. As systems become more complex, "the design problem goes beyond the algorithms and data structures of the computation: designing and specifying the overall system structure emerges as a new kind of problem" [1].

In addition, there is often an existing system that performs some of the functions of the proposed system. Figuring out what that system does, often with little or no documentation, and what legacy code the developers can reuse, adds to development complexity.

We need an architecture in order to

- Understand the system
- Organize development
- Foster reuse
- Evolve the system

### 4.2.1  Understanding the System

For an organization to develop a system, the system must be understandable to all concerned. Making modern systems understandable is a significant challenge for many reasons:

- They encompass complex behavior.
- They operate in complex environments.

- They are technologically complex.
- They often combine distributed computing, commercial products and platforms (such as operating systems and database management systems), and reusable components and frameworks.
- They must satisfy demanding individuals and organizations.
- In some cases, they are so large that management has to divide development work among many projects, which are often geographically separated, adding to the difficulty of coordination.

Moreover, these factors constantly change. It all sums up to a potentially difficult-to-understand situation.

Making development architecture-centric (Appendix C) is the way to prevent this failure of understanding from occurring. Therefore, the first requirement we place on an architecture description is that it must enable developers, managers, customers, and other stakeholders to understand what is to be done in sufficient detail to facilitate their own participation. The models and diagrams we mentioned in Chapter 3 aid in this, and they can be used to describe the architecture. As people become familiar with the UML, they will find architecture easier to grasp when it is modeled using it.

### 4.2.2 Organizing Development

The larger the software project organization, the greater the communications overhead will be among developers trying to coordinate their efforts. The communications overhead increases when the project is geographically dispersed. By dividing the system into subsystems with clearly defined interfaces and by making a group or an individual responsible for each subsystem, the architect can reduce the communications load between groups working on different subsystems, whether they are in the same building or on different continents. A "good" architecture is one that explicitly defines these interfaces, making the reduction of communications possible. A well-defined interface "communicates" efficiently to developers on both sides what they need to know about what other teams are doing.

Stable interfaces permit the software on both sides of the interface to move independently. The right architecture and design **patterns** (Appendix C) help us find the right interfaces between subsystems. One example is the Boundary-Control-Entity pattern (see Section 3.4.1), which helps us separate concerns between use case–specific behavior, boundary classes, and generic classes.

### 4.2.3 Fostering Reuse

Let us use an analogy to explain how architecture is important for reuse. The plumbing industry has long been standardized. Plumbing contractors benefit from standard components. Instead of struggling to match up the dimensions of "creative" components obtained from here and there, the plumber selects from a standardized set that always fit together.

Like the plumber, "reuse-enabled" developers know the **problem domain** (Appendix C) and which components the architecture specifies as suitable. The developers figure out how to connect those components to meet system requirements and realize the use-case model. When reusable components are available, they use them. Like standard plumbing fixtures, reusable software components are designed and tested to fit together, so construction then takes less time and costs less. The result is predictable. As in the plumbing industry, where standardization took centuries, standardizing software components also takes the experience of doing it—but we expect extensive "componentization" to occur within a few years. In fact, it is already well along.

The software industry has yet to reach the level of standardization that many hardware domains have achieved, but good architecture and explicit interfaces are steps in that direction. A good architecture gives developers a stable scaffolding on which they can work. The role of the architect is to define that scaffolding and the reusable subsystems that the developers should use. We get reusable subsystems by carefully designing them so that they can be used together [2]. A good architecture helps developers know where to look for reusable elements cost-effectively and to find the right components to reuse. The UML will accelerate the componentization process, because a standard modeling language is a prerequisite for building domain-specific components that can be presented for reuse.

### 4.2.4  Evolving the System

If there is one thing of which we can be sure, it is that a system of any substantial size is going to evolve. It is going to evolve even as it is undergoing development. Later, when it is in use, the changing environment will call for further evolution. During both of these periods, the system should be easy to change; that is, developers should be able to change parts of the design and implementation without having to worry about the effects of the change reverberating unexpectedly throughout the system. In most cases, they should be able to implement new functionality (i.e., use cases) in the system without seeing a dramatic impact on the existing design and implementation. In other words, the system itself should be resilient to change, or change-tolerant. Another way of stating this goal is to say that the system should be capable of evolving gracefully. Poorly architected systems, in contrast, often degrade with the passage of time and the imposition of many patches until finally they cannot be kept up to date cost-effectively.

---

**Example**    The Ericsson AXE System—
On the Importance of Architecture

The Ericsson AXE telecommunications switching system was initially developed in the early 1970s using an early version of our architectural principles. The software architecture description is an important artifact that has guided the whole development work for the lifetime of the system. The architecture was guided by a few principles that now are incorporated in the Unified Process.

One of these was the principle of function modularity. Classes or their equivalent design elements were grouped into functional blocks, or service subsystems, that customers could treat as optional (even if the elements were delivered to all customers). A service subsystem had strong internal cohesion. Changes to the system would usually be local to one service subsystem and would rarely affect more than one service subsystem.

Another principle was to separate the design of interfaces from the design of the service subsystems. The goal was to achieve "plug-able" designs, wherein several service subsystems could support the same interface. Exchanging one service subsystem with another could be done without changing the clients of the service subsystem (which depend only on the interfaces, not on the actual code of the service subsystem).

A third principle was to map a service subsystem in the design directly to one or more components in the implementation. The components of the service subsystem could be distributed to different computational nodes. There was exactly one component for each processing node on which the service subsystem would be executed. Thus, if the service subsystem would run on the central computer (say, a server), then there would be exactly one component for the service subsystem. If the service subsystem was to be implemented on both a client and a server, there would be two components. This principle made managing changes in software on different installations straightforward.

Yet another principle was to have loose coupling between service subsystems. Signals were the only means of communication between service subsystems. Since signals are asynchronous (i.e., send-no-wait semantics) they support not only encapsulation but distribution.

Because its initial and ongoing development has been guided by a well-designed architecture, the AXE system continues in use to this day, with more than one hundred customers and several thousand installations. It is expected to endure, with changes, for decades.

## 4.3  Use Cases and Architecture

We have already hinted that there is some interplay between use cases and architecture. In Chapter 3 we showed in principle how to develop a system that offers the right use cases to its users. If the system offers the right use cases—use cases with high performance, quality, and usability—then users can use it to carry out their mission. But how do we get there? The answer, as we have already suggested, is to build an architecture that allows us to cost-effectively implement the use cases, now and in the future.

Let us clarify how this interplay occurs, first by looking at what influences the architecture (see Figure 4.1) and then at what influences the use cases.

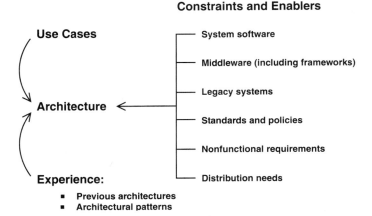

**FIGURE 4.1** Different types of requirements and products influence the architecture, not just the use cases. Also of help in devising an architecture are experience from previous work and structures that we can identify as architectural patterns.

As we have already mentioned, the architecture is influenced by which use cases we want the system to support; the use cases are *drivers* for the architecture. After all, we want an architecture that is suitable when we are implementing our use cases. In the early iterations, we select a few use cases that we think will best allow us to devise the architecture. These architecturally significant use cases include those that the customers need most for the upcoming release and perhaps for future releases.

However, the architecture is influenced not only by the architecturally significant use cases but by the following factors:

■ Which system software products we want to build on, such as an operating system or a particular relational database management system.
■ Which middleware (**middleware layer**; Appendix C) products we want to use. For example, we need to select an object request broker (ORB), which is a mechanism for transparently marshaling and forwarding messages to objects distributed in heterogeneous environments [6], or a platform-neutral framework, that is, a "prefabricated" subsystem, to create graphical user interfaces.
■ Which legacy systems we want to use in our system. By using a legacy system, such as an existing banking system, in our architecture, we can reuse much existing functionality, but we also need to adjust our architecture to match the "old" product.
■ Which standards and company policies we need to adapt to. For example, we might choose OMG's Interface Definition Language (IDL) [7] to specify all interfaces to classes or the telecommunications standard TMN [8] to specify objects in our system.
■ General nonfunctional requirements (i.e., not use case–specific), such as requirements on availability, recovery time, or memory usage.

■ The distribution needs specifies how the system is distributed, perhaps via a client/server architecture.

We can think of the items on the right side of Figure 4.1 as constraints and enablers that lead us to fashion the architecture in a certain way.

The architecture is developed in iterations in the elaboration phase. A simplified, somewhat naive approach—a thought model—could be as follows. We start by deciding on a high-level design for the architecture, such as a **layer**ed architecture (Appendix C). Then we fashion the architecture in a couple of **builds** (Appendix C; see also Chapter 10) within the first iteration.

In the first build, we work with the **application-general** parts (Appendix C), which are general for the domain in question and not specific for the system we plan to develop (i.e., we select system software (system software layer; Appendix C; see also Section 9.5.1.2.2), middleware, legacy systems, standards, and policies to use). We decide on which nodes to have in our deployment model and then how the nodes should interact with each other. We decide on how to deal with general nonfunctional requirements, such as availability requirements. In this first pass it suffices to have a general understanding of the application.

In the second build, we work with the application-specific (application-specific layer; Appendix C) aspect of the architecture. We pick a set of architecturally relevant use cases, capture the requirements, analyze, design, implement, and test them. The result will be new subsystems implemented as components developed to support the use cases we picked. There may also be some changes to the architecturally significant components we implemented in the first build (when we did not think in terms of use cases). The changed and new components are developed to realize the use cases, and in this way the architecture is adapted to suit the use cases better. Then we make another build, and so on, until we finish the iteration. If this finish happens to come at the end of the elaboration phase, the architecture should also be stable.

When we have a stable architecture in place, we can implement the complete functionality by realizing the rest of the use cases during the construction phase. The use cases implemented during the construction phase are mostly developed using customer and user requirements as input (see Figure 4.2). But the use cases are also influenced by the architecture selected in the elaboration phase.

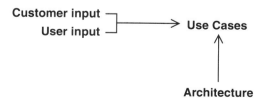

**FIGURE 4.2** The use cases can be developed based on input from customer and users. However, the use cases are also influenced by the architecture that already is in place.

As we capture new use cases, we use our knowledge of the architecture already in place to do our work better. When we assess the value and cost of each suggested use case we do so in the light of the existing architecture. Some use cases will be easy to implement, while others will be difficult.

---

**Example**    Adapting the Use Cases
to the Architecture Already in Place

The customer has requested a function that supervises the processor load. It was specified as a use case that measured the load on a high-priority level of the computer. Implementing that use case would have required some changes to the real-time operating system in use. Instead, the development team suggested that the requested functionality be implemented by a separate external device that makes calls to the system and measures the response time. The customer got a more reliable measure and the development team avoided having to change the critical underlying architecture.

---

We negotiate with the customer and decide if the use cases might be changed to make implementation simpler by aligning the use cases and the resulting design more with the architecture already in place. This alignment means that we must consider what subsystems, interfaces, use cases, use-case realizations, classes, and so on already exist. By aligning the use cases with the architecture, we can create new use cases, subsystems, and classes cost-effectively from what is already there.

So, on the one hand, the architecture is influenced by which use cases we want the system to support. The use cases drive the architecture. On the other hand, we use our knowledge of the architecture to do our work better as we capture the requirements as use cases. The architecture guides the use cases (see Figure 4.3).

What comes first, use cases or architecture? This is a typical chicken-and-egg problem. Such problems are best resolved by iterating. First, we build a tentative architecture based on a good understanding of the **domain area** (Appendix C) but without considering the detailed use cases. Then we pick a few significant use cases and further the architecture by adapting it to support those use cases. Then we pick some more use cases and build an even better architecture, and so on. With each

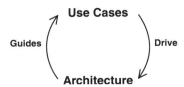

**FIGURE 4.3** The use cases drive the development of the architecture, and the architecture guides which use cases can be realized.

iteration, we pick and implement a set of use cases to validate and, if necessary, to improve the architecture. With each iteration we also further implement the application-specific parts of the architecture based on the use cases we have selected. The use cases thus help us gradually improve the architecture as we iterate our way toward a complete system. This is one benefit of use-case–driven development. We will return to this iterative approach in Chapter 5.

Summing up, a good architecture is one that allows us to provide the right use cases cost-effectively, now and in the future.

## 4.4 The Steps to an Architecture

The architecture is developed in iterations primarily during the elaboration phase. Each iteration is performed as outlined in Chapter 3, starting with requirements, followed by analysis, design, implementation, and test, but focusing on the architecturally relevant use cases and other requirements. The result at the end of the elaboration phase is an architecture baseline—a skeleton of the system with few software "muscles."

Which use cases are architecturally significant? We will elaborate on this question in Section 12.6. For now, let it suffice to say that the architecturally significant use cases are the ones that help us mitigate the most serious risks, those that are the most important to users of the system, and those that help us cover all important functionality so that nothing is left in the shadows. Implementing, integrating, and testing the architecture baseline provide assurance to the architect and other workers that the architecture, as understood at that point, is really operational. This is something that cannot be proven by a "paper" analysis and design. The operational architecture baseline provides a working demonstration to which workers can provide feedback.

### 4.4.1 The Architecture Baseline Is a "Small, Skinny" System

At the end of the elaboration phase we have developed models of the system that represent the most important use cases, from an architectural perspective, and their realizations. We have also, as discussed in Section 4.3, "Use Cases and Architecture," decided on which standards to rely on, which systemware and middleware to use, which legacy systems to reuse, and what distribution needs we have. Thus, we have early versions of the use-case model, the analysis model, the design model, and so on. This aggregate of models (see Figure 4.4) is the architecture baseline; it is a "small, skinny" system.[1] It has versions of all the models that the full-fledged system has at the end of construction phase. It includes the same skeleton of subsystems,

---

1. This is not quite correct. At the end of the elaboration phase, we have a version of the use-case model that contains both the architecturally significant use cases and the use cases (say, up to 80%) we need to have specified in order to make a business case. Thus the architecture baseline has more in the use-case model and the analysis model than Figure 4.4 indicates. However, for the purposes of this discussion, we can make this simplification.

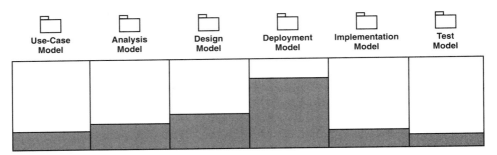

**FIGURE 4.4** The architecture baseline is an internal release of the system that is focused on describing the architecture.

components, and nodes as the eventual system, but not all of the musculature is in place. However, they do have behavior, and they are executable code. The skinny system evolves to become the full-fledged system, perhaps with some minor changes to the structure and behavior. The changes are minor because at the end of the elaboration phase we have by definition a stable architecture; otherwise, the elaboration phase must continue until this goal has been achieved.

In Figure 4.4, the shaded slice of each model represents the version of the model that has been developed at the end of the elaboration phase, that is, the version of the model that is part of the architecture baseline. The whole rectangle (the shaded and unshaded parts) represents the version of the model as developed at the end of the transition phase, that is, the baseline representing the customer release (the reader should not draw too many conclusions from the size of the shaded areas shown in Figure 4.4, which are shown here for purposes of illustration). In between the architecture baseline and the customer-release baseline are several baselines that represent **internal releases** of new versions of the models (Appendix C). We could have illustrated these new versions as increments on top of one another starting from the architecture baseline. Each new version of a model would evolve from the previous version. The different models of Figure 4.4 are, of course, not developed independently of one another. Every use case in the use-case model corresponds, for example, to a use-case realization in the analysis and design models and to test cases in the test model. The process and the node structure must meet the performance required by the use cases. (Otherwise, either the use cases or the deployment model need to be altered, perhaps by changing the way the active classes are allocated to the nodes to get better performance. Such changes in the deployment or the design model may lead to alterations in the use-case model if the changes require us to alter the use cases.) Model elements in the different models are, as we said in Section 2.3.7, related to one another through «trace» dependencies.

However, the architecture baseline, that is, the internal release of the system at the end of the elaboration phase, is represented by more than model artifacts. It also includes an architecture description. This description is actually developed concurrently, often even ahead of the activities that result in the versions of the models that are parts of the architecture baseline. The role of the architecture description is to guide the whole development team throughout the lifetime of the system—not just for iterations within the current cycle but for all the cycles to come. It is the standard to be followed by the developers, now and in the future. Since the architecture should be stable, the standard should be stable as well.

The architecture description can take different shapes. It could be an extract of the (versions of) models that are part of the architecture baseline, or it could be a rewrite of these extracts in an easier-to-read form. We will come back to this in Section 4.4.3, "Describing Architecture." However, it includes extracts, or views, from the models that are part of the architecture baseline. As the system evolves and the models become larger in later phases, it will continue to include views from the new versions of the models. Assuming that the architecture baseline has developed a stable architecture—that is, the architecturally significant model elements are stable and will not change in the iterations to come—the architecture description will also be stable, and it will at every point of time include views of the models of the system.

It is fascinating to see that it is possible to develop a stable architecture during the elaboration phase of the first life cycle when only, say, 30% of the first product release has been invested. This architecture will be the foundation that the system will rest on for its life. Since every change to the foundation will be expensive, and in some cases very painful, it is important to get to a stable architecture early in the development work. Developing an architecture for a particular system is, on the one hand, creating something new. On the other hand, people have developed architectures for years. There is experience in and knowledge of developing good architectures. There are many generic "solutions"—structures, collaborations, and physical architectures—that have evolved over years that every experienced architect should be familiar with. These solutions are usually called "patterns" such as the architectural patterns described in [4] and the design patterns in [5]. Generic patterns are resources the architect will rely upon.

## 4.4.2 Using Architecture Patterns

The ideas of the architect Christopher Alexander about how "pattern languages" are used to systematize important principles and pragmatics in the design of buildings and communities have inspired several members of the object-oriented community to define, collect, and test a variety of software patterns [10]. The "patterns community" defines a pattern as "a solution to a commonly occurring design problem." Many of these design patterns are documented in books, which present patterns using standard documentation templates. These templates assign a name to a pattern and present a summary of the problem and the forces that give rise to it, a solution in terms of a collaboration with participating classes, and interactions among objects of those classes. The templates also provide examples of how the pattern is used in some programming languages, along with variants of the pattern, a summary of the benefits and consequences of using this pattern, and references to related patterns. Following Alexander, it is suggested that software engineers should learn the names and intent of many standard patterns, and apply them to make better, more understandable designs. Design patterns such as Facade, Decorator, Proxy Observer, Strategy, and Visitor are widely quoted and used.

The patterns community has also applied the pattern idea, with a slightly different document template, to collect standard solutions to commonly occurring architectural problems. Some of these patterns include Layers, Pipes and Filters, Broker, Blackboard, Horizontal-Vertical Metadata, and MVC. Others have developed patterns to be used during analysis ("analysis patterns"), during implementation ("idioms" that map common object-oriented structures onto peculiar aspects of languages, such as C++ and Smalltalk), and even for effective organizational structures ("organizational patterns"). Typically, design patterns map fairly directly to object-oriented programming languages. Examples are given in C++, Java, and Smalltalk, while architectural patterns deal mostly with systems or subsystems and interfaces, and examples do not typically include code. For a good classification scheme see [9].

From our model-driven perspective, we will define *pattern* as a template collaboration which is a general collaboration that can be specialized as defined by a **template** (Appendix A). Thus, design patterns become collaborations among classes and instances, with behavior explained by interaction diagrams. We use template collaborations because the solutions are meant to be fairly general. Inheritance, extension, and other mechanisms are used to specialize the pattern (e.g., specifying class names, number of classes, etc. that appear in the template). In many cases, the template collaborations, when specialized, give rise to concrete collaborations that are directly traceable to use cases. See [5] for an extensive treatment of design patterns.

Architectural patterns are used in a similar way but focus on the larger-grained structure and interactions of subsystems and even systems. There are many architectural patterns. Here we will briefly discuss some of the most interesting ones.

The Broker pattern [4] is a generic mechanism for managing object distribution. It allows objects to call other remote objects through a broker that forwards the call to the node and process that holds the desired object. This forwarding is done transparently, which means that the caller does not have to know whether the called object is remote. The Broker pattern often makes use of the Proxy design pattern, which provides a local proxy object with the same interface as the remote object to make the style and details of distributed communication transparent.

There are other patterns that help us understand the hardware of the systems that we build and that help us design our system on top of that hardware. The Client/Server, Three-Tier, and the Peer-to-Peer patterns are examples. These patterns define a structure to the deployment model and suggest how components should be allocated to the nodes. In Section 4.5 we will illustrate how the Client/Server pattern can be applied in the ATM system we described in Chapter 3. In our example, the client/server distribution has one client node that executes all the code for the user interfaces and some of the code for the business logic (control classes) for each physical ATM. The server node holds the actual accounts and the business rules that each transaction is verified against.

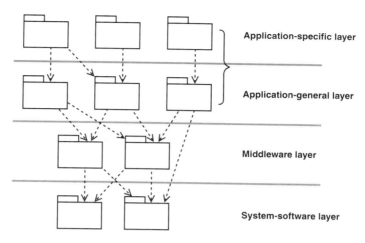

**FIGURE 4.5** The layered architecture organizes systems in layers of subsystems.

The Layers pattern is applicable to many types of systems. It is a pattern that defines how to organize the design model in layers, meaning that components in one layer can reference components only in layers directly below. That pattern is important since it simplifies understanding and organizing the development of complex systems. The layers pattern reduces dependencies in that lower layers are not aware of any details or interfaces in the upper layers. Moreover, it helps us to identify what to reuse, and it provides a structure to help us make decisions about what to buy or to build.

A system with a layered architecture has individual application subsystems at the top. These are built from subsystems in lower layers, such as frameworks and class libraries. See Figure 4.5. The application-general layer contains subsystems that are not specific to a single application but can be reused for many different applications within the same domain or business. The architecture of the lower two layers can be established without considering the details of the use cases because these layers are not business-specific. The architecture of the upper two layers is created from the architecturally relevant use cases (these layers are business-specific).

A **layer** (Appendix C) is a set of subsystems that share the same degree of generality and interface volatility: Lower layers are general to several applications and must have more stable interfaces, while higher layers are more application-specific and may have less stable interfaces. Since the lower layers provide interfaces that change less often, developers who work on the higher layers can build on stable lower layers. Subsystems in different layers can reuse use cases, other lower-level subsystems, classes, interfaces, collaborations, and components from lower layers. Many architecture patterns can be applied within a single system. The patterns that structure the deployment model (e.g., the Client/Server, Three-Tier, or Peer-to-Peer patterns) can be combined with the Layers pattern, which helps structure the design model. Patterns that address structures in different models are often orthogonal to each other. Even patterns that address the same model can often combine well with one another. For instance, the Broker pattern combines well with the Layers pattern, and both are used in the design model. The Broker pattern addresses how to deal with transparent-object distribution, while the Layers pattern suggests how to organize the whole design. In fact, the Broker pattern would be realized as a subsystem in the middleware layer.

Note that sometimes one pattern is predominant. For example, in a layered system, the Layers pattern defines the overall architecture and decomposition of work (layers allocated to different groups), while Pipes and Filters could be used inside one or more layers. By contrast, in a Pipes and Filters system we would show the overall architecture as a flow between filters, while layering would be used explicitly for some filters.

### 4.4.3  Describing Architecture

The architectural baseline developed in the elaboration phase survives, as we observed in Section 4.4.1, in the form of an architecture description. This description is derived from versions of the different models that are the result of the elaboration phase, as depicted in Figure 4.6. The architecture description is an extract or, as we say, a set of views—perhaps with a careful rewrite to make them more readable—of the models in the architecture baseline. The views include the architecturally significant elements. Many model elements that are part of the architecture baseline will, of course, also show up in the architecture description. However, not all of them will, because to get an operational baseline we may need to develop some model elements that are not architecturally interesting but are needed to produce executable code. Since the architecture baseline is used not only to develop an architecture but to specify the requirements of the system to such a level that a detailed plan can be developed, the use-case model of this baseline may also contain more use cases than are interesting from an architectural point of view.

The architecture description will be kept up-to-date throughout the system's lifetime to reflect the changes and additions that are architecturally relevant. These changes are usually minor and may include

- Finding new abstract classes and interfaces.
- Adding new functionality to existing subsystems.
- Upgrading to new versions of reusable components.
- Rearranging the process structure.

The architecture description itself may need to be modified, but it need not grow in size. It is just updated to be relevant (see Figure 4.6).

As discussed earlier, the architecture description presents views of the models. This includes use cases, subsystems, interfaces, some classes and components, nodes, and collaborations. The architecture description also includes architecturally significant requirements that are not described by use cases. The other requirements are nonfunctional and are specified as supplementary requirements, such as those con-

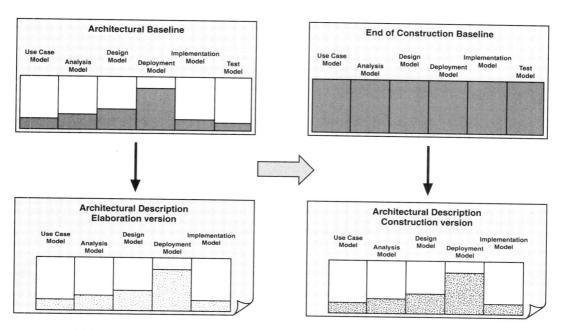

**FIGURE 4.6** During construction, the various models grow to completion (filled shapes in the upper right corner). The architecture description, however, does not grow significantly (lower right) since most of the architecture was defined during the elaboration phase. The few minor changes to the architecture do occur (indicated by a different patterned fill).

cerning security and important constraints regarding **distribution** and **concurrency** (Appendix C; see also Section 9.3.2). The architecture description should also contain a brief description of the platform, the legacy systems, and the commercial software to be used, such as Java's Remote Message Invocation (RMI) for object distribution. Furthermore, it is important to describe frameworks that implement generic **mechanisms** (Appendix C; see also 9.5.1.4), such as storing and retrieving an object from a relational database. Such mechanisms may be reused in several use-case realizations as they have been designed to realize reusable collaborations. The architecture description should also document all architecture patterns that have been used.

The architecture description highlights the most important design issues and brings them out into the open for consideration and feedback from others. These issues then need to be discussed, analyzed, and settled. These analyses may, for example, include estimating performance load or memory requirements and imagining future requirements that might break the architecture.

Although detailed when it counts, the architecture description is still a high-level view. On the one hand, it is not intended to cover everything; it should not inundate the participants with an overwhelming quantity of detail. It is a road map, not a detailed specification of the complete system. On the other hand, it must present what each participant needs, so even 100 pages may not be excessive. People will use a large document if it contains what they need in a form they can readily comprehend. After all, that is what the architecture description should do: It should contain what the developers need to do their jobs.

When reading an architecture description, we may feel that it treats some of the subsystems superficially, while it specifies the interfaces and collaborations of a handful of subsystems in detail. The reason for these differing treatments is that the highly specified subsystems are architecturally significant and should be kept under the architect's control (see Sections 12.4.2 and 14.4.3.1).

It may help to discuss what is *not* architecture. Most classes, with operations, interfaces, and attributes that are private to subsystems or service subsystems (hidden to the rest of the system), are not architecturally significant. Subsystems that are variants of other subsystems are not important from an architecture perspective. Experience indicates that less than 10% of the classes are relevant to the architecture. The remaining 90% are not significant because they are not visible to the rest of the system. A change to one of them does not affect anything substantial outside the service subsystem. Nor are most use-case realizations architecturally significant since they do not impose any additional constraints on the system. That is why architects can plan an architecture from only a fraction of the use cases and other requirements. Most use-case realizations represent simple add-on behavior that is easy to implement even though they constitute most of the functions that the system offers. And this is the point: Most system functionality is really easy to implement once we get the architecture in place.

The architecture description does not include information needed only to validate or verify the architecture. Thus there are no test cases and test procedures, and there is no architectural view of the test model. These matters are not architecture. However, as can be seen in Figure 4.6, the architecture baseline contains a version of all models, including a version of the test model. Thus the baseline underlying the architecture description has undergone tests—all baselines do.

### 4.4.4 The Architect Creates the Architecture

Architecture is created by the architect together with other developers. They work toward a system that will have high performance and high quality, and will be highly functional, testable, user-friendly, reliable, highly available, accurate, expandable, change-tolerant, robust, maintainable, portable, secure, safe, and economical. They know that they have to live within these constraints and have to make trade-offs between them—that is why there is an architect. The architect has the highest technical responsibility in these matters and chooses between architectural patterns and between existing products and arranges subsystem dependencies to separate concerns. Separating concerns here means to create a design where a change in one subsystem does not reverberate to several other subsystems.

The real goal is to meet the needs of the application in the best way available at the current state of technology at a cost the application can bear, in other words, to be able to implement cost-effectively the application functionality (i.e., the use cases) now and in the future. Here the architect is supported by UML and the Unified Process. The UML has powerful constructs to formulate architecture, and the Unified Process gives detailed guidelines on what constitutes a good architecture. Even so, at the end, the chosen architecture is the outcome of judgment based on qualifications and experience. It is the architect who is responsible for making this judgment. When the architect at the end of the elaboration phase presents an architecture description to the development manager at the end of the elaboration phase, it means, "Now I know that we can construct the system without encountering any major technical surprises."

A qualified architect draws upon two kinds of qualifications. One is knowledge of the domain in which he works, for he must work knowledgeably with all stakeholders—not just with developers. The other is knowledge of software development, even down to the ability to write code, for he must communicate the architecture to the developers, coordinate their efforts, and grasp their feedback. It is also valuable if the architect has experience with systems similar to the one being developed.

The architect occupies a difficult post in the software organization. He should not be the project manager, for that position has many duties besides architecture. He does have to have the whole-hearted support of management, both to create the architecture in the first place and to enforce it. Yet he must be sufficiently flexible to accommodate useful feedback from developers and other stakeholders. That is a short summary of what the architect brings to the table. For large systems, one architect may not be sufficient. Instead, it may be wise to have an architecture board develop and maintain the architecture.

Developing the architecture takes considerable calendar time. This time is up front on the development schedule and may be disturbing to managers who are accustomed to seeing development time being devoted largely to implementation and testing. Experience shows, however, that the total duration of development drops markedly when a good architecture guides the later phases. This is something we will touch on in Chapter 5.

## 4.5 Finally, an Architecture Description!

We have been talking about what architecture is for quite some time without giving a substantial example. We will now present a concrete example of what an architecture description looks like. However, before doing so we need to explain why it is not easy.

Recall that the architecture description is just a proper extract of the models of the system (i.e., it does not add anything new). The first version of the architecture description is an extract of the version of the models that we have at the end of the elaboration phase in the first life cycle. Given that we don't try to make a more readable rewrite of those extracts, the architecture description looks very much like ordinary models of the system. This appearance means that the architectural view of the use-case model looks like an ordinary use-case model. The only difference is that the architectural view contains only architecturally significant use cases (see Section 12.6.2), whereas the final use-case model contains all the use cases. The same goes for the architectural view of the design model. It looks like a design model, but it realizes only the use cases that are architecturally interesting.

Another reason it is so difficult to present an example is that architecture is interesting to talk about only for real systems, and when we want to talk about a system in detail here, it must by necessity be a tiny system. However, we will now use the simple ATM example from Chapter 3 to illustrate what the architectural views might entail. We will do that by comparing what will be in the views and what will be in complete models of the system.

The architecture description has five sections, one for each model. There is a view of the use-case model, a view of the analysis model (which is not always maintained), a view of the design model, a view of the deployment model, and a view of the implementation model. There is no view of the test model because it has no role in describing the architecture and is used to verify the architecture baseline only.

### 4.5.1  The Architectural View of the Use-Case Model

The architectural view of the use-case model presents the most important actors and use cases (or scenarios of these use cases). See Section 3.3, "Capturing the Use Cases," regarding the use-case model of the ATM system.

---

**Example**    The Architectural View
of the Use-Case Model of the ATM System

In the ATM example, Withdraw Money is the most important use case. Without it, there would not have been a real ATM system. The Deposit Money and Transfer between Accounts use cases are deemed less important to the average bank customer.

To define the architecture, the architect therefore suggests that the Withdraw Money use case be implemented in full during the elaboration phase, but no other use case (or part of a use case) is deemed interesting for architectural purposes. (In practice, this decision would be a bit farsighted, but is used here for the purposes of discussion).

The architectural view of the use-case model thus should show the full description of the Withdraw Money use case.

---

### 4.5.2  The Architectural View of the Design Model

The architectural view of the design model presents the most architecturally important classifiers of the design model: the most important subsystems, interfaces, as well as a few very important classes, primarily the active classes. It also presents how the most important use cases are realized in terms of these classifiers, that is, as use-case realizations. The active classes are also discussed in Section 4.5.3 as we look at the deployment model (where active classes are allocated to nodes).

| **Example** | The Architectural View of the Design Model of the ATM System |
|---|---|

In Section 3.4.3, we identified three active classes: Client Manager, Transaction Manager, and Account Manager (Figure 4.7). These active classes are included in the architectural view of the design model.

**FIGURE 4.7** The static structure of the architectural view of the design model for the ATM system. This is a class diagram depicting the active classes.

Moreover, from Section 3.4.4, we already know about three subsystems: ATM Interface, Transaction Management, and Account Management; see Figure 4.8. These subsystems are required to realize the Withdraw Money use case, so they are the architecturally significant subsystems. The design model includes many other subsystems, but they are not considered here.

The ATM Interface subsystem handles all input from and output to the bank customer, such as printing the receipts and accepting the commands of the bank customer. The Account Management subsystem maintains all persistent account information and is used for all account transactions. The Transaction Management subsystem contains the classes for use case–specific behavior, such as the behavior specific to the use case Withdraw Money. In Section 3.4.4, the example, we mentioned that the use case–specific classes often end up in different service subsystems, such as a service subsystem for each of the Withdrawal, Transfer, and Deposit classes within the Transaction Management subsystem (not shown in Figure 4.8). In fact, each such service subsystem usually contains several classes, but our example is very simple.

The subsystems in Figure 4.8 provide behavior to each other through interfaces, such as the Transfers interface provided by Account Management. The Transfers, Withdrawal, and Dispensing interfaces are described in Section 3.4.4. There are also the Transferal, Deposits, and History interfaces, but these are not involved in the use case we discuss in this example, so they have not been explained.

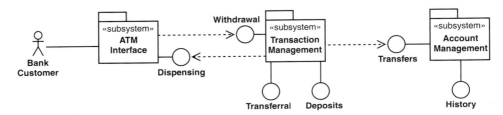

**FIGURE 4.8** The static structure of the architectural view of the design model for the ATM system. This is a class diagram depicting subsystems and interfaces between them.

The static structure is not enough. We also need to show how the architecturally significant use cases are realized by the subsystems in the design model. Therefore, we will once again describe the Withdraw Money use case, this time in terms of interacting subsystems and actors, shown in Figure 4.9 using a collaboration diagram (Appendix A). Objects of classes owned by the subsystems interact with one another to perform a use-case instance. The objects send messages to one another; these exchanges are shown in the diagram. The messages carry names that specify operations owned by interfaces of the subsystems. This is indicated by the :: notation (e.g.,Withdrawal::perform(amount,account), where Withdrawal is an interface provided by a class in the Transaction Management subsystem).

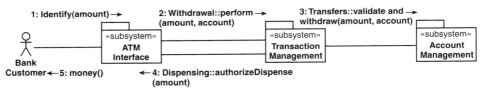

**FIGURE 4.9** The subsystems that collaborate to perform the Withdraw Money use case.

The following list briefly explains the flow in the use-case realization. The text is almost the same as in Section 3.4.1 (the use-case realization description), but here it is presented in terms of subsystems instead of classes.

**Precondition**: The bank customer has a bank account that works for the ATM:

1. The Bank Customer actor chooses to withdraw money and identifies himself to the ATM Interface, maybe by using a magnetic card with a number and a PIN. The Bank Customer also specifies how much to withdraw and from which account. Here we have assumed that the ATM Interface subsystem would be able to validate the identity.
2. ATM Interface asks the Transaction Management subsystem to withdraw the money. The Transaction Management subsystem is responsible for

performing the whole withdrawal sequence as an atomic transaction, so that the money is both deducted from the account and dispensed to the Bank Customer.

3. Transaction Management asks the Account Management subsystem to withdraw the money. The Account Management subsystem determines whether the money can be withdrawn and, if so, deducts the sum from the account and returns a reply that specifies that it is possible to execute the withdrawal.

4. Transaction Management authorizes the ATM Interface subsystem to dispense the money.

5. ATM Interface dispenses the money to the Bank Customer.

### 4.5.3  The Architectural View of the Deployment Model

The deployment model defines the physical system architecture in terms of connected nodes. These nodes are hardware units that software components can execute on. Often we know what the physical system architecture looks like before we start developing the system. The nodes and connections can then be modeled in the deployment model as early as during the requirements workflow.

During design, we decide which classes are active, that is, threads or processes. We decide what each active object should do, what the life cycle of the active objects should be, and how the active objects should communicate, synchronize, and share information. The active objects are allocated to the nodes of the deployment model. When we allocate the active objects to the nodes, we consider the capability of the nodes, such as their processing capacity and memory size, and the characteristics of the connections, such as their bandwidth and availability.

The nodes and connections of the deployment model and the allocation of active objects to the nodes can be depicted in **deployment diagrams** (Appendix A). These diagrams may also show how executable components are allocated to nodes. The ATM system from our example is distributed to three different nodes.

---

| Example | The Architectural View of the Deployment Model of the ATM System |
|---|---|

The Bank Customer accesses the system through an ATM Client node, which accesses the ATM Application Server to perform the transactions (Figure 4.10). The ATM Application Server use, in turn, the ATM Data Server to perform specific transactions on, for example, accounts. This is true not only for the Withdraw Money use case, which we have classified as architecturally significant, but for other use cases, such as Deposit Money and Transfer between Accounts, as well. In Section 3.4.3, we describe which classes we selected to realize the Withdraw Money use case.

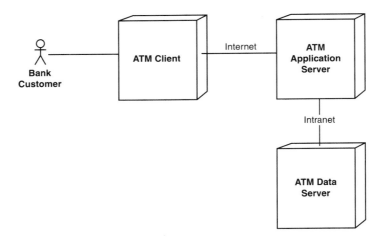

**FIGURE 4.10** The deployment model defines three nodes: ATM Client, ATM Application Server, and ATM Data Server.

When the nodes are defined, it is possible to deploy functionality on them. For simplicity we do this by deploying each subsystem (see Figure 4.8) as a whole to a unique node. The ATM Interface subsystem is deployed onto the ATM Client node, the Transaction Management subsystem is deployed onto the ATM Application Server, and the Account Management subsystem is deployed onto the ATM Data Server. As a consequence, each active class within those subsystems (see Section 3.4.4 and Figure 3.10) is deployed on the corresponding node—representing a process running on the node. Each such process maintains, and keeps in its process space, objects of the other (ordinary, nonactive) classes within the subsystem. The deployment of active objects is shown in Figure 4.11.

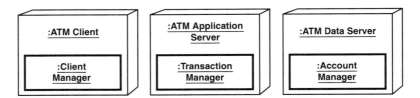

**FIGURE 4.11** The architectural view of the deployment model. The active classes of the ATM system are distributed across the nodes. Active objects are shown as rectangles with heavy borders.

This is a naive example of system distribution. In a real system, the distribution is, of course, more complex. One alternative solution to the distribution problem would have been to use some middleware for object distribution such as an object request broker (ORB).

### 4.5.4 The Architectural View of the Implementation Model

The implementation model is a straightforward mapping from the design and deployment model. Each design service subsystem usually results in one component for each node type that it must be installed on—but not always. Sometimes the same component (e.g., a buffer manager component) may be instantiated and executed on several nodes. Some languages provide a construct for packaging components, such as JavaBeans. Otherwise, the classes are organized into files of code that represent the selected set of components.

In Section 3.4.5, we mentioned that the Withdrawal Management service subsystem possibly could be realized as two components, "Withdrawal on Server" and "Withdrawal on Client." The "Withdrawal on Server" component could implement the Withdrawal class, and Withdrawal on Client could implement a Withdrawal Proxy class. In our simple example, those components would implement only one class each. In a real system, there would be several more classes in each service subsystem, so a component would implement several classes.

## 4.6 Three Interesting Concepts

### 4.6.1 What Is Architecture?

It is what the architect specifies in an architecture description. The architecture description lets the architect control the development of the system from a technical perspective. Software architecture focuses both on the significant structural elements of the system, such as subsystems, classes, components, and nodes, as well as the collaborations that occur among these elements via interfaces.

Use cases drive the architecture to make the system provide the desired usage and functionality while meeting reasonable performance goals. An architecture needs to be comprehensive, but it also needs to be resilient enough to accommodate new functions and it needs to support reuse of existing software.

### 4.6.2 How Is It Obtained?

The architecture is developed iteratively during the elaboration phase through requirements, analysis, design, implementation, and test. The architecturally significant use cases and a range of other input is used to implement the architectural baseline, or "skeleton," system. That range of input includes system software requirements, middleware, which legacy systems to use, nonfunctional requirements, and so on.

### 4.6.3 How Is It Described?

The architecture description is a view of the models of the system, views of the use case, analysis, design, implementation, and deployment models. The architecture description describes the parts of the system that are important for all developers and other stakeholders to understand.

## 4.7 References

[1]    David Garlan and Mary Shaw, *Software Architecture: Perspectives on an Emerging Discipline,* Upper Saddle River, NJ: Prentice-Hall, 1996.

[2]    Ivar Jacobson, Martin Griss, and Patrik Jonsson, *Software Reuse: Architecture, Process and Organization for Business Success,* Reading, MA: Addison-Wesley, 1997.

[3]    P.B. Kruchten. "The 4+1 view model of architecture," *IEEE Software,* November 1995.

[4]    F. Buschmann, R. Meurier, H. Rohnert, P. Sommerlad, M. Stal, *A System of Patterns,* New York: John Wiley and Sons, 1996.

[5]    Erich Gamma, Richard Helm, Ralph Johnson, and John Vlissides, *Design Patterns: Elements of Reusable Object-Oriented Software,* Reading, MA: Addison-Wesley, 1994.

[6]    OMG, Inc. The Common Object Request Broker: Architecture and Specification (CORBA), Framingham, MA. 1996.

[7]    ISO/IEC International Standard 10165-4 = ITU-T Recommendation X.722.

[8]    ITU-T Recommendation M.3010, Principles for a Telecommunication Management Network.

[9]    Thomas J. Mowbray and Raphael C. Malveau, *CORBA Design Patterns*, New York: John Wiley and Sons, 1997.

[10]   Christopher Alexander, Sara Ishikawa, Murray Silverstein, with Max Jacobsen, Ingrid Fiksdahi-King, Shlomo Angel, *A Pattern Language: Towns, Buildings, Construction,* New York: Oxford University Press, 1977.

# *Chapter 5*

---

# An Iterative
# and Incremental Process

To be effective, a software process needs to have a sequence of clearly articulated **milestones** (Appendix C) that provide managers and the rest of the project team with the criteria they need to authorize movement from one phase into the next of a product cycle.

Within each phase the process moves through a series of **iterations** and increments (Appendix C) that lead to these criteria.

In the inception phase the essential criterion is viability, approached by

- Identifying and reducing the **risks** (Appendix C; see also Section 12.5) critical to the system's viability.
- Moving from a key subset of the requirements through use-case modeling into a candidate architecture.
- Making an initial estimate within broad limits, of cost, effort, schedule, and product quality.
- Initiating the business case (see more on the business case in Chapters 12–16), that the project appears to be economically worth doing, again within broad limits.

In the elaboration phase, the essential criterion is the ability to build the system in an economic framework, approached by

- Identifying and reducing the risks significantly affecting system construction.
- Specifying most of the use cases that represent the functionality to be developed.
- Extending the candidate architecture to executable baseline proportions.
- Preparing a **project plan** (Appendix C) in sufficient detail to guide the construction phase.
- Making an estimate within limits narrow enough to justify a business bid.
- Finalizing the business case—the project is worth doing.

In the construction phase, the essential criterion is a system capable of initial operation in the users' environment, approached by

- A series of iterations, leading to periodic builds and increments, so that throughout this phase, viability of the system is always evident in executable form.

In the transition phase, the essential criterion is a system that achieves final operational capability, approached by

- Modifying the product to alleviate problems not identified in the earlier phases.
- Correcting **defects** (Appendix C; see also Section 11.3.6).

One of the goals of the Unified Process is to enable architects, developers, and stakeholders in general to grasp the importance of the early phases. To this end, we can do no better than to cite Barry Boehm's advice from some years ago [1]:

*I can't overemphasize how critical the Life Cycle Architecture milestone [which corresponds to our elaboration-phase milestone] is to your project and your career. If you haven't satisfied the LCA milestone criteria, do not proceed into full-scale development. Reconvene the stakeholders and work out a new project plan that will successfully achieve the LCA criteria.*

The phases and the iterations within them receive more detailed treatment in Part III.

## 5.1 Iterative and Incremental in Brief

As we pointed out in Chapters 3 and 4, that the software development process should be use-case driven and architecture-centric are two of the three keys to the Unified Process. These aspects have a clear technical impact on the product of the process. Being use-case driven means that every phase in the drive to the eventual product refers back to what users actually do. It drives developers to assure that the system meets users' real needs. Being architecture-centric means that development work focuses on achieving the architectural pattern that will guide system construction in the early phases, assuring a smooth progression not only to the current product release, but to the whole product life.

Achieving the right balance between use cases and architecture is much like balancing function and form in the development of any product. It is achieved over time. Which comes first is a chicken-and-egg problem as we said in Section 4.3. The chicken and the egg came about through almost endless iterations during the long process of evolution. Similarly, in the shorter process of software development, developers consciously work out this balance (between use cases and architecture) through a series of iterations. Thus, the iterative-and-incremental development approach constitutes the third key aspect of the Unified Process.

## 5.1.1 Develop in Small Steps

The third key provides the strategy for developing a software product in small manageable steps:

- You plan a little.
- You specify, design, and implement a little.
- You integrate, test, and run each iteration a little.

If you are happy with a step, you take the next step. In between each step you get feedback that permits you to adjust your focus for the next step. Then you take another step, and then another. When you have taken all the steps you planned, you have developed a product that you can release to your customers and users.

The iterations in the early phases are mostly concerned with scoping the project, removing critical risks, and baselining the architecture. Then, as we proceed through the project and gradually reduce the remaining risks and implement the components, the shape of the iterations changes, resulting in increments.

A software development project transforms a "delta" (or change) of users' requirements into a delta (or change) of software product (see Section 2.2). With an iterative and incremental approach this accommodation of change is done little by little. In other words, we split the project into a number of miniprojects, each one being an iteration. Each iteration has everything a software development project has: planning, working through a series of workflows (requirements, analysis and design, implementation, test), and preparation for release.

But, an iteration is not an entirely independent entity. It is a stage within a project. It draws heavily from being part of a project. We say it is a miniproject because it is not, by itself, what the stakeholders have asked us to do. Also, each of these miniprojects is like the old waterfall model because it proceeds through the waterfall activities. We might label each iteration a "miniwaterfall."

The iterative life cycle delivers tangible results in the form of internal (though preliminary) releases, each of which adds an increment and demonstrates the reduction of the risks with which it was concerned. These releases may be shown to customers and users, and thus provide valuable feedback to validate the work.

The planners try to order the iterations to get a straight path where the early iterations provide the knowledge base for the later iterations. Early iterations in the project result in increased knowledge of the requirements, the problems, the risks, and the **solution domain** (Appendix C), whereas later iterations result in additive increments that eventually make up the **external release** (Appendix C), that is, the customer product. The ultimate success—for the planners—is a sequence of iterations that always moves forward; that is, it never has to go back two or three iterations to patch up the model because of something learned in a later iteration. We don't want to climb a mound of melting snow, two steps forward and one step sliding backward.

In summary, a life cycle is made up of a sequence of iterations. Some, particularly the early ones, help us understand the risks, establish feasibility, build the initial core of the software, and make the business case. Others, particularly the later iterations, add increments until we have reached a product ready for external release.

The iterations help management plan, organize, monitor, and control the project. The iterations are organized within the four phases, each with particular needs for staffing, funding, scheduling, and entry and exit criteria. At the beginning of each phase, management can decide how to execute it, what results must be delivered, and what risks must be mitigated.

### 5.1.2  What Iteration Is Not

Some managers think that "iterative or incremental" is a fancy name for "hacking." They fear that the words merely conceal the reality that the developers don't know what they are doing. In the inception phase, even early in the elaboration phase, there may be some truth to this. For example, if the developers have not resolved critical or significant risks, then the assertion is true. If they have not yet proved the underlying concept or established an architectural baseline, the assertion is true. If they have not yet figured out how they can implement the most critical requirements, the assertion is true. Indeed, they might not know what they are doing.

Does it do any good to pretend that they do know what they are doing? Does it do any good to base a plan on insufficient information? Does it do any good to track to this unreliable plan? Of course not.

For the record, let us emphasize what the iterative life cycle is not:

- It is not random hacking.
- It is not a playpen for developers.
- It is not something that affects only developers.
- It is not redesigning the same thing over and over until the developers finally chance on something that works.
- It is not unpredictable.
- It is not an excuse for failing to plan and manage.

In fact, controlled iteration is far from random. It is planned. It is a tool managers can use to control the project. It reduces, early in the life cycle, risks that may threaten the progress of development. **Internal releases** (Appendix C) after iterations enable stakeholder feedback, leading, in turn, to earlier correction of the project course.

## 5.2 Why Iterative and Incremental Development?

In two words: better software. In a few more words, to achieve the major and minor milestones with which we control development. And in still more words,

- To get a handle on the critical and significant risks early.
- To set forth an architecture to guide software development.
- To provide a framework that better handles inevitable requirements and other changes.
- To build up the system over time incrementally rather than all at once near the end when change becomes expensive.
- To provide a development process through which the staff can work more effectively.

### 5.2.1 Mitigating Risks

Software development encounters risks, just as any engineering activity does. "Risk is inherent in the commitment of present resources to future expectations," in the view of the management seer, Peter F. Drucker [2]. In software development, we deal with this reality by identifying the risks as early in development as we can and addressing them promptly. A risk is an exposure that may lead to loss or injury. Risk is a factor, thing, element, or course constituting a danger, the degree of which is uncertain. In software development, we can define risk as a concern that has some degree of probability of endangering the success of a project. For example,

- The **object request broker** (Appendix C) that we initially consider may not be able to deal with 1,000 remote-customer-account object lookups per second.
- A real-time system may have to acquire a number of data inputs that were not specified in the inception phase. It may have to process the data through extensive computations that are not yet spelled out in detail. It may have to issue a command signal within a short but presently unspecified time.
- A telephone switching system may have to respond to various inputs in numbers of milliseconds specified by the client telecommunication operations company.

What the software field needs, as Barry Boehm wrote many years ago, is a process model that "creates a *risk-driven* approach to the software process rather than a primarily *document-driven* or *code-driven* process" [3]. The Unified Process meets these criteria because it addresses important risks in the first two phases, inception and elaboration, and any remaining risks in order of importance early in the construction phase. It identifies, manages, and reduces risks in the early phases by means of iterations. As a result, unidentified or ignored risks do not pop up later and imperil the entire project.

The iterative approach to risk reduction bears little resemblance to the **waterfall approach** (Appendix C). The waterfall model shows development flowing one way through a series of steps: requirements, analysis, design implementation, and test. In this approach, the project would have all of its developers involved when it reached implementation, **integration** (Appendix C), and testing. During integration and testing, problems would start exploding all around them. The project manager would then be forced to reassign people—often the more experienced developers—to resolve these problems before work could proceed. However, with all the developers already engaged, project managers found it difficult to "pry loose" the few who were best qualified to solve the newly discovered problems. To compound these difficulties, reassigning the more experienced developers to "clean-up duty" often left the less experienced developers sitting and waiting. Deadlines passed, and project costs mounted. In the worst case, competitors got to market first.

If we plot risk against development time, as in Figure 5.1, iterative development begins to reduce serious risks in the earliest iterations. By the time work reaches the construction phase, few serious risks remain and work proceeds smoothly. By contrast, using the waterfall model, serious risks are not addressed until the "big bang" of code integration.

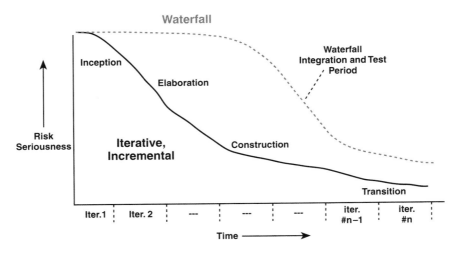

**FIGURE 5.1** Serious risks are identified and reduced early in iterative development in contrast to waterfall development. There, the most serious risks remain until integration and system test address them (dashed line). The iterations indicated at the bottom of the figure are, of course, relevant only for the iterative and incremental approach.

About two thirds of major software projects fail to perform adequate risk assessments, according to Capers Jones [4], so there is room for great improvement! Attacking risks early in the development process is the first step.

### 5.2.2 Getting a Robust Architecture

Achieving a robust architecture is itself the result of iterations in the early phases. In the inception phase, for instance, we seek a core architecture that satisfies the key requirements, overcomes the critical risks, and resolves the central development problems. In the elaboration phase, we establish the architecture baseline that guides further development.

On the one hand, the investment in these phases is still small and we can afford the iterations that assure that the architecture is robust. After the first iteration in the elaboration phase, for example, we are in a position to make an initial evaluation of the architecture. At that time, we can still afford to change it, if that is our finding, to meet the needs of significant use cases and nonfunctional requirements.

If we follow the waterfall approach, by the time we discover the need for an architectural change, we have invested so much in the development that making a change in the architecture incurs a serious financial penalty. Moreover, we would be close to a date of promised delivery. Caught between costs and schedule, we would not be motivated to make major architectural changes. By focusing on architecture in the elaboration phase, we avoid this dilemma. We stabilize architecture at a baseline level early in the life cycle when costs are still low and schedule time still stretches before us.

### 5.2.3 Handling Changing Requirements

Users can comprehend a system that operates, even if it does not yet operate perfectly, more easily than they can a system that exists only as hundreds of pages of documents. Also, they have difficulty recognizing project progress if all that exists is documents. Therefore, from the standpoint of users and other stakeholders, it is more productive to evolve the product through a series of executable releases, or "builds," than to present piles of difficult-to-penetrate documentation. A build is an operational version of part of a system that demonstrates a subset of the system capabilities. Each iteration may work through a series of builds to approach the planned result, that is, the increment.

Having a system in partial operation in an early phase enables users and other stakeholders to provide suggestions on and point out requirements that may have been overlooked. The plan—budget and schedule—is not yet set in stone so the developers can more easily accommodate revisions. In the one-way waterfall model, users do not see a system in operation until integration and testing. At that point, changes, even those that have merit or seem to be small, almost inevitably add to the budget and schedule. Thus the iterative life cycle makes it easier for customers to see the need for additional or changed requirements early in the development cycle and for the developers to work them in. After all, they are building the system as a series of iterations, so responding to feedback or including a revision is just an incremental change.

## 5.2.4 Allowing for Tactical Changes

With the iterative, incremental approach, developers can resolve problems and issues uncovered by the early builds and incorporate changes to correct them almost at once. By using this approach, problems are uncovered in a steady trickle with which developers can easily keep pace. The gush of fault reports that show up in the "big bang" integration of the waterfall often disrupts project progress. If the disruption is severe, the project may come to a halt, with developers kneeling under the pressure, project managers running in circles, and other managers panicking. By contrast, a series of operational builds gives everyone a sense of accomplishment.

Testers, manual writers, toolsmiths, configuration-management staff, and quality-assurance people can all adapt their own plans to the evolving project schedule. They learn of the existence of serious delays early in the project when the developers first encounter the problems that lead to them. They have time to adapt their own schedules. When problems lie hidden until testing, it is too late for them to reschedule efficiently.

When quality assurance has tested an iteration, project managers, architects, and other stakeholders can evaluate it against predefined criteria. They can decide whether the iteration has resulted in the right increment and the risks have been addressed properly. This evaluation allows managers to determine whether the iteration was successful. If it is, they can authorize the next iteration. If the iteration was only partly successful, they can extend it or carry over unresolved issues and necessary rework to the next iteration. In the extreme case, where the evaluation is completely negative, they can cancel the whole project.

## 5.2.5 Achieving Continuous Integration

At the conclusion of each iteration, the project team demonstrates that it has reduced some risks. The team delivers increasing functionality with each iteration, which is evident to stakeholders, who can see that the project is progressing.

Frequent builds force developers to closure at regular intervals—closure in the form of a piece of executable software. The experience of builds makes it hard for them or anyone else to support the "90% completed" attitude. This attitude arises when a count of code or other artifacts (Appendix C) purports to find that the product is almost finished. In the absence of operable builds, however, the most difficult work may still lie ahead. The problems may not yet have been revealed by attempts to integrate and test the system. In contrast, because the successive iterations function, they produce a series of results that accurately indicate the status of the project.

Even if developers fail to achieve the planned result in an early iteration, they still have time to try again and improve the models in subsequent internal releases. Since they work on the critical issues first, they have several opportunities to improve their solutions.

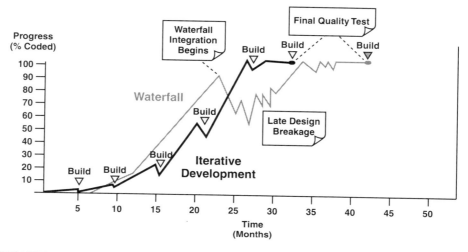

**FIGURE 5.2**  In the waterfall approach (thin line), developers do not begin implementation until they have completed requirements, analysis, and design. They report good progress in implementation because they have no intermediate builds to persuade them otherwise. The problems are actually lying low until integration and testing reveal them all at once (Late Design Breakage). In iterative development, implementation starts earlier and frequent builds not only uncover problems early but also uncover them in small batches that are easier to work on.

The thick line in Figure 5.2 (originally presented in [5]) illustrates how iterative development works out. At early points in the schedule, in this case with only 2% to 4% of the project coded, an increment (or build) is put together. This attempt shows some problems, denoted by the small dip in the progress line, but they are quickly overcome and progress resumes. Thereafter, the project makes frequent builds. Each one may lead to a temporary halt in progress. Because the increments are relatively small, compared to the final integration of the entire product (on the lower line), recovery takes place quickly.

As the diagram suggests, in the waterfall approach, a single integration near the delivery date reveals a host of problems. The large volume of problems and the inevitable haste at this point mean that many of the fixes are not well thought out. Running down the problems and correcting them often delays delivery beyond the planned date. Consequently, iterative development completes in much less schedule time than waterfall development. Moreover, the product of a "waterfall project" may be fragile, that is, it may be difficult to maintain.

## 5.2.6  Attaining Early Learning

After a couple of iterations, everyone on the team has a good understanding of what the different workflows mean. They know what comes after requirements and what comes after analysis. The risk of "analysis paralysis" (too much time spent on analysis) is greatly reduced.

Additionally, it is easier to train new people because they can be trained on the work itself. The project doesn't have to design special pilots just to help people understand what the process is. They can break in directly on mission-related work. Given that they have received appropriate training and that they work with someone who has done it before, they quickly come up to speed. If new people fail to understand a point or make a mistake, their error is not critical to the long-run progress of the project, because it shows up on the next attempt to make a build.

The iterative approach also helps a project address risks of a nontechnical nature, such as organizational risks. For example, developers may not learn quickly enough how to:

- Build applications using an object request broker.
- Use the tools for testing or **configuration management** (Appendix C).
- Work according to the software development process.

As a project iterates, a small team gets acquainted with these new technologies, tools, and processes. In subsequent iterations as the team uses them more, it gains further proficiency. The team grows gradually as the project moves through the iterations, perhaps starting with a small 5 to 10 people, then growing to 25, and finally to some 100 people. As the team grows stepwise, the core team is available to mentor new team members as they come onboard. The iterative approach allows the initial team to fine-tune the process and the tools before most of the developers join the team.

By working in phases and iterations, developers are better able to meet real customer demands and reduce risks. By building in increments, all concerned can observe their level of progress. By reducing late-term difficulties, they hasten time-to-market. Moreover, this iterative approach is beneficial, not only to developers and, ultimately, to users but to their managers. Managers can apprehend real progress by noting the completed iterations.

## 5.3 The Iterative Approach is Risk-Driven

A risk is a project variable that endangers or eliminates success for a project. It is "the probability that a project will experience undesirable events, such as schedule delays, cost overruns, or outright cancellation" (see the glossary in [4]).

We identify, prioritize, and carry out iterations on the basis of risks and their order of importance. This is true when we evaluate new technologies. It is true when we work to fulfill the customers' needs—the requirements—whether they are functional or nonfunctional. It is true when, in the early phases, we are establishing an architecture that will be robust, that is, one that can accommodate changes with little risk of having to redesign anything. Yes, we organize iterations to achieve risk reduction.

Other serious risks are matters of performance (speed, capacity, accuracy), **reliability**, availability, system interface integrity, adaptability, and **portability** (Appendix C). Many of these risks are not exposed until the software that implements the underlying functions is implemented and tested. That is why iterations exploring risks should be carried, even in the inception and elaboration phases, all the way to coding and testing. The objective is to nail the risk in an early iteration.

An interesting observation is that, in principle, all technical risks can be mapped to a use case or a scenario of a use case. Here, *map* means that the risk is mitigated if the use case with its functional and nonfunctional requirements is realized. This is true not just for risks pertaining to requirements and architecture but for verifying the underlying hardware and software. By carefully selecting use cases, we can exercise all the functions of the underlying architecture.

Risk reduction is central for the iterations we do in the inception and elaboration phases. Later, in the construction phase, the risks have, for the most part, been reduced to a routine level, meaning that they yield to ordinary development practices. We try to order the iterations so that each one builds on the previous one. By this phase, we are trying, in particular, to avoid the risk that, if we do not get the order of iterations right, we might have to rework several previous iterations.

### 5.3.1 Iterations Alleviate Technical Risks

Risks have been classified into many categories [3] and [4]. However, for our purposes it is sufficient to be suggestive, not exhaustive. We have identified four broad categories:

1. Risks related to new technologies:
   - Processes may have to be distributed over many nodes, possibly leading to synchronization problems.
   - Some use cases may depend upon computational techniques that are not yet well developed, such as natural language recognition or the use of Web technology.

2. Risks related to architecture. These risks are so important that we have designed the Unified Process to deal with them in a standard way; that is, the elaboration phase and the architectural iterations within it provide an explicit place in the process to deal with them. By establishing a risk-accommodative architecture early, we eliminate the risk of not being able to accommodate changes easily. We eliminate the risk of later having to redo a good deal of work. This risk-resistant architecture is robust. Accepting change gracefully is characteristic of architectural **robustness** (Appendix C). Another advantage of getting a robust architecture early includes showing where reusable components fit in, which allows us early in the project to think about buying instead of making. It also reduces the risk of discovering too late that a system will be too expensive to build. For example,

- The use cases we initially select fail to help us find the subsystem structure we need to evolve the system with later-to-come use cases. In early iterations, say, during the elaboration phase, we may not note that several actors will use the same use case via different interfaces. An example of this situation is several interfaces for cash withdrawal: One employs a graphical user interface and a personal computer; another uses a communication protocol over a network. If we design to meet only one of these use cases, we may end up in an architecture that has no inner interface that will allow us to add new kinds of interactions. The risk is that it will be hard to evolve such a system.
- Certain frameworks (Appendix C) planned for reuse have not, in fact, been used outside the original project on which they were built. The risk is that such a framework will not work well with other frameworks or that it will not be easy to reuse.
- The new version of the operating system we plan to use may not have reached the quality level necessary for us to rely on it. The risk is that we may have to delay release of our own software while we wait for the vendor to upgrade the operating system.

3. Risks related to building the right system, one that supports the mission and the users. This risk underscores the importance of finding the functional and nonfunctional requirements, which essentially means finding the right use cases with the right user interfaces. It is important to find the most important functions early and to make sure that they are implemented early. Here we arrange use cases in order of importance for meeting customer needs and meeting performance requirements. We consider both behavior and capabilities, such as performance. When we select use cases, we base the order of dealing with them on their risk potential, such as the possibility of problems with the performance of the use case. Particularly in the inception and elaboration phases, there is a close correlation between certain requirements (and the use cases that express them) and the risks that lie in them. The use cases the team selects impact the architecture it develops. For example,
   - The Follow Me use case enables a telephone subscriber to redirect calls to another number. Should this redirection apply to all calls? What about a wake-up call? The subscriber will probably be at his or her basic number then and will not want the call to be rerouted.

4. Some risks are related to performance. For example,
   - The response time of a use case must be less than 1 second.
   - The number of concurrent use-case instances exceeds 10,000 an hour.

The identification of problem areas such as these depends largely on people with extensive experience. Since no one person is likely to have all the experience that is necessary, a number of people will have to study the proposed system, make lists of possible problems, and come together for risk-identification sessions. These sessions are not intended to solve the problems, merely to identify them and prioritize the order in which they will be further studied in iterations during the inception and elaboration phases.

### 5.3.2 Management Is Responsible for Nontechnical Risks

Nontechnical risks are those that alert management can detect and divert. Examples in this category include

- The organization presently lacks people with experience in certain unusual aspects of the proposed project.
- The organization plans to implement parts of the proposed system in a language new to it.
- The schedule proposed by the client appears to be too short, unless every step clicks into place with no problems.
- The organization can meet the proposed schedule only if subcontractors who have not been used before can deliver certain subsystems on time.
- The client may not be able to turn around certain approvals within time limits necessary to meet the delivery date.

Risks of this kind lie beyond the scope of this book. Suffice it to say that the software organization should identify them, set up administrative means to follow developments in each risk area, and assure that responsible managers take action when one of the risks materializes.

### 5.3.3 Dealing with Risks

Once the risks have been identified and prioritized, the team next decides how to address each one. Essentially, the team has four choices: avoid it, confine it, mitigate it, or monitor it.

- Some risks can and should be avoided, perhaps by replanning the project or changing the requirements.
- Other risks should be confined, that is, restricted so that they affect only a small part of the project or the system.
- Some risks can be mitigated by trying them out and seeing if they materialize or retire. If a risk materializes, the plus side is that the team has learned more about it. The team may then be in a position to find a way to avoid, confine, or monitor it.
- Some risks, however, cannot be mitigated. The team can only monitor them and see if they materialize. If one does appear, the team has to follow its **contingency plans** (Appendix C). If a "project killer" risk arises, we take a deep breath and assess the situation. Do we want to proceed, or should we cancel the project? At this point we have spent only limited time and money. We

knew a "project killer" could happen—that is why we were doing early itera-tions. So we did a good job by finding a risk of this magnitude before bringing all the developers into the project.

It takes time to address a risk. Avoiding or confining a risk takes replanning or rework. Mitigating a risk might require the team to build something that exposes the risk. Monitoring a risk involves choosing a monitoring mechanism, setting it up, and executing it. Mitigating or monitoring risks, in turn, takes serious development effort, that is, time. Because addressing risks takes time, a project organization can seldom address all risks at the same time. That is why prioritization of iterations is necessary. This is what we mean by risk-driven iterative development. That is sound risk management.

## 5.4 The Generic Iteration

As we have seen, iterations differ markedly in the different phases of the develop-ment cycle because the challenges that developers face in each phase differ. In this section our intention is to present the concept of an iteration on a generic level: what it is, how to plan one, how to sequence it, and what the result of an iteration is. In Part III, we deal with iterations in each of the four phases in separate chapters.

### 5.4.1 What an Iteration Is

An *iteration* is a miniproject—a more or less complete traversal of all core work-flows—resulting in an internal release. This is an intuitive understanding of what an iteration is. However, in order to be able to describe the work going on in an iteration beyond the surface level, we have extended this definition.

We can think of an iteration as a workflow, which means that it is a collaboration between workers (Appendix C) who are using and producing artifacts. In the Unified Process we distinguish between **core workflows** and **iteration workflows** (Appendix C). By now, we are familiar with the five core workflows: requirements, analysis, design, implementation, and test. These core workflows are there for pedagogic rea-sons only, to help us describe the iteration workflows. Thus there is nothing magic about what constitutes a core workflow; another set of core workflows could just as easily have been used, such as one that integrates analysis and design.[1] It is used to simplify the description of more concrete workflows just as an abstract class helps us describe concrete classes. These more concrete workflows are iteration workflows. We describe the core workflows in detail in Chapters 6–11, and we describe the itera-tion workflows using the core workflows in Chapters 12–16.

---

1. Workflows should not be confused with concurrent processes. Workflows are collaborations that are useful for creating descriptions.

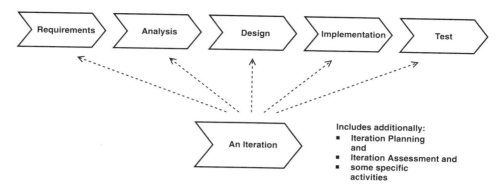

**FIGURE 5.3** Every iteration makes a pass through the five core workflows. It is initiated with a planning activity and finished with assessment.

In Figure 5.3, we describe the generic elements of each iteration workflow. They all pass through the five core workflows. All are initiated with a planning activity and conclude with an assessment. In Part III, we describe four archetypal iterations, one for each phase of the Unified Process. Each reuses the descriptions of the core workflows, but in different ways.

How is this different from a traditional waterfall model? Every core workflow is a collaboration between a set of workers and artifacts. However, there is overlap between iterations. Workers and artifacts may participate in more than one core workflow. For instance, the component engineer participates in three workflows: analysis, design, and implementation. Finally, the iteration workflow is created by superimposing a selected subset of the core workflows on top of each other and then adding what is extra, such as planning and assessment.

Early iterations focus on understanding the problem and the technology. In the inception phase, the iterations are concerned with producing a business case .[2] In the elaboration phase, the iterations are directed at the development of the baseline architecture. In the construction phase, iterations are devoted to building the product via a series of builds within each iteration, culminating with a product ready to be delivered to the user community. However, each iteration follows the same pattern, as shown in Figure 5.3.

Each iteration is assessed at its conclusion. One objective is to determine whether new requirements have appeared or existing requirements have changed in a way that will affect subsequent iterations. In planning the details of the next iteration, the team also examines how the remaining risks will affect the continuing work.

One function deserving special emphasis at this point is **regression testing** (Appendix C). Before finishing an iteration we need to ensure that we did not break

---

2. During the inception phase, an iteration may follow a simplified variant of the workflows when studying particular technology problems.

any other part of the system that worked in previous iterations. Regression testing is particularly important in an iterative, incremental life cycle, since each iteration produces a substantial addition to the previous increment as well as a fair amount of changes. We note that it is impractical to perform regression testing on such a massive scale—every build in every iteration—without appropriate testing tools.

Project managers should not agree to start the next iteration unless the goals of the current iteration have been achieved. If not, the plan will have to change to accommodate the new situation.

### 5.4.2 Planning the Iterations

If anything, the iterative life cycle requires more planning and more thought than the waterfall approach. In the waterfall model all the planning is done up front, often before risks have been reduced and architecture settled. The resulting plans are based on much uncertainty and lacked fidelity. By contrast, the iterative approach does not plan the whole project in detail during the inception phase, it merely takes the first steps. Not until a factual base has been established during the elaboration phase does the project team attempt to plan the construction and transition phases. Of course, there is a working plan during the first two phases, but it is not very detailed.

Ordinarily (except at the very beginning of a project) the planning effort considers the results of preceding iterations, the selection of use cases relevant to the new iteration, the current status of risks that apply to the next iteration, and the state of the latest version of the set of models. It ends with preparation for the internal release.

At the end of the elaboration phase, then, the basis exists for planning the rest of the project and setting forth a detailed plan for every iteration in the construction phase. The plan for the first iteration will be very clear. Later iterations will be in the plan with fewer details, subject to modification, based on the outcome and knowledge gained in earlier iterations. Similarly, there should be a transition-phase plan, but it may have to be modified in light of what the team learns from the construction-phase iterations. This type of planning enables controlled iterative development.

### 5.4.3 Sequencing the Iterations

Evolution in nature occurs without a plan preceding it. This is not the case with software iteration. The use cases set a goal, so to speak. The architecture establishes a pattern. With this goal and pattern in mind, the developers plan the sequence in which they will work product development.

The planners try to order the iterations to get a straight path where the early iterations provide the knowledge basis for the later iterations. Early iterations in the project result in increased knowledge of the requirements, the problems, the risks, and the solution domain, whereas later iterations result in additive increments that eventually make up the external release, that is, the customer product. For the planners, the ultimate success is a sequence of iterations that always move forward, never having to go back to the results of an earlier iteration to patch up the model because of something learned in a later iteration.

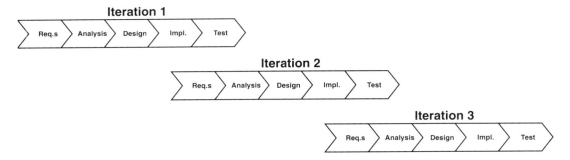

**FIGURE 5.4**  Iterations sweep through the workflows from requirements capture to test.

Iterations can overlap in the sense that one iteration is about to finish while another one is starting, as shown in Figure 5.4. Planning for and early work on the next iteration may begin as we finalize the previous one and prepare it for release. However, we cannot go too far in overlap since one iteration is always the basis for the next one. Remember that the end of an iteration means that we have obtained closure within the development team. All the software of the iteration has been integrated and can be internally released.

To a considerable degree, the order in which we plan iterations depends on technical factors. The most important goal, however, is to sequence the work so that the most important decisions, those that involve new technologies, use cases, and architecture, can be made early.

## 5.5  The Result of an Iteration Is an Increment

An increment is the difference between the internal release of one iteration and the internal release of the next iteration.

At the end of an iteration the set of models that represents the system is in a particular state. This state, or status, is called the *baseline*. Each model has reached a baseline; each essential model element is in a baseline state. For example, the use-case model at the end of each iteration contains a set of use cases that represent the degree to which the iteration has carried through requirements. Some of the use cases in this set are complete, while others are only partially complete. At the same time, the design model has reached a baseline state consistent[3] with the use-case model. The design model's subsystems, interfaces, and use-case realizations are also in baselines that are mutually consistent with one another. To work efficiently with multiple baselines within a project, the development organization needs to maintain consistent and compatible versions of all artifacts within a baseline. When working with iterative

---

3. Not all use cases need to be designed, so here the term *consistent* refers only to those being designed.

development, we cannot overemphasize the need for efficient configuration management tools.

At any given point in the iteration sequence, some subsystems are complete. They contain all the prescribed functionality, and they have been implemented and tested. Other subsystems are only partly finished, and others are still empty, although they do have stubs so that they can work and be integrated with other subsystems. Thus, in more precise terms, an increment is the difference between two successive baselines.

During the elaboration phase, as we have already noted, we build the architectural baseline. We identify the use cases that have a significant impact on the architecture. We realize these use cases as collaborations. It is in this way that we identify most of the subsystems and interfaces—at least, the ones that are architecturally interesting. Once most of the subsystems and interfaces are identified, we flesh them out, that is, write the code that implements them. Some of this work is done before we release the architecture baseline and it continues throughout all of the workflows. However, most of the fleshing out occurs during the iterations in the construction phase.

As we near the transition phase, the level of consistency across models and within the models increases. We build increments by iteratively fleshing out the models, and the integration of the final increment becomes the released system.

## 5.6  Iterations over the Life Cycle

Each of the four phases concludes with a major milestone, as illustrated in Figure 5.5. [1]:

- Inception: life-cycle objectives
- Elaboration: life-cycle architecture
- Construction: initial operational capability
- Transition: product release

The goal of each major milestone is to make sure that the different workflow models evolve in a balanced way over the life cycle of the product. We mean "balanced" in the sense that the most important decisions impacting those models, those concerning risks, use cases, and architecture, are made early in the life cycle. Later, work should be able to proceed at increasing levels of detail with higher quality.

The primary goals of the inception phase are to set the scope of what the product should do, reduce the worst risks, and prepare the initial business case, indicating that the project is worth pursuing from a business standpoint. In other words, we aim to establish the life cycle objectives for the project.

The primary goals of the elaboration phase are to baseline the architecture, capture most of the requirements, and reduce the second worst risks, that is, to establish the life cycle architecture. By the end of this phase, we are able to estimate the costs

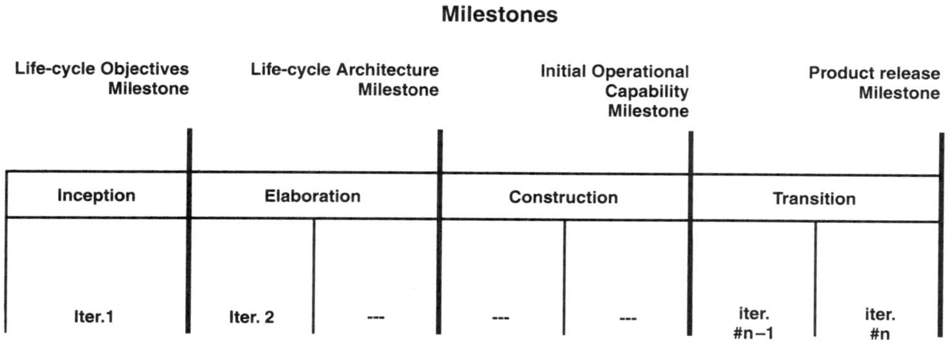

**Milestones**

| Life-cycle Objectives Milestone | Life-cycle Architecture Milestone | Initial Operational Capability Milestone | Product release Milestone |
|---|---|---|---|
| Inception | Elaboration | Construction | Transition |
| Iter.1 | Iter. 2 --- | --- --- | iter. #n−1 | iter. #n |

**FIGURE 5.5** Phases aggregate iterations that result in the major milestones where management makes important business decisions. (The number of iterations is not fixed but varies for different projects.)

and schedule and to plan the construction phase in some detail. At this point, we should be able to bid.

The primary goals of the construction phase are to develop the complete system and to ensure that the product can begin transition to customers, that is, to achieve initial operational capability.

The primary goals of the transition phase are to ensure that we have a product ready to be released to the user community. During this phase of development, the users are trained how to use the software.

Within each phase are lesser milestones, namely, the criteria applicable to each iteration. Each iteration produces results, *model artifacts*. Thus, at the end of each iteration, there will be a new increment to the use-case model, the analysis model, the design model, the deployment model, the implementation model, and the test model. The new increment will be integrated with the result of the previous iteration into a new version of the set of models.

At the minor milestones managers and developers decide how to proceed to the subsequent iterations, as we discussed in the previous sections. At the major milestones at the end of phases, managers make crucial go/no-go decisions and determine schedule, budget, and requirements.

A minor milestone (at the time of an internal release at the end of an iteration) is a planned step toward a major milestone at the end of a phase. The distinction between major and minor is primarily at the business level. The developers iteratively address risks and build software artifacts until they reach the major milestone. At each major milestone management evaluates what the developers have accomplished. Each transition past a major milestone thus represents an important business decision and a commitment to fund the work in (at least) the next phase according to plan. We can think of the major milestones as the synchronization points where the managerial and the technical realms conjunct.

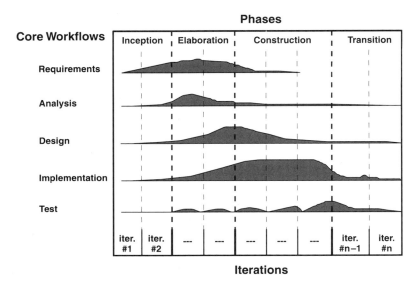

**FIGURE 5.6** Emphasis shifts over the iterations, from requirements capture and analysis toward design, implementation, and testing.

These divisions helps management and other involved stakeholders evaluate what has been done during the low-cost inception and elaboration phases before they decide to commit to the high-cost construction phase.

A software development project can be divided into roughly two chunks: the inception and elaboration phases and the construction and transition phases. During the inception and elaboration phases, we make the business case, mitigate the worst risks, create the architecture baseline, and plan the rest of the project with high precision. A small, low-cost team does this work.

Next, the project moves to the construction phase where economy of scale is the goal. Now the number of people on the project increases. They develop the bulk of the system functionality by building on the architecture baselined during the elaboration phase. They reuse existing software as much as possible.

While each iteration is a sweep through requirements, analysis, design, implementation, and test workflows, the iterations have different emphases in different phases, as illustrated by Figure 5.6. During the inception and elaboration phases, most of the effort is directed toward capturing requirements and preliminary analysis and design. During construction emphasis shifts to detailed design, implementation, and testing. Although it is not shown in Figure 5.6, the early phases are heavy on project management and developing an environment for the project.

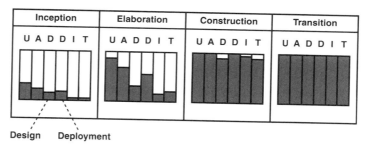

**FIGURE 5.7** Work in all models continues over all phases, as indicated by the increased filling-in of the models. The construction phase ends with an (almost) complete set of models. These models do, however, need to be fine-tuned during transition as they are deployed in the user community.

## 5.7 Models Evolve from Iterations

The iterations build the resulting models increment by increment. Each iteration adds some more to each model, as the iteration takes a sweep through requirements, analysis, design, implementation, and test. Some of these models, such as the use-case model, receive more attention in the early phases, while others such as the implementation model get more attention during the construction phase, as diagrammed in Figure 5.7. In the inception phase, the team perhaps creates the parts of the models that are necessary to support a proof-of-concept prototype. These parts include the most important elements of the (U) use-case model, the (A) analysis model, and the (D) design model, as well as some of the (D) deployment, (I) implementation, and (T) test models. Most of the implementation material is preliminary at this stage. As Figure 5.7 shows, much work remains to be done.

In the elaboration phase, the darker area, which denotes work accomplished, advances quite substantially. At the end of this phase, however, while the team has captured some 80% of the use cases (U) and the deployment model (the second D), less than 10% has been "built into" the system and resulted in implemented (I) and tested (T) functionality. The use-case and deployment models must be this complete after the elaboration phase. Otherwise, we do not know the requirements and implementation preconditions (including the architecture) well enough to plan the construction phase with precision.[4]

The construction phase sees most of the U, A, D, D, I, and T completed, which is to be expected since the exit criterion is a complete system implementation ready to begin transition to the user community. Later, as the system is turned over to operational use in the transition phase, there will be minor fixes and some fine-tuning.

---

4. In Chapter 4, we indicated that the use-case and analysis models had reached a lower level of completion at the end of the elaboration phase than Figure 5.7 indicates. The reason for this discrepancy is that in Chapter 4 we focused exclusively on architecture and did not consider what other work needs to be done (i.e., understanding more about the use cases to be able to make a business case).

## 5.8 Iterations Challenge the Organization

Many software organizations tend to leap right into writing code because lines of code are what their managers count. They tend to resist change, because change slows down the code count. They are not interested in reusing analysis, design, or code because new code is what their managers count.

Moving to iterative development challenges the working practices of these organizations. It requires a change in attitude. The focus of the organization will have to shift from counting lines of code to reducing risks and baselining architectural functionality. Managers must take a fresh look at what they measure. They will need to demonstrate by their actions that they measure progress in terms of risks addressed, use cases prepared, and components realizing those use cases. Otherwise, developers will soon regress to what they used to get credit for, lines of code.

Applying the iterative, incremental approach has some important consequences:

- To make the business case in the inception phase, the organization has emphasized reducing critical risks and demonstrating proof-of-concept.
- To make a business-worthy bid at the end of the elaboration phase, the organization has to know what it is contracting to build (represented by the architecture baseline plus requirements) and be confident that it contains no hidden risks (i.e., insufficiently explored cost and schedule expanders).
- To minimize costs, defects, and time-to-market, the organization has to employ reusable components (an outgrowth of early architectural development based on study of the domain in which the proposed system falls).
- To avoid delivery delay, cost overrun, and poor-quality product, the organization has to "do the hard stuff first."
- To avoid building a product that is out-of-date at delivery, the organization can no longer stubbornly say no to all changes. The phased, iterative approach enables it to work changes into development much further along the development trail.

Iterative and incremental development requires not only a new way of managing projects but tools to support this new approach. It is practically impossible to deal with all the artifacts of a system that concurrently undergoes changes in every build and every increment without the support of tools. An organization undertaking this mode of development needs tool support for the different workflows as well as tools for configuration management and version control.

## 5.9 References

[1] Barry Boehm, "Anchoring the software process," *IEEE Software*, July 1996, pp. 73–82.

[2] Peter F. Drucker, *Management: Tasks, Responsibilities, Practices*, New York: Harper & Row, 1973.

[3] Barry W. Boehm, "A spiral model of software development and enhancement," *Computer,* May 1988, pp. 61–72. (Reprinted in Barry W. Boehm, *Tutorial: Software Risk Management,* IEEE Computer Society Press, Los Alamitos, CA, 1989.)

[4] Capers Jones, *Assessment and Control of Software Risks,* Upper Saddle River, NJ: Prentice-Hall, 1993.

[5] Walker Royce, "TRW's Ada process model for incremental development of large software systems," *Proceedings, 12th International Conference on Software Engineering,* 1990, pp. 2–11.

# Part II

## The Core Workflows

**N**ow that we understand the basic notions underlying the key practices of the Unified Process, we will describe each workflow in detail. Part III will cover the iterations and phases.

In Part II we present the *core* workflows one by one in separate chapters: Chapters 6 and 7 deal with requirements; Chapter 8, analysis; Chapter 9, design; Chapter 10, implementation; and Chapter 11, test. The term *core workflow* is an abstraction, and it is described in detail in Chapter 5. During iterations, we focus on deploying the workflows concretely, a subject to which Part III is devoted.

Describing the core workflows separately, as we are about to do, might mislead the reader, and we want to be sure to avoid that possibility. First, by describing the core workflows one after another, we give the impression that the overall software development process from the beginning of a project to its end goes through this workflow sequence just once. A reader might come away thinking that the core workflows are a one-time-through process, like the old waterfall process. Second, an unwitting reader might conclude that each core workflow is a monolithic step in the process.

Neither of these impressions is correct. We describe the core workflows in separate chapters simply as a means of conveying in full, for pedagogic purposes, the entirety of each workflow.

Regarding the first issue, the waterfall possibility, we do run through the five workflows sequentially, but we do it once in each iteration, not once for the project as a whole. Thus, if we have seven iterations over four phases, we might run through the workflows seven times. To back off a bit, we might not use all five workflows in early inception; that is, we might not reach the later workflows, such as implementation and test, during the first iterations. The principle is clear: We carry the workflows in each iteration as far as required for a particular iteration.

Regarding the second issue, the monolithic step, we do describe each core workflow quite independently of the other workflows. They do, however, interact by producing and using one another's artifacts. In this part, we have tried to simplify each workflow a bit by focusing on its basic activities, again for pedagogic reasons. We have not gone into the alternations with the activities in other core workflows. Of course, these alternations are essential to an iterative software development process, and we do cover them in detail in Part III. For instance, while working on a particular design, a developer might find it desirable to alternate back and forth between the analysis and design workflows.

In Part III we describe how the workflows, which are described separately in this part, are combined in a working project. For example, a limited set of workflows may be appropriate in an early phase, while the full set of workflows is necessary during the construction phase.

*Chapter 6*

---

# Requirements Capture: From Vision to Requirements

For generations, certain Native American tribes built a kind of canoe, called a dugout, made of a hollowed-out log. The canoe builders began by looking for a tree that was several feet in diameter that had already toppled over near the water. Near it, they lit a fire and spread the hot coals on the top of the log. The charred wood was much easier to hollow out with stone tools. After several days of carving, the canoe would appear to be complete, and the builders would push and pull it into shallow water. More than likely, the first rough effort simply rolled over. It was not balanced. More work with those dull stone tools followed, until they had a boat that did not capsize when someone bent over to pull a fish out of the water. Only then did they call it finished. This knowledge had been passed from generation to generation and had made its way to the builders' very backbones.

When a "tribe" of software developers hears the call to develop a new system, they face a far different situation. First of all, the developers will not be the future users of the system. They will not reflexively get immediate feedback about how their "dugout" performs. Second, the system's requirements and constraints have not been ingrained into their "backbones" through continuous product usage since childhood. Instead, they will have to discover for themselves what is needed.

We call this act of discovery *requirements capture*. It is the process of finding out, usually under difficult circumstances, what is to be built. In fact, it is so difficult that it is still not uncommon for project teams to start writing code (which is fairly easy) before they have firmed up just what the code is supposed to do (which is difficult).

## 6.1 Why Requirements Capture Is Difficult

Professional software developers usually build software for someone other than themselves—they build it for users of the software. "Aha," developers used to say, "the users must know what they require." However, a little experience trying to gather requirements from users soon reveals them to be an imperfect source of information. For one thing, any system usually has many users (or types of users), and while each user may know what he or she does, no one can see the whole picture. Users don't know how the operation as a whole can be made more efficient. Most users don't know which aspects of their work can be turned over to software. Frankly, users frequently do not know what the requirements are or how to specify them in a precise manner, either.

The traditional approach to this problem has been to assign intermediaries—analysts—to elicit a list of requirements from each user with the hope that the analyst would be able to see the whole picture and put together a complete, correct, and consistent requirements specification. Analysts typically recorded the requirements in documents that ran to hundreds, sometimes thousands, of pages. But it is absurd to believe that the human mind can come up with a consistent and relevant list of thousands of requirements in the form "The system shall. . . ." What's more, these requirements specifications did not readily transform into design and implementation specifications.

Even with the help of analysts, users did not fully understand what the software system ought to do until the system was almost completed. As projects proceeded and users, intermediaries, and the developers themselves could see what the system would look like and thus came to understand the real needs better, a wealth of changes would be suggested. Many of these changes were desirable, but implementing them usually had a serious impact on schedules and costs.

Over the years we have fooled ourselves into believing that users know what the requirements are and that all we have to do is interview them. It is true that the systems we build should support users and that that we can learn about user interaction from the users themselves. However, it is even more important that systems support the *mission* for which they are built. For example, the system should provide value to the business that uses it and to its customers. Often, it is difficult to identify or understand what this value is, and sometimes it is impossible to have the system satisfy the value. Worse, in a reflection of the ever-changing real world, this elusive value will likely change during the course of the project: The business itself might change, the technology available to build the system might change, the resources (people, money) available to build the system might change, and so on.

Even with this insight, requirements capture remains difficult, and the industry has long sought a good, systematic process to do it. To that we turn our attention in this chapter and the following.

## 6.2 The Purpose of the Requirements Workflow

The essential purpose of the requirements workflow is to aim development toward the right system. This is achieved by describing the system requirements (i.e., the conditions or capabilities to which the system must conform) well enough so that an agreement can be reached between the customer (including the users) and the system developers on what the system should and should not do.

A major challenge with this is that the customer, who we assume to be primarily a noncomputer specialist, must be able to read and understand the results of requirements capture. To meet this challenge we must use *the language of the customer* to describe these results. As a consequence, we should be very careful when introducing formality and structure and when introducing details about the system's internal workings, in the results.

The results of the requirements workflow also helps the project manager plan the iterations and customer releases (this is discussed in Part III).

## 6.3 Overview of Requirements Capture

Every software project is unique. This singularity comes from the variations in the kind of system, the customer, the development organization, the technology, and so on. Similarly, there are different starting points for capturing requirements. In some cases, we start by developing a business model, or we start with a business model already under development by some other organization (see Section 6.6.1, "What Is a Business Model?"). In other cases, the software is an embedded system that does not directly support a business. Then there might be a simple object model, such as a domain model, to serve as input (see Section 6.5.1, "What Is a Domain Model?"). In still other cases, the client may have already developed a complete, detailed requirements specification that is not based on an object model, from which we start and negotiate changes.

At the other extreme are customers who have only a vague notion of what their system should be—perhaps it is derived from a vision statement issued by top management. In between these extremes are all varieties of combinations. We will consider one such starting point, the "vague notion," and introduce the example that we will use in the rest of this book.

---

| **Example** | The Interbank Consortium Considers a Computer System |
|---|---|

The Interbank Consortium, a hypothetical financial institution, is facing major changes due to deregulation, new competition, and capabilities enabled by the World Wide Web. The consortium plans to develop new applications to support the rapidly changing finance markets. It has directed its software development subsidiary, Interbank Software, to initiate the development of these applications.

Interbank Software decides to design the Billing and Payment System in collaboration with some of its main bank customers. The system will use the Internet for sending orders, invoices, and payments between buyers and sellers. The bank's motivation for developing the system is to attract new customers by offering a low payment-processing fee. The bank will also be able to reduce its wage costs by processing payment requests automatically through the Internet instead of manually through cashiers.

The motivations for buyers and sellers are to reduce costs, paperwork, and processing time. For example, they will no longer have to send orders or invoices by paper mail. The payment of invoices will be handled between the buyer's computer and the seller's computer. Buyers and sellers will also have a better overview of the status of their invoices and payments.

---

The possibility of such different starting points as a vague vision statement and a detailed requirements specification suggests that analysts need to be able to adapt their approach to requirements capture to each situation. Different starting points pose different types of risks, so analysts should choose the approach that will best reduce those risks. Risk reduction is discussed in detail in Part III.

Despite the differences in starting points, certain steps are feasible in most cases, which allows us to suggest an archetypal workflow. This workflow includes the following steps, which are not actually performed separately:

- List candidate requirements.
- Understand system context.
- Capture functional requirements.
- Capture nonfunctional requirements.

We will briefly describe these steps in the following paragraphs.

**List candidate requirements**    During the life of a system, customers, users, analysts, and developers come up with many good ideas that might turn into real requirements. We keep a list of these ideas, which we think of as a set of candidate requirements that we may chose to implement in some future release of the system. This *feature list* grows as new items are added and shrinks as features become requirements and are transformed into other artifacts, such as the use cases. The feature list is used only for planning the work.

Each feature has a short name and a brief explanation or definition, just enough information to be able to talk about the feature during product planning. Each feature also has a set of planning values, which might include

- Status (e.g., proposed, approved, incorporated, or validated);
- Estimated cost to implement (in terms of resource types and man-hours);
- Priority (e.g., critical, important, or ancillary); and
- Associated level of risk in implementing the feature (e.g., critical, significant, or ordinary; see Chapter 5).

These planning values are used together with other aspects (as discussed in Chapter 12) to estimate the size of the project and to decide on how to divide the project into a sequence of iterations.

The priority and risk level associated with a feature are, for example, used to decide in which iteration to implement the feature (as discussed in Part III). Moreover, when a feature is scheduled for implementation, it will be traced to one or more use cases or supplementary requirements (discussed shortly).

*Understand system context*    Many of the people involved in software development are specialists in matters pertaining to software. However, to capture the right requirements and to build the right system, key developers—the architect, in particular, and some of the senior analysts—need a firm grasp of the context in which the system is set.

There are at least two approaches to expressing the context of a system in a form usable by software developers: domain modeling and business modeling. A domain model describes the important concepts of the context as domain objects, and it links these objects to one another. Identifying and naming these objects helps us develop a glossary of terms that will enable everyone who is working on the system to communicate better. Later, the domain objects will help us identify some of the classes as we analyze and design our system. As you will see, a business model can be described as a superset of a domain model, and it includes more than just the domain objects.

The goal of business modeling is to describe the processes—existing or perceived—in order to understand them. Business modeling is the only part of business engineering that we will use in this book [3]. Suffice for now to say that business engineering is much like business modeling, but it also has the goal of improving the business processes of the organization.

As analysts model the business they learn a great deal about the context of the software system, and they describe this in a business model. The business model specifies which business processes are to be supported by the system. Apart from identifying the business or domain objects involved in the business, business modeling also establishes the competencies required in each process: the workers, their responsibilities, and the operations they will perform. This knowledge, of course, is crucial in identifying the use cases, as discussed shortly. In fact, the business engineering approach is a most systematic process for capturing requirements for business applications [3].

Together, the architect and project manager decide whether to prepare a domain model, to go all the way and prepare a complete business model, or to prepare neither of these models.

*Capture functional requirements*    The straightforward approach to identifying system requirements is based on use cases (use cases are treated extensively in Chapter 7). These use cases capture both functional and nonfunctional requirements that are specific to individual use cases.

Let us briefly recapitulate how use cases help us capture the right requirements. Each user wants the system to do something for him or her, that is, to perform certain use cases. To the user, a use case is a way of using the system. Consequently, if analysts can describe all the use cases that the users need, then they know what the system is to do.

Each use case represents one way of using the system (e.g., to support a user during a business process). Each user needs several different use cases, each representing the different ways he or she uses the system. Capturing the use cases that are actually wanted from the system, such as those that support the business and that the users think allow them to work in a "comfortable" way, requires that we know the user and customer needs thoroughly. To do so we need to understand the system context, interview users, discuss proposals, and so on.

As an adjunct to the use cases, analysts must also specify what the user interface will look like when the use cases are performed. The best way to develop this user interface specification is to sketch several versions that show the information that is to be transferred, discuss the sketches with users, and make up concrete visualizations or prototypes for users to try out.

**Capture nonfunctional requirements**    Nonfunctional requirements specify system properties, such as environmental and implementation constraints, performance, platform dependencies, maintainability, extensibility, and reliability—all the "ilities." *Reliability* refers to characteristics such as availability, accuracy, mean time between failures, defects per 1,000 lines of code (KLOC), and defects per class. A performance requirement imposes conditions on functional requirements, such as the speed, throughput, response time, and memory usage. Most performance requirements are relevant only to a certain use case and should then be connected (as tagged values) to that use case (Appendix A). In practice, this means that these requirements will be described in the right context, that is, in the use case description (perhaps in a separate Special Requirements section).

---

**Example**    Special Requirements
for the Pay Invoice Use Case

*Performance Requirements*

When a buyer issues an invoice for payment, the system should respond with a verification of the request within 1.0 seconds in 90% of the cases. The time for the verification must never exceed 10.0 seconds unless the network connection is broken (in which case the user should be informed).

---

Some nonfunctional requirements refer to real-world phenomena, such as accounts in a bank system. These requirements can initially be captured on the corresponding business or domain object in the model of the context of the system.

Later, when the use cases and the "concepts" that they actually operate upon are determined, these nonfunctional requirements are related to the concepts instead. By "concepts" we mean here either informal terms in a glossary used for use-case descriptions (see Chapter 7), or, more formally, classes in an analysis model (see Chapter 8). For simplicity, we assume in this chapter the former case, that is, these requirements are related to concepts in the glossary.

Finally, some nonfunctional requirements are more generic and cannot be connected to a particular use case or a particular real-world class. They should instead be managed separately in a list of **supplementary requirements** (Appendix C).

*Summing up*    To capture the requirements effectively, analysts need a suite of techniques and artifacts that help them get a good enough picture of the system to advance to the succeeding workflows. We refer to these artifacts collectively as the *set of requirements*. The traditional requirements specification of the past is then replaced by a set of artifacts: the use-case model and the supplementary requirements. The artifacts required to set the system's context are the business and domain model. This is illustrated in Figure 6.1.

Since the requirements keep changing constantly, we need some way to update them in a controlled way. We do this in iterations, where each iteration will reflect some change to the set of requirements, but the number of changes will usually decrease as we get further into the construction phase and the requirements stabilize. This is elaborated on in Section 6.4. After that we will concentrate on describing the system context as a domain model (Section 6.5) or a business model (Section 6.6). Finally we will discuss the supplementary requirements (Section 6.7).

Capturing requirements as use cases is a much larger topic, and one to which we will return in Chapter 7.

| Work to be done | Resulting Artifacts | |
|---|---|---|
| List candidate requirements | Feature list | |
| Understand system context | Business or domain model | |
| Capture functional requirements | Use-case model | Defines a traditional requirements specification |
| Capture nonfunctional requirements | Supplementary requirements or individual use cases (for use-case specific requirements) | |

FIGURE 6.1 The set of all requirements consists of the different artifacts illustrated in the right column. The work to be done influences one or more of the artifacts. Note that the use cases also contain the nonfunctional requirements that are specific to the use cases.

## 6.4 The Role of Requirements in the Software Life Cycle

The use-case model is developed over several development increments, where the iterations will add new use cases and/or add detail to the descriptions of existing use cases.

Figure 6.2 illustrates how the requirements capture workflow and the resulting artifacts assume different shapes during the different phases and their iterations (see Chapter 12):

- During the inception phase, analysts identify most use cases in order to delimit the system and scope the project and to detail the most critical ones (less than 10%).
- During the elaboration phase, analysts capture most of the remaining requirements so that developers can gauge the size of the development effort that will be required. The goal is to have captured about 80% of the requirements and to have described most of the use cases by the end of the elaboration phase. (Note that only about 5% to 10% of those requirements should be implemented into the architecture baseline at this point.)
- The remaining requirements are captured (and implemented) during the construction phase.
- There is almost no requirements capture during the transition phase, unless there are changing requirements.

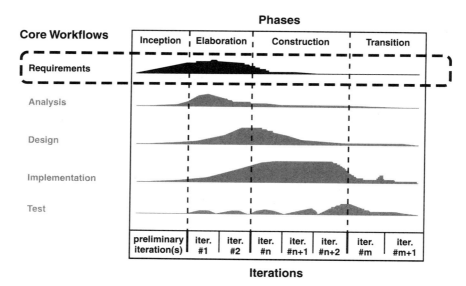

**FIGURE 6.2** Requirements is done primarily during inception and elaboration.

## 6.5 Understanding the System Context Using a Domain Model

### 6.5.1 What Is a Domain Model?

A domain model captures the most important types of objects in the context of the system. The domain objects represent the "things" that exist or events that transpire in environment in which the system works [2, 5].

Many of the domain objects or classes (to use more precise terminology) can be found from a requirements specification or by interviewing domain experts. The domain classes come in three typical shapes:

- Business objects that represent things that are manipulated in a business, such as orders, accounts, and contracts.
- Real-world objects and concepts that a system needs to keep track of, such as enemy aircraft, missiles, and trajectory.
- Events that will or have transpired, such as aircraft arrival, aircraft departure, and lunch break.

The domain model is described in UML diagrams (particularly in class diagrams).

These diagrams illustrate to customers, users, reviewers, and other developers the domain classes and how they are related to one another by association.

---

**Example**    The Domain Classes
Order, Invoice, Item, and Account

The system will use the Internet to send orders, invoices, and payments between buyers and sellers. The system helps the buyer prepare orders, the seller to evaluate orders and send invoices, and the buyer to validate invoices and effect payment from the buyer's account to that of the seller.

An order is the request from a buyer to a seller for a number of items. Each item "occupies a line" in the order. An order has attributes such as date of submission and delivery address. See the class diagram in Figure 6.3.

An invoice is a request for payment sent from a seller to a buyer in response to an order for goods or services. An invoice has attributes such as amount, date of submission, and last date of payment. An invoice may be the request for payment of several orders.

An invoice is paid by transferring money from the buyer's account to the seller's account. An Account has attributes such as balance and owner. The attribute owner identifies the person who owns the account.

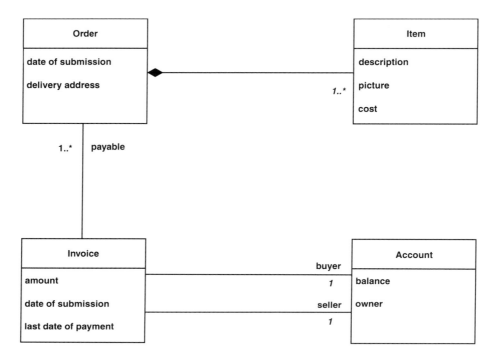

**FIGURE 6.3** A class diagram in a domain model, capturing the most important concepts in the context of the system.

---

### UML Notation

Classes (rectangles), attributes (text in the lower half of the class rectangles), and associations (the lines between the class rectangles). The text at the end of an association path explains the role of one class in relation to another, that is, the role of the association. The multiplicity—the numbers and stars at the end of an association path—tells how many objects of the class at this end are linked to one object at the other end. For example, the association connecting the classes Invoice and Order in Figure 6.3 has a 1..* multiplicity adorned to the Order class end. This means that each Invoice object may be a request for payment of one or more Order objects, as indicated by the payable association **role** (Appendix A).

## 6.5.2 Developing a Domain Model

Domain modeling is usually done in workshops by domain analysts, who use UML and other modeling languages to document the results. To form an effective team, these workshops should include both domain experts and people who are skilled in modeling.

The purpose of domain modeling is to understand and describe the most important classes within the context of the domain. Modest-sized domains usually require between 10 and 50 such classes. Larger domains may require many more.

The remaining hundreds of candidate classes that the analysts may elicit for the domain are kept as definitions in a glossary of terms; otherwise, the domain model will become too large and will require more effort than is appropriate for this stage of the process.

Sometimes, such as for very small business domains, it is not necessary to develop an object model for the domain; instead, a glossary of terms may suffice.

The glossary and domain model help users, customers, developers, and other stakeholders use a common vocabulary. Common terminology is necessary to share knowledge with others. Where confusion abounds, engineering is difficult, if not impossible. And to build a software system of any size, modern engineers must "merge" the language of all the participants into a consistent one.

Finally, a word of caution regarding domain modeling is in order. It can be very easy to start modeling the internal parts of a system and not its context [7]. For example, some domain objects might have a straightforward representation in the system, and some domain analysts might in turn fall into the trap of specifying details regarding this representation. In such cases it is very important to keep in mind that the purpose of domain modeling is to contribute to an understanding of the system's context, and thereby also to an understanding of the system's requirements as they originate from this context. In other words, domain modeling should contribute to an understanding of the *problem* that the system is supposed to solve in relation to its context. The system's internal way of solving this problem will be dealt with in the analysis, design, and implementation workflows (see Chapters 8, 9, and 10).

## 6.5.3 Use of the Domain Model

The domain classes and the glossary of terms are used when developing the use case and analysis models. They are used

- When describing the use cases and when designing the user interface, something which we will return to in Chapter 7.
- To suggest classes internal to the developed system during analysis, something which we will return to in Chapter 8.

However, there is an even more systematic way to identify use cases and to find classes inside the system: develop a business model. As we will see, a domain model is really a special case of a more complete business model. Thus, developing a business model is a powerful alternative to developing a domain model.

## 6.6 Understanding the System Context Using a Business Model

Business modeling is a technique for understanding the business processes of an organization. But what if you work with a system that has nothing to do with what most of us consider a business? For instance, what should we do when developing a pacemaker, an antilock braking system, a camera controller, or a telecom system? In these cases, we can also model the system encompassing the software system that we will develop. That system (part of the human body, part of the car, the camera, the switch) is the "business system" of the embedded software system. It participates in higher-level system use cases that we should outline briefly. The goal is to identify the use cases of the software and the relevant business entities to be supported by the software, so we should just model enough to understand the context. The result of this activity is a domain model derived from understanding the functioning of the encompassing "business system."

Business modeling is supported by two kinds of UML models: use-case models and object models [6]. Both are defined in the business-specific extension to UML.

### 6.6.1  What Is a Business Model?

First, a business use-case model describes the business processes of a company in terms of business use cases and business actors corresponding to business processes and customers, respectively. Like the use-case model for a software system, the business use-case model presents a system (here, the business) from the usage perspective and outlines how it provides value to its users (here its customers and partners) [3, 4, 6].

---

**Example**    **Business Use Cases**

The Interbank Consortium example offers a business use case that involves sending orders, invoices, and payments between a buyer and a seller—Sales: From Order to Delivery. In this business use case, a buyer knows what to buy and from where. In the following sequence Interbank acts as the broker in this business use case, connecting the buyer and seller to each other and providing secure routines for invoice payment:

1. The buyer orders the goods or services.
2. The seller delivers the goods or services.
3. The seller invoices the buyer.
4. The buyer pays.

In this context, the buyer and the seller are the business actors of Interbank, and they use the business use case that Interbank provides.

A business normally provides many business use cases. Interbank is no exception. We will describe two of these use cases here just to get the right context, but we will not discuss the other processes.

In the Loan handling: From Application to Disbursement business use case, a bank customer submits a loan request to the Interbank and receives the funds from the bank.

The bank customer represents a generic customer to the bank. The buyer and the seller are more specific types of customers.

In the Transfer, Withdraw and Deposit Money business use case, a bank customer makes transfers between accounts, withdraws and deposits money. This business use case will also allow a bank customer to set up future automatic transfers.

---

The business use-case model is described in use-case diagrams (see Chapters 4 and 7).

A business-object model is an interior model of a business. It describes how each business use case is realized by a set of workers who are using a set of business entities and work units. Each realization of a business use case can be shown in interaction diagrams (see Chapters 4 and 9) and activity diagrams (such as the workflow diagrams in Chapters 7–11).

A business *entity* represents something, such as an invoice, which workers access, inspect, manipulate, produce, or use in a business use case. A *work unit* is a set of such entities that forms a recognizable whole to an end user.

Business entities and work units are used to represent the same kinds of concepts as domain classes, such as Order, Item, Invoice, and Account. We could therefore prepare a diagram of the business entities, much like Figure 6.3. Then there will be other diagrams to depict the workers, their interactions, and how they use the business entities and work units, such as Figure 6.4.

Each worker, business entity, and work unit may participate in the realization of more than one business use case. As an example, the Account class would probably participate in all three business use-case realizations:

- In Loan Handling: From Application to Disbursement, the money acquired from the loan is disbursed to an account.
- In Transfer, Withdraw, and Deposit Money: Money is withdrawn from or deposited to accounts, and transferred between accounts.
- Sales: From Order to Delivery involves transfer of money from a buyer's to a seller's account.

---

**Example** | **The Sales: From Order to Delivery Business Use Case**

Workers take the following steps in the business use case Sales: From Order to Delivery (see Figure 6.4):

1. A buyer orders goods or services by contacting the seller.
2. The seller sends an invoice to the buyer through the payment handler.
3. The seller delivers the goods or services to the buyer.
4. The buyer pays via the payment handler. This involves transferring money from the account of the buyer to the account of the seller.

The payment handler is a bank employee who helps in Steps 2 and 4. These tasks could be automated by an information system.

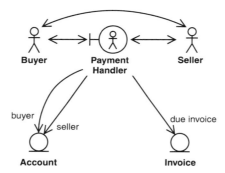

**FIGURE 6.4** Buyer, seller, and payment handler are involved in the Sales: From Order to Delivery business use case. The payment handler transfers money from one account to another as specified by an invoice.

---

The buyer and seller use the (automated) payment handler because that worker adds value to them. The worker payment handler adds value to the seller by sending an invoice to the buyer and by keeping track of outstanding payments. The payment handler worker adds value to the buyer by simplifying payments and by providing a better overview and availability of invoice payment.

### 6.6.2 How to Develop a Business Model

A business model is thus developed in two steps:

1. The business modelers should prepare a business use-case model that identifies the actors to the business and the business use cases that the actors use. This business use-case model allows the modelers to understand better what value the business provides to its actors.

2. The modelers should develop a business object model consisting of workers, business entities, and work units that together realize the business use cases. Business rules and other regulations imposed on the business are associated with these different objects. The goal is to create workers, business entities, and work units that realize the business use cases as effectively as possible— that is, quickly, accurately, and at low cost.

Business modeling and domain modeling are similar in some ways. In fact, we can think of domain modeling as a simplified variant of business modeling, where we focus only on the "things," that is, the domain classes or the business entities that the workers need to work with.[1] Thus domain classes and business entities are very similar concepts, and we use the terms interchangeably.

However, there are some important differences between business modeling and domain modeling that speak strongly for doing the more complete business modeling:

- Domain classes are pulled out of the knowledge base of a few domain experts, or possibly out of the knowledge (e.g., other domain classes, requirements specifications, and so on) associated with systems similar to the one under development. Business entities, on the other hand, are derived by starting from the customers of the business, identifying the business use cases, and then finding the entities. In the business modeling approach, every entity has to be motivated through its use in a business use case. These two approaches usually end up with different sets of classes, associations, attributes, and operations. The domain modeling approach can trace classes back to the experience of the domain experts. The business modeling approach can trace the need for every model element back to the customers.

- Domain classes have attributes but usually no or very few operations. Not so for business entities. The business modeling approach identifies not only the entities but all workers that will participate in realizing the business use cases that use the entities. Moreover, we identify how these workers will use the entities through operations that each entity needs to provide. As for the entities themselves, these operations will also be derived from and can be traced back to the customers.

- The workers found in business modeling are used as a starting point to derive a first set of actors and use cases for the information system to be built. This allows us to trace every use case in the information system through the workers and business use cases back to the customers of the business. This will be elaborated in Chapter 7. Furthermore, every use case can be traced to the components implementing the system, as described in Chapter 3. Thus we can conclude that the combined business modeling and the software engineering approach of the Unified Process allow us to trace customer needs all the way

---

1. Since a domain model is a simplified variant of a business model, we list only the latter as input to the subsequent core workflows as presented in Chapters 7–11.

---

### The Business Modeling Approach Used to Describe the Unified Process (Part One)

The business modeling approach we present for modeling the customer company is basically the same approach we use when we describe the Unified Process for software engineering in this book. We thus use the business-specific extension to UML when we describe the Unified Process for software engineering (see Chapter 2). Although this has a strong theoretical foundation, it is also very practical. It is a kind of bootstrapping or reflexive work. It reveals strengths and weaknesses of the approach.

Thus the Unified Process is a business use case of the software development business. Inside the software development business, the process is organized, or as we say "realized," as a sequence of interlocking workflows: requirements (as discussed in this chapter and in Chapter 7), analysis (Chapter 8), design (Chapter 9), implementation (Chapter 10), and testing (Chapter 11). Each workflow is a realization of a part of the Unified Process business use case, which is described in terms of

- Workers, such as the system analyst and the use-case specifiers.
- Business entities, or as we call them, artifacts, such as use cases and test cases.
- Work units—which are also artifacts—such as the use-case model and the architecture description.

The workers, business entities, and work units of the Unified Process are also depicted in UML class diagrams together with the most important relationships to one another.

(This sidebar will be continued in Chapter 7).

---

through business processes, workers, and use cases, to software code. However, when only a domain model is used, there are no obvious ways of tracing between the domain model and the system use cases.

### 6.6.3  Find Use Cases from a Business Model

Using a business model as input, an analyst employs a systematic technique to create a tentative use-case model.

First, the analyst identifies an *actor*[2] for every worker and business actor (i.e., each customer) who will become a user of the information system.

---

2. We will use the term *actor* to denote a system actor when there is no risk of confusion with the business actors.

**Example**   The Buyer Actor

The buyer uses the Billing and Payment System to order goods or services and to pay invoices. Thus the buyer is both a customer and an actor because he uses the system to order and pay through two use cases: Order Goods or Services and Pay Invoices.

Each worker (and business actor) who will become a user of the information system will need support from it. The support needed is found by going through all the workers, one at a time. For each worker, we identify all the different business use-case realizations in which the worker participates. The worker plays a role in each one, much as a class plays a role in each use-case realization.

Once we have found all the roles of a worker or business actor, one for each business use-case realization in which it participates, we can find use cases for the system actors of the information system. Each worker in and business actor to the business corresponds to an actor of the information system. For each worker or business actor role, a use case is needed by the corresponding system actor.

Thus the most straightforward way to identify a tentative set of use cases is to create a use case for the corresponding actor for each role of each worker and business actor. As a result, for each business use case, there will be one use case for each worker and business actor. Analysts can then detail and adjust these tentative use cases.

The analysts must also decide how many of the workers' or the business actors' tasks should be automated by information systems (as use cases) and rearrange the use cases to fit the needs of the actors better. Note that not all tasks may be appropriate to automate.

**Example**   Identifying Use Cases from a Business Model

Continuing with the preceding example, we could suggest a tentative use case called Buying Goods or Services, which would support the buyer actor when acting as a business actor in the business use case Sales: From Order to Delivery. Upon further analysis, it becomes apparent that Buying Goods or Services would be better realized as several distinct use cases, such as Order Goods or Services and Pay Invoice. The reason for breaking the tentative use case into several smaller use cases is that a buyer does not want to perform a Buying Goods or Services use case in one uninterrupted sequence of actions. Instead, the buyer wants to wait for the delivery of the goods or services before paying the invoice. The payment sequence is therefore represented as a separate Pay Invoice use case, which is performed when the goods have been delivered.

So far we have seen how we can model the context of the system using a domain model or a business model. Then we saw how a use-case model can be derived from a business model, that is, as a use-case model that captures all the functional requirements on a system as well as most of the nonfunctional requirements. Some requirements cannot be associated with any particular use case and are known as *supplementary requirements*.

## 6.7 Supplementary Requirements

The supplementary requirements are primarily nonfunctional requirements that cannot be associated with any particular use case—instead each such requirement have impact on several use cases or none at all. Examples are performance, interfaces, and physical design requirements and architectural, design, and implementation constraints [1]. The supplementary requirements are captured much as the requirements in a traditional requirements specification are, that is, as a list of requirements. They are then used during analysis and design along with the use-case model.

An *interface requirement* specifies the interface to an external item with which a system must interact or sets forth constraints on formats, timings, or other factors relevant in such an interaction.

A *physical requirement* specifies a physical characteristic that a system must possess, such as its material, shape, size, or weight. This type of requirement can, for example, be used to represent hardware requirements such as the required physical network configurations.

---

**Example**    **Hardware Platform Requirements**

*Servers*

SUN SPARC 20 or PC Pentium

*Clients*

PCs (minimum Intel 486 processor) or Sun Sparc 5

---

A *design constraint* constrains the design of a system, such as extensibility and maintainability constraints, or constraints regarding the reuse of legacy systems or essential parts of them.

An *implementation constraint* specifies or constrains the coding or construction of a system. Examples are required standards, implementation guidelines, implementation languages, policies for database integrity, resource limits, and operation environments.

**Example** | **File Format Constraints**

Version 1.2 of the Billing and Payment System shall support long file names.

---

**Example** | **Software Platform Constraints**

*System Software*

Client operating systems: Windows NT 4.0, Windows 95, or Solaris 2.6
Server operating systems: Windows NT 4.0 or Solaris 2.6

*Internet Software*

Netscape Communicator 4.0 or Microsoft Internet Explorer 4.0

---

Furthermore, there are often *other requirements,* such as legal and regulatory requirements.

**Example** | **Other Requirements**

*Security*

The transmission must be secure, meaning that only authorized persons can access the information. The only authorized persons are the bank customer who owns the accounts and the system administrator actors.

*Availability*

The Billing and Payment System must have no more than 1 hour per month of down time.

*Ease of Learning*

The time for 90% of the buyers to learn (through supplied step-by-step instructions) to submit simple orders and to pay simple invoices must not be more than 10 minutes. A simple order is an order with only one item. A simple invoice is an invoice for payment of one simple order.

## 6.8 Summary

At this point, we have provided a good grasp of requirements capture. We have seen how business and domain models help define the system context and how use cases can be derived from a business model. We have seen that use cases are used for capturing the requirements, and we will return to that topic in the next chapter. In subsequent chapters we will see how use cases and supplementary requirements help us analyze, architect, design, implement and test the system to ensure that it meets customer requirements.

## 6.9 References

[1]  IEEE Std 610.12.1990.

[2]  Ivar Jacobson, Magnus Christerson, Patrik Jonsson, and Gunnar Övergaard, *Object-Oriented Software Engineering: A Use-Case–Driven Approach,* Reading, MA: Addison-Wesley, 1992 (Revised fourth printing, 1993).

[3]  Ivar Jacobson, Maria Ericsson, and Agneta Jacobson, *The Object Advantage: Business Process Reengineering with Object Technology,* Reading, MA: Addison-Wesley, 1994.

[4]  Ivar Jacobson, "Business process reengineering with object technology," *Object Magazine,* May 1994.

[5]  James Rumbaugh, M. Blaha, W. Premerlani, F. Eddy, W. Lorensen, *Object-Oriented Modeling and Design,* Englewood Cliffs, NJ: Prentice Hall, 1991.

[6]  OMG Unified Modeling Language Specification. Object Management Group, Framingham, MA, 1998. Internet: www.omg.org.

[7]  Alan M. Davis, *Software Requirements: Objects, Functions, and States,* Englewood Cliffs, NJ: Prentice Hall, 1993.

# *Chapter 7*

# Capturing the Requirements as Use Cases

## 7.1  Introduction

The major effort in requirements is to develop a model of the system that is to be built, and employing use cases is an appropriate way to create such a model. This is because the functional requirements are naturally structured as use cases, and since most of the other nonfunctional requirements are specific to a single use case, they are also dealt with in the context of that use case.

The remaining nonfunctional requirements, those that are common for many or all use cases, are kept in a separate document and are known as the *supplementary requirements*. These requirements were described in Chapter 6 and will not be discussed again until they are used in the analysis, design, implementation, and testing workflows.

Use cases offer a systematic and intuitive way to capture the functional requirements with particular focus on the value added to each individual user or to each external system. By using use cases analysts are forced to think in terms of who the users are and what business or mission needs can be fulfilled through them. However, as we said in Chapter 4, use cases would probably not have become so widely accepted if that was all they did. Their key role in driving the rest of the development work has been an important reason for their acceptance in most approaches to modern software engineering [8].

In this chapter we will detail our understanding of use cases and actors and present stricter definitions than we used in Chapter 3.

We describe the requirements workflow (and we will describe all workflows in Chapters 8–11 in a similar way) in three steps:

- The artifacts created in the requirements workflow
- The workers participating in the requirements workflow
- The requirements capture workflow, including each activity in more detail

To start, we will examine the workers and artifacts illustrated in Figure 7.1.

### The Business Modeling Approach Used to Describe the Unified Process (Part Two)

We identify the workers and the artifacts that participate in each workflow. A *worker* represents a position that can be assigned to a person or a team, and it specifies required responsibilities and abilities (see also Section 2.1.3).

*Artifact* is a general term for any kind of description or information created, produced, changed, or used by workers when working with the system. An artifact can be a model, a model element, or a document. For example, in the requirements workflow, the artifacts are essentially the use-case model and its use cases. Note that in the business model of the Unified Process, an artifact is a business entity or a work unit.

Each worker is responsible for a set of artifacts. This is shown in diagrams with an association named "responsible for" from the worker to the corresponding artifacts (e.g., see Figure 7.1). To make such diagrams more intuitive, we use special symbols for most artifacts. Artifacts that represent documents are shown with a special document symbol. Artifacts that represent models or model elements are shown with their corresponding UML symbol.

Note that to be able to use these special symbols in the business model of the Unified Process, we introduce stereotypes for documents, models, and model elements. Each such stereotype is a subtype of the «business entity» or «work unit» stereotype.

We illustrate how workers collaborate in a *workflow*, where we will see how the work attention moves from worker to worker, and how they work with artifacts as they perform their activities (see also Section 2.4.2). In this context we also look at each activity in more detail. An *activity* is a piece of work that a worker performs in the workflow, that is, it is the execution of one of the worker operations.

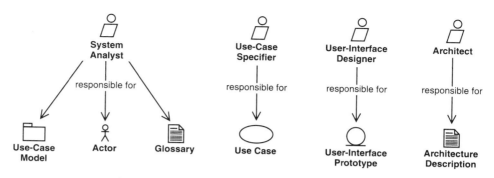

**FIGURE 7.1** The workers and artifacts involved when capturing requirements as use cases.

## 7.2 Artifacts

The primary artifacts used in requirements capture are the use-case model, including the use cases and the actors. There may also be other kind of artifacts, such as user-interface prototypes.

These artifacts were introduced in Chapter 3, but here we will give more precise definitions, which are consistent with those given in [12]. Then we will relax this formalism and show how to apply these constructs in practice in the Unified Process. The definitions are given here to provide a sound foundation, and it is not necessary to apply this formalism in practice. We have included them here for the following reasons:

- It might be important when describing some kinds of use cases, such as using activity diagrams or statecharts, formally. This is particularly valuable for use cases with many states and complex transitions between the states.
- It makes it easier to identify the right use cases and to describe them consistently. Actually, even if you choose not to use the available formalism when describing, for instance, the actors or the use cases, it is good to have it in the back of your mind to help you be complete and consistent.
- It is important to be able to explain the actor and use-case constructs in relation to other UML constructs.

### 7.2.1 Artifact: Use-Case Model

The use-case model allows software developers and the customer to agree on the requirements [6], that is, the conditions or capabilities to which the system must conform. The use-case model serves as an agreement between the customer and the developers, and it provides essential input for analysis, design, and testing.

A use-case model is a model of a system containing actors and use cases and their relationships (see Figure 7.2).

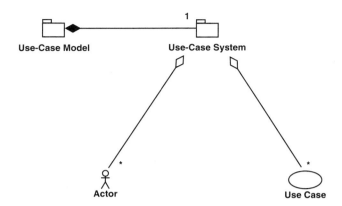

**FIGURE 7.2** The use-case model and its contents. The use-case system denotes the top-level package of the model.

The use-case model can become quite large and difficult to digest in one big bite, so we need some way to help us appreciate the model in smaller chunks. UML allows us to present the model in diagrams that present the actors and use cases from different viewpoints and with different purposes. Also note that if the use-case model is large, that is, if it contains a large number of use cases and/or actors, it may also be useful to introduce packages in the model to manage its size. This is a more or less trivial extension of the use-case model, and it is not dealt with in this book.

### 7.2.2 Artifact: Actor

The use-case model describes what the system does for each type of user. Each type of user is represented as one or more actors. Each external system that the system interacts with is also represented as one or more actors; this includes external devices, such as timers, that are considered external to the system. Thus, actors represent parties outside the system that collaborate with the system. Once we have identified all the actors of a system, we have identified the external environment of the system.

Actors often correspond to workers (or business actors) in a business, as discussed in Chapter 6. Recall that each role (of a worker) defines what the worker does in a particular business process. The roles that a worker plays can then be used to derive (or actually to generate if appropriate tools are provided) the roles that the corresponding system actor will play. Then as suggested in Chapter 6 we supply each worker with one system use case for each of its roles. That use case adds value to the actor when enacting the worker role.

**Example**  Actor

The Interbank Billing and Payment System interacts with a type of user who will use the system to order goods, confirm orders, pay invoices, and so on. This type of user is then represented by the Buyer actor (Figure 7.3).

**Buyer**

**FIGURE 7.3**  The Buyer actor.

An actor plays one role for each use case with which it collaborates. Every time a specific user (a human or another system) interacts with the system, the corresponding actor instance is playing such a role. An instance of an actor is thus a specific user interacting with the system. Any entity that conforms to an actor can act as an instance of the actor.

### 7.2.3  Use Case

Each way the actors use the system is represented as a use case. Use cases are "chunks" of functionality that the system offers to add a result of value to its actors. More strictly, a use case specifies a sequence of actions, including alternatives of the sequence, that the system can perform, interacting with actors of the system.

Thus a *use case* is a specification. It specifies the behavior of dynamic "things," here, use-case instances.

**Example**  The Withdraw Money Use Case

In Chapter 3 we described the use case Withdraw Money, which enables instances of the actor Bank Customer to withdraw money through an ATM (Figure 7.4).

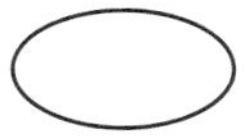

**Withdraw Money**

**FIGURE 7.4**  The Withdraw Money use case.

The Withdraw Money use case specifies the possible instances of that use case, that is, the different legitimate ways in which the use case can be performed by the system and the interaction required with the involved actor instances. Say that a particular person, Jack, first entered his PIN 1234, selected to withdraw $220, and then got the money. The system would have performed one use-case instance. If Jack instead entered the same PIN, selected to withdraw $240, and then got the money, the system would have performed another use-case instance. A third use-case instance would be what the system did if Jack asked to withdraw $480, and the system denied that request due to an insufficient account balance or an incorrect PIN code, and so on.

---

In UML vocabulary, a *use case* is a classifier, which means that it has operations—and attributes. A use-case description can thus include statechart diagrams, activity diagrams, collaborations, and sequence diagrams (see Appendix A, "Overview of the UML," for details).

Statechart diagrams specify the life cycle of use-case instances in terms of states and transitions between states. Each transition is a sequence of actions. Activity diagrams describe the life cycle in more detail by also describing the sequence of actions that occurs within each transition. Collaboration and sequence diagrams are used to describe the interaction between, for instance, a typical actor instance and a typical use-case instance. In practice, we don't always need to be this formal when we describe use cases, as we will discuss in Section 7.4.3, "Detail a Use Case." However, having this more precise understanding of use cases in the back of our minds helps when structuring use-case descriptions.

A *use-case instance* is the performance (or execution) of a use case. Another way of putting it is that a use-case instance is what the system performs as it "obeys a use case." When a use-case instance is performed, it interacts with actor instances, and it performs a sequence of actions as specified by its use case. This sequence is specified in a statechart diagram or an activity diagram; it is one path through the use case. Many paths are possible, and many may be very similar. These are alternatives of the sequence of actions for the use case. Such a path through a use case may look as follows:

1. The use-case instance is initiated and put in a start state.
2. It is invoked by an external message from an actor.
3. It transitions to another state by performing a sequence of actions. Such a sequence contains internal computations, selection of path, and message outputs (to some actor).
4. It awaits (in the new state) another external message from an actor.
5. It is invoked (again) by a new message, and so on. This may go on over many states until the use-case instance is terminated.

Most often it is an actor instance that invokes a use-case instance, as described earlier, but it may also be an event within the system that invokes the instance, such as when a set timer triggers (if the timer is considered internal to the system).

Use cases, like all classifiers, have attributes. These attributes represent the values that a use-case instance uses and manipulates during the performance of its use case. These values are local to a use-case instance, that is, they cannot be used by other use-case instances. For example, the use case Withdraw money could be thought of as having attributes such as PIN, account, and amount to be withdrawn.

Use-case instances do not interact with other use-case instances. The only kind of interactions in the use-case model occur between actor instances and use-case instances [10]. The reason for this is that we want the use-case model to be simple and intuitive to allow fruitful discussions with end-users and other stakeholders without getting us bogged down in details. We don't want to deal with interfaces between use cases, concurrency, and other conflicts (such as sharing of other objects) between different use-case instances. We view use-case instances as atomic, that is, each is performed completely or not at all, without any interference from other use-case instances. The behavior of each use case can thus be interpreted independently of other use cases, which makes use-case modeling much simpler. Viewing use cases as atomic has nothing to do with there being a transaction handler underlying the use cases that takes care of conflicts. This is done only to ensure that we can read and understand the use-case model.

However, we acknowledge that there certainly exist interference issues between different uses of a system. These issues cannot be resolved in use-case modeling but are deferred to analysis and design (described in Chapters 8 and 9, respectively), where we realize the use cases as collaborations between classes and/or subsystems. In the analysis model, we can clearly describe how, for example, one single class can participate in several use-case realizations and how any implied interference issues between use cases are resolved.

---

## *Modeling Large Systems*

In this book we will focus on how to model a single system. However, in many cases we need to develop larger systems, systems that are actually built of other systems. We call them *systems of systems*.

**Example**    **One of The Largest Systems in the World**

The largest system ever built by us humans may be a system with close to 1 billion users, namely the global telecommunications network.

When you make a telephone call from, say, San Francisco to Stockholm, that call will probably go through some 20 systems, including local switches, international switches, satellite systems, transmission systems, and so on. Each such type of system has roughly cost some 1,000 person-years to develop, and the software development effort was a large portion of those costs.

It is amazing that when we make such calls it usually works!

Given the complexity and all the different people, companies, and nations that are involved, why does it work? The primary reason is that each interface

*(continued)*

of the whole network (i.e., the network architecture) has been standardized by a single organization, the ITU (the International Telecommunication Union).

The ITU has specified the interfaces between all types of nodes in the network and the precise semantics of these interfaces.

---

Building systems of systems relies on techniques similar to those used to build the global telecommunication network [9]. The whole system is first specified with its use cases. It is designed in terms of collaborating subsystems. The use cases of the whole system are divided into use cases of the collaborating subsystem, and the subsystems are interconnected through interfaces. These interfaces are defined precisely, after which each separate subsystem can be developed independently (as a system of its own) by a separate organization. UML supports this kind of architecture, and the Unified Process can be extended to develop these kinds of systems [13].

Actually, use cases can be used to specify not only systems but other smaller entities, such as subsystems or classes. Thus a subsystem or a class can have two parts, each describing one perspective: a specification and an implementation. The specification describes what the subsystem or class provides to its environment in terms of use cases. The implementation part describes how the subsystem or the class is structured internally to realize its specification. This environment is usually made up of other subsystems and classes. However, if we want to treat the environment anonymously, we can also represent it by actors.

This approach is used when we want to treat a subsystem like a system in its own right, such as when

- We want to develop the subsystem using different technology than we use for other subsystems. We can do this as long as it offers the right use cases and uses and supports the specified interfaces,
- We want to manage the subsystem separately from other subsystems—perhaps at geographically separated sites.

**7.2.3.1 Flow of Events**    The flow of events for each use case can be captured as a separate textual description of the use case's sequence of actions. The flow of events thus specifies what the system does when the specified use case is performed. The flow of events also specifies how the system interacts with the actors when the use case is performed.

From a management point of view, a flow of events description includes a set of sequences of actions that are suitable to modify, review, design, implement, and test together, and to describe as a section or subsection in the user manual.

We provide examples of a flow of events description of a use case in Section 7.4.3, "Detail a Use Case."

### 7.2.3.2 Special Requirements
The special requirements is a textual description that collects all requirements, such as nonfunctional requirements, on a use case. These are primarily nonfunctional requirements that are related to the use case and that need to be handled in subsequent workflows such as analysis, design, or implementation.

We provide examples of special requirements related to a use case in Section 7.4.3, "Detail a Use Case."

### 7.2.4 Artifact: Architecture Description (View of the Use-Case Model)

The architecture description contains an architectural view of the use-case model, depicting the architecturally significant use cases (Figure 7.5).

The architectural view of the use-case model should include use cases that describe some important and critical functionality or that involve some important requirement that must be developed early in the software's life cycle. This architectural view is used as input when use cases are prioritized to be developed (i.e., analyzed, designed, implemented) within an iteration. This is further elaborated upon in Parts I and III (see Chapter 4, Section 4.3, and Chapter 12, Section 12.6, respectively).

Usually, the corresponding use-case realizations can be found in the architectural views of the analysis and design model (see Chapter 4, Section 4.5, Chapter 8, Section 8.4.5, and Chapter 9, Section 9.3.6).

### 7.2.5 Artifact: Glossary

A glossary can be used to define important and common terms used by analysts (and other developers) when they describe the system. A glossary is very useful in

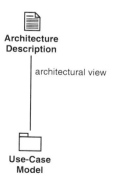

**FIGURE 7.5** The architecture description.

reaching a consensus among developers regarding the definition of various concepts and notions and to reduce the risk of misunderstandings in general.

A glossary can often be derived from a business model or a domain model, but because it is less formal (it includes no classes or explicit relationships), it is easier to maintain and more intuitive to discuss with external parties such as users and customers. Moreover, a glossary tends to be more focused on the system to be built instead of the system's context, as is the case with a business or domain model.

### 7.2.6  Artifact: User-Interface Prototype

The user-interface prototypes help us during requirements capture to understand and specify the interactions between human actors and the system. This helps us not only to develop a better user interface but to understand the use cases better. Other artifacts, such as user-interface models and screen sketches, may also be used when specifying the user interface.

See also [2, 4, 6, 10, 11, 12,] for more details on actors and use cases and [14] for information on user-interface design.

## 7.3  Workers

Earlier in this chapter, we explained the artifacts produced during use-case modeling. The next step is to look at the workers who are responsible for the artifacts.

As discussed in Chapter 2, a worker is a position to which a "real" person can be assigned. With each worker is a description of the responsibilities and the expected behavior of that worker. A worker is not identical to an individual; one person may be assigned as several different workers during a project. Nor does a worker correspond to a particular title or position in an organization—that is a different issue. Rather, you may say that a worker represents an abstraction of a human with certain abilities needed in a business use case, here the Unified Process for software engineering. When a project is staffed, a worker represents the knowledge and the abilities that someone needs to take on the job as that worker in the project. We can identify three workers that participate in use-case modeling, each with its own set of operations and different responsibilities required: system analyst, use-case specifier, and user-interface designer. All these workers will be entitled analysts in this book. There are also other workers, such as reviewers, but we will not consider them in this book.

### 7.3.1  Worker: System Analyst

The system analyst is responsible for the whole set of requirements that are modeled as use cases, which include all functional requirements and the nonfunctional requirements that are use-case specific. The system analyst is responsible for delimiting the system, finding the actors and the use cases, and ensuring that the use-case model is complete and consistent. For consistency, the system analyst can use a glossary to reach agreement on common terms, notions, and concepts when the requirements are captured. The responsibilities of the system analyst are illustrated in Figure 7.6.

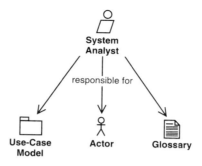

**FIGURE 7.6** The responsibilities of a system analyst when capturing requirements as use cases.

Although the system analyst is responsible for the use-case model and its contained actors, the system analyst is *not* responsible for each individual use case. That is a separate responsibility, held by the use-case specifier worker (Section 7.3.2). The system analyst is also the modeling leader and coordinator in requirements capture.

There is one system analyst for each system. However, in practice, this worker is supported by a team (in workshops or similar events) that includes many other people who also work as analysts.

### 7.3.2  Worker: Use-Case Specifier

Usually, the work of capturing the requirements cannot be accomplished by one individual. Instead, the system analyst is assisted by other workers who each take responsibility for the detailed descriptions of one or more of the use cases. These workers are called *use-case specifiers* (Figure 7.7).

Each use-case specifier needs to work closely with the real users of his or her use cases.

**FIGURE 7.7** The responsibilities of a use-case specifier when capturing requirements as use cases.

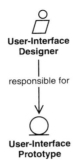

**FIGURE 7.8** The responsibilities of a use-case specifier when capturing requirements as use cases.

### 7.3.3  User-Interface Designer

The *user-interface designers* visually shape[1] the user interface. This may involve developing user-interface prototypes for some use cases, usually one prototype for each actor (Figure 7.8). Thus it is appropriate to let each user-interface designer shape the user interface for one or more actors.

### 7.3.4  Worker: Architect

The architect participates in the requirements workflow to describe the architectural view of the use-case model (Figure 7.9).

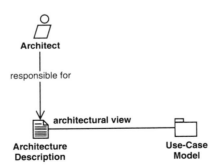

**FIGURE 7.9** The responsibilities of an architect when capturing requirements as use cases.

---

1. By *user-interface design* we mean the visual shaping of the user interface, not the actual implementation of the user interface. The actual implementation is done by other developers during the design and implementation workflows.

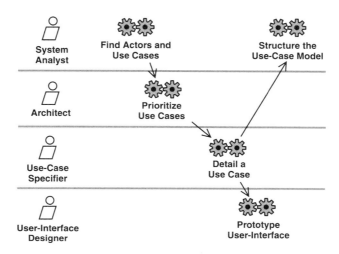

**FIGURE 7.10** The workflow for capturing requirements as use cases, including the participating workers and their activities.

The architectural view of the use-case model is an important input to planning the iterations, as described in Section 7.4.2, "Prioritize Use Cases."

## 7.4 Workflow

In the preceding section we described the requirements capture workflow in static terms. Now we will use an activity diagram (Figure 7.10) to describe its dynamic behavior.

The diagram uses swim lanes to illustrate which worker performs what activities; each activity (represented by cog wheels) is thus positioned in the same field as the worker that performs it. When the workers perform the activities, they create and modify artifacts. We describe the workflow as a sequence of activities, which are ordered so that one activity produces an output that works as an input for the next activity. However, the activity diagram presents only a logical flow. In real life, it is not necessary to work through the activities in sequence. Instead, we can work in any way that produces an "equivalent" end result. We could, for example, start by finding some use cases (the activity Find Actors and Use Cases), then design the user interface (the activity Prototype User Interface), only to realize that a new use case needs to be added (so we jump back to the Find Actors and Use Cases activity, thus breaking the strict sequence), and so on.

An activity may thus be revisited several times, and each visit may entail carrying out only a fraction of the activity. For example, when revisiting the Find Actors and Use Cases activity, the only new result may be that one additional use case was identified. Thus the paths from activity to activity merely illustrate the logical sequence of activities using results from one performed activity as input when performing another.

First, the system analyst (an individual supported by a team of analysts) performs the Find Actors and Use Cases activity to prepare a first version of a use-case model with actors and use cases identified. The system analyst should ensure that the developing use-case model captures the requirements that were input to the workflow, that is, the feature list and the domain or business model. Then the architect(s) will identify the architecturally significant use cases to provide input to the prioritization of use cases (and possibly other requirements) to be developed in the current iteration. Given this, the use-case specifiers (several individuals) describe all use cases that are prioritized. More or less in parallel with this, the user-interface designers (several individuals) suggest suitable user interfaces for each actor based on the use cases. Then, the system analyst restructures the use-case model by defining generalizations between use cases to make it as understandable as possible (generalizations in the Structure the Use-Case Model activity are discussed shortly).

The results of the first iteration through this workflow consists of a first version of the use-case model, the use cases, and any associated user-interface prototypes. The results of any subsequent iteration would then consist of new versions of these artifacts. Recall that all artifacts are completed and improved incrementally over the iterations.

The various activities of use-case modeling take on different shapes in different project phases (see Section 6.4.). For example, when the system analyst performs the Find Actors and Use Cases activity during the inception phase, the system analyst will identify many new actors and use cases. But when the activity is performed during the construction phase, then the system analyst will mostly make minor changes to the set of actors and use cases, such as creating new use-case diagrams that better describe the use-case model from a particular perspective. Next, we will describe the activities as they typically appear in an elaboration iteration.

### 7.4.1 Activity: Find Actors and Use Cases

We identify use cases and actors to

- Delimit the system from its environment.
- Outline who and what (actors) will interact with the system, and what functionality (use cases) is expected from the system.
- Capture and define in a glossary common terms that are essential for creating detailed descriptions of the system's functionality (e.g., use cases).

Identifying actors and use cases is the most crucial activity for getting the requirements right, which is why the system analyst is responsible (Figure 7.11). But the system analyst[2] cannot do this work alone. The analyst requires input from a team

---

2. Actually, we mean here "the person acting as the system analyst." It becomes a bit clumsy to distinguish between a real person and the worker he/she acts as, but it makes the description clearer at the end. We also use the same approach for the other workers discussed.

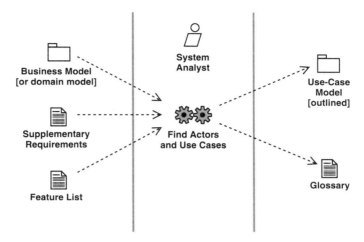

**FIGURE 7.11** The input and result of identifying actors and use cases.

that includes the customer, its users, and other analysts, who participate in modeling workshops led by the system analyst.

Sometimes there may be a business model to start from. If there is, the team can prepare a first draft of a use-case model more or less "automatically." Other times, they may start from a domain model, or the only input may be a brief vision statement or a detailed requirements specification that includes the general features that will be required. There may also be given as input supplementary requirements that cannot be allocated to individual use cases. Refer to Chapter 6 for a discussion of these various input artifacts.

This activity consists of four steps:

- Finding the actors.
- Finding the use cases.
- Briefly describing each use case.
- Describing the use-case model as a whole (this step also includes preparing a glossary of terms).

These steps do not have to be performed in any particular order and are often performed concurrently. For example, the use-case diagrams may be updated as soon as a new actor or use case has been identified.

The result of this activity is a new version of the use-case model with new and changed actors and use cases. The resulting use-case model artifact should be described and diagrammed superficially to the point where each use case can be described in detail, which is the next activity: Detail a Use Case. Figure 7.12 is an illustration of such a use-case diagram (matured and restructured through several iterations). It will be described in more detail shortly.

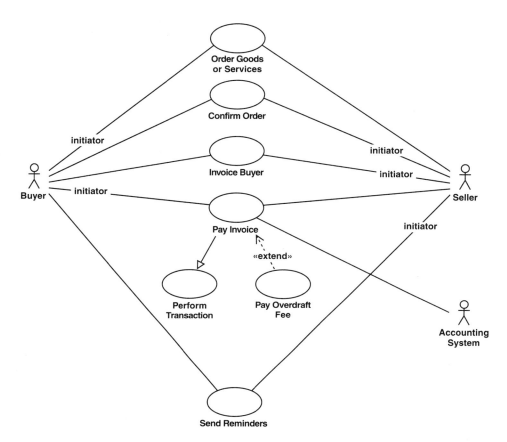

**FIGURE 7.12** Use cases in the Billing and Payment System that support the business use case Sales: From Order to Delivery. The role *initiator,* attached to the associations, indicate which actor starts the use case.

### 7.4.1.1 Finding the Actors    The task of finding the actors depends on the starting point.

When there is a business model to start from, finding the actors is straightforward. The system analyst can suggest one actor for each worker in the business, and one actor for each business actor (i.e., each customer of the business) who will use the information system (see also Chapter 6, Section 6.6.3).

Otherwise, with or without a domain model the system analyst, together with the customer, identifies the users and tries to organize them into categories that represent actors.

In both cases, actors that represent external systems and actors for system maintenance and operation need to be identified.

Two criteria are useful when eliciting candidate actors: First, it should be possible to identify at least one user who can enact the candidate actor. This will help us find only relevant actors and avoid actors that are only ghosts of our imagination. Second, there should be a minimum of overlap between the roles that instances of different actors play in relation to the system. We do not want two or more actors to have essentially the same roles. If that happens, we should either try to combine the roles into a single set of roles for one actor or try to find another generalized actor that has been assigned the roles that are common to the overlapping actors. That new actor can then be specialized using generalizations. For instance, the Buyer and the Seller will be specializations of the Bank Customer actor. It is common, the first time around, to find too many actors with too much overlap. It often takes a few rounds of discussion before the right set of actors and generalizations are stable.

The system analyst names the actors and briefly describes the roles of each actor and what the actor uses the system for. Finding relevant names for the actors is important to convey the desired semantics. The brief description of each actor should outline its needs and responsibilities.

---

**Example**    The Buyer, Seller, and Accounting System Actors

### Buyer

A Buyer represents a person who is responsible for buying goods or services as described in the business use case Sales: From Order to Delivery. This person may be an individual (i.e., not affiliated with a company) or someone within a business organization. The Buyer of goods and services needs the Billing and Payment System to send orders and to pay invoices.

### Seller

A Seller represents a person who sells and delivers goods or services. The Seller uses the system to look for new orders and to send order confirmations, invoices, and payment reminders.

### Accounting System

The Billing and Payment System sends verifications of transactions to the Accounting System.

---

The result of this step is a new version of the use-case model artifact with an updated set of actors, each with a brief description. These briefly described actors can now be used as a starting point for finding the use cases.

### *7.4.1.2 Finding the Use Cases*
When the starting point is a business model, we find the actors and the use cases as discussed in Section 6.6.3, "Find Use Cases from a Business Model," of Chapter 6. A use case is suggested for every role of each worker who participates in a business use-case realization and who will use the information system. Otherwise, the system analyst identifies the use cases through workshops with the customer and its users. The system analyst goes through the actors, one by one, and suggests candidates for use cases for each actor. For example, interviews and storyboarding can be used to understand what use cases are needed; see [16]. The actor will typically need use cases to support its work to create, change, track, remove, or study business objects, such as Orders and Accounts, that are used in business use cases. The actor may also inform the system about certain external events or the other way round—the actor may need the system to inform it about some event that has transpired, such as when an invoice has become overdue. There may also be additional actors that perform system startup, termination, or maintenance.

Some of the candidates won't become use cases by themselves; instead, they may better be parts of other use cases. Recall that we try to create use cases that are easy to modify, review, test, and manage as a unit.

We choose a name for each use case that leads us to think of that particular sequence of actions that adds value to an actor. The name of a use case often starts with a verb, and it should reflect what is achieved in the interaction between the actor and the system. In our example we have use cases such as Pay Invoice and Order Goods or Services.

Sometimes it is difficult to decide on the scope of a use case. A sequence of user-system interaction can be specified either in one use case or in several use cases that the actor invokes one after another. When we decide if a use-case candidate should be a use case by itself, we have to consider if it is complete by itself or if it always follows as a kind of continuation of another use case. Recall that use cases add value to their actors (see Section 7.2.3, "Use Case"). To be more specific, a use case delivers an observable result that is of value to a particular actor. This pragmatic guideline for a "good" use case can help determine the proper scope of the use case.

Note that two key phrases in this guideline, *result of value* and *particular actor,* represent two useful criteria for finding use cases:

- *Result of value:* Each successfully performed use case should provide some value to the actor so that the actor achieves some goal [3]. In some cases, the actor is willing to pay for the value returned. Note that a use-case instance, such as a telephone call, may involve more than one actor. In that case, the criteria for "an observable result of value" should be applied to the *initiating* actor. This "result of values" criteria help us avoid finding use cases that are too small.

---

| **Example** | The Scope of the Pay Invoice Use Case |

The Billing and Payment System offers a use case called Pay Invoice, which is to be used by a buyer to schedule invoice payments for goods he or she has ordered and received. The Pay Invoice use case then executes the payment on the due date.

The use case Pay Invoice includes both the scheduling and execution of a payment. If we split the use case into two parts, one for scheduling and one for executing payment, "Schedule Payment" would not add value by itself. The value gets added as the invoice has been paid (at which point we do not have to worry about receiving reminders).

---

- *Particular actor:* By identifying use cases that provide value to real user individuals, we make sure that the use cases will not become too large.

As for the actors, the use cases that we first identify often need to be restructured and reevaluated a couple of times before the use-case model stabilizes.

As we discussed in Chapter 4, the use cases and the architecture of a system are developed through iterations. Once we have an architecture in place, the new use cases that we capture must be adapted to the existing architecture. Use cases that do not fit with the chosen architecture should be modified to better align with the architecture (we may also need to improve the architecture to better facilitate new use cases). For instance, the initial work on specifying a use case may have had a particular user interaction in mind. Once we have decided on a GUI framework, we may have to modify the use cases, although these adaptations are usually quite small.

More drastic changes can be required. The system analyst may suggest a way to supervise the load of a system by specifying a simulator that acts as an important actor, one that requests use cases from the system. In this way, you can measure response times and other performance requirements. You can also measure the time that a use case halts in internal queues in the system. These two approaches may give similar values, but the costs of implementing them may be very different depending on the existing architecture. Thus the system analyst may need to renegotiate requirements (use cases and so on) with the customer so that a better system, one that is easier to implement and maintain for the developers, can be built. The customer also gains by renegotiating requirements and may be able to get the functionality sooner, with higher quality and at a lower cost.

### 7.4.1.3 Briefly Describing Each Use Case

As analysts identify the use cases, they sometimes scribble down a few words to explain each use case, and sometimes they just write down the names. Later, they describe each use case briefly with, at first, a few sentences that summarize the actions and later a step-by-step description of what the system needs to do when interacting with its actors.

---

**Example** | **Initial Description of the Pay Invoice Use Case**

### Brief Description

The use case Pay Invoice is used by a Buyer to schedule invoice payments. The Pay Invoice use case then effects the payment on the due date.

### Initial Step-by-Step Description

Before this use case can be initiated, the Buyer has already received an invoice (delivered by another use case called Invoice Buyer) and has also received the goods or services ordered:

1. The Buyer studies the invoice to pay and checks that it is consistent with the original order.
2. The Buyer schedules the invoice for payment by the bank.
3. On the day payment is due, the system checks to see if there is enough money in the Buyer's account. If enough money is available, the transaction is made.

---

So far, we have briefly described actors and use cases. However, it is not enough to describe and understand each use case in isolation. We also need to see the whole picture. We need to explain how the use cases and actors are related to each other and how together they make up the use-case model.

### 7.4.1.4  Describing the Use-Case Model as a Whole    We prepare diagrams and descriptions to explain the use-case model as a whole, particularly how the use cases relate to each other and to the actors.

There is no strict rule for what to include in a diagram. Instead, we choose the set of diagrams that will most clearly describe the system. For example, diagrams can be drawn to show the use cases that participate in one business use case (see Figure 7.12) or perhaps to illustrate the use cases that are performed by one actor.

To ensure consistency when describing several use cases concurrently, it is practical to develop a glossary of terms. These terms may be derived from (and traceable to) classes in a domain model or a business model (described in Chapter 6).

The use-case model need not be a flat model as described here. It can also be organized in clusters of use cases called *use-case packages* [12].

The output of this step is also a survey description of the use-case model. This description explains the use-case model as a whole. It describes how actors and use cases interact and how use cases are related to one another. In the UML representation of the use-case model, the survey description is a tagged value of the model itself (see Appendix A, Section A.1.2).

| Example | Survey Description |
|---|---|

The use-case model survey description for the Billing and Payment System (see Figure 7.12) could look like the following. In this description, we have included numbered comments, which are explained at the end of the example.

*The buyer uses the Order Goods or Services use case to look for order items and prices, compile an order, and then to submit the order.*

*Perhaps now or later, the goods or services are delivered to the buyer along with an invoice.*

*The buyer activates the Pay Invoice use case to approve the received invoice and schedule a payment request. On the date scheduled, the Pay Invoice use case automatically transfers money from the buyer's account to the seller's account. {comment 1}*

*Moreover, the Pay Invoice use case is extended by the Pay Overdraft Fee use case if an overdraft occurs. {comment 2}*

*Let us now turn to how the seller may use the system. The seller may study, suggest changes to, and confirm received orders by using the Confirm Order use case. A confirmed order will be followed by a delivery of ordered goods or services (not described in our example use-case model; instead, this is done outside the Billing and Payment System).*

*Later, when the goods or services have been delivered, the seller invoices the buyer through the use case Invoice Buyer. When invoicing, the seller may need to apply an applicable rate of discount and may also choose to combine several invoices into one.*

*If the buyer has not paid by the due date, the seller is informed and may use the case Send Reminders use case. The system could send reminders automatically, but we have chosen a solution in which the seller has a chance to review the reminders before they are sent to avoid embarrassing any customers." {comment 3}*

### Comments

1. Recall that the use-case model is more than a list of use cases. It also describes generalizations between those use cases. For example, the sequence of actions for payment transactions in the Pay Invoice use case can be shared by many use cases (even if only one generalization is shown in Figure 7.12). This sharing can be represented with a separate use case called Perform Transaction that is reused, through generalizations, by several use cases, such as Pay Invoice. The generalization means that the sequence of actions described in the Perform Transaction use case is inserted in the sequence described in Pay Invoice. When the system performs an instance of the Pay Invoice use case, the instance will also follow the behavior described in the Perform Transaction use case.

2. As the system executes an instance of the Pay Invoice use case, the sequence may be extended to include the sequence of actions described in the extending Pay Overdraft Fee use case. We have now briefly mentioned generalization and extend relationships to show that the use-case model can be structured to make it easier to specify and understand the full set of functional requirements; for more information see [7].

3. Send Reminders illustrates a use case that simplifies corrective paths in the business use cases. Such corrective paths help the process "get onto the track again," perhaps to prevent a small issue in the interaction with a customer from growing into a real problem. Thus the actors also need use cases (or alternatives of the basic use cases) that help them correct deviating process paths. This kind of use case often constitutes a good portion of the complete system's responsibilities to deal with the many possible deviations.

### Discussion

There are several ways to shape a use-case model, and this example illustrates just one way. Let us discuss some of the trade-offs we have made. What if the buyer could browse an Internet catalog of *available* goods or services and then make an online order and get a confirmation immediately. Would a separate Confirm Order use case still be necessary? The answer is no, since the direct confirmation of the order would be included in the Order Goods or Services use case.

In this example, however, we have assumed that after an order has been analyzed, it is either confirmed or perhaps an alternative is suggested by the seller. For example, the seller may suggest an alternative set of goods that might be equally useful, cheaper, or delivered earlier. The actual sequence when placing an order may in this case actually be a series of steps in which the seller suggests an alternative order and then confirms it, as illustrated in the following:

1. An initial order is placed by a buyer.
2. An alternative order suggestion is sent from the seller back to the buyer.
3. A final order is placed by the buyer.
4. An order confirmation is sent from the seller to the buyer.

These steps are covered by two use cases: Order Goods or Services and Confirm Order. Why is this not four different use cases—or just one use case? Let us first see why these steps are not described as one large use case: We do not wish to force the seller and the buyer to interact in real time. Instead, we want them to be able to submit requests to one another without having to wait on, or synchronize with, each other. We can assume that a seller wants to collect several new orders from different buyers and then analyze and confirm them all at the same time. This would not be possible if all four steps were one use case because each use case is considered atomic and is therefore always completed before another use case is begun. As a result a seller could not have several initial orders pending (after Step 1), while waiting for an alternative order to be sent back (Step 2 in the example).

The four steps could of course become four different use cases, but an initial and a final order (Steps 1 and 3) are so similar that they can be expressed as alternatives of the Order Goods or Services use case. After all, we do not wish the set of use cases to grow beyond comprehension. Too many use cases make the use-case model difficult to understand and use as input to analysis and design.

Similarly, suggesting an alternative order (Step 2) involves confirming parts of an order and suggesting alternatives for other parts, while confirming an order (Step 4) involves confirming all parts. Both of these steps can be expressed as a single use case, Confirm Order, which allows the seller both to confirm parts and to suggest alternatives. So there will be a use case called Order Goods or Services, which provides the services corresponding to Steps 1 and 3, and another use case called Confirm Order, which corresponds to Steps 2 and 4.

---

When the use-case model survey is prepared, we let people who are not part of the development team (e.g., users and customers) approve the use-case model by conducting an informal review to determine if:

- All necessary functional requirements have been captured as use cases.
- The sequence of actions is correct, complete, and understandable for each use case.
- Any use cases that provide little or no value have been identified. If so, these use cases should be reconsidered.

### 7.4.2 Activity: Prioritize Use Cases

The purpose of this activity is to provide input to the prioritization of use cases to determine which of them need to be developed (i.e., analyzed, designed, implemented, etc.) in early iterations, and which can be developed in later iterations (Figure 7.13).

The results are captured in an architectural view of the use-case model. This view is then considered together with the project manager and used as an input when planning what to be developed within an iteration. Note that this planning also needs to take into consideration other nontechnical aspects, such as business or economical aspects of the system to be developed (see Chapter 12, Section 12.4.2).

The architectural view of the use-case model should depict the architecturally significant use cases. Refer to Section 7.2.4, "Architecture Description (View of the Use-Case Model)" for details.

### 7.4.3 Activity: Detail a Use Case

The main purpose of detailing each use case is to describe its flow of events in detail, including how the use case starts, ends, and interacts with actors (Figure 7.14).

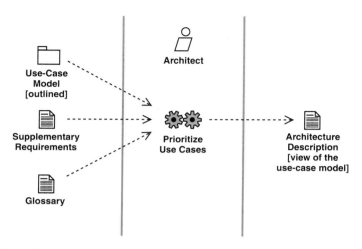

**FIGURE 7.13** The input and result of prioritizing use cases.

With the use-case model and the associated use-case diagrams as a starting point, the individual use-case specifiers can now describe each use case in detail. The use-case specifiers detail the step-by-step description of each use case into a precise specification of the sequence of actions. In this section, we will see

- How to structure the description to specify all alternative paths of the use case.
- What to include in a use-case description.
- How to formalize the use-case description when necessary.

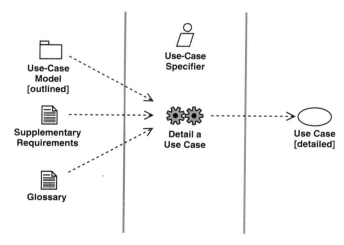

**FIGURE 7.14** The input and result of detailing each use case.

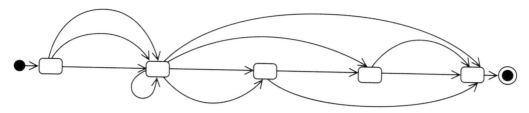

**FIGURE 7.15** A use case can be thought of as having a start state (the leftmost rounded rectangle), intermediary states (the subsequent rounded rectangles), end states (the rightmost rounded rectangle), and transitions from one state to another. (Refer to Appendix A for statechart notation.) The straight arrows illustrate the basic path, and the curved arrows are other paths.

Each use-case specifier needs to work closely with the real users of the use cases. The use-case specifier needs to interview the users, perhaps write down their understanding of the use cases and discuss proposals with them, and ask them to review the use case descriptions.

The result of this activity is a detailed description of a particular use case in text and diagrams.

### 7.4.3.1 *Structuring the Use-Case Description*

We have already mentioned that a use case defines the states that use-case instances may enter and the possible transitions between those states (see Figure 7.15). Each such transition is a sequence of actions that is performed by a use-case instance when triggered by an event such as a message.

The graph of state transitions illustrated by Figure 7.15 can become quite intricate. Still, we must describe the possible state transitions (sequences of actions) simply and precisely. A proven technique is to choose one complete basic path (the straight arrows in Figure 7.15) from the start state to the end state and to describe that path in one section of the description. Then we can describe the rest of the paths (the curved arrows) as alternatives or deviations from that basic path, each in a separate section. Sometimes, however, the alternatives or deviations are small enough to be explained "inline" as part of the basic path description. Common sense determines whether to inline the description of an alternative or to create a separate section for it. Recall that the goal is to make a description that is precise but easy to read. Whatever technique we choose, we still have to describe all alternatives, otherwise we have not specified the use case.

The alternatives, deviations, or exceptions from the basic path can occur for many reasons:

- The actor may choose to take different paths through the use case. For example, during the Pay Invoice use case, the actor may decide to pay an invoice or to reject it.

- If more than one actor is involved in the use case, the actions of one of the actors may influence the path of actions for other actors.
- The system may detect erroneous input from the actor.
- Some system resources may be malfunctioning, thus preventing the system from doing its job properly.

The basic path chosen should be a "normal" path, that is, one that the users perceive as the one most commonly followed and the one that yields the most obvious value to the actor. Generally, such a basic path should involve few exceptions and few peculiarities that the system seldom needs to deal with.

---

## Example    Paths of the Pay Invoice Use Case

Please note how the text has changed from the draft earlier in this chapter when we had only a sketch at a use case description (see Section 7.4.1.3, "Briefly Describing Each Use Case"). This change reflects how we detail the use cases as we proceed to model them, although complete use-case descriptions are in reality likely to be larger and cover more paths.

**Precondition:** The buyer has received the goods or services ordered and at least one invoice from the system. The buyer now plans to schedule the invoice(s) for payment.

### Flow of Events

Basic Path
1. The buyer invokes the use case by beginning to browse the invoices received by the system. The system checks that the content of each invoice is consistent with order confirmations received earlier (as part of the Confirm Order use case) and somehow indicates this to the buyer. The order confirmation describes which items will be delivered, when, where, and at what price.
2. The buyer decides to schedule an invoice for payment by the bank, and the system generates a payment request to transfer money to the seller's account. Note that a buyer may not schedule the same invoice for payment twice.
3. Later, if there is enough money in the buyer's account, a payment transaction is made on the scheduled date. During the transaction, money is transferred from the buyer's account to the seller's account, as described by the abstract use case Perform Transaction (which is used by Pay Invoice). The buyer and the seller are notified of the result of the transaction. The bank collects a fee for the transaction, which is withdrawn from the buyer's account by the system.
4. The use-case instance terminates.

### Alternative Paths

In Step 2, the buyer may instead ask the system to send an invoice rejection back to the seller.

In Step 3, if there is not enough money in the account, the use case will cancel the payment and notify the buyer.

**Postcondition:** The use-case instance ends when the invoice has been paid or when the invoice payment was canceled and no money was transferred.

Since use cases need to be understood by developers as well as by customers and users, they should always be described using plain English as illustrated in this example.

#### 7.4.3.1.1 What to Include in a Use-Case Description
As illustrated by the preceding example, a use-case description must include the following:

- A use-case description should define the start state (see Figure 7.15) as a precondition.
- How and when the use case starts (i.e., the first action to perform; Step 1).
- The required order (if any) in which actions must be performed. Here, the order is defined by the numbered sequence (Steps 1–4).
- How and when the use case ends (Step 4).
- A use-case description should define the possible end states (see Figure 7.15) as postconditions.
- Paths of execution that are not allowed. The note in Step 2 tells us about a path that is *not* possible—paying an invoice twice. It is a path that the user cannot take.
- Alternative path descriptions that are inlined in the basic path description. All of Step 3 is an action that is performed only if there is enough money in the account.
- Alternative path descriptions that have been extracted from the basic path description (Step 5).
- System interaction with the actors and what they exchange (Steps 2 and 3). Typical examples are when the buyer decides to schedule payment of the invoice in Step 2 and when the buyer and seller are notified of the results of the transaction in Step 3. In other words, we have described the sequence of actions of the use case, how these actions are invoked by actors, and how the their execution results in requests to actors.
- Usage of objects, values, and resources in the system (Step 3). In other words, we have described the sequence of actions in a use-case use and have assigned values to the use-case attributes. A typical example is when money is transferred from the buyer's account to the seller's account in Step 3. Another is the usage of invoices and order confirmations in Step 1.
- Note that we must explicitly describe what the system does (the actions it performs) and what the actor does. We need to be able to separate the

responsibilities of the system from those of the actors, otherwise the use-case description will not be precise enough to use as a system specification. For example, in Step 1, we write "*The system* checks that the content of each invoice is consistent with the order confirmations received," and in Step 3, "This fee is withdrawn from the buyer's account *by the system.*"

The attributes of a use case can be used as inspiration for finding classes and attributes later in analysis and design, such as suggesting a design class called Invoice derived from a use-case *invoice* attribute. During analysis and design, we will also consider that some objects will be used in several use cases, but it is not necessary to consider this in the use-case model. Instead (as discussed in Section 7.2.3, "Use Case"), we keep the use-case model simple by forbidding interactions among the use-case instances and instances from accessing one another's attributes.

So far, we have mostly talked about the functional requirements and how to represent them as use cases, but we also need to specify the nonfunctional requirements. Most nonfunctional requirements are related to a specific use case, such as requirements that specify the speed, availability, accuracy, response time, recovery time, or memory usage with which the system must perform a given use case. Such requirements are attached as special requirements (tagged values in UML) to the use case in question. This can, for example, be documented in a separate section in the use-case description.

### Example    Special (Performance) Requirement

When a buyer issues an invoice for payment, the system should respond with a verification of the request within 1.0 second in 90% of the cases. The time for the verification must never exceed 10.0 seconds, unless the network connection is broken (in which case the user should be notified).

If the system interacts with some other system (nonhuman actors), it is necessary to specify this interaction (e.g., by referring to a standard communication protocol). This must be done in early iterations, during the elaboration phase, since the realization of intersystem communication usually has architectural impacts.

The use-case descriptions are finished when they are deemed understandable, correct (i.e., they capture the right requirements), complete (e.g., they describe all possible paths), and consistent. The descriptions are evaluated by analysts as well as users and customers at review meetings that are held at the end of requirements capture. Only the customers and users can verify whether the use cases are the right ones.

### 7.4.3.2 Formalizing the Use-Case Descriptions

Figure 7.15 illustrates how transitions move use-case instances from one state to another. Often, as when the use case has only a few states, we do not need to describe the states explicitly. Instead, we may choose to use the style employed in the Pay Invoice example. Still, it is a good idea to have the state machine in the back of our minds when we describe a use case, just to ensure that we cover all possible cases. Sometimes however, as in complex real-time systems, the use cases may be so complex that it becomes necessary to use a more structured description technique. The interaction between the actors and the use cases may, for example, go through so many states and alternative transitions that it is almost impossible to keep a textual use-case description consistent. It may then be useful to use a visual modeling technique to describe the use cases. Such techniques can help the system analyst to better understand the use cases:

- UML statechart diagrams can be used to describe the states of the use case and the transitions between those states; see Figure 7.16.
- Activity diagrams can be used to describe the transitions between states in more detail as sequence of actions. Activity diagrams can be described as a generalized form of SDL state transition diagrams [15], which is a well-proven technique used in telecommunications.
- Interaction diagrams can be used to describe how an instance of a use case interacts with an instance of an actor. The interaction diagram then shows the use case and the participating actor (or actors).

See [2, 11, 12, 17] for explanations of statechart, interaction, and activity diagrams.

---

**Example**   **Using Statechart Diagrams to Describe Use Cases**

Figure 7.16 is a statechart diagram for the Pay Invoice use case. The black dot at the top of the diagram denotes the beginning of the use case. This is where the state machine starts from when a use-case instance is instantiated. The arrow from the black dot shows where the state machine immediately "moves" when it is instantiated, in this case, to the first state, Browsing. States are shown as rectangles with rounded corners. State transitions are shown as arrows from one state to another.

First, the user browses the invoices (cf. Step 1 in the preceding Pay Invoice example) and then decides to schedule (cf. Step 2) or reject (cf. Step 5) an invoice. The use case moves from the state Invoice Scheduled to Invoice Paid when the scheduled invoice is paid on the due date (cf. Step 3). The use case immediately terminates (the circle with the black dot in it) after it has reached the Invoice Paid or the Invoice Canceled state.

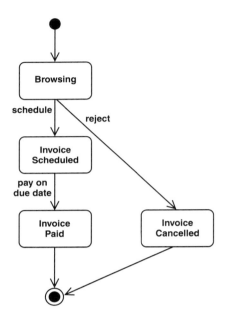

**FIGURE 7.16** The statechart diagram for the Pay Invoice use case showing how an instance of the Pay Invoice use case moves over several states (rounded rectangles) in series of state transitions (arrows).

Note that using these diagrams in a use-case context may sometimes lead to large and complex diagrams that are very hard to read and understand. For example, a single use case may involve many states that are difficult to name in a meaningful fashion. This is especially delicate if stakeholders who are not software developers are to read the diagrams. Also, it is costly to develop detailed diagrams and to keep them consistent with other models of the system.

Thus our basic recommendation is to use these kinds of diagrams with care and that purely textual descriptions (i.e., flow-of-events descriptions) of the use case are often enough. Also, in many cases the textual descriptions and the diagrams can complement each other.

### 7.4.4  Activity: Prototype User Interface

The purpose of this activity is to build a prototype of the user interface (see Figure 7.17).

Up to now the system analyst has developed a use-case model that specifies who the users are and what they need to use the system for. This has been presented in use-case diagrams, in survey descriptions of the use-case model, and in detailed descriptions for each use case.

We now need to design user interfaces that let the user perform the use cases effectively. We do that in several steps. We start with the use cases and try to discern

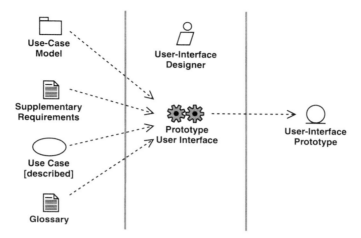

**FIGURE 7.17** The input and result of prototyping the user interface.

what is needed from the user interfaces to enable the use cases for each actor. That is, we do a logical user-interface design. Then we create the physical user-interface design and develop prototypes that illustrate how users can use the system to perform the use cases [1]. By starting to specify what is needed before we decide how to realize the user interface, we are compelled to understand the needs before we try to realize them [1].

The end result of this activity is a set of user-interface sketches and user-interface prototypes that specify the look and feel of the user interfaces for the most important actors.

### 7.4.4.1 Creating a Logical User-Interface Design    When actors interact with the system, they will use and manipulate user-interface elements that represent attributes (of the use cases). Often, these are terms from the glossary (e.g., *account balance*, *due date*, and *account owner*). The actors may experience these user-interface elements as icons, list items, folders, or objects on a 2D map, and they may manipulate them by selecting, dragging, or speaking to them. The user-interface designer identifies and specifies these elements for one actor at a time by going through all the use cases that the actor can access and identifying the proper user-interface elements for each use case. A single user-interface element may participate in many use cases,[3] playing a role in each one. Thus the user-interface element must be designed to provide all these roles. The following questions should be answered for each actor:

- Which user-interface elements are needed to enable the use cases?
- How should they be related to each other?

---

3. In much the same way that a class can participate in several collaborations to realize different use cases, the class plays a role in each such collaboration.

- How will they be used in the different use cases?
- What should they look like?
- How should they be manipulated?

To determine which user-interface elements needed in each use case accessible from the actor, we can ask the following questions:

- Which of the domain classes, business entities, or work units are suitable as user-interface elements for the use case?
- What user-interface elements does the actor work with?
- What actions can the actor invoke, and what decisions can the actor make?
- What guidance and information does the actor need before invoking each action in the use case?
- What information does the actor need to supply to the system?
- What information does the system need to supply to the actor?
- What are the average values for all input/output parameters? For example, how many invoices will an actor normally deal with during a session, and what is the average account balance? We need rough estimates of these figures because we will optimize the graphical user interface for these figures (even though we must enable a wide enough range).

---

**Example**    **User-Interface Elements
Employed in the Pay Invoice Use Case**

For the Pay Invoice use case we will illustrate how we can find the user-interface elements that the actor needs to work with on the screen as well as what kind of guidance an actor might need while being at work.

The actor will certainly work with user-interface elements like Invoices (found from a domain class or a business entity). Invoice is therefore a user-interface element as illustrated by Figure 7.18. Note that invoices have a due date, an amount to pay, and a destination account. All of these attributes are needed by an actor who must decide whether or not to pay the invoice.

Also, as the actor is deciding which invoices to pay, he or she may want to keep an eye on the amount of money in the account to avoid overdrafts. This is an example of the kind of guidance and information that the actor needs. The user interface must therefore display invoices as they are scheduled over time and how the scheduled payment of the invoices will affect the balance of the account (as indicated by the association *buyer account*, which is derived from the domain class association *buyer* in Chapter 6). The account is thus another aspect of the user interface. The account balance and how it is expected to change over time as invoices are paid are indicated in Figure 7.18 by the *account* attribute and by the *invoice to pay* association between the Account to the Invoice user-interface elements (see Figure 7.18).

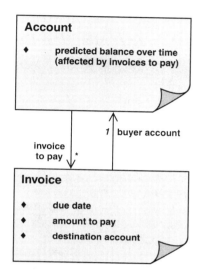

**FIGURE 7.18** User-interface elements for Invoice and Account, with some of their attributes indicated.

A practical way of working is to represent the user-interface elements as sticky notes[4] (as shown in Figure 7.18), attach them to a whiteboard, and arrange them to illustrate the appearance of the user interface. Next, the user-interface designers describe how the actors can use these elements as they work with the use cases. The advantage of using sticky notes is that they can present the necessary amount of data. Also, the sticky notes do not look permanent—it is easy to move them around or even to throw them away—which makes the users comfortable in proposing changes.

Thus the user-interface designers make sure that each use case is accessible through its user-interface elements. However, they also need to make sure that the whole set of use cases accessible from an actor has a well-integrated, easy-to-use, and consistent user interface.

So far, we have looked only for what the actors need from the user interface. We will now look at how the physical user interface can deliver this.

### 7.4.4.2 Creating a Physical User-Interface Design and Prototype     The
user-interface designers first prepare rough sketches of the constellation of user interface elements that form useful user interfaces to the actors. Then they sketch additional elements that are needed to combine the various user-interface elements into complete user interfaces. These additional elements might include containers of the

---

4. For the sake of formality, such a "sticky note" can be seen as a stereotype on class within the UML. However, it is beyond the scope of this book to dwell on the details regarding a formal (object) model of the user-interface elements.

## Essential Use-Case Modeling

Detailed use-case descriptions are a good starting point when designing the user interface—sometimes too good a starting point. The problem is that the descriptions often contain implicit decisions about the user interfaces. Later, when the user-interface designers suggest suitable user interfaces for the use cases, they may be limited by those implicit decisions. However, to create the best user interface for the use cases, they must avoid falling into this trap. For example, the Pay Invoice use case begins "The buyer invokes the use case by beginning to *browse* the invoices received. . . ." Such a description may fool the user-interface designer into creating a user interface that includes a *list* of received invoices that the actor may browse. But that may not be the best way to study the received invoices. Instead, the buyers may find it easier to browse the invoices in a less obvious way, such as through icons positioned horizontally according to the *payment date* and vertically according to the *amount to pay.*

Larry Constantine suggests a remedy to the problem of implicit user-interface decisions [14]. He proposes that use-case specifiers first prepare lightweight use-case descriptions—essential use cases—that do not contain any implicit user-interface decisions. The preceding example could then be rewritten "The buyer invokes the use case by beginning to *study* the invoices received. . . ." Then the user-interface designers can use these essential use cases as input to create the user interface, without being bound by any implicit decisions.

This example is a naive illustration of what might be entailed in distilling a use-case description to its essential meaning. In reality, to do so would entail much more than replacing a word in a description. The important thing is to avoid making premature decisions about

- The technique to be used to present some user-interface element, such as whether to use a list or a text field.
- The sequence of actor input, such as entering one attribute before another.
- The devices needed for input and output, such as using the mouse to select something or the monitor to present something.

Then, if appropriate, the use-case specifiers can make a second pass through the use-case descriptions to add the details that were left out in the essential style descriptions.

user-interface elements (e.g., folders), windows, tools and controls; see Figure 7.19. These sketches can be prepared after (or sometimes concurrently with) the sticky notes developed during the logical user-interface design.

| **Example** | **Physical User-Interface Design and Prototype** |
| --- | --- |

The user-interface designer sketches the following physical design of the visualized account balance as it is affected over time by the scheduled invoices. The invoices are shown as white trapezoids that will reduce the account balance when they are supposed to be paid. The user-interface designer chose the trapezoid shape because it is wide enough to be visible and selectable, but it also has a sharp point that is used to indicate when the payment will occur. The scheduled invoices, such as the invoice for the rent, will result in a reduced balance in the account on the due date, as illustrated in Figure 7.19. Likewise, the sketch illustrates how money gets added to the account, perhaps when the owner gets his salary. The figure also illustrates user-interface controls such as the scroll and zoom buttons.

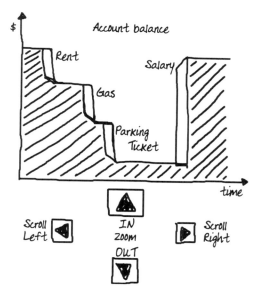

**FIGURE 7.19** A suggested user interface for the related interface elements Account and Invoice. The interface shows how payment of invoices and receipt of deposits will result in account deductions and increases. The scroll left and right buttons move the "time window" in which the actor can study the account balance. The zoom in and out buttons affect the scale of the diagram.

Now we are prepared to build executable prototypes for the most important constellations of user-interface elements. These prototypes can be built with a rapid-prototyping tool.

There may be several prototypes, perhaps one for each actor, to verify that each actor can perform the use cases that he or she needs. The prototyping effort must be scaled to the expected return value. We develop executable GUI prototypes when there is a lot to gain in usability value (e.g., a prototype for the most important actors), and use the paper sketches when there is not as much to gain.

Validating the user interface through reviews of prototypes and sketches at an early point can prevent many mistakes that will be expensive to correct later. The prototypes may also reveal oversights in the use-case descriptions and allow them to be corrected before the use cases are brought into design. The reviewers should verify that each user interface

- Allows the actor to navigate properly.
- Provides a consistent look and feel and a consistent way of working with the user interface, such as tab ordering and accelerator keys.
- Complies with relevant standards such as colors, size of buttons, and placement of toolbars.

Note that the implementation of the real user interface (as opposed to the prototype we have developed here) is constructed in parallel with the rest of the system, that is, during the analysis, design, and implementation workflows. The user-interface prototype we have developed here will then work as a specification of the user interface. This specification will be realized in terms of production-quality components.

### 7.4.5 Activity: Structure the Use-Case Model

The use-case model is structured to

- Extract general and shared (use-case) descriptions of functionality that can be used by more specific (use-case) descriptions.
- Extract additional or optional (use-case) descriptions of functionality that can extend more specific (use-case) descriptions.

Before this activity takes place, the system analyst has identified the actors and use cases, depicted them in diagrams, and explained the use-case model as a whole. The use-case specifiers have developed a detailed description of each use case. At this point, the system analyst can restructure the whole set of use cases to make the model easier to understand and work with (see Figure 7.20). The analyst should look for shared behavior and extensions.

#### *7.4.5.1 Identifying Shared Descriptions of Functionality*    As we identify and outline the actions of each use case, we should also be looking for actions or parts of actions that are common to or shared by several use cases. In order to reduce

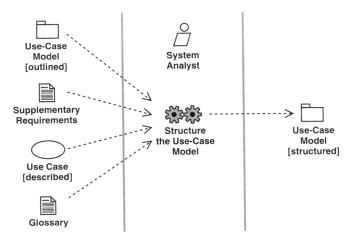

**FIGURE 7.20** The input and result of finding generalizations in the use-case model.

redundancy, this sharing can be extracted and described in a separate use case that can then be reused by the original use cases. We show this reuse relation with a generalization (it is called a *uses relationship* in [7]). Generalization between use cases is a kind of inheritance, since instances of the generalized use cases can perform all behavior described in the generalizing use case. In other words, a generalization from use case A to use case B indicates that an instance of the use case A will also include the behavior as specified by B.

| Example | Generalization between Use Cases |
|---|---|

Recall from Figure 7.12 earlier in this chapter, in which the Pay Invoice use case is generalized by the Perform Transaction use case. The sequence of actions described in the Perform Transaction use case is thus inherited in the sequence described in Pay Invoice (Figure 7.21).

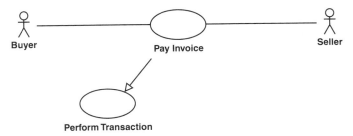

**FIGURE 7.21** The generalization relationship between the Pay Invoice and the Perform Transaction use cases.

The generalization is employed to simplify the work with and the understanding of the use-case model and to reuse "semimanufactured" use cases when putting together complete use cases requested by customers. Such complete use cases are called *concrete use cases*. They are initiated by an actor, and their instances constitute a complete sequence of actions performed by the system. The "semimanufactured" use cases exist only for other use cases to reuse and are known as *abstract use cases*. An abstract use case will not be instantiated by itself, but an instance of a concrete use case also exhibits the behavior specified by the abstract use cases that it (re)uses. For the purpose of understanding, we call this instance the "real" use case that the actor(s) perceive when interacting with the system.

---

**Example**    "Real" Use Cases

We can conceptualize a "real" use case, as shown in Figure 7.22, when Pay Invoice is generalized by Perform Transaction.

**Buyer A**          **Pay Invoice + Perform Transaction**          **Seller B**

**FIGURE 7.22** The "real" use case instance formed by the Pay Invoice and Perform Transaction use cases, as perceived by the actor instances, Buyer A and Seller B.

This "real" use case is the result that we get after applying the generalization to the two use cases, one concrete, the other abstract. This real use case represents the behavior of the use-case instance that an actor interacting with the system is perceiving. If the model contained more concrete use cases generalized by the Perform Transaction use case, then there would be more real use cases. These real use cases would have specifications with overlap, the overlap is what is specified in the Perform Transaction use case.

Note that this example does not expose the whole truth, since there is also a use case (Pay Overdraft Fee) that extends the Pay Invoice use case, thereby yielding other real use cases. To that we turn our attention in the next section.

---

### 7.4.5.2 Identifying Additional and Optional Descriptions of Functionality

The other relationship between use cases is the *extend relationship* [7]. Extend models additions to a use case's sequence of actions. An extension "behaves" as if it is something that is added into the original description of a use case. In other words, an extend relationship from use case A to use case B indicates that an instance of use case B may include (subject to specific conditions specified in the extension) the behavior specified by A. Behavior specified by several extensions of a single target use case may occur within a single use-case instance.

The extend relationship includes both a condition for the extension and a reference to an extension point in the target use case, that is, a position in the use case where additions may be made. Once an instance of a (target) use case reaches an extension point to which an extend relationship is referring, the condition of the relationship is evaluated. If the condition is fulfilled, the sequence obeyed by the use-case instance is extended to include the sequence of the extending use case.

---

**Example**  Extend Relationship between Use Cases

Recall Figure 7.12 earlier in this chapter and the example given in Section 7.4.1.4, "Describing the Use-Case Model as a Whole," in which the Pay Invoice use case is extended by the Pay overdraft fee use case. The sequence of actions described in the Pay Overdraft Fee use case (Figure 7.23) is thus inserted in the sequence described in Pay Invoice if an overdraft occurs (this is the condition for the extension).

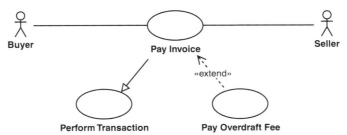

**FIGURE 7.23**  The extend relationship between the Pay Invoice and the Pay Overdraft Fee use cases.

Note that with the extend relationship we can go a step further when discussing the real use cases perceived by the actors. By applying the extend relationship from the extension use case Pay Overdraft Fee to the target use case (i.e., Pay Invoice generalized by Perform Transaction), we get another real use case that is a merging of the three use cases (see Figure 7.24).

170    Chapter 7    Capturing the Requirements as Use Cases

**FIGURE 7.24** The "real" use case instance formed by the Pay Invoice and Perform Transaction use cases extended with the Pay Overdraft Fee use case, as perceived by the actor instances, Buyer A and Seller B.

We can say that the real use cases, which are use cases in their own right, are obtained by applying generalization and extend relationships to the use cases in the model. The real use cases are those that yield values to the users. Thus the criteria for good use cases that were mentioned in the Section 7.4.1, "Find Actors and Use Cases" (a use case delivers an observable result of values to a particular actor), are relevant only for real use cases. Thus we must identify separate criteria for good concrete use cases, abstract use cases, and extension use cases. Concrete use cases should not describe (significant) behavior that is shared with other concrete use cases. An abstract use case makes it easy to specify concrete use cases by offering shared, reusable behavior. An extension use case specifies additional behavior to other use cases, regardless of whether this behavior is optional or mandatory.

Thus to understand generalization and extend relationships, we have introduced the notion of real use cases. Once we have identified the concrete, abstract, and extension use cases, we can combine them to get real use cases. However, when we start modeling a new system, we typically work the other way around, starting from real use cases and identifying shared behavior, which separates concrete use cases from abstract use cases, and additional behavior, which we treat as extensions to other use cases.

See [7] for a more thorough discussion of generalizations (which are also called *uses relationships*) and extend relationships, and when to use which kind of relationship.

### 7.4.5.3 Identifying Other Relationships between Use Cases

There also exist other relationships between use cases, such as the *include* relationship [12]. This relationship can for simplicity be thought of as a reversed extend relationship that provides explicit and unconditioned extensions to a use case. Moreover, when including a use case, the behavior sequence and the attributes of the included use case are encapsulated and cannot be changed or accessed—only the result (or function) of the included use case can be exploited; this is a difference as compared to using the generalization relationship. However, in this book we will not dwell on too many details about these relationships. But we provide some words of caution:

- The structure of the use cases and their relationships should reflect the real use cases (as discussed earlier) as much as possible. The more this structure diverges from the real use cases, the harder it will be to understand the use cases and their purpose, not only for external parties such as users and customers but also for the developers themselves.
- Each single use case needs to be treated as a separate artifact. Someone, that is, a use-case specifier, needs to be responsible for its description; and in subsequent workflows—analysis and design—the use case needs to be realized with separate use-case realizations (as we will see in Chapters 8 and 9). For this reason, the use cases should not be too small or too many, thereby implying a significant management overhead.
- Avoid decomposing the use cases functionally in the use-case model. This is much better done by refining each use case in the analysis model. This is because, as we will see in Chapter 8, the functionality defined by the use cases will instead be decomposed, in an object-oriented fashion, as collaborations of conceptual analysis objects. This decomposition will yield an in-depth understanding of the requirements, if necessary.

## 7.5 Summary of the Requirements Workflow

In this and the preceding chapter, we have described how to capture the requirements on a system as

- A business model or a domain model to set the context of the system.
- A use-case model that captures the functional requirements and the nonfunctional requirements that are specific to individual use cases. The use-case model is described by a survey description, a set of diagrams, and a detailed description of each use case.
- A set of user interface sketches and prototypes for each actor representing the design of the user interfaces.
- A supplementary requirements specification for the requirements that are generic and not specific for a particular use case.

This result is a very good starting point for the subsequent workflows: analysis, design, implementation, and testing. The use cases will drive the work through these workflows iteration by iteration. For every use case in the use-case model we will identify a matching use-case realization in the analysis and design phases and a set of test cases in the testing phase. Thus the use cases will link the different workflows seamlessly.

In Chapter 8 we move on to the next step in our chain of workflows—analysis—where we will reformulate the use cases as objects to gain a better understanding of the requirements and also to prepare for the design and implementation of the system.

## 7.6 References

[1]  Ahlqvist Stefan and Jonsson Patrik, "Techniques for systematic design of graphical user interfaces based on use cases," *Proceedings OOPSLA 96.*

[2]  Grady Booch, James Rumbaugh, and Ivar Jacobson, *Unified Modeling Language User Guide.* Reading, MA: Addison-Wesley, 1998.

[3]  Alistair Cockburn, "Structuring use cases with goals," *Report on Analysis and Design (ROAD),* 1997.

[4]  Ivar Jacobson, Magnus Christerson, Patrik Jonsson, and Gunnar Övergaard, *Object-Oriented Software Engineering: A Use-Case–Driven Approach.* Menlo Park, CA: Addison-Wesley, 1992. (Revised fourth printing, 1993).

[5]  Ivar Jacobson, Maria Ericsson, and Agneta Jacobson, *The Object Advantage— Business Process Reengineering with Object Technology.* Menlo Park, CA: Addison-Wesley, 1994.

[6]  Jacobson I., "Basic use case modeling," *Report on Analysis and Design (ROAD),* July–August, vol. 1 no. 2, 1994.

[7]  Jacobson I., "Basic use case modeling (continued)," *Report on Analysis and Design (ROAD),* vol. 1 no. 3, September–October 1994.

[8]  Ivar Jacobson and Magnus Christerson, "Modeling with use cases—A growing consensus on use cases." *Journal of Object-Oriented Programming,* March–April 1995

[9]  Jacobson I., K Palmqvist, and S. Dyrhage, "Systems of interconnected systems," *Report on Analysis and Design (ROAD),* May–June 1995.

[10] Ivar Jacobson, "Modeling with use cases—Formalizing use-case modeling," *Journal of Object-Oriented Programming*, June 1995.

[11] James Rumbaugh, Ivar Jacobson, and Grady Booch, *Unified Modeling Language Reference Manual,* Reading, MA: Addison-Wesley, 1998.

[12] OMG Unified Modeling Language Specification. Object Management Group, Framingham, MA, 1998. Internet: www.omg.org.

[13] Ivar Jacobson, Martin Griss, and Patrik Jonsson, *Software Reuse: Architecture, Process and Organization for Business Success.* Reading, MA: Addison-Wesley, 1997.

[14] L.L. Constantine and L.A.D. Lockwood, *Software for Use: A Practical Guide to the Models and Methods of Usage-Centered Design.* Reading, MA: Addison-Wesley, 1999.

[15] CCITT, Specification and Description Language (SDL), Recommendation Z.100. Geneva, 1988.

[16] John Carrol, *Scenario-Based Design,* New York: John Wiley & Sons, 1995.

[17] David Harel, Michal Politi, *Modeling Reactive Systems With Statecharts: The STATEMATE Approach*, New York:  McGraw-Hill, 1998.

# *Chapter 8*

## Analysis

### 8.1 Introduction

In analysis we analyze the requirements as described in requirements capture by refining and structuring them. The purpose of doing this is to achieve a more precise understanding of the requirements and to achieve a description of the requirements that is easy to maintain and that helps us give structure to the whole system—including its architecture.

Before we state exactly what this means, let us reflect a little on the results of requirements capture. Recall that the number one rule in requirements capture is to use the language of the customer (see Section 6.2). Also, as discussed in Chapter 7, we believe that use cases form a good basis for this language. But even if we manage to reach an agreement with the customer on what the system should do, *it is likely that unresolved issues regarding the system requirements remain.* This is the price we have to pay for using the intuitive but imprecise language of the customer during requirements capture. To bring some light on what "unresolved issues" there may be left regarding the system requirements described in requirements capture, recall that to communicate the system's function efficiently to the customer:

1. *Use cases must be kept as independent of each other as possible.* This is achieved by not getting bogged down in details regarding interference,

concurrency, and conflicts among use cases when they, for example, compete for shared resources that are internal to the system (see Section 7.2.3). For example, the Deposit and Withdrawal use cases both access the same customer account. Or, a conflict would occur if an actor combines use cases that result in undesirable behavior, such as when a telephone subscriber uses an Order Wake-Up Call use case followed by a Redirect Incoming Calls use case to order a wake-up call for another subscriber. Issues regarding interference, concurrency, and conflicts among use cases may thus be unresolved in requirements capture.

2. *Use cases must be described using the language of the customer.* This is achieved primarily by using natural language in use-case descriptions and by being careful when using more formal notations such as statechart, activity, and interaction diagrams (see Section 7.4.3.2). But by using only natural language, we lose expressive power, and many details that we could have made precise with more formal notations may thus be unresolved—or only vaguely described—in requirements capture.

3. *Each use case must be structured to form a complete and intuitive specification of functionality.* This is achieved by structuring the use cases (and thereby the requirements) so that they intuitively reflect the "real" use cases provided by the system. One should not structure them into small, abstract, non-intuitive use cases, for example, to remove redundancies. Although this is possible, we must achieve a compromise between understandable and maintainable use-case descriptions (see Section 7.4.5.3). Thus, issues regarding such redundancies among described requirements may not be resolved during requirements capture.

Given those unresolved issues, the primary purpose of analysis is to resolve them by analyzing the requirements more in-depth but with the major difference (as compared to requirements capture) that *the language of the developers* can be used when describing the results.

As a consequence, we can in analysis reason more about the internals of the system, and thereby resolve issues regarding use-case interference and the like (item 1 above). We can also, in analysis, use a more formal language to pinpoint details regarding the system requirements (item 2 above). We refer to this as "refining the requirements."

Furthermore, in analysis we can structure the requirements in a way that facilitates understanding them, preparing them, changing them, reusing them, and, in general, maintaining them (item 3 above). This structure (based on analysis classes and packages) is orthogonal to the structure provided by requirements (based on use cases). However, there is a seamless traceability between these different structures, so we can trace different descriptions—on different levels of detail—of the same requirement and easily keep the descriptions consistent with each other. In fact, this seamless traceability is defined between use cases in the use-case model and use-case realizations in the analysis model; we will discuss this in detail later in this chapter (see also Table 8.1).

**TABLE 8.1**  Brief Comparison of the Use-Case Model and the Analysis Model

| Use-Case Model | Analysis Model |
| --- | --- |
| Described using the language of the customer | Described using the language of the developer |
| External view of the system | Internal view of the system |
| Structured by use cases; gives structure to the external view | Structured by stereotypical classes and packages; gives structure to the internal view |
| Used primarily as a contract between the customer and the developers on what the system should and should not do | Used primarily by developers to understand how the system should be shaped, i.e., designed and implemented |
| May contain redundancies, inconsistencies, etc. among requirements | Should not contain redundancies, inconsistencies, etc., among requirements |
| Captures the functionality of the system, including architecturally significant functionality | Outlines how to realize the functionality within the system, including architecturally significant functionality; works as a first cut at design |
| Defines use cases that are further analyzed in the analysis model | Defines use-case realizations, each one representing the analysis of a use case from the use-case model |

Finally, the structure of requirements provided by analysis also works as an essential input to shaping the system as a whole (including its architecture); this is because we want to make the system as a whole maintainable, and not just describe its requirements.

In this chapter we will present a more detailed explanation of what we mean by analysis and refining and structuring the requirements. We will start with a brief "positioning" of analysis (Section 8.2) and then describe the role of analysis during

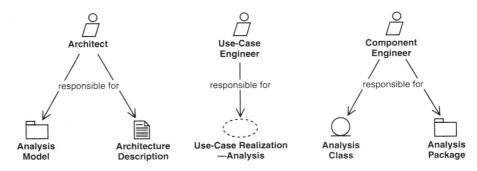

**FIGURE 8.1**  The workers and artifacts involved in analysis.

different phases of the software life cycle (Section 8.3). Next, we will present the artifacts (Section 8.4) and workers (Section 8.5) involved in analysis (see Figure 8.1). Finally we will describe the analysis workflow (Section 8.6).

## 8.2 Analysis in Brief

The language that we use in analysis is based on a conceptual object model, called the *analysis model*. The analysis model helps us refine the requirements along the lines mentioned earlier (Section 8.1) and lets us reason about the internals of the system, including its internal shared resources. In fact, an internal resource can be represented as an object in the analysis model, such as the customer account accessed by the Deposit and Withdrawal use cases. Moreover, the analysis model provides more expressive power and formalism, such as interaction diagrams that are used to describe the dynamics of the system.

The analysis model also helps us structure the requirements as discussed earlier (Section 8.1) and provides a structure that focuses on maintenance, such as resilience to changes in the requirements and reusability. (Later in this chapter we discuss principles that will make the analysis model resilient to such changes and contain reusable elements.) This structure not only is useful for the maintenance of the requirements as such but is also used as an input to design and implementation activities (as we describe in Chapters 9 and 10). We strive to preserve this structure as we shape the system and decide on its design and implementation. Given this, the analysis model can be viewed as a first cut at the design model, although it is a model of its own. By preserving the structure of the analysis model in design, we will get a system that, as a whole, should also be maintainable: It will be resilient to changes in the requirements, and it will include elements that can be reused when related systems are built.

However, it is important to note here that the analysis model makes abstractions and avoids solving some problems and handling some requirements that we think are better postponed to design and implementation (Appendix C; see also Section 8.2.1). Because of this, the structure provided by the analysis model may not always be preserved but needs to be negotiated and compromised on during design and implementation, as we will see in Chapters 9 and 10. The reason that this "preserving of structure" doesn't always work in practice is simply that in design we need to consider the implementation platform: programming language, operating systems, prefabricated frameworks, legacy systems, and so on. For cost-efficiency, a better architecture may be achieved by modifying the structure of the analysis model when transitioning to the design model and shaping the system.

### 8.2.1  Why Analysis Is not Design or Implementation

You may now ask why we do not analyze the requirements at the same time we design and implement the system. The answer we give is that *design and implementation are so much more than analysis (refining and structuring the requirements), so a separation of concern is needed.* In design, we have to shape the system and find its form, including its architecture; a form that lives up to all requirements made on the system; a form that includes code components that are compiled and integrated into executable releases of the system; and hopefully a form that we can maintain in the long run—a form that can stand straight under the pressures of time, change, and evolution; a form with integrity.

In design we thus have to make decisions regarding how the system should handle, for example, performance and distribution requirements, and answer questions such as "How can we optimize this procedure so it will take a maximum of 5 milliseconds to execute?" and "How can we deploy this code on that network node without overloading the network traffic?" And there are still many other similar issues that must be dealt with in design, such as how to exploit acquired components such as databases and object request brokers efficiently, and how to integrate them into the system's architecture, how to use the programming language in an appropriate way, and so on. We will not give an extensive list of all additional issues that arise during design and implementation here, but will instead return to this in Chapters 9 and 10. We hope that we have made our point, namely, that *design and implementation is so much more than just analyzing the requirements by refining and structuring them; design and implementation are actually about shaping the system so that it lives up to all requirements—including all nonfunctional requirements—made on them.* To give some ideas on the abstractions made in the analysis model as compared to the richness of detail in the design model, a 1:5 ratio among their model elements is common.

Given this, we simply think that before one starts to design and implement, one should have a precise and detailed understanding of the requirements—a level of preciseness and detail that the customer (in most cases) does not bother about. Moreover, if one also has a structure of the requirements that can be used as an input to the shaping of the system, it is even better. All this is achieved through analysis.

Simply put, by performing analysis we achieve a separation of concern that prepares for and simplifies the subsequent design and implementation activities by delimiting the issues that need to be resolved and the decisions that need to be taken in those activities. Also, by separating these concerns, developers are able to "face the cliff" in the beginning of the software development effort, and thereby avoid the paralysis that may occur when trying to solve too many problems at once—including problems that may not have to be solved at all because the requirements were vague and not understood correctly!

### 8.2.2 The Purpose of Analysis: Summary

Analyzing the requirements in the form of an analysis model is important for several reasons, as we explained earlier:

- An analysis model yields a more precise specification of the requirements than we have in the results from requirements capture, including the use-case model.

- An analysis model is described using the language of the developers, and can thereby introduce more formalism and be used to reason about the internal workings of the system.
- An analysis model structures the requirements in a way that facilitates understanding them, preparing them, changing them, and, in general, maintaining them.
- An analysis model can be viewed as a first cut at a design model (although it is a model of its own), and is thus an essential input when the system is shaped in design and implementation. This is because the system as a whole should be maintainable, not just the description of its requirements.

### 8.2.3 Concrete Examples of When to Employ Analysis

In addition to what we said earlier, we provide more concrete examples of when to employ analysis and how to exploit its result (i.e., the analysis model):

- By performing analysis separately, instead of performing it as an integrated part of design and implementation, we can inexpensively analyze a large part of the system. We can then use the result to plan the subsequent design and implementation work; maybe as several successive increments, where each increment only designs and implements a *small part* of the system; or maybe as several concurrent increments, possibly designed and implemented by geographically distributed development teams. Finding and planning these increments may be harder without the results of analysis.
- Analysis provides an overview of the system that may be harder to get by studying the results of design or implementation since too many details are introduced (recall the 1:5 ratio discussed in Section 8.2.1). Such an overview can be very valuable to newcomers to the system or to developers who maintain the system in general. For example, an organization had developed a large system (one with thousands of service subsystems) using principles similar to those we described in Chapters 3 and 4. We introduced, after the fact, an analysis model in order to get a better understanding of the system already developed. The CIO summarized their experience: "Thanks to the analysis model, we are now able to train system architects in two years instead of five." For a smaller system the training period would be measured in months instead of years, but the proportions should be the same.
- Some parts of the system have alternative designs and/or implementations. For example, life-critical systems, such as aircraft control systems or railway control systems, may consist of several different programs that concurrently calculate the same operations, and a maneuver of importance can take place only if these computations give the same results. Another example is when a customer wants two or more vendors—or subcontractors—to provide software at different sites; the customer wants to have two competing software houses give bids based on the same specification. In general, this is the case

when a part of the system is implemented more than once by the use of different technology such as programming languages or components running on different platforms. The analysis model can then offer a conceptual, precise, and unifying view of these alternative implementations. In this case the analysis model obviously should be maintained throughout the life of the system.

■ The system is built using a complex legacy system. This legacy system, or a part of it, can then be reengineered in terms of an analysis model so that the developers can understand the legacy system without having to delve into the details of its design and implementation, and build the new system using the legacy system as a reusable building block. A complete reengineering of the design and the implementation of such a legacy system may be very complicated, expensive, and not very helpful—especially if the legacy system does not have to be changed and is implemented using obsolete technologies.

## 8.3  The Role of Analysis in the Software Life Cycle

Analysis is the focus during the initial elaboration iterations (see Figure 8.2). It contributes to a sound and stable architecture and facilitates an in-depth understanding of the requirements. Later, during the end of elaboration and in construction when the architecture is stable and requirements are understood, the focus is on design and implementation instead.

The purpose and goal of analysis must somehow be achieved in every project. But exactly how to view and employ analysis may differ from project to project, and we see three basic variants:

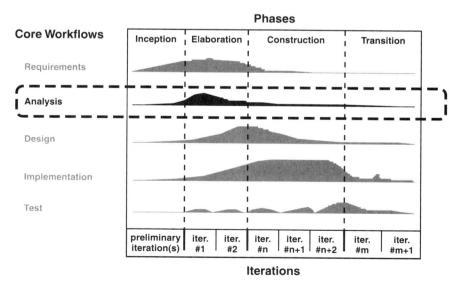

FIGURE 8.2  The focus of analysis.

1. The project uses the analysis model (as will be presented in detail later in this chapter) to describe the results of analysis, and maintains the consistency of this model throughout the entire software life cycle. This can, for example, be done continually—through every iteration in the project—to achieve some of the benefits outlined in Section 8.2.3.

2. The project uses the analysis model to describe the results of analysis but views the analysis model as a transient and intermediate tool—maybe with a focus in the elaboration phase. Later, when design and implementation are up to speed during the construction phase, the analysis model is no longer maintained. Instead, any remaining "analysis issues" are resolved as an integrated part of the design work in the resulting design model (to which we turn our attention in Chapter 9).

3. The project does not use the analysis model at all to describe the results of analysis. Instead, the project analyzes the requirements as an integrated part of either requirements capture or design. The first case would require more formalism in the use-case model. This may be justifiable if the customer is capable of understanding the results, although we believe this is seldom the case. The second case would complicate the design work as we explained in Section 8.2.1. However, this may still be justifiable if, for example, the requirements are very simple and/or well known if, the system's form (including its architecture) is easy to find, or if the developers have some intuitive but correct understanding of the requirements and are capable of constructing a system that lives up to these requirements in a fairly straightforward manner. We believe that this is also seldom the case.

When choosing between the first two variants, the advantages of keeping the analysis model have to be weighed against the cost of maintaining it through several iterations and generations. We therefore need to make the right cost/benefit trade-off and decide if we should stop keeping the analysis model up-to-date—perhaps as early as after the elaboration phase—or if we should keep it and maintain it for the rest of the system's lifetime.

Regarding the third variant we acknowledge that the project can not only avoid the cost of maintaining the analysis model, but avoid the cost of introducing the analysis model in the first place (such as the cost in time and resources it takes to train the developers—and to have them gain experience—in how to use the model). However, as we believe we have pointed out already, usually the benefits of working with an analysis model at least initially in a project outweigh the costs of introducing it; thus this variant should be employed only in rare cases for extraordinarily simple systems.

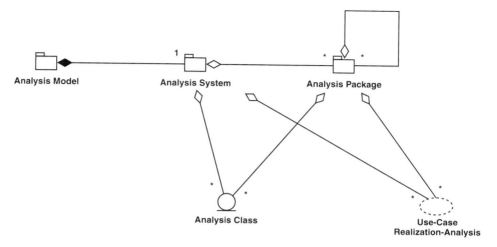

**FIGURE 8.3** The analysis model is a hierarchy of analysis packages containing analysis classes and use-case realizations.

## 8.4  Artifacts

### 8.4.1 Artifact:  Analysis Model

We introduced the analysis model in the beginning of Section 8.2. The structure imposed by the analysis model is defined by a hierarchy as illustrated in Figure 8.3.

The analysis model is represented by an analysis system denoting the top-level package of the model. Using other analysis packages are then a way of organizing the analysis model into more manageable pieces that represent abstractions of subsystems and possibly complete layers in the system's design. Analysis classes represent abstractions of classes and possibly subsystems in the system's design. Within the analysis model, use cases are realized by analysis classes and their objects. This is represented by collaborations within the analysis model and are denoted *use-case realizations—analysis*. The artifacts in the analysis model are presented in detail in Sections 8.4.2–8.4.5.

### 8.4.2 Artifact:  Analysis Class

An analysis class represents an abstraction of one or several classes and/or subsystems in the system's design. This abstraction has the following characteristics:

- An analysis class focuses on handling functional requirements and postpones the handling of nonfunctional requirements until subsequent design and implementation activities have been addressed by designating them as special requirements of the class. This makes an analysis class more obvious in a problem domain context, more "conceptual," and often of a larger granularity than its corresponding design and implementation class counterparts.

■ An analysis class seldom defines or provides any interface in terms of operations and their signatures. Instead, its behavior is defined by responsibilities on a higher, less formal level. A responsibility is a textual description of a cohesive subset of the behavior defined by a class.

■ An analysis class defines attributes, although those attributes are also on a fairly high level. The types of those attributes are often conceptual and recognizable from the problem domain, whereas the types of attributes on design and implementation classes often are programming language types. Moreover, attributes found during analysis commonly become classes by themselves in design and implementation.

■ An analysis class is involved in relationships, although those relationships are more conceptual than their design and implementation counterparts. For example, the navigability of associations is not very important in analysis, but it is essential in design. Or, generalizations can be used in analysis, but it might not be possible to use them in design if they are not supported by the programming language.

■ Analysis classes always fit one of three basic stereotypes: boundary, control, or entity (see Figure 8.4). Each stereotype implies specific semantics (described shortly), which results in a powerful and consistent method of finding and describing analysis classes and contributes to the creation of a robust object model and architecture. However, it is much harder to stereotype

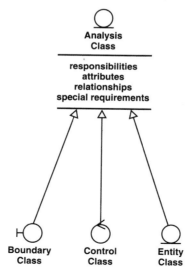

**FIGURE 8.4** The key attributes and subtypes (i.e., stereotypes) of an analysis class.

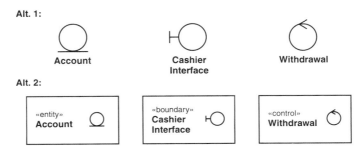

**FIGURE 8.5** UML provides three standard class stereotypes that we use in analysis.

design and implementation classes in this clear and intuitive way. Because they handle nonfunctional requirements, they "live in a solution domain context," and are often described using programming language syntax and similar low-level technologies.

These three stereotypes are standardized in the UML and are used to help developers distinguish concerns among different classes [3]. Each stereotype has its own symbol, as illustrated in Figure 8.5.

### 8.4.2.1 Boundary Classes
A boundary class is used to model interaction between the system and its actors (i.e., users and external systems). The interaction often involves receiving (and presenting) information and requests from (and to) users and external systems.

Boundary classes model the parts of the system that depend on its actors, implying that they clarify and collect the requirements on the system's boundaries. Thus, a change in a user interface or in a communication interface is usually isolated in one or more boundary classes.

Boundary classes often represent abstractions of windows, forms, panes, communication interfaces, printer interfaces, sensors, terminals, and (possibly non-object-oriented) APIs. Still, boundary classes should be kept on a fairly high and conceptual level and, for example, should not delve into every widget of a user interface. Note that it is enough if the boundary classes describe what is achieved by the interaction (i.e., the information and requests that are passed back and forth between the system and its actors). The boundary classes need not describe how the interaction is physically realized, since this is considered in subsequent design and implementation activities.

Each boundary class should be related to at least one actor and vice versa.

## Example    The Payment Request UI Boundary Class

The following boundary class, called Payment Request UI, is used to support the interaction between the Buyer actor and the Pay Invoice use case (Figure 8.6).

**FIGURE 8.6**  The boundary class Payment Request UI.

Payment Request UI allows a user to browse invoices that are due, check particular invoices in more detail, and then ask the system to pay an invoice (by scheduling it). Payment Request UI also allows a user to discard an invoice that the buyer does not want to pay.

Next, we will give examples of how this boundary class relates to the "inside" of the system, that is, to the control and entity classes.

### 8.4.2.2 Entity Classes    An entity class is used to model information that is long-lived and often persistent. Entity classes model information and associated behavior of some phenomenon or concept such as an individual, a real-life object, or a real-life event.

In most cases, entity classes are derived directly from a corresponding business entity class (or domain class) within the business-object model (or domain model). However, a major difference between entity classes and business entity classes is that the former represents objects handled by the system under consideration, whereas the latter represents objects in the business (and in the problem domain) in general. As a result, entity classes reflect the information in a way that benefits the developers when designing and implementing the system, including its support for persistence. This is not really the case for the business entity classes (or domain classes), which instead describe the context of the system and thereby may capture information that is not handled within the system at all.

An entity object need not be passive and may sometimes have complex behavior related to the information it represents. Entity objects isolate changes to the information they represent.

Entity classes often show a logical data structure and contribute to the understanding of what information the system is dependent upon.

## Example    The Invoice Entity Class

The following entity class, called Invoice, is used to represent invoices. The entity class is associated with the Payment Request UI boundary class by which the user browses and handles invoices; see Figure 8.7.

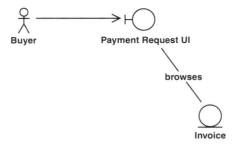

**FIGURE 8.7**  The Invoice entity class and its relationship with the Payment Request UI boundary class.

### 8.4.2.3  Control Classes    Control classes represent coordination, sequencing, transactions, and control of other objects and are often used to encapsulate control related to a specific use case. Control classes are also used to represent complex derivations and calculations, such as business logic, that cannot be related to any specific, long-lived information stored by the system (i.e., a specific entity class).

The dynamics of the system are modeled by control classes, since they handle and coordinate the main actions and control flows, and delegate work to other objects (i.e., boundary and entity objects).

Note that control classes do not encapsulate issues related to interactions with the actors, nor do they encapsulate issues related to long-lived, persistent information handled by the system; this is encapsulated by boundary and entity classes, respectively. Instead, control classes encapsulate, and thereby isolate, changes to control, coordination, sequencing, transactions, and sometimes complex business logic that involve several other objects.

---

**Example**    **The Payment Scheduler Control Class**

To refine the preceding example, we introduce a control class called Payment Scheduler, which is responsible for coordination between Payment Request UI and Invoice; see Figure 8.8.

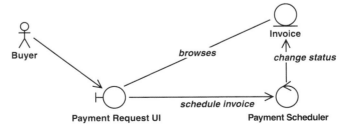

**FIGURE 8.8**  Introducing the control class Payment Scheduler and its relationships with boundary and entity classes.

Payment Scheduler accepts a payment request, such as a request to pay an invoice, and a date when the invoice is to be paid. Later, on the date of payment, Payment Scheduler performs the payment by requesting a transfer of money between the appropriate accounts.

### 8.4.3 Artifact:  Use-Case Realization—Analysis

A *use-case realization—analysis* is a collaboration within the analysis model that describes how a specific use case is realized and performed in terms of analysis classes and their interacting analysis objects. A use-case realization thus provides a straightforward trace to a specific use case in the use-case model (Figure 8.9).

A use-case realization has a textual flow-of-events description, class diagrams that depict its participating analysis classes, and interaction diagrams that depict the realization of a particular flow or scenario of the use case in terms of analysis object interactions (see Figure 8.10). Also, because a use-case realization here is described in terms of analysis classes and their objects, it has a natural focus on functional requirements. Thus it can, just as analysis classes themselves, postpone the handling of nonfunctional requirements until subsequent design and implementation activities by designating them as special requirements on the realization.

***8.4.3.1  Class Diagrams***    An analysis class and its objects often participate in several use-case realizations, and some responsibilities, attributes, and associations of a specific class are often relevant to only one use-case realization. It is thus important during analysis to coordinate all the requirements on a class and its objects that different use-case realizations may have. To do so, we attach class diagrams to use-case realizations, showing their participating classes and their relationships (see Figure 8.11).

***8.4.3.2  Interaction Diagrams***    The sequence of actions in a use case begins when an actor invokes the use case by sending some form of message to the system. If here we consider the "inside" of the system, a boundary object will receive this message from the actor. The boundary object then sends a message to some other object, and so the involved objects interact to realize the use case. In analysis we prefer to depict this with collaboration diagrams since our primary focus is on finding requirements and responsibilities on objects and not on finding detailed and

**FIGURE 8.9**  A trace exists between a use-case realization—analysis in the analysis model and a use case in the use-case model.

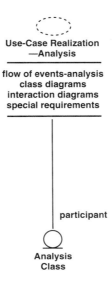

**FIGURE 8.10** The key attributes and associations of a use-case realization—analysis.

chronological sequences of interactions (in which case we would use sequence diagrams instead).

Using collaboration diagrams, we illustrate object interaction by creating links between the objects and by attaching messages to these links. The name of a message should denote the intent of the invoking object when interacting with the invoked object.

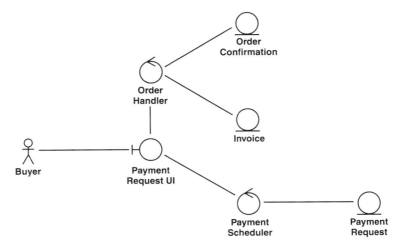

**FIGURE 8.11** A class diagram for a realization of the Pay Invoice use case.

**Example**    A Collaboration Diagram Showing the Realization
of a Use Case

Figure 8.12 is a collaboration diagram realizing the first part of the Pay Invoice use
case.

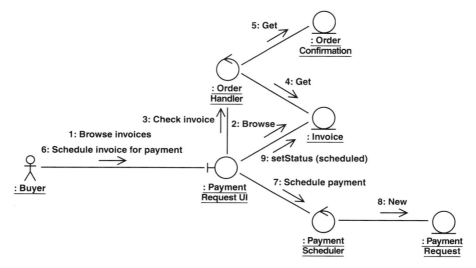

**FIGURE 8.12**  A collaboration diagram for a realization of the Pay Invoice use case.

Regarding the creation and termination of analysis objects within a use-case
realization, different objects have different life cycles (Appendix C):

- A boundary object need not be specific to one use-case realization if, for
  example, it must appear in a window and participate in two or more use-case
  instances. However, boundary objects are often both created and terminated
  within a single use-case realization.
- An entity object is often not specific to one use-case realization. Instead, an
  entity object is often long-lived and participates in several use-case realizations before it is terminated.
- Control classes often encapsulate control related to a specific use case, implying that a control object would be created when the use case starts and that the
  control object would be terminated when the use case ends. However, there
  are exceptions where a control object participates in more than one use-case
  realization, where several control objects (of different control classes) participates in one use-case realization, and where a use-case realization does not
  require any control object at all.

**8.4.3.3 Flow of Events—Analysis** The diagrams—especially the collaboration diagrams—of a use-case realization can be hard to read by themselves, so additional text that explains the diagrams can be useful. The text should be written in terms of objects, particularly control objects, that interact to perform the use case. The text should not, however, mention any of the object attributes, responsibilities, and associations, which would be difficult to maintain because they change quite frequently.

| **Example** | **A Flow of Events—Analysis That Explains a Collaboration Diagram** |
| --- | --- |

The following textual description complements the collaboration diagram shown in the preceding example (see Figure 8.12):

> *The buyer browses the invoices managed by the system to find those received (1, 2), through the Payment Request UI. The Payment Request UI uses the Order Handler to check the invoices against their related order confirmations (3, 4, 5), before showing the list of invoices to the buyer. What this check entails depends on the business rules that the buyer organization sets up and might include comparing the price, delivery date, and contents of the invoice with the order confirmation. The Order Handler object uses these business rules to decide what questions (illustrated by the Get messages 4, 5) to ask the Order Confirmation and Invoice objects how to analyze the answers. Any suspect invoice is somehow flagged for the buyer by the Payment Request UI, perhaps by using a different color to highlight them.*
>
> *The buyer selects an invoice via the Payment Request UI and schedules the invoice for payment (6). The Payment Request UI asks the Payment Scheduler to schedule the payment of the invoice (7). The Payment Scheduler then creates a payment request (8). The Payment Request UI then changes the state of the invoice to "scheduled" (9).*
>
> *The Payment Scheduler initiates the payment on the due day (not shown in the diagram).*

It is interesting to compare this description with the flow of events of the use case as described in Chapter 7, Section 7.2.3.1. The description in Chapter 7 is that of the externally observable behavior of the use case, whereas the description here focuses on how the use case is realized by the system in terms of (logical) objects that collaborate.

---

**8.4.3.4 Special Requirements** The special requirements are textual descriptions that collect all nonfunctional requirements, on a use-case realization. Some of these requirements were already captured in some form during the requirements workflow (as described in Chapters 6 and 7), and are just changed to a use-case realization—analysis. However, some of them may also be new or derived requirements that are found as the analysis work progresses.

---

**Example**    Special Requirements
for the Realization of a Use Case

The following is an example of special requirements on a realization of the Pay Invoice use case:

- When the buyer asks to view received invoices, it should not take more than 0.5 seconds to show invoices on the screen.
- Invoices should be paid using the SET standard.

---

### 8.4.4 Artifact: Analysis Package

Analysis packages provides a means of organizing the artifacts of the analysis model in manageable pieces. An analysis package can consist of analysis classes, use-case realizations, and other analysis packages (recursively). See Figure 8.13.

Analysis packages should be cohesive (i.e., their contents should be strongly related), and they should be loosely coupled (i.e., their dependencies on each other should be minimized).

In addition, analysis packages have the following characteristics:

- Analysis packages can represent a separation of analysis concerns. For example, in a large system some analysis packages may be analyzed separately—possibly concurrently by different developers with different domain knowledge.

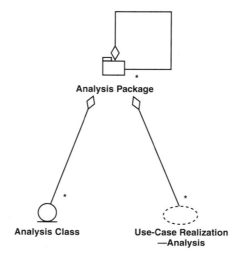

**FIGURE 8.13** Analysis package contents.

- Analysis packages should be created based on functional requirements and on the problem domain (i.e., the application or the business), and they should be recognizable by people with domain knowledge. Analysis packages should not be based on nonfunctional requirements and the solution domain.
- Analysis packages are likely to become, or be distributed among, subsystems in the two top application layers in the design model. In some cases, an analysis package might even reflect a complete top-level layer in the design model.

### 8.4.4.1 Service Packages

Apart from providing use cases to its actors, every system also provides a set of services to its customers. A customer acquires a suitable mix of services to give its users the necessary use cases to carry out its business:

- A use case specifies a sequence of actions: a thread is initiated by an actor, followed by interactions between the actor and the system, and completed and stopped after having returned a value to the actor. Usually, use cases don't exist in isolation. For instance, the Invoice Buyer use case assumes that another use case has created an invoice and that the buyer's address and other customer data are accessible.
- A service represents a coherent set of functionally related actions—a package of functionality—that are employed in several use cases. A customer of a system usually buys a mix of services to give its users the necessary use cases. A service is indivisible in the sense that the system needs to provide it completely or not at all.
- Use cases are for users, and services are for customers. Use cases cross services, that is, a use case requires actions from several services.

In the Unified Process, the service concept is supported by service packages. Service packages are used at a lower level of the analysis package (containment) hierarchy to structure the system according to the services it provides. The following can be noted about service packages:

- A service package contains a set of functionally related classes.
- A service package is indivisible. Each customer gets either all classes in the service package or none at all.
- When a use case is realized, one or more service packages may be participants in the realization. Moreover, it is common for a specific service package to participate in several different use-case realizations.
- A service package often has very limited dependencies toward other service packages.
- A service package is usually of relevance to only one or a few actors.
- The functionality defined by a service package can, when designed and implemented, be managed as a separate delivery unit. A service package can thus represent some "add-in" functionality of the system. When a service package

is excluded, so is every use case whose realization requires the service package.

- Service packages may be mutually exclusive, or they may represent different aspects or variants of the same service. For example, "spell checking for British English" and "spell checking for American English" may be two different service packages provided by a system.
- The service packages constitute an essential input to subsequent design and implementation activities, in that they will help structure the design and implementation models in terms of service subsystems. In particular, the service subsystems have a major impact on the system's decomposition into binary and executable components.

By structuring the system according to the services it provides, we prepare for changes in individual services, since such changes are likely to be localized to the corresponding service package. This yields a robust system that is resilient to change.

A method for identifying service packages, together with examples of service packages, is provided in Section 8.6.1.1.2.

Note that the general way of organizing the artifacts of the analysis model is still by using ordinary analysis packages as discussed in the preceding section. However, here we introduce a «service package» stereotype to be able to mark explicitly those packages representing services. It is especially important in large systems (which have many packages) to be able to discriminate among different types of packages in an easy way. This is also an illustration of how stereotypes may be used and exploited within the UML.

### 8.4.4.1.1 Service Packages Are Reusable

As discussed in the previous section, service packages have many nice characteristics, such as being cohesive (Appendix C), indivisible, loosely coupled, delivered separately, and so on. This makes most service packages primary candidates for being reused, both within a system and across (more or less) related systems. More specifically, service packages whose services are centered around one or more entity classes (see Section 8.4.2.2) are likely to be reusable in different systems that support the same business or domain. This is because entity classes are derived from business entity classes or domain classes, which make the entity classes and related services candidates for reuse within the business or domain as a whole and most systems supporting it—not just candidates for a specific system. Service packages, and services, are orthogonal to use cases in the sense that a service package can be employed in several different use-case realizations. This is particularly true when the service package resides in a general layer with common and shared functionality (see Section 8.6.1.1.3). Such a service package is then likely to be reused in several different applications (configurations) of the system, where each application provides use cases whose realizations require the service package. Service packages trace to service subsystems in design (see Section 9.3.4.1) and then to components in the implementation (see Section 10.3.2). Those components are reusable for the same reasons as service packages are.

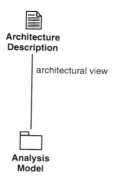

**FIGURE 8.14** The architecture description contains an architectural view of the analysis model.

Thus, service packages manifest our primary instrument to build for reuse during analysis. This impacts both the design and the implementation of the system, and ultimately yields reusable components.

### 8.4.5 Artifact:  Architecture Description (View of the Analysis Model)

The architecture description contains an **architectural view of the analysis model** (Appendix C), depicting its architecturally significant artifacts (Figure 8.14).

The following artifacts in the analysis model are usually considered to be architecturally significant:

- The decomposition of the analysis model into analysis packages and their dependencies. This decomposition often impacts the subsystems in top-level layers during design and implementation and is thus significant for the architecture in general.
- Key analysis classes such as entity classes that encapsulate an important phenomenon of the problem domain; boundary classes that encapsulate important communication interfaces and user-interface mechanisms; control classes that encapsulate important sequences with large coverage (i.e., those that coordinate significant use-case realizations); and analysis classes that are general, central, and have many relationships with other analysis classes. It is usually sufficient to consider an abstract class but not its subclasses as architecturally significant.
- Use-case realizations that realize some important and critical functionality; involve many analysis classes and thereby have a large coverage, possibly across several analysis packages; or focus on some important use case that needs to developed early in the software's life cycle and is thereby likely to be found in the **architectural view of the use-case model** (Appendix C).

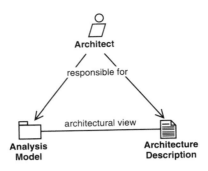

FIGURE 8.15 The responsibilities of the architect in analysis.

## 8.5 Workers

### 8.5.1 Worker: Architect

During the analysis workflow, the architect is responsible for the integrity of the analysis model, ensuring that the analysis model as a whole is correct, consistent, and readable (see Figure 8.15). For large and complex systems these responsibilities may, after some iterations, require more maintenance, and the work involved may become fairly routine. In such cases, the architect may delegate this work to another worker, possibly a "higher-level" component engineer (see Section 8.5.3). However, the architect will remain responsible for what is architecturally significant—the architecture description. The other worker will be responsible for the top-level package of the analysis model, which needs to be compliant with the architecture description.

The analysis model is correct when it realizes the functionality described in the use-case model, and only that functionality.

The architect is also responsible for the architecture of the analysis model, that is, for the existence of its architecturally significant parts as depicted in the architectural view of the model. Recall that this view is a part of the architecture description of the system.

Note that the architect is not responsible for the continuous development and maintenance of the various artifacts within the analysis model. Instead, these are the responsibility of the corresponding use-case engineer and component engineer (see Sections 8.5.2 and 8.5.3).

### 8.5.2 Worker: Use-Case Engineer

A use-case engineer is responsible for the integrity of one or several use-case realizations, ensuring that they fulfill the requirements made on them (see Figure 8.16). A use-case realization must correctly realize the behavior of its corresponding use case in the use-case model, and only that behavior. This includes ensuring that all textual descriptions and diagrams that describe the use-case realization are readable and that they suit their purpose.

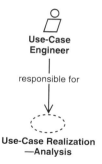

**FIGURE 8.16**  The responsibilities of a use-case engineer in analysis.

Note that the use-case engineer is not responsible for the analysis classes and relationships employed in the use-case realization. Instead, these are the corresponding component engineer's responsibilities (see Section 8.5.3).

As we will see in the next chapter, the use-case engineer is also responsible for the design of the use-case realizations. Thus the use-case engineer is responsible for both analyzing and designing the use case, which makes for a seamless transition.

### 8.5.3 Worker:  Component Engineer

The component engineer defines and maintains the responsibilities, attributes, relationships, and special requirements of one or several analysis classes, making sure that each analysis class fulfills the requirements made on it from the use-case realizations in which it participates (see Figure 8.17).

The component engineer also maintains the integrity of one or several analysis packages. This includes making sure that their contents (e.g., classes and their relationships) are correct and that their dependencies on other analysis packages are correct and minimal.

It is often appropriate to let the component engineer who is responsible for an analysis package also be responsible for its contained analysis classes. Moreover, if

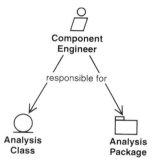

**FIGURE 8.17**  The responsibilities of the component engineer in analysis.

there is a direct mapping (a straightforward trace) between an analysis package and the corresponding design subsystems (see Section 8.4.4), the component engineer should also be responsible for those subsystems and use the knowledge acquired during analysis when designing and implementing the analysis package. If there is no such direct map, additional component engineers may be involved in designing and implementing the analysis package.

## 8.6  Workflow

Earlier in this chapter, we described the analysis work in static terms. Now we use an activity diagram to reason about its dynamic behavior (see Figure 8.18).

The creation of the analysis model (as defined earlier in this chapter) is initiated by the architects, who begin by identifying major analysis packages, obvious entity classes, and common requirements. Then, use-case engineers realize each use case in terms of the participating analysis classes by stating the behavioral requirements of each class. These requirements are then specified by component engineers and integrated into each class by creating consistent responsibilities, attributes, and relationships for each class. During analysis, the architect continually finds new analysis packages, classes, and common requirements as the analysis model evolves, and component engineers responsible for individual analysis packages continually refine and maintain those packages.

### 8.6.1 Activity:  Architectural Analysis

The purpose of architectural analysis is to outline the analysis model and the architecture by identifying analysis packages, obvious analysis classes, and common special requirements (see Figure 8.19).

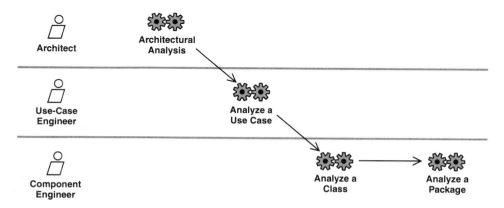

**FIGURE 8.18** The workflow in analysis, including the participating workers and their activities.

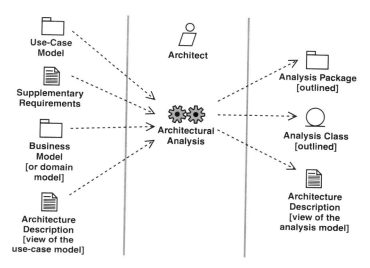

**FIGURE 8.19** The input and result of architectural analysis.

### 8.6.1.1 Identifying Analysis Packages

Analysis packages provide a way to organize the analysis model into smaller, more manageable pieces. They can either be identified initially as a way of dividing the analysis work or be found as the analysis model evolves and "grows" into a large structure that needs to be decomposed.

An initial identification of analysis packages is naturally done based on functional requirements and the problem domain, that is, the application or business under consideration. Since we capture functional requirements as use cases, a straightforward way to identify analysis packages is to allocate the main portion of a number of use cases to a specific package and then realize the corresponding functionality within that package. Appropriate "allocations" of use cases to a specific package include the following:

- The use cases required to support a specific business process.
- The use cases required to support a specific actor of the system.
- The use cases that are related via generalizations and extends-relationships. Such sets of use cases are coherent in the sense that the use cases either specialize or "extend" each other.

Such packages will localize changes to a business process, an actor's behavior, and a set of closely related use cases, respectively. This approach simply helps initially to allocate use cases to packages. Use cases are usually not local to one package but cross several packages. Therefore, as the work proceeds in analysis, when use cases are realized as collaboration among classes, possible in different packages, a more refined package structure evolves.

**Example**    Identifying Analysis Packages

This example illustrates how Interbank Software might identify some of its analysis packages from the use-case model. The use cases Pay Invoice, Send Reminder, and Invoice Buyer are all involved in the same business process, Sales: From Order to Delivery. Therefore, they could be provided by one analysis package.

However, Interbank Software needs to be able to offer their system to different customers with different needs. Some customers use the system only as buyers, others only as sellers, and some customers use the system both as buyers and sellers. They therefore choose to separate the realization of the use cases that the seller needs from the realization of the use cases that the buyer needs. Here we can see that an initial assumption of one analysis package for the business process Sales: From Order to Delivery has been adjusted to meet the customer requirements. The result is two analysis packages that can be delivered separately to customers depending on their needs: Buyer's Invoice Management and Seller's Invoice Management (see Figure 8.20).

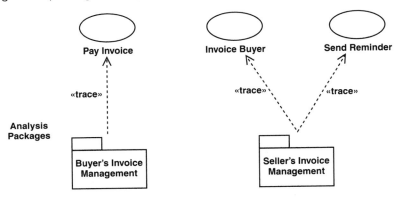

**FIGURE 8.20** Finding analysis packages from use cases.

Note that other use cases also support the business process Sales: From Order to Delivery, but they have been ignored to make the example simpler.

**8.6.1.1.1 Handling Commonality among Analysis Packages** It is often the case that commonalties can be found among the packages as identified in the preceding section. An example is when two or more analysis packages need to share the same analysis class. An appropriate way to handle this is to extract the shared class, put it into its own package or just outside the other packages, and then let the other packages be dependent on this more general package or class.

Such shared classes that represent commonalties are very likely to be entity classes that can be traced to domain or business entity classes. It is thus worth studying the domain or business entity classes if they are shared, and general analysis packages are to be found initially in analysis.

## Example    Identifying General Analysis Packages

This example illustrates how Interbank Software might identify general analysis packages from the domain model. Each of the domain classes Bank Customer and Account represent important and complex entities in the real world. Interbank realizes that those classes require sophisticated information system support and that they are shared by other and more specific analysis packages. Interbank Software thus creates separate packages, Account Management and Bank Customer Management, for each class (see Figure 8.21).

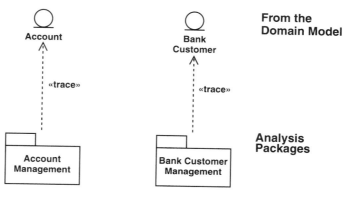

FIGURE 8.21  Finding general analysis packages from domain classes.

Note that the Account Management and the Bank Customer Management packages will probably contain many analysis classes such as control and boundary classes related to account and bank customer management, respectively. It is thus unlikely that these packages will contain only one or a few entity classes traceable to the corresponding domain classes.

**8.6.1.1.2  Identifying Service Packages**  An appropriate service package identification is often done late in the analysis work, when the functional requirements are well understood and most of the analysis classes exist. The analysis classes within the same service package all contribute to the same service.

When identifying service packages, do the following:

■ Identify one service package for each optional service. The service package will be an ordering unit.

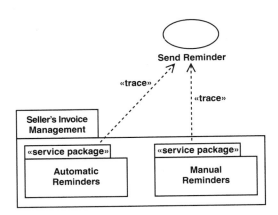

**FIGURE 8.22** The service packages, Automatic Reminders and Manual Reminders, located within the Seller's Invoice Management package.

**Example**    Optional Service Packages

Most sellers who use the Interbank system want a service for sending reminders. This service is described in the (optional) use case Send Reminder. Some sellers want reminders to be sent automatically as soon as there is an overdue invoice, while others prefer to be notified when an invoice is overdue and then decide themselves whether to send a reminder. This variability is represented as two optional and mutually exclusive service packages: Automatic Reminders are used for automatic reminders, and Manual Reminders notify the seller, who decides whether to contact the buyer; see Figure 8.22. When a seller wants no support whatsoever for reminders, none of the service packages is delivered with the system. The service packages are contained by the Seller's Invoice Management package.

■ Identify one service package for each service that *could* be made optional, even though every customer always wants it. Since service packages contain functionally related classes, this will result in a package structure that has localized most changes to individual service packages. This criteria could also have been described as: Identify one service package for each service provided by functionally related classes. Examples of when class A and class B are functionally related are the following:

• A change in A is very likely to require a change in B.
• Removing A makes B superfluous.
• Objects of A interact heavily with objects of B, possibly via several different messages.

**Example** | Identifying Service Packages that Encapsulate Functionally Related Classes

The Account Management package includes a general service package called Accounts which is used to access accounts for such activities as transferring money and extracting transaction histories. The package also includes a service package called Risks for estimating the risks associated with a particular account. These different service packages are common and are used by several different use-case realizations. See Figure 8.23.

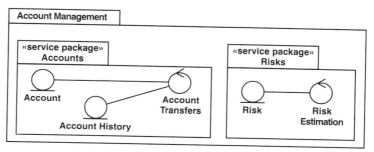

**FIGURE 8.23** The service packages, Accounts and Risks, each encapsulating functionally related classes.

**8.6.1.1.3 Defining Analysis Package Dependencies** Dependencies between analysis packages should be defined if their contents have relationships to each other. The direction of the dependency should be the same as the (navigability) direction of the relationship.

The aim is to find packages that are relatively independent and loosely coupled but have a high internal cohesion. High cohesion and loose coupling makes the packages easier to maintain since changing some classes within a package will primarily affect classes within the package itself. It is therefore wise to try to reduce the number of relationships between classes in different packages since that reduces package dependencies.

To clarify the dependencies, it can be useful to layer the analysis model by having application-specific packages in one top layer and more general packages in a lower layer. This makes the distinction between specific and general functionality clear.

**Example** | Analysis Package Dependencies and Layers

The Account Management package contains several classes, such as Account, that classes in other packages use. For example, the Account class is used by classes in the packages Buyer's Invoice Management and Seller's Invoice

Management. These packages therefore depend on the Account Management package (see Figure 8.24).

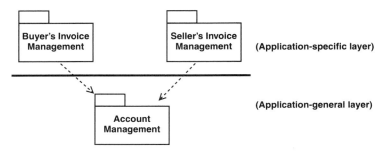

**FIGURE 8.24** Dependencies and layers of analysis packages.

During design and implementation, we will refine those layers and add more lower-level layers as we consider the implementation environment and the nonfunctional requirements in general.

### 8.6.1.2 *Identifying Obvious Entity Classes*     It is often appropriate to prepare a preliminary proposal of the most important (10 to 20) entity classes based on the domain classes or business entities that were identified during requirements capture. However, most classes will be identified when use-case realizations are created (in the use-case analysis activity, see Section 8.6.2). Because of this, one should be careful about identifying too many classes at this stage and to delve into too many details. An initial outline of the architecturally significant classes should suffice (see Section 8.4.5). Otherwise, one will probably have to redo much of the work when the use cases are used later on to identify the truly needed entity classes, that is, those participating in use-case realizations. An entity class that does not participate in a use-case realization is unnecessary.

The aggregations and associations between domain classes in the domain model (or between business entities in the business model) can be used to identify a tentative set of associations between the corresponding entity classes.

**Example     An Entity Class Identified from a Domain Class**

Invoice is a domain class mentioned in Chapter 6. We will use that domain class to suggest one of the initial entity classes. As a starting point, we can suggest the same attributes for the Invoice class: amount, date of submission, and last date of payment. We can also define associations between the entity classes from the domain model, associations such as the payable association between an Order and an Invoice.

### 8.6.1.3 Identifying Common Special Requirements
A special requirement is a requirement that occurs during analysis and is important to capture so that it can be handled appropriately in subsequent design and implementation activities. Examples are restrictions or constraints on the following:

- Persistence
- Distribution and concurrency
- Security features
- Fault tolerance
- Transaction management

The architect is responsible for identifying the common special requirements so that developers can refer to them as special requirements on individual use-case realizations and analysis classes. In some cases the special requirement cannot be found up front and are instead found as use-case realizations and analysis classes are explored. Note also that it is not uncommon for a class or use-case realization to specify several different special requirements.

To further support the subsequent design and implementation, the key characteristics of each common special requirement should be identified.

---

**Example**    Identifying the Key Characteristics of a Special Requirement

A persistency requirement has the following characteristics:

- *Size range*: The range of size of the objects to keep persistent.
- *Volume*: The number of objects to keep persistent.
- *Persistency period*: The time period an object typically needs to be kept persistent.
- *Update frequency*: The update frequency of objects.
- *Reliability*: Reliability issues such as whether objects should survive a crash of the software or hardware.

---

The characteristics of each special requirement will then be qualified for each class or use-case realization referring to the special requirement.

### 8.6.2 Activity: Analyze a Use Case

We analyze a use case to (see Figure 8.25)

- Identify the analysis classes whose objects are needed to perform the use case's flow of events.

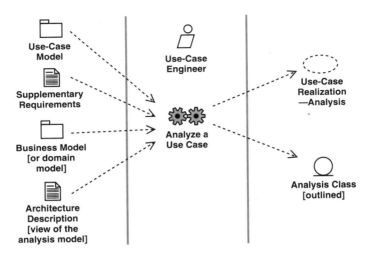

**FIGURE 8.25** The input and result of analyzing a use case.

- Distribute the behavior of the use case to interacting analysis objects.
- Capture special requirements on the realization of the use case.

Another term for use-case analysis would be *use-case refinement*. We refine each use case as a collaboration of analysis classes.

### 8.6.2.1 Identifying Analysis Classes    In this step, we identify the control, entity, and boundary classes needed to realize the use case and outline their names, responsibilities, attributes, and relationships.

The use cases described in requirements are not always detailed enough for identifying analysis classes. Information about the inside of the system is usually not of interest during requirements capture and may therefore have been left out. Thus to identify the analysis classes you may have to refine the descriptions of the use cases with respect to the inside of the system. This refinement should be captured in the textual flow of events—analysis description of the use-case realization.

The following general guidelines can be used to identify analysis classes:

- Identify entity classes by studying the use-case description and any existing domain model in detail, and then consider what information needs to be involved and manipulated in the use-case realization. However, be aware of information that is better to capture as an attribute (see Section 8.6.3.2, "Identifying Attributes"), that is better to be related with boundary or control classes, or that simply is not needed by the use-case realization; such "information" should not be modeled as an entity class.
- Identify one central boundary class for each human actor, and let this class represent the primary window in the user interface that the actor is interacting

with. If the actor already interacts with a boundary class, you should consider reusing that class to achieve a good usability of the **user interface** (Appendix C) and to minimize the number of primary windows that each actor needs to interact with. Moreover, these central boundary classes are often considered as aggregates of more primitive boundary classes.

- Identify one primitive boundary class for each entity class found earlier. These classes represent logical objects that the (human) actor interacts with in the user interface during the use case. These primitive boundary classes can then be refined according to various usability criteria and contribute to the creation of a "good" user interface.
- Identify one central boundary class for each external system actor, and let this class represent the communication interface. Recall that a system actor may be anything from software to hardware units that interact with the current system, such as printers, terminals, alarm devices, sensors, and so on. If the system communication is divided into several protocol levels, it may be necessary for the analysis model to discriminate some of these levels. If so, identify separate boundary classes for each level of interest.
- Identify one control class responsible for handling the control and coordination of the use-case realization, and then refine this control class according to the requirements of the use case. For example, in some cases the control is better encapsulated within a boundary class, especially if the actor handles large parts of the control. In such cases the control class is not needed. In other cases the control is so complex that it is better encapsulated in two or more control classes. In such cases the control class needs to be divided.

When performing this step, the analysis classes already in the analysis model should, of course, be taken into consideration. Some are likely to be reused in the current use-case realization, and several use cases are realized nearly simultaneously, which makes it easier to find analysis classes that participate in several use-case realizations.

Collect the analysis classes participating in a use-case realization in a class diagram. Use this class diagram to show the relationships that are employed in the use-case realization.

### 8.6.2.2 Describing Analysis Object Interactions

When we have an outline of the analysis classes needed to realize the use case, we need to describe how their corresponding analysis objects interact. This is done by using collaboration diagrams that contain the participating actor instances, analysis objects, and their links. If the use case has different and distinct flows or subflows, it is often of value to create one collaboration diagram for each flow. This can make the use-case realization clearer, and it also makes it possible to extract collaboration diagrams that represent general and reusable interactions.

A collaboration diagram is created by starting from the beginning of the flow of the use case, and then going through the flow one step at a time and deciding which analysis object and actor instance interactions are necessary to realize it. Usually the objects naturally find their place in the sequence of interactions in the use-case realization. The following can be noted about such a collaboration diagram:

- The use case is invoked by a message from an actor instance to a boundary object.
- Each analysis class identified in the preceding step should have at least one analysis object participating in a collaboration diagram. If it does not, the analysis class is superfluous since it does not participate in any use-case realization.
- Messages are not assigned to operations since we don't specify operations for analysis classes. Instead, a message should denote the intent of the invoking object when interacting with the invoked object. This "intent" is a seed of a responsibility of the receiving object and might even become the name of the responsibility.
- The links in the diagram often need to be instances of associations between analysis classes. Either those associations already exist or the links define requirements on associations. All obvious associations should be outlined in this step and depicted in the class diagram associated with the use-case realization.
- The sequence in the diagram should not be in primary focus and can be excluded if it is hard to maintain or if it clutters the diagram. Instead, the relations (links) between objects and the requirements (as captured on messages) on each particular object should be in primary focus.
- The collaboration diagram should handle all relationships of the use case that is realized. For example, if a use case A is specializing another use case B via a generalization relationship, the collaboration diagram realizing use case A may need to refer to the realization (e.g., to a collaboration diagram) of use case B.

In some cases it is appropriate to complement the collaboration diagrams with textual descriptions, especially if there are many diagrams realizing the same use case or if there are diagrams representing complex flows. Such textual descriptions should be captured in the flow of events—analysis of the use-case realization.

### 8.6.2.3 *Capturing Special Requirements*     In this step we capture all requirements, such as nonfunctional requirements, on a use-case realization that is identified in analysis but that should be handled in design and implementation.

| Example | Special Requirements on a Use-Case Realization |

Special requirements posed by the realization of the Pay Invoice use case include the following:

- The Invoice class must be persistent.
- The Order Handler class must be able to manage 10,000 transactions per hour.

When capturing these requirements, refer to any common special requirements that have been identified by the architect if possible.

### 8.6.3 Activity:  Analyze a Class

The purposes of analyzing a class (see Figure 8.26) are to:

- Identify and maintain the responsibilities of an analysis class, based on its role in use-case realizations.
- Identify and maintain the attributes and relationships of the analysis class.
- Capture special requirements on the realization of the analysis class.

#### 8.6.3.1 *Identifying Responsibilities*    The responsibilities of a class can be compiled by combining all the roles that it plays in different use-case realizations. We can find all the use-case realizations in which the class participates by studying their class and interaction diagrams. Also recall that each use-case realization's requirements with regard to its classes are sometimes described textually in the flow of events—analysis of the use-case realization.

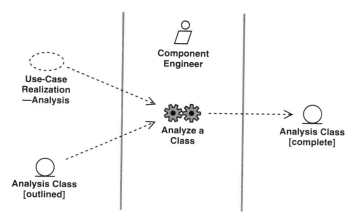

**FIGURE 8.26**  The input and result of analyzing a class.

**Example**    **Class Roles**

Invoice objects are created during the Invoice Buyer use case. The seller performs this use case to ask a buyer to pay for an order (an order that was created during the Order Goods and Service use case). During the use case, the invoice is passed to the buyer, who can later decide to pay for it.

Payment is effected in the Pay Invoice use case, where the Payment Scheduler object schedules an Invoice object for payment. Later the invoice is paid, and the Invoice object is closed.

Note, however, that the same instance of Invoice participates in both the Invoice Buyer use case and in the Pay Invoice use case.

There are several ways we can compile the responsibilities of a class. A simple approach is to extract the responsibilities from one role at a time, adding additional or changing existing responsibilities based on one use-case realization at a time.

**Example**    **Class Responsibilities**

The Payment Scheduler has the following responsibilities:

- Create a payment request.
- Track the payments that have been scheduled and send a notification when payment has been effected or aborted.
- Initiate the transfer of money on the due date.
- Notify an Invoice when it has been scheduled for payment and when it has been paid (i.e., closed).

**8.6.3.2 Identifying Attributes**    An attribute specifies a property of an analysis class, and it is often implied and required by the responsibilities of its class (as considered in the preceding step). The following general guidelines should be kept in mind when attributes are identified:

- The name of an attribute should be a noun [1,2].
- Recall that attribute types should be conceptual in analysis, and, if possible, they should not be restricted by the implementation environment. For example, "amount" can be an appropriate type in analysis, whereas its design counterpart could be "integer."
- When choosing an attribute type, try to reuse one that exists already.
- A single attribute instance cannot be shared by several analysis objects. If this is required, the attribute needs to be defined in its own class.

- If an analysis class becomes too complicated to understand because of its attributes, some of these attributes may be separated into classes of their own.
- Attributes of entity classes are often fairly obvious. If an entity class traces to a domain class or business entity class, the attributes of those classes are a valuable input.
- Attributes of boundary classes that interact with human actors often represent information items manipulated by the actors, such as labeled text fields.
- Attributes of boundary classes that interact with system actors often represent properties of a communication interface.
- Attributes of control classes are rare because of their short life span. However, control classes can have attributes that represent accumulated or derived values during the realization of a use case.
- Sometimes formal attributes are not needed. Instead, a simple explanation of a property handled by an analysis class may be sufficient, and it can be put in the description of the responsibilities of the class.
- If there are many or complex attributes of a class, you can illustrate this in a separate class diagram that shows only the attribute compartment.

### 8.6.3.3 Identifying Associations and Aggregations

Analysis objects interact with each other via links in collaboration diagrams. These links are often instances of associations between their corresponding classes. The component engineer should thus study the links used in the collaboration diagrams to determine which associations are needed. The links may imply the need for references and aggregations among objects.

The number of relationships between the classes should be minimized. It is not primarily real-world relationships that should be modeled as aggregations or associations but relationships that must exist in response to demands from the various use-case realizations. In analysis the focus should not be on modeling optimal search routes through aggregations or associations. This is best handled during design and implementation.

The component engineer also defines association multiplicities, role names, self-associations, association classes, ordered roles, qualified roles, and **n-ary associations** (Appendix A). Refer to [2, 3].

---

**Example**   An Association between Analysis Classes

An invoice is a request for payment for one or more orders (see Figure 8.27). This is represented by an association with the "1..*" multiplicity (there is always at least one order associated with an invoice) and the role name order to pay.

**FIGURE 8.27**  An invoice is the requested payment for one or more orders.

Aggregations should be used when objects represent:

- Concepts that physically contain each other, such as a car that contains the driver and the passengers.
- Concepts that are composed of each other, such as when a car consists of an engine and wheels.
- Concepts that form a conceptual collection of objects, such as a family that consists of a father, mother and children.

*8.6.3.4 Identifying Generalizations*    Generalizations should be used during analysis to extract shared and common behavior among several different analysis classes. The generalizations should be kept on a high and conceptual level, and their primary purpose should be to make the analysis model easier to understand.

**Example**    **Identifying Generalizations**

Invoices and Orders have similar responsibilities. Both are specializations of a more general Trade object; see Figure 8.28.

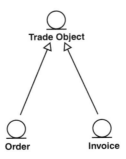

**FIGURE 8.28**  The Trade Object generalizes Invoice and Order.

During design, generalizations will be adjusted to fit better with the chosen implementation environment, e.g., the programming language. A generalization might disappear and instead become realized by other relationships, such as associations.

### 8.6.3.5 *Capturing Special Requirements*

In this step we capture all requirements of an analysis class that are identified in analysis but should be handled in design and implementation (e.g., nonfunctional requirements). When executing this step, be sure to study the special requirements of the use-case realization, which may contain additional (nonfunctional) requirements on the analysis class.

---

**Example**    **Capturing Special Requirements on an Analysis Class**

The characteristics of the persistency requirement of the Invoice class could be qualified as follows:

- *Size range*: 2 to 24 Kbyte per object
- *Volume*: Up to 100,000
- *Update frequency*:
  - Creation/deletion: 1,000 per day
  - Update: 30 updates per hour
  - Read: 1 access per hour

---

When capturing these requirements, refer to any common special requirements identified by the architect if possible.

### 8.6.4 Activity: Analyze a Package

The purpose of analyzing a package, as shown in Figure 8.29, is to

- Ensure that the analysis package is as independent of other packages as possible.
- Ensure that the analysis package fulfills its purpose of realizing some domain classes or use cases.
- Describe dependencies so that the effect of future changes can be estimated.

The following are some general guidelines for this activity:

- Define and maintain the dependencies of the package on other packages whose contained classes are associated with it.

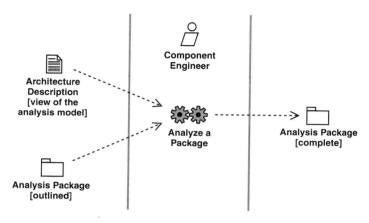

**FIGURE 8.29**  The input and result of analyzing a package.

- Make sure the package contains the right classes. Try to make the package cohesive by including only functionally related objects.
- Limit the dependencies to other packages. Consider relocating to these packages contained classes that are too dependent on other packages.

## Example    Package Dependencies

The Seller's Invoice Management package contains an Invoice Processing class that is associated with the Account class in the Account Management package. This requires a corresponding dependency between the packages (see Figure 8.30).

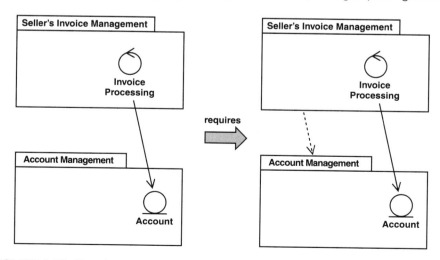

**FIGURE 8.30**  Required package dependencies.

## 8.7  Summary of Analysis

The result of the **analysis workflow** (Appendix C) is the analysis model, which is a conceptual object model that analyzes the requirements by refining and structuring them. The analysis model includes the following elements:

- Analysis packages and service packages, and their dependencies and contents. Analysis packages can localize changes to a business process, an actor's behavior, or a set of closely related use cases. Service packages will localize changes to individual services offered by the system, and they manifest a primary instrument to build for reuse during analysis.
- Analysis classes, their responsibilities, attributes, relationships, and special requirements. Each of the control, entity, and boundary classes will localize changes to the (stereotypical) behavior and information they represent. A change in the user interface or in a communication interface is usually localized to one or more boundary classes; a change in the long-lived, and often persistent, information handled by the system is usually localized to one or more entity classes; a change in the control, coordination, sequencing, transactions, and sometimes complex business logic, that involve several (boundary and/or entity) objects is usually localized to one or more control classes.
- Use-case realizations—analysis, which describes how use cases are refined in terms of collaborations within the analysis model and their special requirements. Use-case realizations will localize changes in use cases, since if a use case changes, its realization may also need to be changed.
- The architectural view of the analysis model, including its architecturally significant elements. The **architectural view** (Appendix C) will localize changes to the architecture.

As we will present in the following chapter, the analysis model is considered the primary input to subsequent design activities. When using the analysis model for this purpose, we preserve as much as possible of the structure that it defines as we design the system by handling a major part of the nonfunctional requirements and other constraints related to the implementation environment. More specifically, the analysis model will impact the design model as follows:

- Analysis packages and service packages will have a major impact on the design subsystems and service subsystems, respectively, in the application-specific and application-general layers. In many cases there will be a one-to-one (isomorphic) trace between packages and the corresponding subsystems.
- Analysis classes will serve as specifications when classes are designed. Different technologies and skills will be required when analysis classes with different stereotypes are designed; for example, the design of entity classes often requires the use of database technologies, whereas the design of boundary classes often requires the use of user-interface technologies. However, the analysis classes and their responsibilities, attributes, and relationships serve as

a (logical) input to the creation of the corresponding operations, attributes, and relationships in the design classes. Also, most special requirements captured on an analysis class will be handled by the corresponding design classes when technologies such as database and user-interface technologies are considered.

- Use-case realizations—analysis have two major purposes. One is that they will help create more precise specifications for the use cases. Instead of detailing each use case in the use-case model with statecharts or activity diagrams, describing each use case as a collaboration among analysis classes will result in a comprehensive formal specification of the requirements of the system. Use-case realizations—analysis also serve as inputs when use cases are designed. They will help identify the design classes that need to participate in the corresponding use-case realizations—design. They will also help by outlining an in initial sequence of interactions among the design objects. Also, most special requirements captured on a use-case realization—analysis will be handled by the corresponding use-case realization—design when technologies such as database and user-interface technologies are considered.

- The architectural view of the analysis model is used as an input when the architectural view of the design model is created. It is very likely that elements in the different views (of the different models) trace to each other. This is because the notion of architectural significance tends to flow smoothly through the various models via trace dependencies.

## 8.8 References

[1] Ivar Jacobson, Magnus Christerson, Patrik Jonsson, and Gunnar Övergaard, *Object-Oriented Software Engineering: A Use-Case–Driven Approach,* Reading, MA: Addison-Wesley, 1992. (Revised fourth printing, 1993.)

[2] James Rumbaugh, M. Blaha, W. Premerlani, F. Eddy, W. Lorensen, *Object-Oriented Modeling and Design,* Englewood Cliffs, NJ: Prentice Hall, 1991.

[3] OMG Unified Modeling Language Specification. Object Management Group, Framingham, MA, 1998. Internet: www.omg.org.

# *Chapter 9*

# Design

## 9.1 Introduction

In design we shape the system and find its form (including its architecture) that lives up to all requirements—including all nonfunctional requirements and other constraints—made on it. An essential input to design is the result of analysis, that is, the analysis model (see Table 9.1, page 219). The analysis model provides a detailed understanding of the requirements. Most important it imposes a structure of the system that we should strive to preserve as much as possible when the system is shaped (refer to Chapter 8, Section 8.2). In particular, the purposes of design are to

- Acquire an in-depth understanding of issues regarding nonfunctional requirements and constraints related to programming languages, component reuse, operating systems, distribution and concurrency technologies, database technologies, user-interface technologies, transaction management technologies, and so on.
- Create an appropriate input to and point of departure for subsequent implementation activities by capturing requirements on individual subsystems, interfaces, and classes.
- Be able to decompose implementation work into more manageable pieces handled by different development teams, possibly concurrently. This is useful

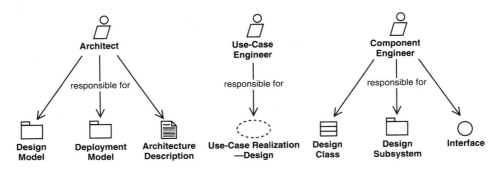

**FIGURE 9.1** The workers and artifacts involved in design.

in cases where such decomposition cannot be done based on the results from requirements capture (including the use-case model) or analysis (including the analysis model). An example would be cases when implementation of those results is not straightforward.

- Capture major interfaces between subsystems early in the software's life cycle. This is helpful when we reason about architecture and when we use interfaces as synchronization instruments between different development teams.
- Be able to visualize and reason about the design by using a common notation.
- Create a seamless abstraction of the system's implementation, in the sense that the implementation is a straightforward refinement of the design by filling in the "meat" but not changing the structure. This permits the use of techniques like code generation and round-trip engineering between the design and implementation.

In this and the following chapters we will present how to achieve these goals. We approach the design workflow in a similar way as we did for the analysis workflow (see Figure 9.1).

## 9.2 The Role of Design in the Software Life Cycle

Design is in focus during the end of elaboration and the beginning of construction iterations (see Figure 9.2). It contributes to a sound and stable architecture and creates a blueprint for the implementation model. Later, during the construction phase, when the architecture is stable and requirements are well understood, the focus shifts to implementation.

Since the design model is very close to implementation, it is natural to keep and maintain the design model through the complete software life cycle. This is especially true in round-trip engineering, where the design model can be used to visualize the implementation and to support graphical programming techniques.

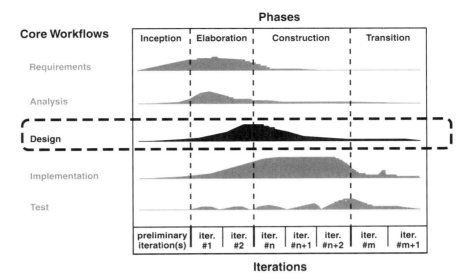

**FIGURE 9.2** The focus of design.

## 9.3 Artifacts

### 9.3.1 Artifact: Design Model

The design model is an object model that describes the physical realization of use cases by focusing on how functional and nonfunctional requirements, together with other constraints related to the implementation environment, impact the system under consideration. In addition, the design model serves as an abstraction of the system's implementation and is thereby used as an essential input to activities in implementation.

The design model defines a hierarchy as illustrated in Figure 9.3.

The design model is represented by a design system that denotes the top-level subsystem of the model. Using other subsystems is then a way of organizing the design model into more manageable pieces.

Design subsystems and design classes represent **abstractions** (Appendix C) of subsystems and components in the system's implementation. Those abstractions are straightforward and represent a simple mapping between design and implementation.

Within the design model, use cases are realized by design classes and their objects. This is represented by collaborations within the design model and denoted *use-case realizations—design*. Note that a use-case realization—design is different from a use-case realization—analysis. The former describes how a use case is realized in terms of interacting design objects, whereas the latter describes how a use case is realized in terms of interacting analysis objects.

The artifacts in the design model are presented in detail in the following sections.

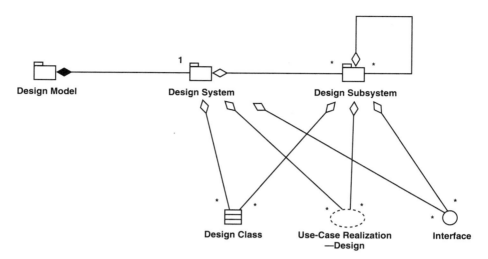

**FIGURE 9.3** The design model is a hierarchy of design subsystems containing design classes, use-case realizations—design, and interfaces.

### 9.3.2 Artifact:  Design Class

A design class is a seamless abstraction of a class or similar construct in the system's implementation (see Figure 9.4). This abstraction is seamless in the following sense:

- The language used to specify a design class is the same as the programming language. Consequently, operations, parameters, attributes, types, and so on are specified using chosen programming language syntax.
- The visibility of attributes and operations of a design class is often specified. For example, the keywords *public*, *protected*, *private* are commonly used in C++.
- The relationships in which a design class is involved with other classes often has a straightforward meaning when the class is implemented. For example, generalization or any stereotypes of generalizations have semantics that correspond to the meaning of generalization (or inheritance) in the programming language. That is, associations and aggregations often map to corresponding variables (attributes) of classes in the implementation to provide references among objects.
- The methods (that is, the realizations of operations) of a design class have straightforward mappings to the corresponding methods in the implementation of the class (that is, the code). If methods are specified in design they are often specified in natural language, or in pseudocode, and can thereby be used as annotations to the method implementations. This is one of the few major abstractions between design and implementation and is seldom necessary

**TABLE 9.1**  Brief Comparison of the Analysis Model and the Design Model

| Analysis Model | Design Model |
|---|---|
| Conceptual model, because it is an abstraction of the system and avoids implementation issues | Physical model, because it is a blueprint of the implementation |
| Design-generic (applicable to several designs) | Not generic, but specific for an implementation |
| Three (conceptual) stereotypes on classes: «control», «entity», and «boundary» | Any number of (physical) stereotypes on classes, depending on implementation language |
| Less formal | More formal |
| Less expensive to develop (1:5 ratio to design) | More expensive to develop (5:1 ratio to analysis) |
| Few layers | Many layers |
| Dynamic (but not much focus on sequence) | Dynamic (much focus on sequence) |
| Outlines the design of the system, including its architecture | Manifests the design of the system, including its architecture (one of its views) |
| Primarily created by "leg work," in workshops and the like | Primarily created by "visual programming" in round-trip engineering environments; the design model is "round-trip engineered" with the implementation model (described in Chapter 10) |
| May not be maintained throughout the complete software life cycle | Should be maintained throughout the complete software life cycle |
| Defines a structure that is an essential input to shaping the system—including creating the design model | Shapes the system while trying to preserve the structure defined by the analysis model as much as possible |

since we recommend that the same developer both designs and implements a class (see Section 9.4.3).

- A design class can postpone the handling of some requirements to subsequent implementation activities by noting them as *implementation requirements* on the class. This makes it possible to postpone decisions that are inappropriate to handle in the design model, such as those having to do with the coding of the class.

- A design class is often given a stereotype that is seamlessly mapped to a construct in the given programming language. For example, a design class for a Visual Basic application could be stereotyped as «class module», «form», «user control», and so on.

- A design class can realize—and thus provide—interfaces if it makes sense to do so in the programming language. For example, a design class that represents a Java class can provide an interface.

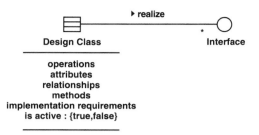

**FIGURE 9.4** The key attributes and associations of a design class.

- A design class can be active, implying that objects of the class maintain their own thread of control and run concurrently with other active objects. However, design classes are normally not active, implying that their objects "run" in the address space and under the control of another active object. Again, the detailed semantics of this is dependent on the programming language and any concurrency or distribution technologies in use. Note that there is a significant difference between the semantics of active classes and ones that are not active. Because of this, the active classes could, as an alternative, reside in their own process model instead of in the design model. In particular, this can be appropriate when there are many active classes whose objects have complex interactions—as, for example, in some real-time systems.

### Example    The Invoice Design Class

Figure 9.5 illustrates the Invoice design class as it has been elaborated in design. The Account attribute suggested during analysis has been turned into an association with an Account class.

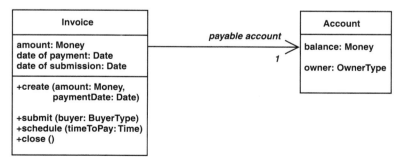

**FIGURE 9.5** The Invoice design class with its attributes, operations, and an association that associates Invoice objects with Account objects.

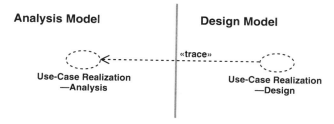

**FIGURE 9.6** Traces exist between use-case realizations in different models.

### 9.3.3 Artifact: Use-Case Realization—Design

A use-case realization—design is a collaboration within the design model that describes how a specific use case is realized, and performed, in terms of design classes and their objects. A *use-case realization—design* provides a straightforward trace to a *use-case realization—analysis* within the analysis model (see Figure 9.6). Note that a use-case realization—design thereby also can be traced to a use case in the use-case model via the use-case realization—analysis.

When the analysis model will not be maintained throughout the software life cycle but is used only to create a good design, there will be no use-case realizations—analysis. The trace dependency from a use-case realization—design will then go directly to the use case in the use-case model instead.

A use-case realization—design has a textual flow-of-events description, class diagrams depicting its participating design classes, and interaction diagrams depicting the realization of a particular flow or scenario of the use case in terms of interactions between design objects (see Figure 9.7). If needed, the diagrams can also depict the subsystems and interfaces involved in the use-case realization (i.e., the subsystems containing the participating design classes).

A use-case realization—design provides a physical realization of the use-case realization—analysis it traces to, and it also handles most nonfunctional requirements (i.e., special requirements) captured on the use-case realization—analysis. However, a use-case realization—design can, just as design classes can, postpone the handling of some requirements until subsequent implementation activities by noting them as *implementation requirements* on the realization.

*9.3.3.1 Class Diagrams* A design class and its objects, and thereby also the subsystem containing the design class, often participate in several use-case realizations. It can also be the case that some operations, attributes, and associations on a specific class are relevant to only one use-case realization. It is thus important to coordinate all the requirements on a class and its objects, and on the containing subsystem, that different use-case realizations impose. To handle this, we use class diagrams attached to a use-case realization, showing its participating classes,

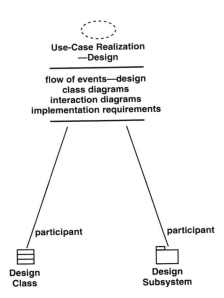

**FIGURE 9.7** The key attributes and associations of a *use-case realization—design.*

subsystems, and their relationships. This way we can keep track of the participating elements in a use-case realization.

Examples of such class diagrams are provided in Sections 9.5.2.1 and 9.5.2.3.

### 9.3.3.2 Interaction Diagrams
The sequence of actions in a use case begins when an actor invokes the use case by sending some form of message to the system. If we consider the "inside" of the system, there will be some design object receiving this message from the actor. Then the design object calls some other object, and so the involved objects interact to realize and carry out the use case. In design, we prefer to depict this with sequence diagrams since our primary focus is on finding detailed, chronological sequences of interactions.

In some cases we include subsystems in sequence diagrams to describe which subsystems are participating in a use-case realization and, possibly, which interfaces provided by those subsystems (i.e., realized) are participating. By doing this, use cases can be designed on a high level before the internal designs of the participating subsystems are developed. This is, for example, useful when there is a need to identify interfaces on subsystems early in the software's life cycle before their internal designs are developed.

Using sequence diagrams, we illustrate object interaction with message transmissions between object or subsystem lifelines. When we say that a message is "received" by a subsystem lifeline, we mean that it is actually an object of a class within the subsystem that receives the message. When a message is "sent" from a subsystem lifeline, it is actually an object of a class within the subsystem that sends the message. The name of a message should indicate an operation of the invoked object or of an interface provided (realized) by the object.

Examples of such interaction diagrams are provided in Sections 9.5.2.2.

### 9.3.3.3 Flow of Events—Design

The diagrams, especially the interaction diagrams, of a use-case realization are often hard to read by themselves. Because of this, the flow-of-events—design, which is a textual description that explains and complements the diagrams and their labels, can be useful. The text should be written in terms of objects that interact to perform the use case, or in terms of the participating subsystems. The description should not, however, mention any of the object attributes, operations, or associations, since the description would then be difficult to maintain because the attributes, operations, and associations of the design classes change frequently. Also, the description should not mention any interface operations, if interfaces are employed in the diagrams. Following this approach, we minimize the need of having to update the flow-of-events—design description if the described diagrams, especially the operations shown on messages in interaction diagrams, are updated.

The flow-of-events—design is especially useful if there are many sequence diagrams describing the same use-case realization or if there are diagrams representing complex flows. Note the following:

- The flow-of-events—design of a use-case realization is not local to a specific sequence diagram. It can thus be used to describe how several diagrams are related.
- The labels (e.g., timing marks or descriptions of actions during an activation) of a sequence diagram are local to the diagram. However, if there are many labels they may clutter the diagram. If this happens, the text of some of the labels might be included in the flow-of-events—design instead.

When using both, flow-of-events—design and labels, they should complement each other.

Examples of flow-of-events—design descriptions are provided in Sections 9.5.2.2.

### 9.3.3.4 Implementation Requirements

The implementation requirements are a textual description that collects requirements, such as nonfunctional requirements, on a use-case realization. Those are requirements that are captured only in design but that are better handled in implementation. Some of these requirements may already have been captured in the previous workflows and are thus just changed to a use-case realization. However, some of them may also be new or derived requirements that are found as the design work progresses.

Examples of implementation requirements on a use-case realization—design are provided in Section 9.5.2.5.

### 9.3.4 Artifact: Design Subsystem

Design subsystems provide a means of organizing the artifacts of the design model in more manageable pieces (see Figure 9.8). A subsystem can consist of design classes, use-case realizations, interfaces, and other subsystems (recursively). Moreover, a subsystem can provide interfaces that represent the functionality they export in terms of operations.

A subsystem should be cohesive; that is, its contents should be strongly related. Also, subsystems should be loosely coupled; that is, their dependencies on each other, or on each other's interfaces, should be minimal.

In addition, design subsystems should have the following characteristics:

- Subsystems can represent a separation of design concerns. For example, in a large system some subsystems may be designed separately, and possibly concurrently, by different development teams with different design skills.
- The two top application layers and their subsystems in the design model often have straightforward traces to analysis packages and/or analysis classes.
- Subsystems can represent large-grained components in the system's implementation; that is, components that provide several interfaces are created out of several other finer-grained components, such as those that specify individual implementation classes, and manifest themselves as executables, binaries, or similar entities that can be deployed on different nodes.
- Subsystems can represent reused software products by wrapping them. Subsystems can thereby be used to reason about the integration of reused software products in the design model. Such subsystems reside in the middleware and system-software layers.

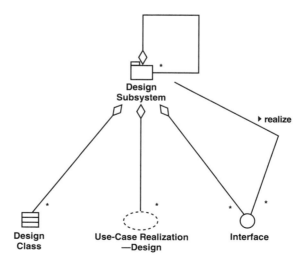

**FIGURE 9.8** Subsystem contents and key associations.

- Subsystems can represent legacy systems by wrapping them (or parts of them). Subsystems can thereby be used to incorporate legacy systems into the design model.

In Section 9.5.1.2, we provide more details regarding subsystems and their pragmatics, together with a method of how to identify them and their interfaces.

### 9.3.4.1 Service Subsystems
Service subsystems are used at a lower level of the design subsystem hierarchy for the same reason service packages are used in the analysis model, namely, to prepare for changes in individual services by localizing the changes to the corresponding service subsystem. For a discussion of what a service is, refer to Section 8.4.4.1 in Chapter 8.

The identification of service subsystems is based on the service packages in the analysis model, and there is usually a one-to-one (isomorphic) trace between them. Consequently, service subsystems are most common in the upper two layers (i.e., the application-specific and application-general layers). However, the service subsystems need to handle more issues than their corresponding service packages, for the following reasons:

- Service subsystems may need to provide their services in terms of interfaces and their operations.
- Service subsystems contain design classes instead of analysis classes. Service subsystems thus deal with many nonfunctional requirements and other constraints that are related to the implementation environment. As a result, service subsystems tend to contain more classes than their service package counterparts and may then need to be decomposed further into (smaller) subsystems just to manage their size.
- A service subsystem often leads to a binary or executable component in the implementation. But in some cases, a service subsystem needs to be partitioned, and having each part deployed onto different nodes may imply that a binary or executable component is needed for each node. In such cases, the service subsystem may need to be decomposed further into (smaller) subsystems, each one encapsulating the functionality deployed to a specific node.

Examples of service subsystems are provided in Section 9.5.1.2.1.

Note that the general way of organizing the artifacts of the design model is still by using ordinary design subsystems as discussed in the preceding section. However, we here introduce a «service subsystem» stereotype to be able to mark explicitly those subsystems representing services. This is especially important in large systems (which have many subsystems) to be able to discriminate among different types of subsystems in an easy way. Recall that a similar reasoning holds for the «service package» stereotype we introduced in Chapter 8.

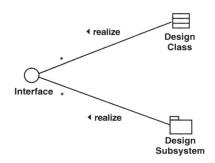

**FIGURE 9.9**  The key associations of an interface.

### 9.3.5 Artifact:  Interface

Interfaces are used to specify the operations provided by design classes and subsystems (see Figure 9.9).

A design class that provides an interface must also provide methods that realize the operations of the interface. A subsystem that provides an interface must also contain design classes or other subsystems (recursively) that provide the interface.

Interfaces provide a means of separating the specification of functionality in terms of operations from their implementation in terms of methods. This separation makes any client that is dependent on, or using, an interface independent of the implementation of the interface. A particular implementation of an interface, such as a design class or subsystem, can then be substituted with another implementation without having to change the client.

Most interfaces between subsystems are considered architecturally significant since they define how the subsystems are allowed to interact. In some cases, it is also useful to outline stable interfaces early in the software's life cycle before the functionality they represent is implemented by the subsystems. These interfaces can then be considered as requirements for the development teams designing the subsystems, and they can also be used as synchronization instruments between different teams, which may be working concurrently with different subsystems [2].

In Section 9.5.1.2.4, we provide more details regarding interfaces and their pragmatics, together with a method of how to identify them.

### 9.3.6 Artifact:  Architecture Description (View of the Design Model)

The architecture description contains an **architectural view of the design model** (Appendix C), depicting its architecturally significant artifacts (Figure 9.10).

The following artifacts in the design model are normally considered as architecturally significant:

- The decomposition of the design model into subsystems, their interfaces, and dependencies between them. This decomposition is very significant for the

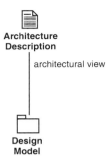

**FIGURE 9.10** The architecture description contains an architectural view of the design model.

architecture in general since the subsystems and their interfaces make up the fundamental structure of the system.

- Key design classes such as classes that trace to architecturally significant analysis classes, active classes,[1] and design classes, that are general and central, represent generic design mechanisms, and have many relationships with other design classes. It is normally sufficient to consider an abstract class as architecturally significant, and not its subclasses, unless the subclasses manifest some interesting and architecturally significant behavior different from the abstract class.

- Use-case realizations—design that realize some important and critical functionality that needs to be developed early in the software's life cycle, involve many design classes and thereby have a large coverage, possibly across several subsystems, or involve key design classes such as those in the previous bulleted item. It is normally the case that the corresponding use cases can be found in the architectural view of the use-case model and that the corresponding use-case realizations—analysis can be found in the architectural view of the analysis model.

In Sections 9.5.1.2, 9.5.1.3, and 9.5.1.4, we provide examples of what might be included in the architectural view of the design model.

### 9.3.7 Artifact: Deployment Model

The deployment model is an object model that describes the physical distribution of the system in terms of how functionality is distributed among computational nodes (see Figure 9.11). The deployment model is used as an essential input to activities in design and implementation since the system's distribution has a major impact on its design.

---

1. If active classes were to reside in their own process model (as noted earlier), they would instead be depicted in an architectural view of the process model.

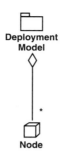

**FIGURE 9.11** The deployment model contains nodes.

The following can be noted about the deployment model:

- Each node represents a computational resource, often a processor or similar hardware device.
- Nodes have relationships that represent means of communication between them, such as *Internet, intranet, bus,* and so on.
- The deployment model can describe several different network configurations, including test and simulation configurations.
- The functionality (or processes) of a node is defined by the components deployed on the node.
- The deployment model itself manifests a mapping between the *software* architecture and the *system* architecture (the hardware).

In Section 9.5.1.1, we provide examples of the deployment model.

### 9.3.8 Artifact: Architecture Description (View of the Deployment Model)

The architecture description contains an **architectural view of the deployment model** (Appendix C), which depicts its architecturally significant artifacts (see Figure 9.12).

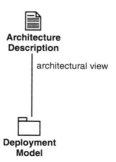

**FIGURE 9.12** The architecture description contains an architectural view of the deployment model.

Because of its importance, all aspects of the deployment model should be shown in the architectural view, including the mapping of components onto nodes as found during implementation.

In Section 9.5.1.1, we provide examples of what might be included in the architectural view of the deployment model.

## 9.4 Workers

### 9.4.1 Worker: Architect

In design, the architect is responsible for the integrity of the design and deployment models, ensuring that the models as a whole are correct, consistent, and readable (see Figure 9.13). As for the analysis model, for large and complex systems a separate worker may be introduced to take over the responsibilities of the top-level subsystem of the design model (i.e., the design system).

The models are correct when they realize the functionality, and only this functionality, as described in the use-case model, the supplementary requirements, and the analysis model.

The architect is also responsible for the architecture of the design and deployment models, that is, for the existence of their architecturally significant parts as depicted in the architectural views of the models. Recall that these views are a part of the architecture description for the system.

Note that the architect is not responsible for the continuous development and maintenance of the various artifacts within the design model. Instead, these are under the corresponding use-case engineer's and component engineer's responsibilities (see Sections 9.4.2 and 9.4.3).

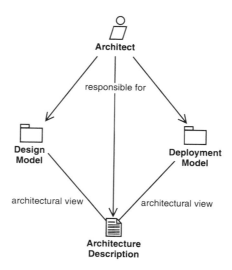

**FIGURE 9.13** The responsibilities of the architect in design.

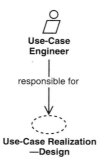

FIGURE 9.14 The responsibilities of the use-case engineer in design.

### 9.4.2 Worker:  Use-Case Engineer

The use-case engineer is responsible for the integrity of one or several use-case realizations—design, ensuring that they fulfill the requirements made on them (see Figure 9.14). A use-case realization—design must correctly realize the behavior, and only this behavior, of its corresponding use-case realization—analysis in the analysis model as well as the behavior of the corresponding use case in the use-case model.

This includes making all textual descriptions and diagrams describing the use-case realization readable and suited to their purpose.

Note that the use-case engineer is not responsible for the design classes, subsystems, interfaces, and relationships employed in the use-case realization. Instead, these are the responsibility of the corresponding component engineer.

### 9.4.3 Worker:  Component Engineer

The component engineer defines and maintains the operations, methods, attributes, relationships, and implementation requirements of one or several design classes, making sure that each design class fulfills the requirements made on it from the use-case realizations in which it participates (see Figure 9.15).

The component engineer may also maintain the integrity of one or more subsystems. This includes making sure that their contents (e.g., classes and their relationships) are correct, that their dependencies on other subsystems and/or interfaces are correct and minimized, and that they correctly realize the interfaces they provide.

It is often appropriate to let the component engineer who is responsible for a subsystem also be responsible for its contained model elements. Moreover, to achieve a smooth and seamless development, it is natural that the artifacts in the design model (e.g., the design classes and subsystems) are carried over to the implementation workflow and implemented by the same component engineer.

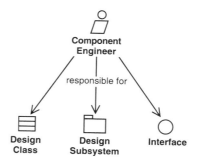

**FIGURE 9.15** The responsibilities of the component engineer in design.

## 9.5 Workflow

Earlier in this chapter, we described the design work in static terms. Now we use an activity diagram to reason about its dynamic behavior; see Figure 9.16.

The creation of the design and deployment models (as defined earlier in this chapter) is initiated by the architects, who outline the nodes in the deployment model, major subsystems and their interfaces, important design classes including active ones, and generic design mechanisms in the design model. Then, use-case engineers realize each use case in terms of participating design classes and/or subsystems and their interfaces. The resulting use-case realizations state behavioral requirements for each class or subsystem participating in use-case realizations. These requirements are then specified by component engineers and integrated into each class either by the creation of consistent operations, attributes, and relationships on each class or by the

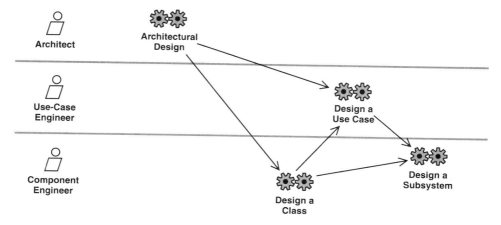

**FIGURE 9.16** The workflow in design, including the participating workers and their activities.

creation of consistent operations on each interface provided by the subsystem. Throughout the design workflow, the developers will identify candidates for new subsystems, interfaces, classes, and generic design mechanisms as the design model evolves, and the component engineers responsible for individual subsystems will refine and maintain those subsystems.

### 9.5.1 Activity: Architectural Design

The purpose of architectural design is to outline the design and deployment models and their architecture by identifying the following (see Figure 9.17):

- Nodes and their network configurations.
- Subsystems and their interfaces.
- Architecturally significant design classes, such as active classes.
- Generic design mechanisms that handle common requirements, such as the special requirements on persistency, distribution, performance, and so on as captured during analysis on analysis classes and use-case realizations—analysis.

Throughout this activity the architects consider various reuse possibilities, such as reusing parts of similar systems or general software products. The resulting subsystems, interfaces, or other design elements, are then incorporated into the design model. The architect also maintains, refines, and updates the architecture description and its architectural views of the design and deployment models.

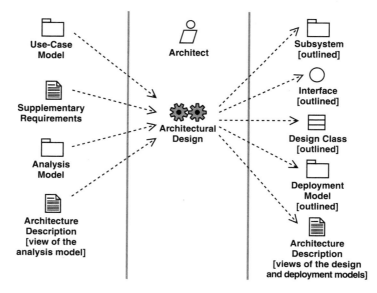

**FIGURE 9.17**  The input and result of architectural design.

### 9.5.1.1 *Identifying Nodes and Network Configurations*   The physical network configurations often have a major impact on the software's architecture, including the active classes required and the distribution of functionality among network nodes. Common network configurations use a three-tier pattern where clients (user interactions) are partitioned onto one tier, database functionality onto one tier, and business/application logic onto one tier. The simple client/server pattern is a special case of the three-tier pattern where the business/application logic is relocated to one of the other tiers (i.e., the client or the database tier).

Aspects of the network configurations include:

- Which nodes are involved, and what are their capacities in terms of processing power and memory size?
- What type of connections are between the nodes, and what communication protocols will be used over them?
- What are the characteristics of the connections and communication protocols, such as bandwidth, availability, and quality?
- Is there any need for redundant processing capacity, fail-over modes, process migration, keeping backup of data, and so on?

By knowing both the limits and the possibilities of the nodes and their connections, the architect can incorporate technologies such as object request brokers and data replication services, which will make it easier to realize the system's distribution.

---

**Example**   Network Configuration for the Interbank System

---

The Interbank system will execute on three server nodes and a number of client nodes. First of all, there is one server node for the buyer and one for the seller, since the seller and buyer organizations each need a central server for their business objects and processing. End users access the system through client nodes, such as the Buyer client. The nodes communicate using the Internet and intranet TCP/IP protocol; see Figure 9.18.

There is also a third server node for the bank itself. This is where the actual payment of invoices occurs (i.e., it is where money is transferred between accounts).

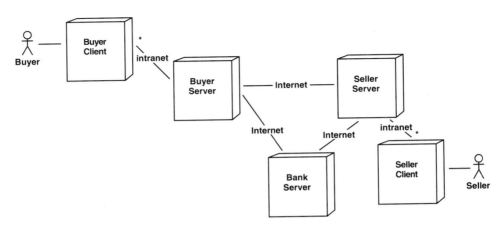

**FIGURE 9.18** Deployment diagram for the Interbank system.

Each network configuration, including special configurations for tests and simulations, should be depicted in separate deployment diagrams. Given these network configurations, it is possible to start reasoning about how to distribute functionality among them (see Section 9.5.1.3.2).

### 9.5.1.2 Identifying Subsystems and Their Interfaces
Subsystems provide a way of organizing the design model into manageable pieces. They can either be identified initially as a way of dividing the design work or found as the design model evolves and "grows" into a large structure that needs to be decomposed.

Note also that not all subsystems are developed in-house by the current project. Instead, some subsystems represent reused products and other existing company assets. Including such subsystems in the design model makes it possible to reason about and evaluate reuse opportunities.

**9.5.1.2.1 Identifying Application Subsystems** In this step we identify the subsystems in the application-specific and application-general layers (i.e., the subsystems in the two top layers). See Figure 9.19.

If an appropriate analysis package decomposition is found during analysis, we can use those packages as much as possible and identify corresponding subsystems within the design model. This is especially important when it comes to the service packages, so that we identify corresponding service subsystems that do not break the structuring of the system according to the services it provides. However, this initial identification of subsystems will be slightly refined during design to handle issues related to the design, implementation, and deployment of the system, as we will discuss shortly.

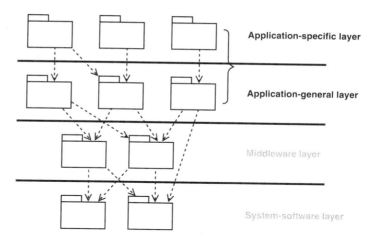

**FIGURE 9.19** Subsystems in the application-specific and application-general layers.

**Example**    Identifying Design Subsystems
from Analysis Packages

The Buyer's Invoice Management and Account Management packages in the analysis model are used to identify corresponding subsystems in the design model (see Figure 9.20).

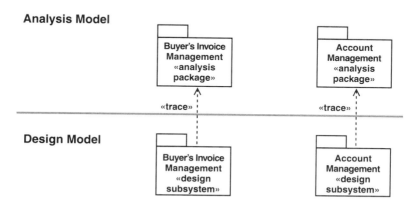

**FIGURE 9.20**  Finding subsystems based on existing analysis packages.

Moreover, the Accounts and Risks service packages within the Account Management package in the analysis model are used to identify corresponding service subsystems in the design model (see Figure 9.21).

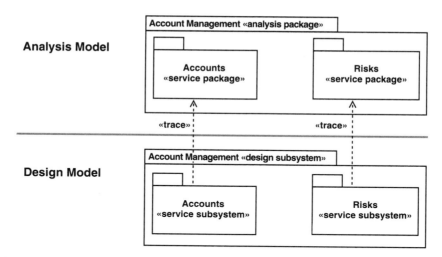

**FIGURE 9.21**  Finding service subsystems based on existing service packages.

A refinement of this initial subsystem decomposition, as compared to the (former) analysis packages in the analysis model, may be needed when:

- Part of the (former) analysis package is mapped onto a subsystem of its own (e.g., if it is found that the part can be shared and used by several other subsystems).

| Example | Refining the Subsystems to Handle Shared Functionality |
|---|---|

Interbank Software considered implementing all the service packages for paying invoices in the Buyer's Invoice Management subsystem, where they seem to belong after having analyzed the use cases related to invoicing. Then the developers realized that several future use cases might benefit from a general payment service subsystem. They therefore decided to keep the functionality for payment in one service subsystem by itself, called Payment Scheduling Management. This means that the Buyer's Invoice Management subsystem uses the functionality for scheduling payments from the Payment Scheduling Management service subsystem. Later, when the scheduled payment is due, the Payment Scheduling Management subsystem uses the Account Management subsystem for the actual transfer of the money from one account to another. See Figure 9.22.

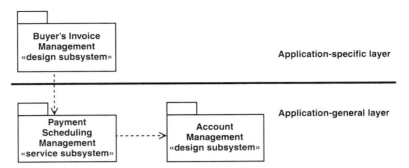

**FIGURE 9.22** During design, the Payment Scheduling Management service subsystem is found to provide a general service that can be used by several use-case realizations.

- Some parts of the (former) analysis package are realized by reused software products. Such functionality might then be allocated to middleware or system-software subsystems (see Section 9.5.1.2.2).
- The (former) analysis packages do not reflect an appropriate division of work.
- The (former) analysis packages do not reflect the incorporation of a legacy system. A legacy system, or part of it, may then be wrapped as a separate design subsystem.
- The (former) analysis packages are not prepared for a straightforward deployment onto nodes. The subsystem decomposition may then need to handle such deployment issues by letting some subsystems be further decomposed into (smaller) subsystems, in which each one can be allocated to individual nodes. Then these (smaller) subsystems need to be refined to minimize network traffic, and so on.

**Example**    **Distributing a Subsystem Among Nodes**

The Buyer's Invoice Management subsystem needs to be distributed among several different nodes when deployed. To handle this, the subsystem is in turn decomposed into three subsystems: Buyer's UI, Payment Request Management, and Invoice Management (see Figure 9.23). The components created from each of these three (smaller) subsystems can then be deployed onto the Buyer Client, Buyer Server, and Seller Server nodes, respectively.

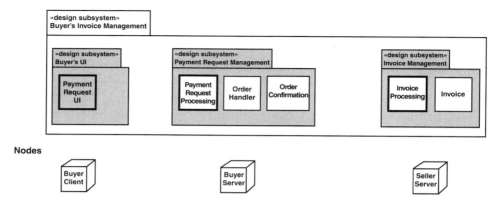

**FIGURE 9.23** A subsystem decomposed into three new subsystems recursively to handle deployment.

**9.5.1.2.2  Identifying Middleware and System-Software Subsystems**  Middleware and system software is the foundation of a system, since all functionality rests on top of software such as operating systems, database management systems, communication software, object distribution technologies, GUI design kits, and transaction management technologies [3] (see Figure 9.24). Choosing and integrating software products that are acquired or built are two of the primary concerns during the inception and elaboration phases. The architect validates that the chosen software products fit the architecture and that they provide a cost-effective implementation of the system.

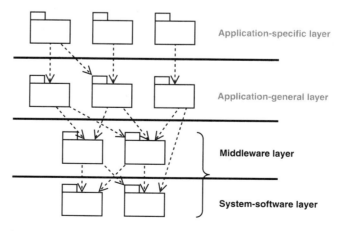

**FIGURE 9.24** Subsystems in the middleware and system-software layers encapsulate acquired software products.

A note of caution: When middleware and system software are acquired, there is little or no control over their evolution. It is then important to maintain appropriate freedom of action and avoid becoming "cornered" and totally dependent on some product and vendor that the project has little influence over. Try to limit the dependencies on acquired products, and thereby the risk related with using them, in case they change in the future, or be able to choose a different vendor if need be.

One way to control the dependencies is to treat each acquired software product as a separate subsystem with explicit interfaces to the rest of the system. For example, if there is a need to implement a mechanism for transparent object distribution, it should be done by defining a strict interface to a subsystem that will realize the mechanism. This preserves the freedom of choosing between different products, since the cost of updating the system is thereby delimited.

### Example · Using Java When Building the Middleware Layer

Several of the application subsystem implementations developed by Interbank Software may need to execute on different types of machines, such as PCs and UNIX workstations, and therefore need to interoperate across different platforms. Interbank Software chose to implement this interoperability using middleware, in this case, Java's Abstract Windowing Toolkit (AWT), Remote Message Invocation (RMI), and Applet packages. These Java packages are represented as subsystems in Figure 9.25. These subsystems are built on the Java Virtual Machine, which is the Java interpreter that has to be installed for a machine to be able to execute Java code. A Web browser is used in our examples for loading Web pages that fetch applets.

At the lowest level, Interbank Software will build on system software such as the TCP/IP protocol for Internet communication (see Figure 9.25).

The Java Applet subsystem is a middleware that enables Interbank to create Java *applets.*

Each user interface window is designed using the Java Applet class together with other user interface classes such as Lists, which is provided by the AWT subsystem. The Java Abstract Windowing Toolkit package (java.awt) is built to enable the creation of platform-independent user interfaces. The AWT package includes classes such as Fields, Scrollbars, and Check Boxes.

The Java RMI is a mechanism for object distribution integrated in the standard Java class libraries. We have here chosen RMI for object distribution to make the examples simple and to avoid mixing several techniques and languages. CORBA or an ActiveX/DCOM solution could just as well have been used.

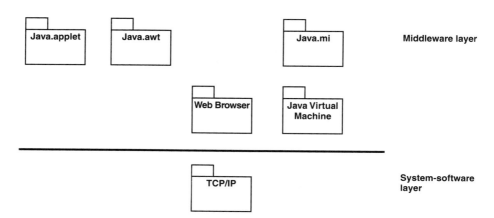

**FIGURE 9.25** Java middleware provides platform-independent graphical user interfaces (java.awt) and distributed object computing (java.rmi). The figure does not show any subsystem dependencies (these are presented in Figure 9.26).

Figure 9.25 illustrates how Java services can be organized into subsystems in the middleware layer. Each subsystem contains classes that are designed to be used in conjunction with each other to offer certain services. Similarly, ActiveX components such as spreadsheets, multimedia, image processing, security management, persistence, distribution, inference engines, processes, and concurrency support can also be represented as subsystems. It is also often practical to create a separate subsystem for standard data-types or fundamental classes that all other subsystems can import and use (e.g., java.lang, which provides many of the core classes in Java, such as Boolean, Integer, and Float).

**9.5.1.2.3 Defining Subsystem Dependencies**  Dependencies between subsystems should be defined if their contents have relationships to each other. The direction of the dependency should be the same as the (navigability) direction of the relationship. If dependencies need to be outlined before the contents of the subsystems are known, we consider the dependencies between the analysis packages corresponding to the design subsystems. These dependencies are likely to be similar in the design model. Also, if interfaces between subsystems are used, dependencies should be toward interfaces, not toward the subsystems themselves (see Section 9.5.1.2.4).

**Example**    Dependencies and Layers

The subsystems and some of their (initial) dependencies in the Interbank system are illustrated in Figure 9.26.

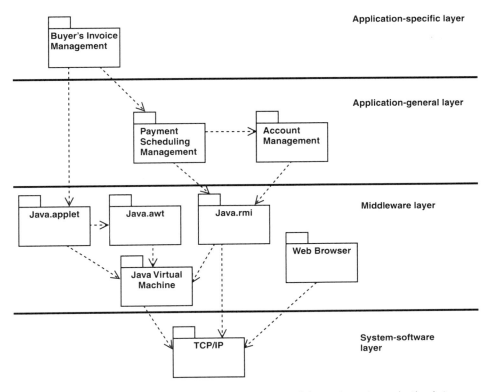

**FIGURE 9.26** Dependencies and layers of some of the subsystems in the Interbank system.

Note that some of these dependencies, especially those in the middleware and system-software layers, can be more or less implicit in the implementation environment (Java in this case). But when the dependencies have an impact on the system's architecture, especially when they "go" between layers, it is useful to make them explicit in the design model and to depict them in class diagrams like Figure 9.26. Such diagrams can then be referred to by both use-case and component engineers when they design use cases, classes, and subsystems.

**9.5.1.2.4 Identifying Subsystem Interfaces** The interfaces provided by a subsystem define operations that are accessible from "outside" of the subsystem. These interfaces are either provided by classes or other subsystems (recursively) within the subsystem.

To outline interfaces initially, and before the contents of the subsystems are known, we start by considering the dependencies between subsystems as found in the preceding step (Section 9.5.1.2.3). When a subsystem has a dependency directed toward it, it is likely that it needs to provide an interface. Moreover, if there is an analysis package that can be traced from the subsystem, then any analysis class that is referenced from the outside of the package may imply an interface candidate provided by the subsystem (as shown in the following example).

**Example** | **Finding Candidate Interfaces Based on the Analysis Model**

The Accounts service package contains an analysis class called Account Transfers, that is referenced from outside of the package. We can therefore identify an initial interface, called Transfers, which is provided by the corresponding Accounts service subsystem in the design model (see Figure 9.27).

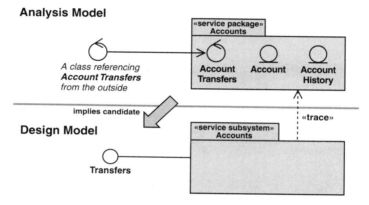

**FIGURE 9.27** An interface initially identified based on the analysis model.

Using this approach, we initially identify the interfaces shown in Figure 9.28 in the two top layers of the design model.

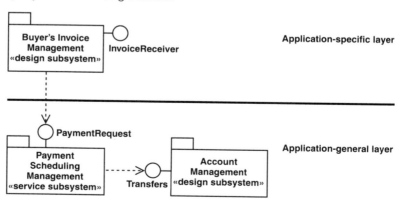

**FIGURE 9.28** The interfaces in the two top layers of the design model.

The Account Management subsystem provides the Transfers interface for transferring money between accounts. This is the same interface provided by the Accounts service subsystem within Account Management (see the preceding example). The Payment Scheduling Management subsystem provides the PaymentRequest interface that is used to schedule payments. The Buyer's Invoice Management subsystem provides the InvoiceReceiver interface for receiving new invoices from a seller. This interface is used in the use case Invoice Buyer, where a new invoice is sent to the buyer.

---

Note that the interfaces identified here let us refine the dependencies between subsystems as discussed in Section 9.5.1.2.3 in that dependencies can be on interfaces instead of subsystems.

Regarding interfaces in the two lower layers (i.e., the middleware and system-software layers) the issue of identifying interfaces is simpler because subsystems in those layers encapsulate software products, and such products often have some form of predefined interfaces.

However, it is not enough to identify the interfaces; we must also identify the operations that need to be defined by each interface. This is done by designing use cases in terms of subsystems and their interfaces, as described in Sections 9.5.2.3 and 9.5.2.4, in the following use-case design activity. This will state requirements on the operations that need to be defined by interfaces. The requirements from the various use-case realizations are then handled and integrated for each interface, as described in Section 9.5.4.2.

### 9.5.1.3 Identifying Architecturally Significant Design Classes

It is often practical to identify architecturally significant design classes early in the software's life cycle, to initiate the design work. However, most design classes will be identified when classes are designed in the class design activity and refined based on the results from the use-case design activity (see Sections 9.5.2 and 9.5.3). For this reason, developers should be careful not to identify too many classes at this stage or to delve into too many details. An initial outline of the architecturally significant classes would suffice (see Section 9.3.6). Otherwise, much of the work will likely have to be done over when the use cases are used later to justify the design classes (i.e., the classes participating in use-case realizations are justified). A design class that does not participate in a use-case realization is unnecessary.

#### 9.5.1.3.1 Identifying Design Classes from Analysis Classes

Some design classes can be initially outlined from the architecturally significant analysis classes as found during analysis. Also, the relationships between these analysis classes can be used to identify a tentative set of relationships between the corresponding design classes.

---

**Example**    Outlining a Design Class from an Analysis Class

The Invoice design class is initially outlined from the Invoice entity class in the analysis model (see Figure 9.29).

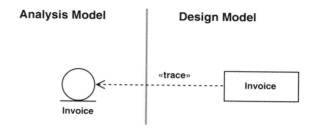

**FIGURE 9.29** The Invoice design class is initially outlined from the Invoice entity class.

---

**9.5.1.3.2 Identifying Active Classes**   The architect also identifies the active classes required by the system by considering the concurrency requirements on the system, as for example,

- The performance, throughput, and availability requirements different actors have as they interact with the system. If, for example, a certain actor has high requirements on response time, then that might be managed by a dedicated active object for taking input from and providing output to that actor—an object that does not get halted just because other active objects are heavily loaded (provided that there is enough processor capacity and memory resources to exploit).
- The system's distribution onto nodes. The active objects need to support distribution onto several different nodes, which, for example, may require at least one active object per node and separate active objects to handle node intercommunication.
- Other requirements such as requirements on system startup and termination, liveliness, deadlock avoidance, starvation avoidance, reconfiguration of nodes, and the capacity of the connections.

Each active class is outlined by considering the life cycle of its active objects and how the active objects should communicate, synchronize, and share information. The active objects are then allocated to the nodes of the deployment model. When allocating the active objects to the nodes, it is necessary to consider the capacity of the nodes, such as their processors and memory size, and the characteristics of the connections, such as their bandwidth and availability. When doing this, a basic rule is that network traffic often has a substantial impact on the computational resources (including both hardware and software) required by the system, and thus needs to be kept under careful control. This may have a major impact on the design model.

To outline active classes initially it is possible to use the results of analysis and the deployment model as input and then map the corresponding designs of analysis classes (or parts of them) to nodes via active classes.

---

## Example — Using Analysis Classes to Outline Active Classes

As stated earlier, the Interbank system needs to be distributed onto nodes such as Buyer client, Buyer server, Bank server, and so on. Moreover, we have identified analysis classes such as Payment Request UI, Order Handler, Order Confirmation, Invoice, and so on (see Figure 9.30). Now, we find that a buyer is interested in the functionality provided by the analysis classes Order Confirmation and Order Handler, but this functionality requires more computational power than can be provided by a Buyer client node. Instead, the major parts of these two analysis classes need to be allocated onto the Buyer Server and managed by a separate active class (Payment Request Processing) on that node.

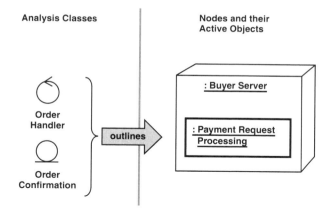

FIGURE 9.30  An active class, Payment Request Processing, is outlined by considering the analysis classes Order Handler and Order Confirmation and the Buyer Server node. It is decided that when the analysis classes are designed, the major parts of the corresponding design classes will be allocated to the Buyer server node. The Payment Request Processing class is then identified to encapsulate the thread of control of those design classes on the node.

---

Another possibility to outline active classes is to use the subsystems identified earlier and allocate a whole subsystem to a specific node by identifying an active class within the subsystem (see Section 9.5.1.2.1). Recall that the subsystem decomposition may need to be refined to make this possible.

Any active class that represents a heavyweight process is a candidate for an executable component to be identified during implementation. Thus the allocation of active classes to nodes in this step is an important input to the allocation of (executable) components to nodes during implementation. Moreover, when a whole subsystem is allocated to a node, all the constituents of the subsystem will often together contribute to an (executable) component allocated to the node.

### 9.5.1.4 *Identifying Generic Design Mechanisms*    In this step, we study common requirements, such as the special requirements as identified during analysis on use-case realizations—analysis and analysis classes, and decide how to handle them, given the available design and implementation technologies. The result of this is a set of generic design mechanisms, which can manifest themselves as design classes, collaborations, or even subsystems, similar to what is described in [1].

The requirements that need to be handled are often related to issues such as:

- Persistency
- Transparent object distribution
- Security features
- Error detection and recovery
- Transaction management

In some cases, the mechanism cannot be found up front but is instead found as use-case realizations and design classes are explored.

---

**Example**    **A Design Mechanism for Transparent Object Distribution**

Some objects, such as Invoice objects, need to be accessed from several nodes so they must be designed for a distributed system. Interbank Software decides to implement such object distribution by making each distributed class a subclass of the abstract Java class, java.rmi.UnicastRemoteObject, which supports Remote Message Invocation (RMI); see Figure 9.31. RMI is the technique used by Java to achieve transparent object distribution (i.e., objects distributed in such a way that the client object does not have to know where the object resides).

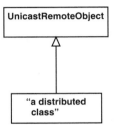

**FIGURE 9.31**  Any class that needs to be distributed should be a subtype of UnicastRemoteObject.

---

**Example**   Design Mechanisms for Persistency

Some objects, such as Invoice and Order objects, need to be persistent. To handle this, Interbank Software can use an object database management system, a relational database management system, or even plain binary files. What is best depends on how the objects need to be accessed and updated, and what is easiest to implement and evolve in the future. A relational database generally offers better performance for tabular data, while an object database offers better performance for complex structures of objects. Relational database management systems are also more mature than object-database systems, but it may be costly to build a system using a relational database management system and then have to upgrade it to an object database later (when mature enough). Whatever solution is selected, it is documented by the architect as a generic design mechanism for the handling of persistency issues.

---

The last example illustrates that each mechanism can often be handled in several different ways and that each approach has its pros and cons. If no single mechanism is feasible in all situations, it may be necessary to provide more than one mechanism and use the most suitable one in each situation.

The architect should also identify generic collaborations that can work as patterns and be used by several use-case realizations within the design model.

---

**Example**   A Generic Collaboration Used
in Several Use-Case Realizations

During the work with use cases and their realizations, the architects identify a pattern in which a Trade object, such as an Order or an Invoice, is created by an actor and sent to another actor:

- When a Buyer decides to order some goods or services from a seller, the buyer invokes the use case Order Goods or Services. The use case allows a buyer to specify and electronically send an order to a seller.
- When a Seller decides to invoice a buyer, the seller invokes the use case Invoice Buyer, which electronically sends an invoice to a buyer.

This is a common type of behavior that can be represented by a generic collaboration, as shown by the collaboration diagram in Figure 9.32.

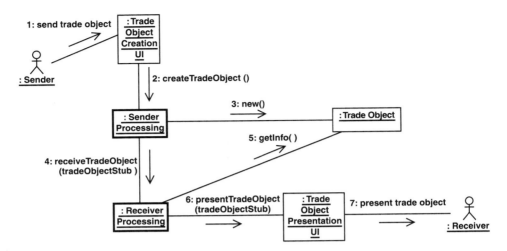

**FIGURE 9.32** Collaboration diagram exemplifying a generic collaboration to create, send, receive, and present trading objects.

First, the Trade Object Creation UI receives information from the Sender actor, which is used as input to creating a Trade object (1) (numbers within parenthesis refer to Figure 9.32). The Trade Object Creation UI then asks Sender Processing to create a Trade object (2). Sender Processing asks the corresponding Trade Object class to create an instance (3). Invoice Processing submits the Trade object reference to Receiver Processing (4). Receiver Processing can then query the Trade object for more information as required (5). Receiver Processing then sends the Trade object for presentation to the Trade Object Presentation UI (6), which then presents the Trade object to the Receiver actor (7).

Then, when, for example, the Invoice Buyer use case is realized, each of the abstract classifiers participating in the generic collaboration can be subtyped by concrete classifiers as illustrated in Figure 9.33.

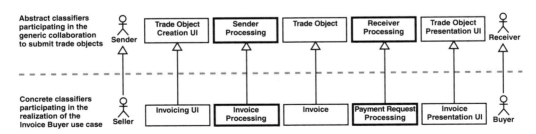

**FIGURE 9.33** Abstract classifiers participating in a generic collaboration are subtyped by concrete classifiers participating in a specific use-case realization.

Given this, the realization of the Invoice Buyer use case need only refer to the generic collaboration, but it need not duplicate or specialize it, provided that the (virtual) operations on the abstract classifiers are realized by methods on the concrete classifiers that subtype them.

---

The same approach can be followed when the Order Goods or Services use case is realized.

Note that using generalizations is not the only way to employ a generic collaboration. For example, patterns, which are parameterized collaborations (e.g., parameterized classes), are also generic and can be employed by associating concrete classes to the parameters.

Most generic mechanisms should be identified and designed during the elaboration phase. By doing this carefully, the architect can often devise a set of mechanisms that will resolve the most complex design issues and make most use cases fairly simple and straightforward to realize during the construction phase. Mechanisms related to acquired software products are natural candidates for the middleware layer. Other mechanisms are likely to find a more natural home in the application-general layer.

### 9.5.2 Activity:  Design a Use Case

The purposes of designing a use-case are to

- Identify the design classes and/or subsystems whose instances are needed to perform the use case's flow of events.
- Distribute the behavior of the use case to interacting design objects and/or to participating subsystems.
- Define requirements on the operations of design classes and/or subsystems and their interfaces.
- Capture implementation requirements for the use case.

#### 9.5.2.1 Identifying the Participating Design Classes    In this step we identify the design classes needed to realize the use case (see Figure 9.34). Do as follows:

- Study the analysis classes that participate in the corresponding use-case realization—analysis. Identify the design classes that trace to those analysis classes, as created by the component engineer during class design or by the architect during architectural design.
- Study the special requirements of the corresponding use-case realization—analysis. Identify the design classes that realize those special requirements. These are found either by the architect during architectural design (i.e., as generic mechanisms) or by the component engineer during class design.
- As a result, the required class should be identified, and some component engineer should be assigned responsibility for it.

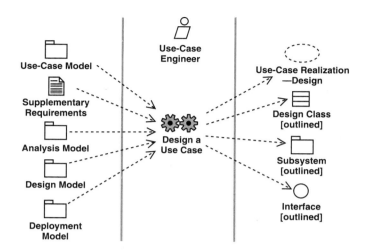

**FIGURE 9.34** The input and result of use-case design. The corresponding use-case realization—analysis in the analysis model is an essential input to this activity.

- If some design class to design the specific use case is still missing, the use-case engineer should communicate this to the architects or the component engineers. The required class should be identified, and a component engineer should be assigned to it.

Collect the design classes participating in a use-case realization in a class diagram associated with the realization. Use this class diagram to show the relationships that are employed in the use-case realization.

| Example | Classes Participating in the Realization of the Pay Invoice Use Case |
| --- | --- |

Figure 9.35 shows a class diagram that depicts the classes that participate in the realization of the Pay Invoice use case and their associations to each other.

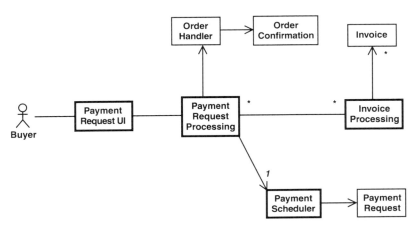

**FIGURE 9.35** The classes participating in the realization of the Pay Invoice use case and their associations. In the diagram, active classes have thicker borders.

Some active classes, like Payment Request Processing and Invoice Processing, keep the Interbank system running. They do this by passing trade objects between the different nodes from an issuer to a recipient, such as invoices from the seller to the buyer.

### 9.5.2.2 Describing Design Object Interactions

When we have an outline of the design classes needed to realize the use case, we need to describe how their corresponding design objects interact. This is done using sequence diagrams containing the participating actor instances, design objects, and message transmissions between them. If the use cases have different and distinct flows or subflows, it is often of value to create one sequence diagram for each flow. This can make the use-case realization clearer, and it also makes it possible to extract sequence diagrams that represent general and reusable interactions.

To initiate this step, study the corresponding use-case realization—analysis. It can be used to get an outline of the sequence of messages required between the design objects, although many new design objects may have been added. In some cases, it may even be worthwhile to transform a collaboration diagram of the use-case realization—analysis to an initial outline of a corresponding sequence diagram.

A sequence diagram is created by starting from the beginning of the flow of the use case, and then going through the flow one step at a time and deciding which design object and actor instance interactions are necessary to realize it. In most cases, the objects naturally find their places in the sequence of interactions in the use-case realization. The following can be noted about such a sequence diagram:

- The use case is invoked by a message from an actor instance to a design object.
- Each design class identified in the preceding step should have at least one design object participating in a sequence diagram.

- Messages are sent between **object lifelines** (Appendix A) to realize the use case. A message may have a temporary name that will become the name of an operation after it has been identified by the component engineer responsible for the receiving object's class.
- The sequence in the diagram should be in primary focus because the use-case realization—design is the primary input when the use case is implemented. It is important to understand the chronological order of message transmissions between objects.
- Use labels and the flow-of-events—design to complement the sequence diagrams.
- The sequence diagram should handle all relationships of the use case that is realized. For example, if a use case A is specializing another use case B via a generalization relationship, the sequence diagram realizing use case A may need to refer to the realization (e.g., to a sequence diagram) of use case B. Note that such references also are likely to occur in the corresponding use-case realizations—analysis.

## Example    Sequence Diagram for the First Part of the Pay Invoice Use Case

Figure 9.36 shows the sequence diagram for the first part of the Pay Invoice use case.

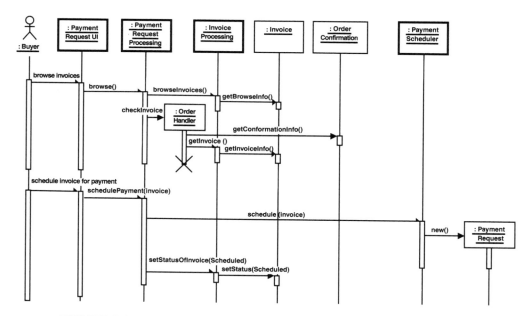

**FIGURE 9.36**  Sequence diagram for the design objects that perform part of the Pay Invoice use-case realization.

The flow-of-events—design description complementing this sequence diagram might look like the following:

> *The buyer uses the system, through the Payment Request UI applet and the Payment Request Processing application, to browse the invoices received. Payment Request Processing uses the Order Handler to check the invoices against their related order confirmations, before the Payment Request UI shows the list of invoices to the buyer.*
>
> *The buyer selects an invoice via the Payment Request UI and schedules it for payment, whereby the Payment Request UI passes this request to Payment Request Processing. Payment Request Processing asks the Payment Scheduler to schedule payment of the invoice. The Payment Scheduler then creates a payment request. The Payment Request Processing application then asks the Invoice Processing application to change the state of the invoice to "Scheduled."*

As we detail the interaction diagrams, we will most likely find new alternative paths that the use case can take. Such paths can be described in the labels of the diagrams or in interaction diagrams of their own. While adding more information, the use-case engineer will often discover new exceptions that were not thought of during requirements capture or analysis. These types of exceptions include:

- Handling time-outs when nodes or connections cease to work.
- Erroneous input that human and machine actors might provide.
- Error messages generated by middleware, system software, or hardware.

### 9.5.2.3 Identifying the Participating Subsystems and Interfaces  So far, we have designed a use case as a collaboration of classes and their objects. Sometimes, however, it is more appropriate to design a use case in terms of participating subsystems and/or their interfaces. For example, during top-down development, it may be necessary to capture the requirements on the subsystems and their interfaces before their internals are designed. Or, in some cases it should be easy to substitute a subsystem and its specific internal design with another subsystem that has another internal design. In such cases, a use-case realization—design can be described at several levels in the subsystem hierarchy (see Figure 9.37).

To start, it is necessary to identify the subsystems needed to realize the use case:

- Study the analysis classes participating in the corresponding use-case realization—analysis. Identify the analysis packages that contain those analysis classes, if there are any. Then, identify the design subsystems that trace to those analysis packages.
- Study the special requirements of the corresponding use-case realization—analysis. Identify the design classes that realize those special requirements, if there are any. Then, identify the design subsystems that contain those classes.

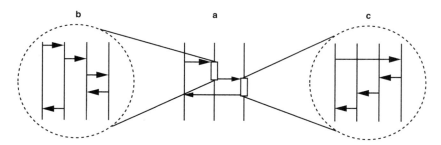

**FIGURE 9.37**  The lifelines in the middle diagram (a) represent subsystems, and show the messages that are received and sent by subsystems. The other diagrams (b,c) represent the internal designs of the subsystems, and show how those messages (in a) are received and sent by the internal elements of the subsystems. Diagram (a) can be designed before (b,c).

Collect the subsystems that participate in a use-case realization in a class diagram that is associated with the realization. Use this class diagram to show the dependencies between those subsystems and any interfaces that are employed in the use-case realization.

---

**Example**   Subsystems and Interfaces Participating in the Realization of the Pay Invoice Use Case

Figure 9.38 shows a class diagram that includes subsystems, interfaces, and their dependencies, involved in the first part of the Pay Invoice use case.

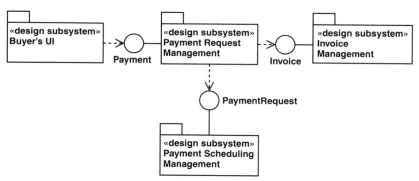

**FIGURE 9.38**  Class diagram with subsystems, interfaces, and their dependencies.

**9.5.2.4 Describing Subsystem Interactions**   When we have an outline of the subsystems needed to realize the use case, we need to describe how their contained classes' objects interact on a subsystem level. This is done by using sequence diagrams that contain the participating actor instances, subsystems, and message transmissions between them. When doing this, we use an approach similar to that described in Section 9.5.2.2, with the following differences:

- The **lifelines** (Appendix A) in the sequence diagrams denote subsystems instead of design objects.
- Each subsystem identified in Section 9.5.2.3 should have at least one lifeline denoting it in a sequence diagram.
- If a message is assigned to an operation of an interface, it may be appropriate to qualify the message with the interface providing the operation. This is needed when a subsystem provides several interfaces, and there is a need to distinguish which interface is used in the message.

*9.5.2.5 Capturing Implementation Requirements*    In this step, we capture on a use-case realization all requirements, such as nonfunctional requirements, that are identified in design but that should be handled in implementation.

| Example | Implementation Requirements on the Pay Invoice Use Case |
| --- | --- |

The following is an example of an implementation requirement posed by the realization of the Pay Invoice use case:

*An object of the (active) class Payment Request Processing should be able to handle 10 different buyer clients without a perceivable delay for any individual buyer.*

### 9.5.3 Activity: Design a Class

The purpose of designing a class is to create a design class that fulfills its role in use-case realizations and the nonfunctional requirements that apply to it (see Figure 9.39). This includes maintaining the design class itself, and the following aspects of it:

- Its operations
- Its attributes
- The relationships it participates in
- Its methods (that realize its operations)
- Its imposed states
- Its dependencies to any generic design mechanisms
- Requirements relevant to its implementation
- The correct realization of any interface that it is required to provide

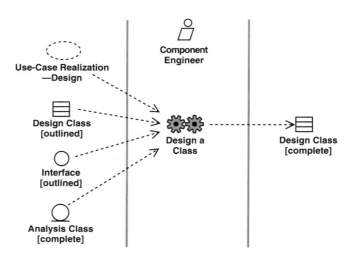

**FIGURE 9.39** The input and result of designing a class.

### 9.5.3.1 *Outlining the Design Class*    As a first step, we need to outline one or several design classes given the input in terms of analysis classes and/or interfaces. When an interface is given as input, it is often simple and straightforward to assign one design class to provide the interface.

When one or several analysis classes are given as input, the method used depends on the stereotype of the analysis class:

- Designing boundary classes is dependent on the specific interface technologies in use. For example, boundary classes designed in Visual Basic would imply design classes stereotyped as «form» together with other design classes representing "controls," possibly ActiveX controls, in the user interface. Also note that in some modern user-interface design tools, the user interface can be visually created directly on screen, thereby making the creation of corresponding design classes implicit. Any existing user-interface prototype is an essential input to this step.
- Designing entity classes that represent persistent information (or classes that have other persistence requirements) often implies using a specific database technology. For example, this can include creating design classes that map to tables in a relational data model. This step can be partially automated by using currently available modeling tools, although it can also be quite delicate and require the adoption of a persistency strategy. There may be many design issues involved in adopting such a strategy, especially when mapping the object-oriented design model to a relational data model. Those issues may in turn require separate workers (e.g., database designers), activities (e.g.,

database design), and models (e.g., data models) in the development process—these cases are beyond the scope of this book.

■ Designing control classes is delicate. Since they encapsulate sequences, coordination of other objects, and sometimes pure business logic, the following need to be considered:

  • Distribution issues. If the sequence needs to be distributed and managed among several different nodes in a network, separate design classes on different nodes might be required to realize the control class.

  • Performance issues. It might not be justifiable to have separate design classes realizing the control class. Instead, the control class could be realized by the same design classes that are realizing some related boundary and/or entity classes.

  • Transaction issues. Control classes often encapsulate transactions. Their corresponding design must then incorporate any existing transaction management technology in use.

The design classes identified in this step should be assigned trace dependencies to the corresponding analysis classes that they design. It is important to keep in mind the "origins" of the design class as it is refined in the following steps.

### 9.5.3.2 *Identifying Operations*

In this step we identify the operations that need to be provided by the design class and describe those operations using the syntax of the programming language. This includes specifying the visibility of each operation (e.g., *public*, *protected*, *private* in C++). Important inputs to this step are

■ The responsibilities of any analysis class that the design class traces to. A responsibility often implies one or several operations. Moreover, if inputs and outputs are described for the responsibilities, they can be used as a first outline of formal parameters and result values of operations.

■ The special requirements of any analysis class that the design class traces to. Recall that those requirements often need to be handled in the design model, possibly by incorporating some generic design mechanism or technology such as a database technology.

■ The interface(s) that the design class needs to provide. The operations of the interface also need to be provided by the design class.

■ The use-case realizations—design in which the class participates (see Section 9.5.2).

The operations of a design class need to support all the roles that the class plays in different use-case realizations. These roles are found by going through the use-case realizations and seeing if the class and its objects are included in the diagrams and the flow-of-events—design descriptions of the realizations.

## Example    Operations of the Invoice Class

The Invoice class participates in several use-case realizations, such as those for Pay Invoice, Send Reminder, and Invoice Buyer. Each of these realizations reads or changes the state of Invoice objects. The Invoice Buyer use case creates and submits Invoices. The Pay Invoice use case schedules Invoices, and so on. Each of these use-case realizations thus uses Invoice objects differently; in other words, the Invoice class and its objects play different roles in these use-case realizations.

First, the component engineers thought of implementing these state changes as one operation called setStatus, which had a parameter that indicated the desired action and the target state (e.g., setStatus(Scheduled)). But then they decided that they preferred to implement explicit operations for each of the state transitions. Moreover, they decided to use this approach not only for the Invoice class but also for the Trade Object class, of which the Invoice class is a subtype (see Figure 9.40). The Trade Object class thus supports the following operations (each of which changes the state of the Trade Object): Create, Submit, Schedule, and Close. However, these operations are only virtual operations that define a signature. The classes that are subtypes of the Trade Object class each have to define a concrete method that realizes those operations.

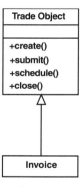

**FIGURE 9.40** The Invoice class, its supertype Trade Object, and the operations it supports.

For some classes the behavior of their objects depends highly on the object state. These classes are best described using statechart diagrams. See Section 9.5.3.7.

***9.5.3.3 Identifying Attributes***    In this step, we identify the attributes required by the design class and describe them using the syntax of the programming language. An attribute specifies a property of a design class and is often implied and required by the operations of the class (as considered in the preceding step). The following general guidelines can be kept in mind when attributes are identified:

- Consider the attributes on any analysis class that the design class traces to. Sometimes these attributes imply the need for one or several attributes of the design class.
- The available attribute types are restricted by the programming language.
- When choosing an attribute type, try to reuse an existing one.
- A single attribute instance cannot be shared by several design objects. If this is required, the attribute needs to be defined as a separate class.
- If a design class becomes too complicated to understand because of its attributes, some of these attributes may be separated out into classes of their own.
- If there are many or complex attributes of a class, you can illustrate this in a separate class diagram that shows only the attribute compartment.

### 9.5.3.4 Identifying Associations and Aggregations

Design objects interact with each other in sequence diagrams. These interactions often require associations between their corresponding classes. The component engineer should thus study the message transmissions in the sequence diagrams to determine which associations are required. Instances of associations might be used to hold references to other objects, and to group objects into aggregations for the purpose of sending messages to them.

The number of relationships between the classes should be minimized. It is not primarily real-world relationships that should be modeled as associations or aggregations, but relationships that must exist in response to demands from the various use-case realizations. Also note that since performance issues need to be handled during design, the modeling of optimal search routes through associations or aggregations might be required.

The following general guidelines can be kept in mind when associations and aggregations are identified and refined:

- Consider the associations or aggregations involving the corresponding analysis class (or classes). Sometimes these relationships (in the analysis model) imply the need for one or several corresponding relationships (in the design model) that involve the design class.
- Refine association multiplicities, role names, association classes, ordered roles, qualified roles, and $n$-ary associations according to the support of the programming language in use. For example, role names may become attributes of the design class when code is generated, thereby restricting the form of role names. Or, an association class may become a new class between the other two (original) classes, thereby requiring new associations with appropriate multiplicity between the "association" class and the other two classes.
- Refine the navigability of associations. Consider the interaction diagrams in which the association is employed. The direction of message transmissions between design objects implies corresponding navigabilities of associations between their classes.

### 9.5.3.5 *Identifying Generalizations*    Generalizations should be used with the same semantics as defined by the programming language. If the programming language does not support generalization (or inheritance), associations and/or aggregations could be used instead to provide delegation (e.g., sending a message requesting work to be done, get the work done, and an acknowledgment message back) from objects of the more specific class to objects of the more generic class.

---

### Example    Generalizations in the Design Model

Both Invoices and Orders change state in a similar way and support similar operations. They are both specializations of a more general Trade object (see Figure 9.41).

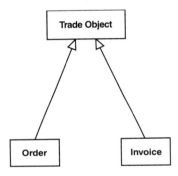

FIGURE 9.41  Trade Object generalizes Invoice and Order. Note that these generalizations also exist in the analysis model between the corresponding analysis classes.

---

### 9.5.3.6 *Describing Methods*    Methods can be used during design to specify how operations are realized. For example, a method can specify an algorithm to be used to realize an operation. The method can be specified using natural language or using pseudocode if appropriate.

However, most of the time methods are not specified during design. Instead, they are created during implementation by using the programming language directly. This is because the same component engineer should design and implement the class, thereby eliminating the need for handing over specifications such as method specifications.

Note that if the design tool supports a smooth code generation from methods on design classes, the methods may be specified directly in the design tool using the programming language, but this is then considered an implementation activity, and it is not dealt with in design. Please refer to Chapter 10 and the discussion of the class implementation activity (Section 10.5.4) for details.

### 9.5.3.7 Describing States
Some design objects are state controlled, meaning that their state determines their behavior when they receive a message. In such cases, it is meaningful to use a statechart diagram to describe the different state transitions of a design object. Such a statechart diagram is then a valuable input to the implementation of the corresponding design class.

---

**Example**    Statechart Diagram for the Invoice Class

Invoice objects change states as they are created, submitted, scheduled, and closed. As for all trade objects, these state changes follow a strict sequence. For example, an invoice may not be scheduled before it has been submitted. This sequence of state changes can be defined using a statechart diagram, see Figure 9.42.

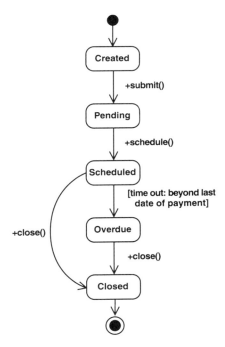

**FIGURE 9.42** A statechart diagram for the Invoice class.

An invoice is created when a seller wants a buyer to pay for an order. Then the invoice is submitted to the buyer, and the state is changed to pending. When the buyer decides to pay, the invoice state is changed to scheduled. Then, if the buyer does not pay in time, the invoice state is changed to overdue. Finally, as the invoice is paid, the state is changed to closed.

---

*9.5.3.8 Handling Special Requirements*   In this step any requirements that have not been considered in the preceding steps are handled. When doing this, study the requirements posed by the use-case realizations in which the class participates. These may state (nonfunctional) requirements for the design class. It is also necessary to study the special requirements on any analysis class that the design class traces to. Those special requirements often need to be handled by the design class.

**Example**   Employing a Design Mechanism to Handle a Special Requirement

Invoice objects need to be accessed from several nodes, both from the Buyer Server and from the Seller Server. Invoice is not an active class, but it has to be designed for a distributed system. In our example, we implement this object distribution by making the Invoice class a subclass of the abstract Java class, java.rmi.UnicastRemoteObject, that supports Remote Message Invocation (RMI), see Figure 9.43. Note that this design mechanism is identified and described by the architect in the architectural design activity.

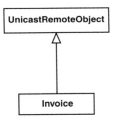

**FIGURE 9.43**  Objects of the Invoice class must be distributed. This is done by making them subtypes of UnicastRemoteObject.

When handling these requirements, use any proposed generic design mechanisms as identified by the architect if possible.

However, it may be appropriate to postpone the handling of some requirements until implementation. Such requirements should then be noted as *implementation requirements* for the design class.

**Example**   Implementation Requirement for an Active Class

The following is an example of an implementation requirement for the Payment Request Processing class.

- An object of the Payment Request Processing class should be able to handle 10 different Buyer clients without a perceivable delay for buyers.

### 9.5.4 Activity:  Design a Subsystem

The purposes of designing a subsystem are to (see Figure 9.44)

- Ensure that the subsystem is as independent as possible of other subsystems and/or their interfaces.
- Ensure that the subsystem provides the right interfaces.
- Ensure that the subsystem fulfills its purpose in that it offers a correct realization of the operations as defined by the interfaces it provides.

#### 9.5.4.1  *Maintaining the Subsystem Dependencies*    Dependencies should be defined and maintained from the subsystem to other subsystems whose contained elements are associated from elements within the subsystem. However, if those other subsystems provide interfaces, (uses) dependencies should be declared toward those interfaces instead. It is better to be dependent on an interface than on a subsystem since a subsystem might be substituted with another subsystem containing another internal design, whereas the interface need not be substituted in that case.

Try to minimize the dependencies to other subsystems and/or interfaces. Consider relocating contained classes that are too dependent on other subsystems of these subsystems.

#### 9.5.4.2  *Maintaining the Interfaces Provided by the Subsystem*    The operations defined by the interfaces provided by a subsystem need to support all the roles that the subsystem plays in different use-case realizations. Even if the interfaces are outlined by the architects, these interfaces may need to be refined by the component

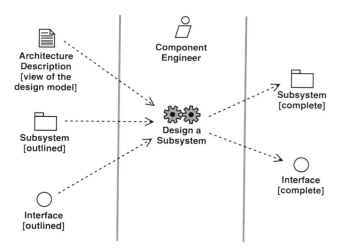

**FIGURE 9.44** The input and result of designing a subsystem.

engineer as the design model evolves and use cases are designed. Recall that a subsystem and its interfaces may be employed within various use-case realizations by the use-case engineers, thereby providing further requirements on the interfaces (see Section 9.5.2.4).

The approach of maintaining interfaces and their operations is similar to the approach of maintaining design classes and their operations as described in Section 9.5.3.2.

### 9.5.4.3 *Maintaining the Subsystem Contents*    A subsystem fulfills its purpose when it offers a correct realization of the operations as defined by the interfaces it provides. Even if the content of the subsystem is outlined by the architects, it may need to be refined by the component engineer as the design model evolves. Some general issues related to this include

- For each interface provided by the subsystem, there should be design classes or other subsystems within the subsystem that also provide the interface.

- To clarify how the internal design of a subsystem realizes any of its interfaces or use cases, collaborations can be created in terms of the elements contained by the subsystem. This can be done to justify the elements contained by the subsystem.

---

**Example**    A Design Class Providing an Interface within a Subsystem

The Buyer's Invoice Management subsystem provides the Invoice interface. The component engineer responsible for the subsystem decides to let the Invoice class realize that interface, see Figure 9.45. An alternative realization would have been to let some other design class realize the interface and then use the Invoice class.

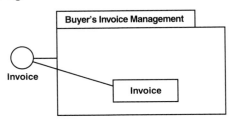

**FIGURE 9.45** The Invoice class provides the Invoice interface that the Buyer's Invoice Management subsystem provides.

---

## 9.6  Summary of Design

The primary result of design is the design model which strives to preserve a structure of the system as imposed by the analysis model, and which works as a blueprint of the implementation. The design model includes the following elements:

- Design subsystems and service subsystems and their dependencies, interfaces, and contents. Design subsystems in the two top layers (i.e., the application-specific and application-general layers) are outlined based on analysis packages (Section 9.5.1.2.1). Some of the design subsystem dependencies are outlined based on corresponding analysis package dependencies (Section 9.5.1.2.3). Some of the interfaces are outlined based on analysis classes (Section 9.5.1.2.4).
- Design classes, including active classes, and their operations, attributes, relationships, and implementation requirements. Some architecturally significant design classes are outlined based on architecturally significant analysis classes (Section 9.5.1.3.1). Some active classes are outlined based on analysis classes (Section 9.5.1.3.2). In general, analysis classes are used as specifications when design classes are outlined (Section 9.5.3.1).
- Use-case realizations—design, which describe how use cases are designed in terms of collaborations within the design model. In general, use-case realizations—analysis are used as specifications when design use-case realizations—design are outlined (Section 9.5.2).
- The architectural view of the design model, including its architecturally significant elements. As pointed out earlier, the architecturally significant elements of the analysis model are used as specifications when architecturally significant elements of the design model are outlined.

Design also results in the deployment model, describing any network configurations on which the system should be distributed. The deployment model includes:

- Nodes, their characteristics, and connections
- An initial mapping of active classes onto nodes
- The architectural view of the deployment model, including its architecturally significant elements

As we will present in the following chapters, the design model and the deployment model are considered as the primary input to subsequent implementation and test activities. More specifically,

- Design subsystems and service subsystems will be implemented by implementation subsystems that contain actual components such as source code files, scripts, binaries, executables, and the like. These implementation subsystems will be traced one-to-one (isomorphically) to the design subsystems.

- Design classes will be implemented by file components that contain the source code. It is common that several design classes are implemented in one single file component, although this depends on the programming language in use. Also, active design classes denoting heavyweight processes will be used as an input when executable components are to be found.
- Use-case realizations—design will be used when the implementation effort is planned and done in small and manageable steps, resulting in "builds." Each build will primarily implement a set of use-case realizations or parts of them.
- The deployment model and the network configurations will be used when the system is distributed by deploying executable components onto nodes.

## 9.7 References

[1]  Erich Gamma, Richard Helm, Ralph Johnson, and John Vlissides, *Design Patterns: Elements of Reusable Object-Oriented Software*, Reading, MA: Addison-Wesley, 1994.

[2]  Ivar Jacobson, Stefan Bylund, Patrik Jonsson, Staffan Ehnebom, "Using contracts and use cases to build plugable architectures," *Journal of Object-Oriented Programming,* June, 1995.

[3]  Ivar Jacobson, Martin Griss, and Patrik Jonsson, *Software Reuse: Architecture, Process and Organization for Business Success*, Reading, MA: Addison-Wesley, 1997.

# Chapter 10

---

# Implementation

## 10.1 Introduction

In implementation, we start with the result from design and implement the system in terms of components, that is, source code, scripts, binaries, executables, and the like.

Fortunately, most of the system's architecture is captured during design. The primary purpose of implementation is to flesh out the architecture and the system as a whole. More specifically, the purposes of implementation are to

- Plan the system integrations required in each iteration. Our approach to this is incremental, which results in a system that is implemented as a succession of small and manageable steps.
- Distribute the system by mapping executable components onto nodes in the deployment model. This is primarily based on active classes found during design.
- Implement the design classes and subsystems found during design. In particular, design classes are implemented as file components that contain source code.
- Unit test the components, and then integrate them by compiling them and linking them together into one or more executables, before they are sent to integration and system tests.

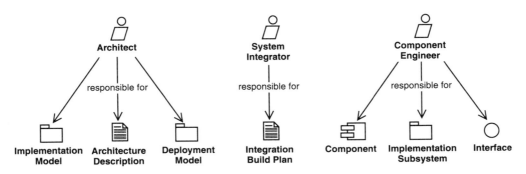

**FIGURE 10.1**  The workers and artifacts involved in implementation.

In this and the following chapters we will present how implementation is carried out and which workers and artifacts are involved (see Figure 10.1). We approach the workflow much as we did the design workflow.

## 10.2  The Role of Implementation in the Software Life Cycle

Implementation is the focus during the construction iterations. Implementation is also done during elaboration to create the executable architectural baseline and during transition to handle late defects such as those found when beta releasing the system (as indicated in Figure 10.2 by a peak in the transition column).

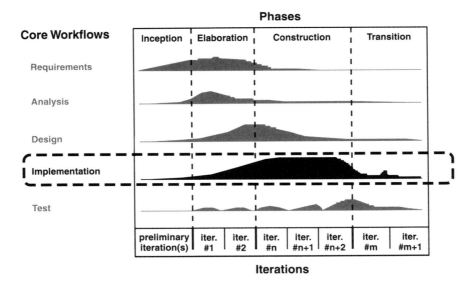

**FIGURE 10.2**  The focus of implementation.

Since the implementation model denotes the actual implementation of the system in terms of components and implementation subsystems, it is natural to maintain the implementation model through the complete software life cycle.

## 10.3 Artifacts

### 10.3.1 Artifact: Implementation Model

The implementation model describes how elements in the design model, such as design classes, are implemented in terms of components such as source code files, executables, and so on. The implementation model also describes how the components are organized according to the structuring and modularization mechanisms available in the implementation environment and the programming language(s) in use, and how the components depend on each other.

The implementation model defines a hierarchy as illustrated in Figure 10.3.

The implementation model is represented by an implementation system that denotes the top-level subsystem of the model. Using other subsystems is then a way of organizing the implementation model into more manageable pieces.

The artifacts in the implementation model are described in detail in the following sections.

### 10.3.2 Artifact: Component

A component is the physical packaging of model elements, such as design classes in the design model [5]. Some standard stereotypes of components include the following:

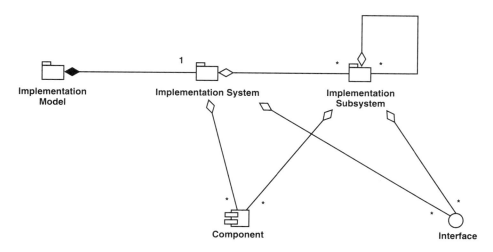

**FIGURE 10.3** The implementation model is a hierarchy of implementation subsystems containing components and interfaces.

- «executable» is a program that may be run on a node.
- «file» is a file containing source code or data.
- «library» is a static or dynamic library.
- «table» is a database table.
- «document» is a document.

When creating components in a particular implementation environment, these stereotypes may be modified to reflect what the components actually stand for. Components have the following characteristics:

- Components have trace relationships to the model elements they implement.
- It is common for a component to implement several elements, such as design classes; however, exactly how this trace is created depends on how source code files are to be structured and modularized, given the programming language in use.

## Example    A Component Tracing to a Design Class

In the Interbank system, the design class Account Transfers is implemented in the AccountTransfers.java source code component. This is because it is a convention and common use of Java to create one ".java" source code file for each class, although this is not enforced. Anyway, this is modeled by a trace dependency between the design and the implementation model (see Figure 10.4).

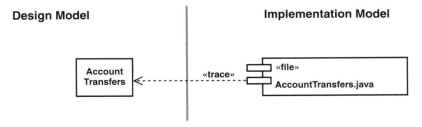

**FIGURE 10.4**  Trace dependencies between components and design classes.

- Components provide the same interfaces as the model elements they implement.

## Example    Interfaces in Design and Implementation

In the Interbank system, the Account Transfers design class provides a Transfers interface. This interface is also provided by the AccountTransfers.java component, which implements the Account Transfers class (see Figure 10.5).

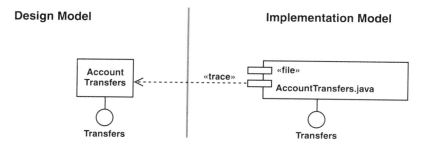

**FIGURE 10.5** Components provide the same interfaces as the classes they implement.

- There can be compilation dependencies between components, denoting which components are required to compile a specific component.

---

**Example**   Compilation Dependencies between Components

---

In the Interbank system, the AccountTransfers.java (file) component compiles into an AccountTransfers.class (executable)[1] component (see Figure 10.6).

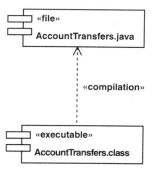

**FIGURE 10.6** Compilation dependencies between two components.

---

*10.3.2.1 Stubs*   A stub is a component with a skeletal or special-purpose implementation that can be used to develop or test another component depending on the stub; a similar definition is given in [1]. Stubs can be used to minimize the number of new components required in each new (intermediate) version of the system, thereby simplifying integration problems and integration tests (see Section 10.5.2, "Integrate System").

---

1. To be more specific, the component is actually *interpretable* in the Java virtual machine.

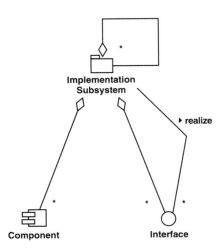

**FIGURE 10.7** Subsystem contents and key associations.

### 10.3.3 Artifact:  Implementation Subsystem

Implementation subsystems provide a means of organizing the artifacts of the implementation model into more manageable pieces (see Figure 10.7). A subsystem can consist of components, interfaces, and other subsystems (recursively). Moreover, a subsystem can realize—and thus provide—interfaces that represent the functionality they export in terms of operations.

It is important to understand that an implementation subsystem is manifested by an actual "packaging mechanism" in the implementation environment, such as

- A *package* in Java [2].
- A *project* in Visual Basic [3].
- A *directory* of files in a C++ project.
- A *subsystem* in an integrated development environment such as Rational Apex.
- A *component view package* in a visual modeling tool such as Rational Rose.

Thus the notion of an *implementation subsystem* will get slightly refined semantics when manifested in a specific implementation environment. However, in this chapter we discuss implementation on a generic level, applicable to most implementation environments.

Implementation subsystems are very strongly related to design subsystems in the design model (see Chapter 9, Section 9.3.4, "Design a Subsystem"). In fact, an implementation subsystem should be traced one-to-one (isomorphic) to a corresponding design subsystem. Recall that a design subsystem already defines:

- Dependencies on other subsystems and/or interfaces of other subsystems.
- What interfaces are to be provided by the subsystem.

■ Which design classes or, recursively, other design subsystems within the sub-system should provide the interfaces provided by the subsystem itself.

These aspects are important to the corresponding implementation subsystem for the following reasons:

■ The implementation subsystem should define analog dependencies toward other (corresponding) implementation subsystems and/or interfaces.
■ The implementation subsystem should provide the same interfaces.
■ The implementation subsystem should define which components or, recursively, other implementation subsystems within the subsystem should provide the interfaces that are provided by the subsystem itself. Moreover, these contained components (or implementation subsystems) should trace to the corresponding classes (or design subsystems) that they implement from the design subsystem.

Figure 10.8 clarifies the relationship between the design and implementation models.

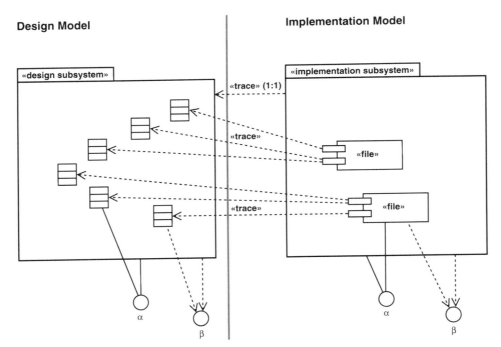

**FIGURE 10.8**  An implementation subsystem in the implementation model tracing one-to-one to a design subsystem in the design model. The subsystems in the different models provide the same interface (α) and is dependent on the same inter-face (β). Components in the implementation subsystem implement classes in the design subsystem.

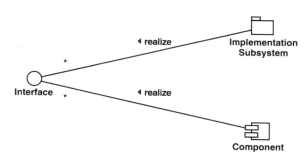

**FIGURE 10.9** The key associations of an interface.

Any changes to the way the subsystems provide and use interfaces, or changes to the interfaces themselves, are described in the design workflow (please refer to Chapter 9, Section 9.5.4, "Design a Subsystem"). Consequently, those changes are not dealt with in the implementation workflow, although they also affect the implementation model.

Note that the mapping just described also holds for service subsystems in the design model. As a result, implementation subsystems that trace to service subsystems will reside at a lower level in the implementation model hierarchy and fulfill the same purpose as service subsystems, namely, to structure the system according to the services it provides. Because of this, implementation subsystems that trace to service subsystems in the design model are likely to encapsulate executable components that provide the various services of the system.

### 10.3.4 Artifact: Interface

Interfaces are described in detail in Chapter 9. However, the same interfaces can be used within the implementation model to specify the operations implemented by components and implementation subsystems. Moreover, as noted earlier, components and implementation subsystems can have "uses dependencies" on interfaces (Figure 10.9).

A component that realizes (and thus provides) an interface must implement all operations defined by the interface in a correct manner. An implementation subsystem that provides an interface must also contain components that provide the interface or other subsystems (recursively) that provide the interface.

**Example**    An Implementation Subsystem Providing an Interface

The Interbank system has an implementation subsystem called AccountManagement (a Java package), which provides the Transfers interface (see Figure 10.10).

**FIGURE 10.10** The AccountManagement subsystem provides the Transfers interface.

The Java code for the Transfers interface is given in Figure 10.11.

### 10.3.5 Artifact: Architecture Description (View of the Implementation Model)

The architecture description contains an **architectural view of the implementation model** (Appendix C), depicting its architecturally significant artifacts (see Figure 10.12).

The following artifacts in the implementation model are usually considered architecturally significant:

- The decomposition of the implementation model into subsystems, their interfaces, and the dependencies between them. Generally speaking, this decomposition is very significant for the architecture. However, because implementation subsystems trace to design subsystems one-to-one and design subsystems are likely to be depicted in the architectural view of the design model, it is usually unnecessary to depict the implementation subsystems in the architectural view of the implementation model.
- Key components, such as components that trace to architecturally significant design classes, executable components, and components that are general, central, implement generic design mechanisms that many other components depend upon.

```
package AccountManagement;

// provided interfaces:

public interface Transfers {

        public Account create(Customer owner, Money balance,

                                        AccountNumber account_id);

        public void Deposit (Money amount, String reason);

        public void Withdraw (Money amount, String reason);

}
```

**FIGURE 10.11** The Java code for the Transfers interface provided by the AccountManagement subsystem.

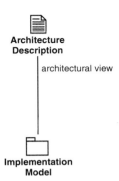

**FIGURE 10.12** The architectural view of the implementation model.

In Section 10.5.1.1, "Identifying Architecturally Significant Components," we provide examples of what might be included in the architectural view of the implementation model.

### 10.3.6 Artifact:  Integration Build Plan

It is important that the software is built incrementally in manageable steps so that each step yields small integration or test problems. The result of each step is called a "build," which is an executable version of the system, usually a specific part of the system. Each build is then subject to integration tests (as described in Chapter 11), before any subsequent build is created. To prepare for a failing build (e.g., if it does not pass the integration tests) each build is put under version control so that it is possible to roll back to an earlier build. The benefits of this incremental approach are that

- An executable version of the system can be created early on, instead of having to wait for a more complete version. The integration tests start early, and the executable version can be used to demonstrate system features to internal project members as well as external stakeholders.
- Defects are easier to locate during integration tests because only a small and manageable part of the system is added to or refined in an existing build. Even better, defects are probably (but not always) related to the new or refined part.
- Integration tests tend to be more thorough than systemwide tests because they can focus on smaller, more manageable parts.

**Incremental integration** (Appendix C) is to system integration as controlled iterative development is to software development in general. Both focus on a fairly small and manageable increment of functionality.

Putting this in an iterative development context, each iteration will result in at least one build. However, the functionality to be implemented in a specific iteration is often too complex to be integrated in a single build. Instead, a sequence of builds may be created within the iteration, each representing a manageable step forward by adding a small increment to the system. Each iteration will result in a larger increment added to the system, possibly accumulated over several builds (see Chapter 5).

An *integration build plan* describes the sequence of builds required in an iteration. More specifically, such a plan describes the following for each build:

- The functionality that is expected to be implemented in the build. This is a listing of use cases and/or scenarios or parts of them, as discussed in earlier chapters. This listing can also refer to other supplemental requirements.
- Which parts of the implementation model are affected by the build. This is a listing of the subsystems and components required to implement the functionality expected by the build.

In Section 10.5.2, "Integrate System," we describe a systematic approach to creating an integration build plan.

## 10.4 Workers

### 10.4.1 Worker: Architect

During the implementation phase, the architect is responsible for the integrity of the implementation model and ensures that the model as a whole is correct, consistent, and readable. As for analysis and design, for large and complex systems a separate worker may be introduced to take over the responsibilities of the top-level subsystem (i.e., the implementation system) of the implementation model.

The model is correct when it implements the functionality described in the design model and in any (relevant) supplementary requirements—and only this functionality.

The architect is also responsible for the architecture of the implementation model, that is, for the existence of its architecturally significant parts as depicted in the architectural views of the model. Recall that this view is part of the architecture description for the system. See Figure 10.13.

Finally, an important result of implementation is the mapping of executable components onto nodes. The architect is responsible for this mapping, which is depicted in the architectural view of the deployment model. Please refer to Chapter 9, Section 9.3.7, "Deployment Model," for details.

Note that the architect is not responsible for the ongoing development and maintenance of the various artifacts within the implementation model; instead, these are the responsibility of the corresponding component engineer.

### 10.4.2 Worker: Component Engineer

The component engineer defines and maintains the source code of one or several file components, making sure that each component implements the correct functionality (e.g., as specified by design classes).

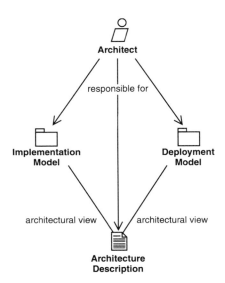

**FIGURE 10.13**  The responsibilities of the architect in implementation.

The component engineer often also maintains the integrity of one or several implementation subsystems. Because implementation subsystems trace one-to-one to design subsystems, most of the changes to these subsystems are handled during design. However, the component engineer needs to make sure that the contents (e.g., components) of the implementation subsystems are correct, that their dependencies to other subsystems and/or interfaces are correct, and that they correctly implement the interfaces they provide. See Figure 10.14.

It is often appropriate for the component engineer who is responsible for a subsystem to be responsible for its contained model elements (e.g., components) as well. Moreover, to achieve a smooth and seamless development, it is natural that a

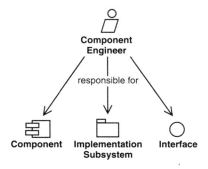

**FIGURE 10.14**  The responsibilities of a component engineer in implementation.

**FIGURE 10.15** The responsibilities of a system integrator.

component engineer carries the responsibility for a subsystem and its contents through the design and implementation workflows. A component engineer should thus both design and implement the classes under his or her responsibility.

### 10.4.3 Worker: System Integrator

Integrating the system is beyond the scope of each individual component engineer. Instead, this responsibility lies with the system integrator. This includes planning the sequence of builds required in each iteration and integrating each build when its parts have been implemented. The planning results in an integration build plan. See Figure 10.15.

## 10.5 Workflow

In the preceding sections we described the implementation work in static terms. Now we will use an activity diagram to reason about its dynamic behavior (see Figure 10.16).

The main goal of implementation is to implement the system. This is initiated by the architect[2] by outlining the key components in the implementation model. Then, the system integrator plans the system integrations required by the current iteration as a sequence of builds. For each build, the system integrator describes the functionality that should be implemented and which parts of the implementation model (i.e., subsystems and components) will be affected. The requirements made on the subsystems and components in the build are then implemented by component engineers. The resulting components are unit tested and passed to the system integrator for integration. The system integrator then integrates the new components into a build and passes it to integration testers for integration tests (refer to Chapter 11). Then the developers initiate the implementation of the subsequent build, taking into consideration the defects of the previous build.

---

2. That is, by a number of individuals acting together as the architect worker, possibly on an architecture team.

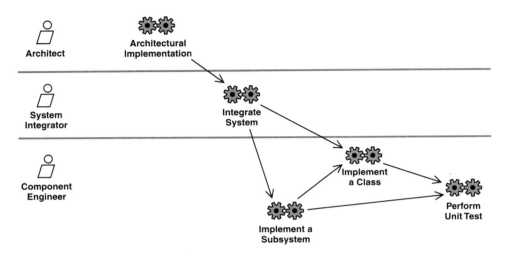

**FIGURE 10.16** The workflow in implementation, including the participating workers and their activities.

### 10.5.1 Activity: Architectural Implementation

The purpose of architectural implementation is to outline the implementation model and its architecture by

- Identifying architecturally significant components, such as executable components.
- Mapping components to nodes in the relevant network configurations.

Recall that during architectural design (see Chapter 9, Section 9.5.1, "Architectural Design"), the design subsystems, their contents, and interfaces are outlined. During implementation we use implementation subsystems that trace one-to-one to these design subsystems and provide the same interfaces. Identifying the implementation subsystems and their interfaces is thus more or less trivial and not dealt with here. Instead, the major challenge during implementation is to create within the implementation subsystems components that implement the corresponding design subsystems.

During this activity, the architect maintains, refines, and updates the architecture description and its architectural views of the implementation and deployment models.

#### 10.5.1.1 Identifying Architecturally Significant Components    It is often practical to identify architecturally significant components early in the software's life cycle, to initiate the implementation work (see Figure 10.17). However, many com-

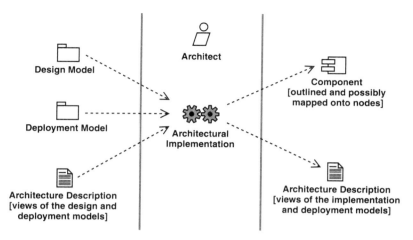

**FIGURE 10.17** The input and result of architectural implementation.

ponents, especially file components, are fairly trivial to create initially when classes are implemented because basically these components just provide a means for packaging the implementation of the classes into source code files. For this reason, developers should be careful not to identify too many components at this stage or delve into too many details. Otherwise, much of the work will have to be done over when the classes are implemented. An initial outline of the architecturally significant components would suffice (see Section 10.3.4, "Architecture Description (View of the Implementation Model)").

**10.5.1.1.1 Identifying Executable Components and Mapping Them onto Nodes** To identify the executable components that can be deployed onto nodes, we consider the active classes found during design and assign one executable component per active class, denoting a heavyweight process. This might also include identifying other file and/or binary components that are required to create the executable components, although this is of secondary importance.

**Example**    Identifying Executable Components

In the design model, there is an active class called Payment Request Processing. In the implementation, we identify a corresponding executable component called PaymentRequestProcessing (see Figure 10.18).

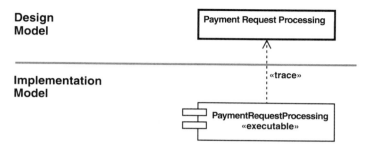

**FIGURE 10.18** Active classes are used to identify executable components.

Continuing to consider the design and deployment model, we can examine if there are any active objects allocated to nodes. If this is the case, the components tracing to the corresponding active classes should be deployed onto the same nodes.

---

**Example**    Deploying Components onto Nodes

An active object of the Payment Request Processing class is allocated to the Buyer server node.

Since the PaymentRequestProcessing component implements the Payment request processing class (see the preceding example), it should also be deployed onto the Buyer server node (see Figure 10.19).

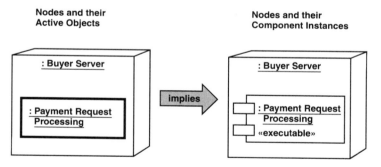

**FIGURE 10.19** Active objects allocated to nodes imply a corresponding deployment of components.

---

The mapping of components onto nodes is very significant to the architecture of the system and should be depicted in the architectural view of the deployment model.

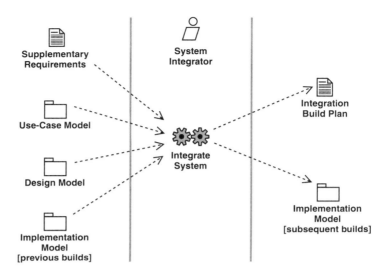

**FIGURE 10.20** The input and result of system integration. The use-case realizations—design in the design model is an essential input to this activity.

### 10.5.2 Activity: Integrate System

The purposes of system integration are to

- Create an integration build plan describing the builds required in an iteration and the requirements on each build. (See Figure 10.20).
- Integrate each build before it is subject to integration tests.

***10.5.2.1 Planning a Subsequent Build***    In this section, we discuss how to plan the contents of a subsequent build, whether we have a previous build to start from or we start from scratch. We also assume that we are given a number of use cases and/or scenarios (i.e., paths through use cases) and other requirements that are to be implemented in the current iteration.

Some criteria for a subsequent build include:

- The build should add functionality to the previous build by implementing complete use cases and/or scenarios of them. (For simplicity, in the rest of this list we will let *use case* stand for *use case and/or scenario.*) The integration tests of the build will be based on these use cases, and it is easier to test complete use cases than fragments of them (see Chapter 11).
- The build should not include too many new or refined components. Otherwise, it may be very hard to integrate the build and perform integration testing. If

necessary, some components can be implemented as stubs to minimize the number of new components introduced in the build (see Section 10.3.2.1, "Stubs").

■ The build should be based on the previous build, and it should expand upwards and to the sides in the layered subsystem hierarchy. This means that the initial builds should start in the lower layers (e.g., the middleware and system-software layers). Subsequent builds then expand upwards to the application-general and application-specific layers. The rationale behind this is simply that it is hard to implement components in the upper layers before the required components in the lower layers are in place and functioning properly.

Keeping these criteria in mind, one can start to evaluate the requirements, such as the use cases (and/or scenarios of them), that are to be implemented. Note that a compromise will probably be needed to fulfill the criteria in an appropriate manner. For example, implementing a complete use case (bullet one) may require many new components (bullet two), but it may be done anyway if the use case is important to implement in the current build. In any case, it is crucial to identify the right requirements to be implemented in a build and to leave the rest of the requirements for future builds. For each potential use case to be implemented, do the following:

1. Consider the design of the use case by identifying its corresponding use-case realization—design in the design model. Recall that the use-case realization—design can be traced to the use case (and thereby implicitly to any of its scenarios) via trace dependencies.
2. Identify the design subsystems and classes that participate in the use-case realization—design.
3. Identify the implementation subsystems and components in the implementation model tracing to those design subsystems and classes as found in Step 2. These are the implementation subsystems and components that are required to implement the use case.
4. Consider the impact that implementing the requirements made on these implementation subsystems and on the components on top of the current build. Note that these requirements are specified in terms of design subsystems and classes, as noted in Step 3. Evaluate whether this impact is acceptable according to the criteria described earlier. If so, plan to implement the use case in the subsequent build. Otherwise, leave it for a future build.

The results should be captured in the integration build plan and communicated to the component engineers responsible for the affected implementation subsystems and components. The component engineers can then begin implementing the requirements of the implementation subsystems and components in the current build (as described in Sections 10.5.3, "Implement a Subsystem," and 10.5.4, "Implement a Class"), and unit test them (as described in Section 10.5.5, "Perform Unit Test").

Then, the implementation subsystems and components are passed to the system integrator for integration (see Section 10.5.2.2, "Integrating a Build").

**10.5.2.2 Integrating a Build**   If the build has been carefully planned as described in the preceding step, it should be fairly straightforward to integrate the build. This is done by collecting the right versions of the implementation subsystems and components, compiling them, and linking them into a build. Note that compilation may need to be done bottom up in the layered hierarchy since there may be compilation dependencies from upper layers to lower layers.

The resulting build is then made subject to integration tests and to system tests if it passed the integration tests and is the last build created within an iteration (see Chapter 11).

### 10.5.3 Activity:  Implement a Subsystem

The purpose of implementing a subsystem is to ensure that a subsystem fulfills its role in each build, as stated in the integration build plan. This means ensuring that the requirements (e.g., scenarios and/or use cases) be implemented in the build and those that affect the subsystem are correctly implemented by components or other subsystems (recursively) within the subsystem (see Figure 10.21).

**10.5.3.1 Maintaining the Subsystem Contents**   A subsystem fulfills its purpose when the requirements to be implemented in the current build and those that affect the subsystem are correctly implemented by components within the subsystem.

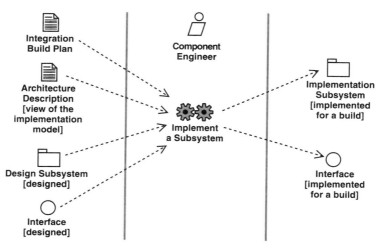

**FIGURE 10.21** The input and result of subsystem implementation.

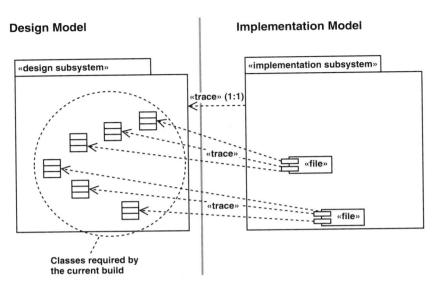

**FIGURE 10.22** The design classes required in a build are implemented by components.

Even if the subsystem contents (e.g., its contained components) are outlined by the architects, it may need to be refined by the component engineer as the implementation model evolves. Aspects of this refinement include the following:

■ Each class in the corresponding design subsystem that is required in the current build should be implemented by components in the implementation subsystem (see Figure 10.22).

Note that if the design subsystem contains other design subsystems (recursively) required by the current build, the method is analogous: Each such contained design subsystem should be implemented by a corresponding implementation subsystem that is contained by the implementation subsystem under consideration.

■ Each interface provided by the corresponding design subsystem that is required in the current build should also be provided by the implementation subsystem. Consequently, the implementation subsystem must contain either a component or an implementation subsystem (recursively) that provides the interface (see Figure 10.23).

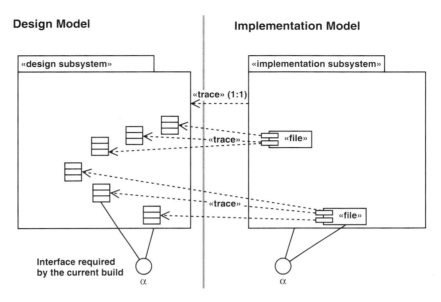

**FIGURE 10.23** An interface required in a build (α) should also be provided by an implementation subsystem.

## Example    A Subsystem Providing an Interface

The subsystem Buyer's Invoice Management needs to provide the Invoice interface in the current build. The component engineer responsible for the subsystem then decides to let the Invoice Processing component realize that interface (see Figure 10.24).

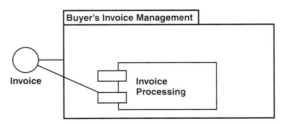

**FIGURE 10.24** The Invoice Processing component provides the Invoice interface.

Given this, the component engineers can start to implement what is required by the components within the subsystem (as described in Section 10.5.4, "Implement a Class") and unit test them (as described in Section 10.5.5, "Perform Unit Test").

The resulting subsystem is then passed to the system integrator for integration (as described in Section 10.5.2, "Integrate System").

### 10.5.4 Activity:  Implement a Class

The purpose of implementing a class is to implement a design class in a file component. This includes the following (see Figure 10.25):

- Outlining a file component that will contain the source code.
- Generating source code from the design class and the relationships in which it participates.
- Implementing the operations of the design class in terms of methods.
- Ensuring that the component provide the same interfaces as the design class.

Although not described here, this activity also includes handling various maintenance aspects of the implemented class, such as fixing defects when the class has been tested.

***10.5.4.1 Outlining the File Components***    The source code that implements a design class resides in a file component. Thus we must outline the file component and consider its scope. It is common to implement several design classes in a single file component. Recall, however, that the file-modularization approach and the conventions of the programming language in use will restrict how the file components are outlined (see Section 10.3.2, "Component"). For example, when using Java, we create a '.java' file component for each class implementation. In general, the chosen file components should support the compilation, installation, and maintenance of the system.

***10.5.4.2 Generating Code from a Design Class***    During design, many of the details regarding the design class and its relationships are described using the syntax

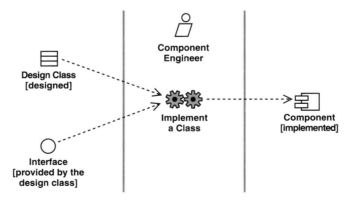

**FIGURE 10.25** The input and result of implementing a class.

of the programming language, which makes generating parts of the source code that implements the class straightforward. In particular, this holds for the operations and attributes of the class, as well as the relationships in which the class participates. However, only the signatures of operations are generated; the operations themselves must still be implemented (see Section 10.5.4.3, "Implementing Operations").

Note also that it can be quite delicate to generate code from associations and aggregations, and how this is done depends very much on the programming language in use. For example, it is common for an association that is navigable in one way to be implemented by a "reference" between objects; this reference would be represented as an attribute on the referring object, and the name of the attribute would be the role name of the opposite association end. The multiplicity of the opposite association end would, in turn, indicate whether the attribute type (of the reference) should be a simple pointer (if the multiplicity is less than or equal to one) or be a collection of pointers (if the multiplicity is greater than one) [6].

### 10.5.4.3 *Implementing Operations*    Every operation defined by the design class must be implemented, unless it is "virtual" (or "abstract") and implemented by descendants (such as subtypes) of the class. We use the term *methods* to denote the implementation of operations [5]. Examples of methods in real life file components are *methods* in Java [2], *methods* in Visual Basic [3], and *member functions* in C++ [4].

Implementing an operation involves choosing a suitable algorithm and supporting data structures (such as local variables of the method), and then coding the actions required by the algorithm. Recall that the method may have been specified using natural language or by using pseudocode during design of the design class (although this is rare and often a waste of time; see Section 9.5.3.6); however, any "design method" should of course be used as input for this step. Note also that any states described for the design class can impact the way operations are implemented since its state determines its behavior when it receives a message.

### 10.5.4.4 *Making the Component Provide the Right Interfaces*    The resulting component should provide the same interfaces as the design class(es) it implements. See Section 10.3.2, "Component" for an example.

## 10.5.5 Activity:  Perform Unit Test

The purpose of performing a unit test is to test the implemented components as individual units (see Figure 10.26). The following types of unit testing are done:

- *Specification testing*, or "black-box testing," verifies the unit's externally observable behavior.
- *Structure testing*, or "white-box testing," verifies the unit's internal implementation.

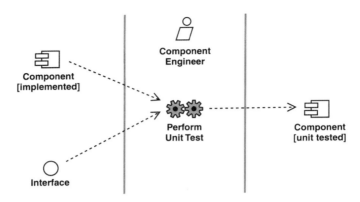

**FIGURE 10.26** The input and result of testing a unit.

Note that there may also be other tests to perform for some units, such as tests of performance, memory usage, load, and capacity. Also, integration and system tests must be done to ensure that several components behave correctly when integrated (see Chapter 11).

**10.5.5.1 Performing Specification Tests**    Specification testing is done to verify the component's behavior without considering *how* that behavior is implemented within the component. The specification tests thus look at what output the component will return when given certain input and when starting in a particular state. The range of combinations of possible inputs, starting states, and outputs is often considerable, which makes it impractical to test all individual combinations. Instead, the ranges of inputs, outputs, and states are divided into *equivalence classes*. An equivalence class is a set of input, state, or output values for which an object is supposed to behave similarly. By testing a component for each combination of the equivalence classes of inputs, outputs, and starting states, it is possible to achieve almost the same "effective" test coverage as when testing all individual value combinations, but at a dramatically reduced effort.

---

**Example    Equivalence Classes**

The state of an account has three equivalence classes: *empty*, *negative balance* (perhaps overdrawn), and *positive balance*. Similarly, the input arguments can be divided into two equivalence classes: *zero* and *positive numbers*. Finally, the output arguments fall into two equivalence classes: *positive amount withdrawn* and *nothing withdrawn*.

The component engineer should choose values for the tests based on heuristics:

- Normal values in the allowed range for each equivalence class, such as withdrawing 4, 3.14, or 5,923, from an account.
- Values that are on the boundary of the equivalence classes, such as withdrawing 0, the smallest possible positive number (e.g., 0.00000001) and the largest possible number.
- Values outside the eligible equivalence classes, such as withdrawing a value greater or smaller than the possible range.
- Illegal values, such as withdrawing −14, and *A*.

When choosing the tests, the component engineer should try to cover all the combinations of input, state, and output equivalence classes, such as withdrawing $14 from

- An account with $−234.13, resulting in nothing being withdrawn.
- An account with $0, resulting in nothing being withdrawn.
- An account with $13.125, resulting in nothing being withdrawn.
- An account with $15, resulting in $14 being withdrawn.

The net result of these four test cases is that all eligible combinations of equivalence classes for state (*positive balance* and *negative balance*) and output (*positive amount withdrawn* and *nothing withdrawn*) are tested for one value in one equivalence class. The component engineer should then choose to test cases with similar state (perhaps $−234.13, 0, 3, and 15) and output values ($0 and 14), but with another value from the same input equivalence class, such as 3.14.

Then the component engineer prepares similar ranges of test cases for other equivalence classes of input values, such as trying to withdraw $0, 4, 3.14, 5,923, 0.00000001, 37,000,000,000,000,000,000,000 (if that is the largest possible number), 37,000,000,000,000,000,000,001, −14, and *A*.

### 10.5.5.2 Performing Structure Tests

Structure testing is done to verify that a component works internally as intended. During structure testing, the component engineer should be sure to test all code. This means that every statement has to be executed at least once. The component engineer should also be sure to test the most interesting paths through the code. These paths include those most commonly followed, the most critical paths, the least-known paths through the algorithms, and other paths that are associated with high risks.

**Example    Java Source Code for a Method**

Figure 10.27 shows a (simplified) implementation of the *withdraw* method defined by the Account class:

```
public class Account {
1       // In this example the Account has a balance only
2       private Money balance = new Money (0);
3       public Money withdraw(Money amount) {
4                   // First we must ensure that the balance is at least
5                   // as big as the amount to withdraw
6                   if balance >= amount
7                   // Then we check that we will not withdraw negative amount
8                       then { if amount >= 0
9                               then {
10                                  try {
11                                          balance = balance – amount;
12                                          return amount
13                                      }
14                                  catch (Exception exc) {
15                                      // Deal with failures reducing the balance
16                                      // ... to be defined ...
17                                  }
18                              }
19                          else {return 0}
20                      }
21                  else {return 0}
22      }
    }
```

**FIGURE 10.27** The Java source code for a simple withdraw method defined by the Account class.

When we test this code, we must ensure that all if-statements evaluate to both true and false, and that all code is executed. For example, we may test the following:

- Withdrawing $50 from an Account with a balance of $100, where the system will execute rows 10–13.
- Withdrawing $–50 from an Account with a balance of $10, where the system will execute row 21.
- Withdrawing $50 from an Account with a balance of $10, where the system will execute row 19.
- Triggering an exception when the system executes the statement *balance = balance – amount,* where the system will execute rows14–17.

## 10.6 Summary of Implementation

The primary result of implementation is the implementation model, which includes the following elements:

- Implementation subsystems and their dependencies, interfaces, and contents.
- Components, including file and executable components, and their dependencies on each other. The components are unit tested.
- The architectural view of the implementation model, including its architecturally significant elements.

Implementation also results in a refinement of the architectural view of the deployment model, when executable components are mapped onto nodes.

As we will present in the next chapter, the implementation model is considered as the primary input to subsequent testing activities. More specifically, each particular build released from implementation is integration tested, and possibly also system tested, during testing.

## 10.7 References

[1]  IEEE, Std 610.12-1990.

[2]  Ken Arnold and James Gosling, *The Java™ Programming Language*, Reading, MA: Addison-Wesley, 1996.

[3]  Anthony T. Mann, *Visual Basic5—Developer's Guide,* Indianapolis, IN: SAMS Publishing, 1997.

[4]  Bjarne Stroustrup, *The C++ Programming Language*, Third Edition, Reading, MA: Addison-Wesley, 1997.

[5]  The Unified Modeling Language for Object-Oriented Development, Documentation set, ver. 1.1, Rational Software Corp., September 1997.

[6]  James Rumbaugh, M. Blaha, W. Premerlani, F. Eddy, and W. Lorensen, *Object-Oriented Modeling and Design.* Englewood Cliffs, NJ: Prentice Hall, 1991.

# *Chapter 11*

# Test

## 11.1 Introduction

In the test workflow, we verify the result from implementation by testing each build, including both internal and intermediate builds, as well as final versions of the system to be released to external parties. A good, general overview of testing is provided in [2]. More specifically, the purposes of testing are to

- Plan the tests required in each iteration, including integration tests and system tests. Integration tests are required for every build within the iteration, whereas system tests are required only at the end of the iteration.
- Design and implement the tests by creating test cases that specify what to test, creating test procedures that specify how to perform the tests, and creating executable test components to automate the tests if possible.
- Perform the various tests and systematically handle the results of each test. Builds found to have defects are retested and possibly sent back to other core workflows, such as design and implementation, so that the significant defects can be fixed.

In this chapter we will present how testing is done, and which workers and artifacts are involved (see Figure 11.1). We approach the workflow in much as we did the implementation workflow.

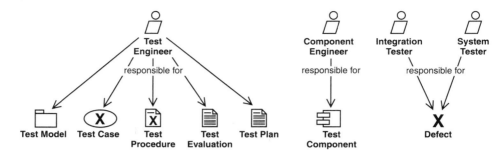

**FIGURE 11.1**  The workers and artifacts involved in testing.

## 11.2  The Role of Testing in the Software Life Cycle

Some initial test planning may occur during inception when the system is scoped. However, testing is primarily employed when each build (as an implementation result) is integration and system tested. This means that testing is a focus both during elaboration, when the executable architectural baseline is tested, and during construction, when the bulk of the system is implemented. During the transition phase, the focus shifts toward fixing defects detected during early usage and toward regression testing. See Figure 11.2.

Due to the iterative nature of the development effort, some of the test cases that specify how to test earlier builds can also be used as regression test cases that specify how to regression test subsequent builds. The number of regression tests required

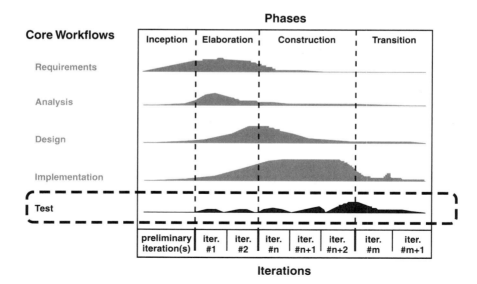

**FIGURE 11.2**  The focus of testing.

thus grows steadily over the iterations, which means that the late iterations will involve a substantial amount of regression testing. As a consequence, it is natural to maintain the test model throughout the complete software life cycle, although the test model constantly evolves by

- Removing obsolete test cases (and corresponding test procedures and test components).
- Refining some test cases into regression test cases.
- Creating new test cases for each subsequent build.

## 11.3 Artifacts

### 11.3.1 Artifact: Test Model

The test model primarily describes how executable components (such as builds) in the implementation model are tested by integration and system tests. The test model can also describe how specific aspects of the system are to be tested (e.g., whether the user interface is usable and consistent or whether the system's user manual fulfills its purpose). The test model is a collection of test cases, test procedures, and test components, as illustrated in Figure 11.3.

The artifacts in the test model are presented in detail in the following sections. Note that if the test model is large, that is, if it contains a large number of test cases, test procedures, and/or test components, it may be useful to introduce packages in the model to manage its size. This is a more or less trivial extension of the test model and is not dealt with in this chapter.

### 11.3.2 Artifact: Test Case

A test case specifies one way of testing the system, including what to test with which input or result, and under which conditions to test (see Figure 11.4). In practice, what to test can be any system requirement or collection of requirements whose

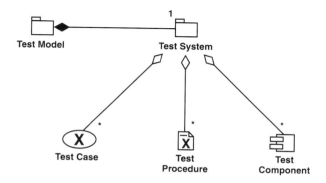

**FIGURE 11.3** The test model.

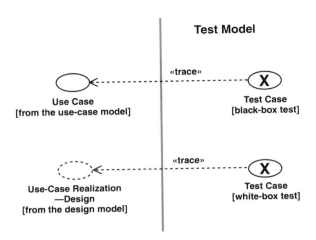

**Test Model**

«trace»

Use Case
[from the use-case model]

Test Case
[black-box test]

«trace»

Use-Case Realization
—Design
[from the design model]

Test Case
[white-box test]

**FIGURE 11.4** A test case can be derived from, and thereby traceable to, a use case in the use-case model or a use-case realization in the design model.

implementation justifies a test that is possible to perform and that is not too expensive to perform. The following are common test cases:

- A test case that specifies how to test a use case or a specific scenario of a use case. Such a test case includes verifying the result of the interaction between the actors and the system, that the pre- and postconditions specified by the use case is satisfied, and that the sequence of actions specified by the use case is followed. Note that a test case based on a use case typically specifies a "black-box" test of the system (i.e., a test of the externally observable behavior of the system).
- A test case that specifies how to test a use-case realization—design or a specific scenario of the realization. Such a test case can include verifying the interaction between the components implementing the use case. Note that test cases based on a use-case realization typically specify a "white-box" test of the system (i.e., a test of the internal interaction between components of the system).

## Example    Test Case

Test engineers suggest a set of test cases to test the Pay Invoice use case, in which each test case will verify one scenario of the use case. One of the proposed test cases is the payment of an invoice for a $300 order of one mountain bike They call this test case Pay 300–Mountain Bike.

To be complete, the test case must specify the input, expected result, and other conditions relevant for verifying the scenario of the use case.

### Input

- A valid order of a mountain bike exists and has been submitted to the seller, Crazy Mountaineer, Inc. The list price of the bike is $300, including shipping and handling.
- An order confirmation (ID 98765) of a mountain bike has been received by the buyer. The confirmed price of the bike is $300, including shipping and handling.
- An invoice (ID 12345) has been received by the buyer. The invoice complies with the mountain bike order confirmation. This is the only invoice present in the system. The invoiced amount should be a total $300, and the invoice should be in the Pending state. The invoice should point to an account 22-222-2222, which should receive the money. The account has a current balance of $963,456.00. The account should be owned by the seller.
- The buyer's account 11-111-1111 shows a balance of $350.

### Result

- The invoice state should be set to Closed (to indicate that it has been paid).
- The buyer's account 11-111-1111 should show a balance of $50.
- The balance of the seller's account 22-222-2222 should have increased to $963,756.00.

### Conditions

- No other use cases (instances) are allowed to access the accounts during this test case.

---

Note that some test cases may be similar and differ only in a single input or result value. This often holds for test cases that verify different scenarios of the same use case. In these cases, it may be appropriate to specify the test cases in a matrix format, where each test case is represented as a row and each range of input and result values is represented as a column. Such a matrix can provide a good overview of similar test cases and provide a usable input to the subsequent creation of test procedures and test components (refer to Sections 11.3.3 and 11.3.4).

Other test cases can be specified for testing the system as a whole. Examples are

- *Installation tests* verify that the system can be installed on the customer platform and that the system operates correctly when installed.
- *Configuration tests* verify that the system works correctly in different configurations, such as different network configurations.

- *Negative tests* try to cause the system to fail in order to reveal its weaknesses. Test *engineers* identify test cases that try to use the system in ways for which it is not designed, perhaps using incorrect network configurations, insufficient hardware capacity, or an "impossible" work load.[1]
- *Stress tests* identify problems with the system when it suffers from insufficient resources or when resources are competed for.

Many of these test cases can be found by considering the use cases of the system. We provide more details in Section 11.5.2.

### 11.3.3  Artifact: Test Procedure

A *test procedure* specifies how to perform one or several test cases or parts of them. For example, a test procedure may be an instruction for an individual on how to perform a test case manually, or it may be a specification of how to interact with a test automation tool manually to create executable test components (see Section 11.3.4).

How to perform one test case may be specified by one test procedure, but it is often useful to reuse a test procedure for several test cases and to reuse several test procedures for one test case (see Figure 11.5).

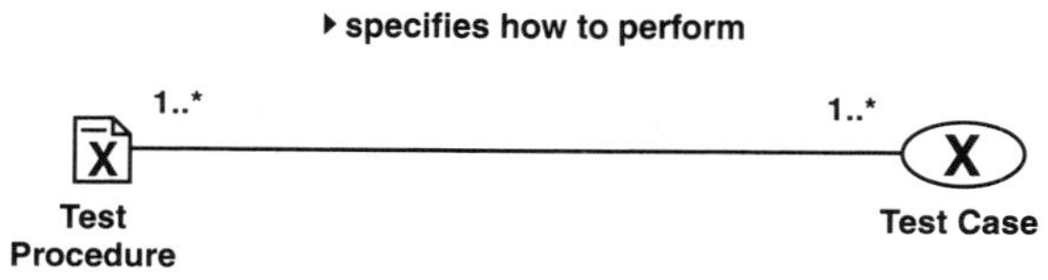

**FIGURE 11.5**  There are many-to-many associations between test procedures and test cases.

---

**Example**    **Test Procedure**

A test procedure is required for an individual to perform the Pay 300–Mountain Bike test case as discussed in the last example (in Section 11.3.2). The first part of the test procedure is specified as follows (text enclosed in square brackets need not be included in the specification since it is already specified in the test case):

Test case supported: Pay 300–Mountain Bike

1. From the main window, select **Browse Invoices** the menu. The Browse Invoice Query dialog window opens.

---

1. Also called "abuse cases."

2. In the Invoice Status field, select **Pending** and click the **Query** pushbutton. The Query Results window is displayed. Verify that the invoice specified in the test case [ID 12345] is listed in the Query Results window.

3. Select the specified invoice to be paid by double-clicking it. The Invoice Details window for the selected invoice is displayed. Verify the following fields:
   - Status is Pending
   - Payment Date is empty
   - Order Confirmation ID matches the ID specified in the test case [ID 98765]
   - Invoice Amount matches the amount specified in the test case [$300]
   - Account matches the account specified in the test case [22-222-2222]

4. Select the Authorize to Pay checkbox to initiate payment of this invoice. The Invoice Payment dialog box is displayed.

5. Etc. (it is specified how the complete path of the Pay Invoice use case is performed via the user interface by giving certain inputs to the system, and what to verify in the system's output.)

Note that this test procedure also can be used for other similar test cases whose input and result values differ (i.e., the values enclosed in square brackets). Note also that the test procedure is similar to the flow-of-events description of the Pay Invoice use case (see Section 7.4.3.1), but that the test procedure includes additional information such as what input values to use from the test case, how to input these values in the user interface, and what to verify.

## Example  General Test Procedures

When test designers suggest test procedures, they note that several use cases (and the test cases for verifying them) begin by validating objects at the start of the use case, such as comparing the received invoice with the order confirmation.

The test designers then suggest a general test procedure called Validate Business Objects to test such sequences. The test procedure specifies that the objects to be validated first should be created (by reading in the values they should have from a file and then creating them in the database). Then the test procedure specifies that the active object that validates the business objects should be invoked (such as Order Handler in the Pay Invoice use case). Finally, the test procedure specifies that the result of the validation should be compared with the expected result (as described in the mentioned file).

The test designers also suggest a test procedure called Verify Scheduling that specifies how to test the scheduling of an invoice and later verifies that the scheduling of the invoice triggers an account transfer.

The test designers know that several use cases perform account transfers, so they create a separate test procedure called Verify Account Transfer that specifies how to verify account transfers.

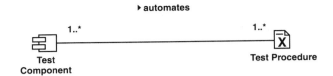

**FIGURE 11.6**  There are many-to-many associations between test components and test procedures.

### 11.3.4 Artifact: Test Component

A *test component* automates one or several test procedures or parts of them (see Section 10.3.2). See Figure 11.6.

Test components can be developed using a scripting language or a programming language, or they can be recorded with a test automation tool.

Test components are used to test the components in the implementation model (see Chapter 10) by providing test inputs, controlling and monitoring the execution of the tested component, and possibly reporting the test results. Test components are also sometimes called *test drivers*, *test harnesses* [1], and *test scripts*.

Note that test components can be implemented using object technology. If several test components have complex internal interactions or complex interactions with the ordinary components in the implementation model, a separate "test design model" (similar to the design model; see Section 9.3.1) may be used to model the test components and to depict high-level views of them. Although it can be useful, such a model is not discussed further in this book.

### 11.3.5 Artifact: Plan Test

The test plan describes the testing strategies, resources and schedule. The test strategy includes defining what kind of tests to perform for each iteration and their objectives, the required level of test and code coverage, and the percentage of tests that should execute with a specific result.

### 11.3.6 Artifact: Defect

A defect is a system anomaly, such as a symptom of a software fault or a problem discovered in a review meeting. A defect can be used to capture anything that the developers need to register as a symptom of a problem in the system that they need to track and resolve.

### 11.3.7 Artifact: Evaluate Test

A test evaluation is an evaluation of the results of the testing efforts such as test-case coverage, code coverage, and the status of defects.

## 11.4 Workers

### 11.4.1. Worker: Test Designer

A test designer is responsible for the integrity of the test model, ensuring that the model fulfills its purpose. Test designers also plan the tests, which means that they decide on appropriate test goals and a test schedule. Moreover, the test designers select and describe the test cases and the corresponding test procedures required, and they are responsible for evaluating the integration and system tests when they have been executed. See Figure 11.7.

Note that the test designers do not actually perform the tests but instead concentrate on test preparation and evaluation. Two other kinds of workers, integration testers and system testers, perform the tests.

### 11.4.2 Worker: Component Engineer

Component engineers are responsible for test components that automate some of the test procedures (not all test procedures can be automated). This is because the creation of such components may require substantial programming skills (i.e., skills that are also required by the component engineer in the implementation workflow; see Section 10.4.2).

### 11.4.3 Worker: Integration Tester

Integration testers are responsible for performing the integration tests that are required for each build produced in the implementation workflow (see Section 10.5.2). Integration testing is performed to verify that the components integrated into a build operate together properly. Because of this, integration tests are often derived from test cases that specify how to test use-case realizations—design (see Section 11.3.2).

The results of integration tests are defects issued by the integration tester.

Note that an integration tester is testing the result (i.e., a build) created by a system integrator in the implementation workflow. As a consequence, some projects choose to staff these workers with the same individual(s) to minimize the overlap of knowledge required.

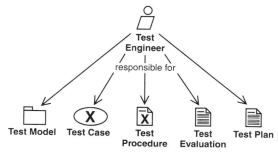

FIGURE 11.7  The responsibilities of a test designer in the testing workflow.

### 11.4.4 Worker: System Tester

A system tester is responsible for performing the system tests required for a build manifesting the (executable) result of a complete iteration (see Section 10.5.2). System testing is performed primarily to verify interactions between the actors and the system. Because of this, system tests are often derived from test cases that specify how to test use cases, but other kinds of tests also apply to the system as a whole (see Section 11.3.2).

The results of system tests are defects issued by the system tester.

Due to the nature of system tests, the individuals acting as system testers need not know much about the internal workings of the system. Instead, they should be familiar with the externally observable behavior of the system. As a consequence, some system tests may be performed by other project members, such as use-case specifiers, or even by external parties, such as beta customers.

## 11.5  Workflow

In the preceding sections we described testing in static terms. Now we will use an activity diagram (Figure 11.8) to reason about its dynamic behavior:

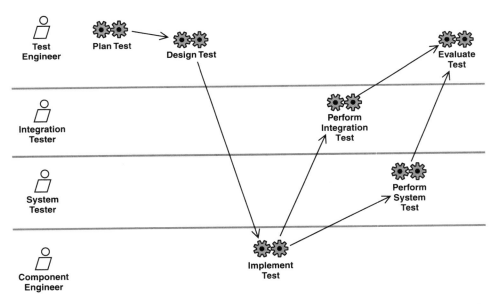

**FIGURE 11.8** The workflow during testing, including the participating workers and their activities.

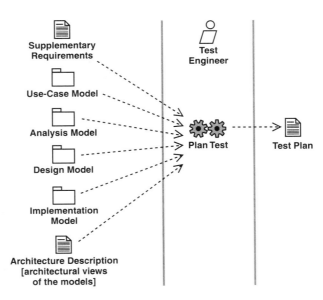

**FIGURE 11.9** The input and result of planning test.

The main goal of testing is to perform and evaluate the tests as described in the test model. This is initiated by test engineers who plan the testing effort within each iteration. The test engineers then describe the required test cases and corresponding test procedures for performing the tests. Component engineers then create test components to automate some of the test procedures, if possible. This is done for each build as it is released from the implementation workflow.

With these test cases, procedures, and components as input, the integration and system testers test each build and capture any defects they find. The defects are then fed back both to the other workflows, such as design and implementation, and to the test engineers for a systematic evaluation of the test results.

### 11.5.1 Activity: Plan Test

The purpose of test planning (see Figure 11.9) is to plan the testing efforts in an iteration by

- Describing a testing strategy.
- Estimating the requirements for the testing effort, such as the human and system resources needed.
- Scheduling the testing effort.

Test engineers draw upon a range of input when preparing the test plan. The use-case model and the supplemental requirements help them to decide on a suitable order of tests and to estimate the effort required for the testing. The test designer will also use other artifacts as input, such as the design model.

The test designers develop a general test strategy for the iteration, that is, what type of tests to run, how to run them, when to run them, and how to determine whether the testing effort is successful.

---

**Example**  **System Test Strategy**
**for the Last Iteration in the Elaboration Phase**

At least 75% of the tests should be automated, and the rest should be manual. Each subject use case will be tested for its normal flow and three alternative flows.

Success criteria: 90% of test cases passed. No medium-to-high priority defects unresolved.

---

Each test case, test procedure, and test component takes time and costs money to develop, to perform, and to evaluate when it has been performed. No system can ever be completely tested. We should therefore identify test cases, procedures, and components that give the best return on investment in terms of improved quality [3]. The general principle is to develop test cases and procedures with a minimum overlap to test the most important use cases, and to test requirements that are associated with the highest risks.

### 11.5.2  Activity: Design Test

The purposes of designing tests (see Figure 11.10) are to

- Identify and describe test cases for each build.
- Identify and structure test procedures specifying how to perform the test cases.

### 11.5.2.1.  *Designing Integration Test Cases*    Integration test cases are used to verify that the components interact properly with each other after they have been integrated into a build (see Section 10.5.2). Most integration test cases can be derived from use-case realizations—design, since the use-case realizations describe how classes and objects (and thereby also components) interact.

The test engineers should create a set of test cases that makes it possible to achieve the goals established in the test plan with a minimum effort. To do this, the test designers try to find a set of test cases with a minimum overlap, each of which tests an interesting path or scenario through a use-case realization.

When the test designers create the integration test cases, they primarily consider the interaction diagrams of the use-case realizations as input. The test designers look for combinations of actor input, output, and system start state that lead to interesting scenarios that employ the classes (and thereby components) that participate in the diagrams.

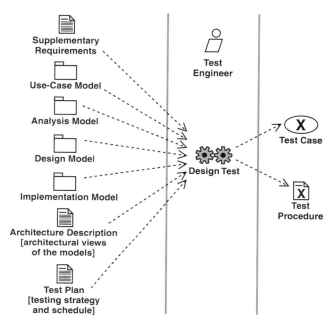

**FIGURE 11.10** The input and result of design test.

---

**Example**   **Integration Test Case**

The test *designers* start by considering a sequence diagram that is part of a use-case realization—design for the Pay Invoice use case. Figure 11.11 shows the first part of the diagram (see Section 9.5.2.2).

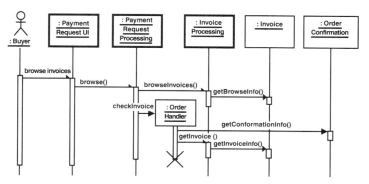

**FIGURE 11.11** First part of a sequence diagram for the use-case realization—design of the Pay Invoice use case.

Note that there can be several different "sequences" through a sequence diagram, depending, for example, on the "start" state of the system and the input from the actor. For example, considering the sequence diagram in Figure 11.11, we can note that many messages would not be sent if there were no Invoices in the system.

A test case derived from a sequence diagram such as the one shown in Figure 11.11 should describe how to test one interesting sequence through the diagram, by capturing the required start state of the system, the input from the actor, and so on that makes the sequence happen.

---

Later, when the corresponding integration test is performed, we capture the actual interactions of objects within the system (e.g., by creating trace-printouts of or by single-stepping its execution). Then we compare those actual interactions with the interaction diagram. They should be the same; otherwise, a defect is spotted.

### 11.5.2.2 Designing System Test Cases

System tests are used to test that the system functions properly as a whole. Each system test primarily tests combinations of use cases instantiated under different conditions. These conditions include different hardware configurations (processors, primary memory, hard disks, etc.), different levels of system loads, various numbers of actors, and different sizes of the database. When developing system test cases, test designers should prioritize combinations of use cases that:

- Are required to function in parallel.
- Are likely to be performed in parallel.
- Are likely to influence each other if performed in parallel.
- Involve multiple processes.
- Frequently use system resources, such as processes, processors, databases, and communication software, perhaps in complex and unpredictable ways.

Many system test cases can thus be found by considering the use cases, especially their flow of events and special requirements (such as performance requirements).

### 11.5.2.3 Designing Regression Test Cases

Some test cases from earlier builds may be used for regression tests in subsequent builds, but not all test cases are suitable for regression testing. To be suitable and to continually contribute to the quality of the system, the test cases must be flexible enough to be resilient to changes of the software that is tested. The flexibility required from a regression test case can cost some extra development effort, which means that we must be careful and turn them into regression test cases only when it is worth the effort.

### 11.5.2.4 Identifying and Structuring Test Procedures

Test designers can work test case by test case and suggest testing procedures for each one. We try to reuse existing test procedures as much as possible, which means that we may need to modify them so that they may be used to specify how to perform a new and/or changed test case. The test designers also try to create test procedures that are reusable for several test cases. This allows the test designers to use a compact set of test procedures quickly and accurately for many test cases.

Most test cases will test several classes from several service subsystems (since test cases are based on use cases or use-case realizations), but each test procedure should, if possible, specify how to test classes from one service subsystem only; however, several test procedures may specify how to test one service subsystem. Each test case will then involve several test procedures, perhaps one for each service subsystem tested in the test case. Aligning the test procedures with the service subsystems makes the test procedures easier to maintain. When changing a service subsystem, the effects of the change regarding test procedures can then be limited to the test procedures used for verifying the service subsystem, and all other test procedures would be unaffected.

**Example** | **Test Procedure**

The Accounts service subsystem provides functionality for moving money between accounts. This functionality is involved in several use-case realizations, such as those for Pay Invoice and Transfer between Accounts. How to test the moving of money between accounts will be specified by a test procedure called Verify Account Transfer. The procedure specified by Verify Account Transfer takes as in-parameters two account identities and an amount to transfer, and validates the transfer by asking for the balance of the two involved accounts before the transfer and after the transfer.

The test designers create 8 test cases for the Pay Invoice use case and 14 test cases for the Transfer between Accounts use case. The test procedure Verify Account Transfer specifies how (parts of) all those test cases are performed.

### 11.5.3 Activity: Implement Test

The purpose of implementing tests is to automate test procedures by creating test components, if possible (not all test procedures can be automated); see Figure 11.12.

Test components are created using the test procedures as input:

- When using a test automation tool, we perform or specify the actions as described by the test procedures. These actions are then recorded, yielding as output a test component, such as a Visual Basic test script.
- When programming the test components explicitly, we use the test procedures as the primary specifications of the programming effort. Note that such a programming effort might require individuals with advanced programming skills.

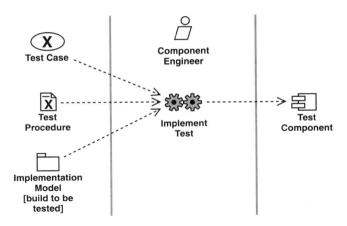

**FIGURE 11.12**  The input and result of test implementation.

The test components often use large amounts of input data to be tested and produce large amounts of output data as results of the tests. It is useful to be able to visualize this data in a clear and intuitive way so it can be specified correctly and the test results can be interpreted. We use spreadsheet and database applications for this purpose.

### 11.5.4  Activity: Perform Integration Test

In this activity, the integration tests (see Section 11.5.2.1) required for each build created within an iteration are performed (see Section 10.5.2), and the test results are captured. See Figure 11.13.

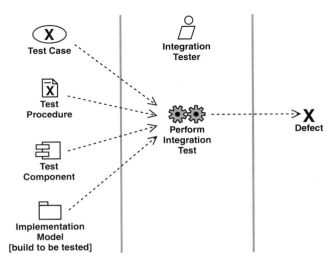

**FIGURE 11.13**  The input and result of integration testing.

Integration testing is done in the following sequence:

1. Perform the integration tests relevant to the build by manually performing the test procedures for each test case or by executing any test components automating the test procedures.
2. Compare the test results with the expected results and investigate test results that deviate from the expected.
3. Report defects to the component engineer who is responsible for the components that are likely to contain the fault.
4. Report the defects to the test designers, who then use the defects to evaluate the overall results of the testing effort (as described in Section 11.5.6).

### 11.5.5 Activity: Perform System Test

The purpose of system testing is to perform the system tests (see Section 11.5.1.2) required in each iteration and to capture the test results (see Figure 11.14).

System testing can begin when integration tests indicate that the system meets the integration quality goals set in the test plan for the current iteration (e.g., 95% of the integration test cases execute with an expected result).

System testing is analogously performed as integration testing (see Section 11.5.4).

### 11.5.6 Activity: Evaluate Test

The purposes of test evaluation is to evaluate the testing efforts within an iteration (see Figure 11.15).

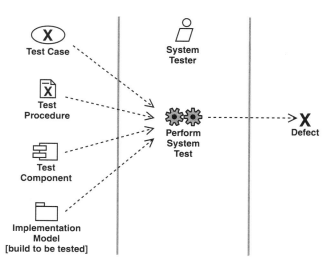

**FIGURE 11.14** The input and result of system test.

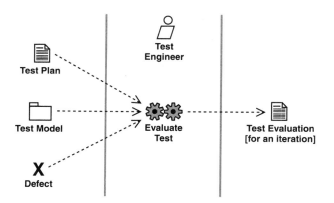

**FIGURE 11.15** The input and result of test evaluation.

The test designers evaluate the results of the testing effort by comparing the results with the goals outlined in the test plan. They prepare metrics that let them determine the quality level of the software and determine how much more testing needs to be done.

The test engineer looks at two metrics in particular:

- *Testing completeness*, which is derived from the coverage of test cases and the coverage of the tested components. This indicates what percentage of the test cases have been executed and the percentage of the code that has been tested.
- *Reliability*, which is based on analyses of trends in the discovered defects and on trends in the tests that execute with an expected result.

To determine the reliability of the system, the test designers create defect trend diagrams where they illustrate the distribution of specific kinds of defects (such as new or fatal defects) over time. The test may also create trend diagrams that depict the ratio of successfully executed tests (i.e., test executions that generate the expected results) over time.

The defect trends often follow patterns that repeat from project to project. For example, the number of new defects generated when testing a system usually rises fairly quickly as soon as the testing commences, then flattens out after some time, and finally begins to fall slowly. By then comparing the actual trend with similar trends from earlier projects, it is possible to predict how much effort will be needed to reach an acceptable quality level.

Based on the defect trend analysis, the test designers may suggest further actions, such as:

- Performing additional tests to locate more defects, if the measured reliability suggests that the system is not mature enough.

- Relaxing the criteria for the tests, if the quality goals were set too high for the current iteration.
- Isolating the parts of the system that seem to be of acceptable quality and deliver them as a result of the current iteration. The parts that did not meet the quality criteria must then be revised and tested again.

The test designers document testing completeness, reliability, and suggested actions in a test evaluation description.

## 11.6 Summary of Testing

The primary result of testing is the test model, which describes how the system is tested. The test model includes:

- Test cases, which specify what to test in the system.
- Test procedures, which specify how to perform the test cases.
- Test components, which automate the test procedures.

Testing also results in a test plan, evaluations of the performed tests, and defects that can be fed back to other core workflows, such as design and implementation.

## 11.7 References

[1]  IEEE, Std 610.12-1990.

[2]  Bill Hetzel, *The Complete Guide to Software Testing,* Second Edition, Wellesley, MA: QED Information Sciences, Inc., 1988.

[3]  Robert V. Binder, "Developing a test budget," *Object Magazine*, 7(4), June 1997.

# Part III

## Iterative and Incremental Development

**A** software system goes through a number of development cycles during its lifetime. Each cycle results in a new release of the product to customers and users, and the first one may very well be the most difficult. It lays the foundation, the architecture, for the system; it explores a new area that may contain serious risks. A development cycle, thus, has a different content depending on where the system is in the overall life cycle. In later releases, if the architecture changes seriously, that may mean more work in the early phases. In most later releases, however, if the original architecture is extendable, the new project simply builds on top of what was already there; that is, a later release of the product will be built on top of the previous release.

More and more people seize the idea of working on problems earlier rather than later within each development cycle. They are applying the term *iteration* to problem-solving sequences in the inception and elaboration phases, as well as to each series of builds in the construction phase.

Risks do not come in a neat package with an identification card tucked under a pink bow. They must be identified, delimited, monitored, and mitigated—and it is best to tackle the most significant risks first. Similarly, the order in which the iterations are added has to be thought out carefully so that the most serious problems are solved first. In short, *do the hard stuff first.*

In Part II we described each workflow separately. For example, Figure 6.2 describes how the requirements workflow is in focus throughout the different phases. Similarly, Figure 8.2 does this for analysis, Figure 9.2 for design, Figure 10.2 for implementation, and Figure 11.2 for test.

In this part we show how the workflows are combined in different ways, depending on where we are in the life cycle. We describe first, in Chapter 12, what is common for all phases, that is, things that cross all phases, such as planning an iteration, setting the evaluation criteria for one, establishing a risk list, prioritizing the use cases, and assessing the iterations. Successive chapters focus on each phase.

In the inception phase (Chapter 13) activity is concentrated in the first workflow, requirements, with a little work carrying over to the second and third workflows (analysis and design). This phase seldom carries work as far as the final two workflows, implementation and test.

In the elaboration phase (Chapter 14), while activity is still heavy in completing requirements, the second and third workflows, analysis and design, see more activity, as they underlie the creation of the architecture. To reach the executable architecture baseline, there is necessarily some activity in the final workflows, implementation and test.

In the construction phase (Chapter 15), the requirements workflow tapers off, analysis lightens, and the last three workflows represent the bulk of the work.

In the transition phase (Chapter 16), the mix of workflows depends on the feedback from acceptance or beta test. For instance, if the beta tests uncover defects in the implementation, there will be considerable activity in revived implementation and test workflows.

The final chapter, Chapter 17, returns to the central theme of the book. In a single chapter we show how the many strands—workflows, phases, iterations—come together to form a well-designed process for developing mission-critical software. This chapter also devotes a few paragraphs to how these relationships should be managed and to how an organization can transition from where it is now to the Unified Process.

# *Chapter 12*

# The Generic Iteration Workflow

I n this chapter we return to the idea of the generic iteration, discussed in Chapter 5. The intent of this chapter is to distill the common pattern that characterizes all iterations from the variety of iterations that occur during the four phases.

We employ this generic pattern as a base on which to build the concrete iterations where, in each phase, the content changes to accommodate the special goals of that phase (see Figure 12.1).

The generic iteration workflow includes the five core workflows: requirements, analysis, design, implementation, and test. It also includes planning, which precedes the workflows, and assessment, which follows them (Chapters 6–11 describe each core workflow separately). In this chapter we will focus on planning, assessment, and other activities that are common to all the workflows.

Planning is necessary throughout the entire development cycle. But before we can plan, we need to know what to do. The five core workflows provide a starting point. Risk management, that is, identifying and then mitigating risks by realizing the corresponding set of use cases, is another key aspect of planning. Of course, no plan can be complete without estimating the resources that will be required, and finally, the execution of each iteration and phase has to be assessed.

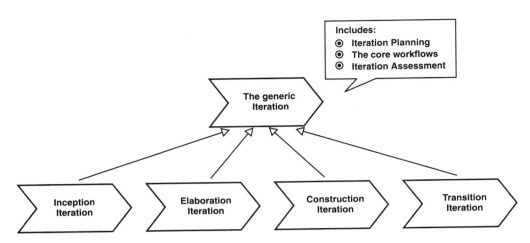

**FIGURE 12.1** The generic iteration workflow is used to describe concrete iteration workflows for each phase. (The intent of this figure is to illustrate the way in which we have structured Part III, with the iteration generics in Chapter 12 and the specializations for each phase in Chapters 13–16).

## 12.1 The Need for Balance

At every moment in the life cycle of a software development project many different sequences of activities go on. We work on new functions, we architect, we receive feedback from users, we mitigate risks, we plan the future, and so on. We must at every moment balance and synchronize these different sequences of activities streaming through this complexity.

Developers split up the work, which is overwhelmingly complex in its entirety, into smaller, more comprehensible pieces. Over the development life cycle, they divide the work into phases and, within the phases, into iterations, as we outline in Part I.

Within each iteration the project strives to achieve a balance among the sequences of activities running through the iteration. That means we should work on the right things in each iteration. What the right things to work on are depends on where we are in the life cycle. A project's task is to select the right things to work on for each sequence of activity. In determining the balance of the sequences of activities it is also important to ensure that they are of comparable importance, so that they can be efficiently prioritized and synchronized. Failure to achieve this sort of balance and efficient execution seems to be the undoing of many iterative, incremental development life cycles.

In an early iteration we work with critical risks, key use cases, architectural issues, the selection of the development environment, all activities that are research-oriented, whereas in later iterations we work on development-oriented activities with implementing and testing, evaluating performance problems, and deploying the system. Relating all these activities to each other is a delicate balancing act. It is the fact of this delicacy that makes software development extraordinarily difficult.

Understanding these different sequences of activities and balancing them is what we do in each iteration. In the Unified Process some of these sequences of activities have been identified and described as the core workflows. There are other sequences that we have not identified formally, but that could very well be treated in much the same way as we treat the workflows. For instance,

- Interacting with customers on new requirements.
- Preparing a bid to clients.
- Understanding the context of a system by making a business model.
- Planning and managing the project.
- Establishing and managing the development environment, that is, the process and tools.
- Managing the risks.
- Deploying of a product to a customer site.
- Responding to user feedback.

## 12.2  The Phases Are the First Division of Work

The first step toward dividing the software development process into pieces is to separate it timewise into four phases: inception, elaboration, construction, and transition. Each phase is further divided into one or more iterations. This chapter outlines the general nature of these phases and iterations. The next four chapters consider each phase in detail.

### 12.2.1.  Inception Phase Establishes Feasibility

The primary goal of this phase is to establish the business case—the case for going forward with the project. This case will be further developed in the elaboration phase as more information becomes available. The inception phase is not a complete study of the proposed system. We seek out only the small percentage of use cases we need to support the initial business case. To make this case, we take four steps:

1. Delimit the scope of the proposed system, that is, define the system boundary and begin to identify the interfaces to related systems outside the boundary.
2. Describe or outline the candidate architecture of the system, especially those parts of the system that are new, risky, or difficult. We carry this step only to an architecture description, rarely to an executable prototype. The architecture description consists of first cuts of views of the models. Here the goal is to make it believable that we can create a stable architecture of the proposed

system in the next phase. We don't build this architecture in this phase; we simply make it so believable that we can build one. Building it is the major product of the elaboration phase.

3. Identify critical risks, those that affect the ability to build the system, and determine whether we can see a way to mitigate them, perhaps in a later phase. In this phase we consider only the risks that affect feasibility, that is, those that threaten the successful development of the system. Any noncritical risks that we happen to identify are placed on the risk list for detailed consideration in the next phase.

4. Demonstrate to potential users or customers that the system proposed is capable of solving their problem or supporting their business objective by building a proof-of-concept prototype. In the inception phase we may build a prototype to demonstrate a solution to the problem of the potential customers and users. The prototype demonstrates the basic ideas of the new system with focus on its use—user interfaces and/or some interesting new algorithms. This latter prototype tends to be exploratory, that is, it demonstrates a possible solution, but it may not evolve into the final product. It is usually a throw-away prototype. In contrast, an architectural prototype, developed in the elaboration phase, tends to be evolutionary, that is, one capable of being further evolved in the next phase.

We carry these efforts to the point at which it appears to be economically worthwhile to develop the product. They show that the system is likely to provide, within fairly broad limits, income or other values commensurate with the investment required to build it. In other words, we have made the first cut at the business case. We will further refine it in the next phase, elaboration.

The intent is to minimize expenditures of schedule time, effort, and funds in this phase until we find that the system is, indeed, feasible. In the case of a largely new system in a little explored domain, that determination may take considerable time and effort and may extend to several iterations in that event. For a well-known system in an established domain or the extension of an existing system to a new release, risks and unknowns may be minimal, enabling this first phase to be completed in a few days.

## 12.2.2 Elaboration Phase Focuses on "Do-Ability"

The primary product of the elaboration phase is a stable architecture, to guide the system through its future life. This phase also carries the study of the proposed system to the point of planning the construction phase with high fidelity. With these two overall goals—the architecture and the high-fidelity cost estimate—the team does the following:

1. Creates an architectural baseline that covers the architecturally significant functionality of the system and features important to the stakeholders, as

described in Chapter 4. This baseline consists of the model artifacts, architecture description, and executable implementation. It not only demonstrates that we can build a stable architecture, it also encompasses the architecture.

2. Identifies significant risks, meaning risks that could upset plans, costs, and schedules of later phases, and reduces them to activities that can be timed and priced.
3. Specifies the levels to be attained by quality attributes such as reliability (defect rates) and response times.
4. Captures use cases to about 80% of functional requirements, sufficient to plan the construction phase. (We will clarify what we mean by 80% later in this chapter.)
5. Prepares a bid covering schedule, staff needed, and cost within the limits set by business practices.

Requirements and architecture (in analysis, design, and implementation) represent the bulk of the effort in the inception and elaboration phases.

### 12.2.3 Construction Phase Builds the System

The general objective of the construction phase is indicated by its major milestone: initial operational capability. That signifies a product ready for beta testing. This phase employs more staff over a longer period of time than any of the other phases. That is why it is so important to get everything of importance straightened out before entering it. It generally is carried out through a greater number of iterations than the earlier phases.

In many cases it seems that construction takes an excessive amount of time because of poor requirements, analysis, and design work. As a result the developers hack out the system, which takes longer than it should to satisfy requirements and eliminate defects (bugs). One of the big advantages of a software engineering approach that uses multiple phases and iterative, incremental development is that it allows you to balance resources and time allocations over the life cycle (see Section 12.1).

The activities of the construction phase include:

1. Extending use-case identification, description, and realization to the entire body of use cases.
2. Finishing analysis (perhaps more than half of the use cases still remain to be analyzed when the construction phase begins), design, implementation, and test (perhaps 90% remains).
3. Maintaining the integrity of the architecture; modifying it when necessary.
4. Monitoring critical and significant risks carried over from the first two phases and, if they materialize, mitigating them.

### 12.2.4 Transition Phase Moves into the User Environment

The transition phase often begins with the beta release, that is, the development organization distributes the software product, now capable of initial operation, to a representative sample of the community of actual users. Operation in the harsh environment of user organizations is often a more severe trial of the product's state of development than operation in the developer's realm.

Transition activities include:

- Preparation activities, such as site preparation.
- Advising the customer on updating the environment (hardware, operating systems, communications protocols, etc.) in which the software is to operate.
- Preparation of manuals and other documentation for product release. In the construction phase we prepared preliminary documentation for beta users.
- Adjusting the software to operate under the actual parameters of the user environment.
- Correcting defects found after feedback from the beta tests.
- Modifying the software in the light of unforeseen problems.

The transition phase ends with formal product release. However, before the project team relinquishes the project, team leaders conduct a postmortem devoted to two goals:

- To find, discuss, evaluate, and record for future reference "lessons learned."
- To record matters of use in the next release or the next generation.

## 12.3 The Generic Iteration Revisited

We make a distinction between core workflows and iteration workflows. The core workflows—requirements, analysis, design, implementation, and test—are described in Chapters 6–11. In the Unified Process, these core workflows occur not just once, as is theoretically the case in the waterfall model. Rather, they recur in each iteration, time after time, as iteration workflows. In each recurrence, however, they differ in detail—they address the issues central to that iteration.

### 12.3.1 Core Workflows Repeat in Each Iteration

The generic iteration consists of the five workflows: requirements, analysis, design, implementation, and test, and it also includes planning and assessment. See Figure 12.2.

In Sections 12.4–12.7, we discuss the planning that precedes the iteration, and in Section 12.8, the assessment of each iteration. Then in Chapters 13–16 we show in detail how the five workflows are applied in each phase.

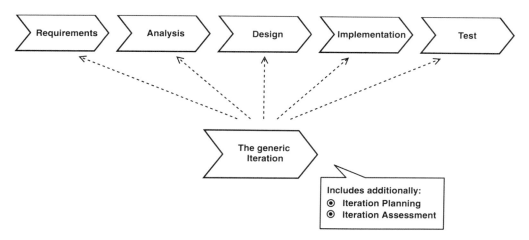

**FIGURE 12.2** The five core workflows are repeated in each iteration, preceded by planning and followed by assessment.

## 12.3.2 Workers Participate in the Workflows

We have talked of software development from time to time as "complex." Figure 12.3 provides a simplified overview of the process. Even so, the figure is far from simple, and the reality, as you know, is still more complicated. In this chapter, we are not going to describe in detail how each worker produces the artifacts for which he or she is responsible, nor just what these artifacts are. The small cogwheels in the figure symbolize that work, and the arrows between these activities represent temporal relationships. See Chapters 6–11 for details.

Still, Figure 12.3 gives you an impression of what falls within an iteration. For example, starting in the upper-left corner, a system analyst identifies the use cases and actors and structures them into a use-case model. Then, a use-case specifier details each use case, and a user-interface designer prototypes the user interfaces. The architect prioritizes the use cases to be developed within the iteration, taking risks into consideration.

You can see that the particular activities performed within the requirements "circle" would vary with the location of the iteration in the entire development process. In the inception phase, for instance, the workers limit use-case detailing and prioritization to the small proportion of use cases needed in that phase. The first four of the workflows follow, largely in time sequence, although there may be some overlapping. The three workers involved in the analysis workflow carry the work on into design.

The test workflow, however, begins very early, with the test engineer planning what to do. As soon as sufficient detail becomes available, in the implementation workflow, the test engineer designs tests. As components that have passed unit testing are integrated, the system tester and the integration tester test the results of several levels of integration. The test engineer evaluates whether the testing he has prescribed has been adequate.

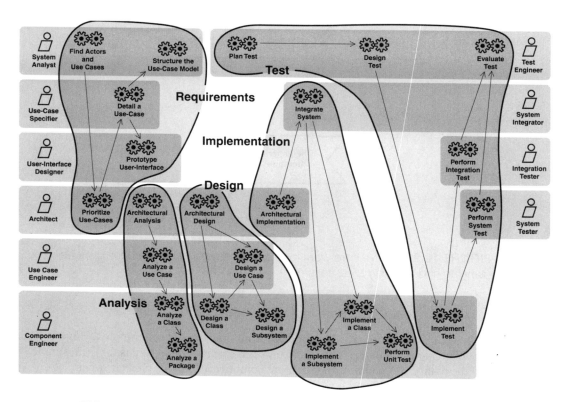

**FIGURE 12.3**  The worker titles are listed vertically at the left and right, identifying each "swim lane." Time advances from left to right. The core workflows, embracing the workers and the activities they perform, are depicted within the free-hand "circles." The component engineer, for example, analyzes a class and a package in the analysis workflow, designs a class and a subsystem in the design workflow, implements a class and a subsystem, and performs a unit test in the implementation workflow.

In the following chapters, we add on top of Figure 12.3 what we need to represent the iteration workflows in each phase. These workflows are all patterned on this generic figure. Since the focus varies in different phases, the corresponding iteration workflows differ in degree.

## 12.4  Planning Precedes Doing

As we sit down at the beginning of the inception phase, we know three things:

- We are going to carry out the project in a series of iterations in four phases.
- We have the information about the proposed system that our predecessors collected (and that led to initiating a project).

- We have our own background information about the domain and about similar systems on which we worked in the past.

From this information, we must plan both the project (project plan) and each iteration (iteration plan). In the beginning, with limited information with which to work, both plans contain little detail. As we work through the inception and elaboration phases, the plans become more detailed.

First, we describe how to plan the phases and iterations and how to evaluate the iteration. In Section 12.5 we discuss how risks affect the plan and in Section 12.6 how we mitigate these risks by selecting the right use cases. Finally, we discuss resource allocation in Section 12.7.

### 12.4.1 Plan the Four Phases

We know, from the prescriptions of the Unified Process, what each phase involves. Our task, in the project plan, is to reduce these prescriptions to concrete terms:

- Time allocation. We decide how much time to assign to each phase and the date by which each phase is to be completed. These times, while set precisely, may be rather uncertain at the beginning of the inception phase, but they will be firmed up as we learn more. After all, it is not until the end of the elaboration phase that we make a firm bid.
- Major milestones. A phase ends when the preset criteria have been met. At first, these criteria may be little more than educated guesses, but they are informed by our past experience in the domain, by the extent to which the proposed system differs from earlier ones, by performance specifications the new system is intended to achieve, and by the capability of our software development organization.
- Iterations per phase. Within each phase, we advance the work through one or more iterations. The general character of each iteration is contained in the coarse-grained project plan.
- Project plan. The project plan outlines an overall "road map," covering the schedule, major milestone dates and criteria, and the breakdown of the phases into iterations.

You can expect the first iteration in the inception phase to be difficult. In addition to the iteration itself, you have to cope with

- Tailoring the Unified Process to fit the project and selecting tools to automate the process.
- Beginning to assemble people with the talents required by the project.
- Building the relationships that make an effective team.
- Understanding the domain, which is often new to the team.
- Perceiving the nature of the project, which will be more difficult in green-field development than in extending an existing product into a new generation.

- Familiarizing the team with tools appropriate to the tailored process and the project.

## 12.4.2 Plan the Iterations

Each phase consists of one or more iterations. Planning the iterations proceeds through a set of steps roughly comparable to those followed in planning the phases:

- Iteration schedule. We decide how much time each iteration is allowed to require and its date of completion, at first roughly and then with increasing precision as we learn more.
- Iteration content. While the project plan outlines the iterations planned in general terms, as the date of beginning an iteration approaches, we plan what is to be done in more detail. The content of an iteration is based on the following:
  - Which use cases are to be at least partially filled out during the iteration.
  - Which technical risks it is time to identify, translate into use cases, and mitigate.
  - Any changes in requirements that have occurred or defects that may have been corrected.
  - Which subsystems are to be implemented partly or completely. (This point varies depending on the phase under consideration. In the elaboration phase, for example, we identify most of the subsystems and all of the architecturally significant classes. In the construction phase, we fill the subsystems with more and more behavior, resulting in more complete components.)

The plan of the current iteration is fully detailed, and that of the next one becomes more detailed as we learn more. The detail for later iterations may be limited by the knowledge available at the time.

- **Minor milestones** (Appendix C). The attainment of preset criteria (preferably on the planned date) signals the completion of each iteration.
- **Iteration plan** (Appendix C). The activities of each iteration are recorded in a fine-grained iteration plan. At the beginning of every iteration we allocate the individuals available to act as the workers.

The number of iterations planned for each phase varies, essentially, with the complexity of the proposed system. A very simple project might be carried out with only one iteration per phase. A more complex project might require more iterations. For example,

- **Inception phase** (Appendix C): One iteration, primarily devoted to scoping the system.
- **Elaboration phase** (Appendix C): Two iterations, the first for an initial pass at the architecture, the second culminating in the architectural baseline.

- **Construction phase** (Appendix C): Two iterations, to assure that the resulting increments operate satisfactorily.
- **Transition phase** (Appendix C): One iteration.

As the project under consideration becomes larger and more complex and involves more novel considerations, we can expect the size of the development organization to grow. There will be more iterations, and their length will vary with the size of the system from a week to, say, three months for each iteration.

### 12.4.3 Think Long Term

The long period that the system may last may see extensive changes, such as new technologies, new interfaces to the system's environment, and advanced platforms. Also, the planners should examine whether the business will need to be adapted to other organizations, such as affiliates or merger partners. However, don't speculate on the future to the point of absurdity. You don't want to construct a rigid system architecture if you can already see that it will have to be changed in the future, but on the other hand, you don't want to introduce unnecessary flexibility in the system, i.e., flexibility that will never be used.

### 12.4.4 Plan the Evaluation Criteria

Iterations are short compared to traditional projects. To keep them from running on indefinitely, project leaders, in addition to setting a schedule, outline the key objectives of each iteration. To carry out the objectives, they establish criteria that indicate the completion of the iteration. These criteria, such as the minimal feature set at a given point, give focus to the iteration and help bring it to a timely close. Examples of criteria include

- Functional requirements, expressed in the form of use cases.
- Nonfunctional requirements, attached to the use cases to which they apply.
- Nonfunctional requirements, not specific to a particular use case, listed in supplementary requirements, as detailed in Section 6.7.

One of the objectives in an early iteration, for instance, might be to resolve ambiguities in the client's current expression of the requirements. The criteria specify what the planners intend the iteration to achieve in terms that can be measured, such as performance, or observed, such as a desirable feature.

The project manager sets evaluation criteria in advance for each iteration and the phase itself. Each needs a clear end point that enables the developers themselves to see that they have finished. In addition, these end points provide milestones that managers can use to gauge the progress of the work.

Broadly speaking, evaluation criteria fall into two categories, verifiable requirements and more general criteria.

Test engineers have been participating in the development from the inception phase onward, as detailed in Chapter 11. They identify which characteristics of the use cases can be confirmed by testing. They plan the test cases that define the integration and regression tests, as well as the system tests. In iterative development, the testing cycle is also iterative. Each build created within an iteration is a target for testing. The test engineers add to and refine the tests that are executed for each build, thus accumulating a body of tests used for regression testing at later stages. Early iterations introduce more new functions and new tests than later iterations. As the integration of builds continues, the number of new tests diminishes, and a growing number of regression tests is executed to validate the accumulated system implementation. Consequently, the early builds and iterations require more test planning and design, while the later ones are weighted toward test execution and evaluation.

General criteria are not reducible to paths through the code that testers can test. They can, however, be perceived, first, in prototypes and, later, in the series of working builds and iterations. Users, stakeholders, and developers can view displays and graphical user interfaces with more insight than they can the static information contained in model artifacts.

The evaluation criteria tell how to verify that the requirements for an iteration have been developed correctly. They specify in terms that can be observed or verified what the project manager intends for the iteration to achieve. Their original inspiration is the vision statement. The criteria become more detailed as use cases, use-case scenarios, performance requirements, and test cases express concretely what successive increments are to be.

## 12.5 Risks Affect Project Planning

The way in which we plan the development of a new system is to a considerable extent influenced by the risks we perceive. Therefore, one of the first steps, early in the inception phase, is to create a risk list. At first, we may be hampered by lack of information, but we probably have some sense of what the critical risks—those that will determine whether we will be able to build the system—are. As we proceed with the early work, we will come to appreciate what the significant risks—those that have to be mitigated in order to bid a schedule and cost and to attain a quality goal—will be.

### 12.5.1 Manage a Risk List

It is one thing to know in a vague sort of way that software development involves risks. It is another thing to get them out in the open where everyone can see them, be guided by them, and do something about them. That is the purpose of the risk list. It is not just something that gets filed away in a drawer or computer folder. Everything you need to know about a risk in order to work with it, including its unique identifier, would be on the list. That includes:

- Description: Start with a brief description and add to it as you learn more.
- Priority: Assign a priority to it, beginning with critical, significant, and routine. As the list develops, you will probably want to add a few more categories.

- Impact: Which parts of the project or system will the risk affect?
- Monitor: Who is responsible for keeping track of a continuing risk?
- Responsibility: What individual or organization unit is responsible for retiring the risk?
- Contingency: What is to be done if the risk materializes?

On a project of some size, people may eventually find hundreds of risks. In large projects, the risks should probably be items in a database so that they can be sorted and searched efficiently. The team cannot focus on everything at once. That is one reason for iterative development. Risks are sorted by degree of seriousness or by their effect on development and attacked in order. As we have emphasized many times, the risks to attack first are those that could cause the project to fail. Some risks do not yield to easy resolution and remain on the risk list for some time. Some organizations have found it helpful to lead off the list with the "Top Ten" as a means of focusing attention.

The risk list is not a static instrument. As risks are discovered, the list grows. As risks are retired or as we pass the point in development at which a particular risk could materialize, they are removed from the list. The project manager conducts periodic meetings, often in concert with iteration assessments, to review the status of the most important risks. Other leaders conduct sessions on lesser risks.

### 12.5.2  Risks Affect the Iteration Plan

During the inception phase the critical risks are identified and the team tries to mitigate them. They explore their nature to the point of preparing an iteration plan. To know enough to make the plan, for example, they may have to develop the small set of use cases related to the risk and implement it in the proof-of-concept prototype. Then, with certain inputs, they find that the prototype generates an unacceptable output—premature firing, for example—a critical risk. (These inputs have to be within the specified input range, perhaps on its fringes, but still cause unacceptable outputs.)

In addition to the effect that the most serious risks have on the success of a project, all risks have some impact on schedule, cost, or quality. Some of these risks may be serious enough to extend the schedule or increase the effort beyond those planned—unless they are mitigated before these undesired results materialize. In nearly all cases an impact on schedule also affects effort and cost. In a few cases, while a risk may have little impact on schedule or cost, it adversely affects other factors, such as quality or performance.

### 12.5.3  Schedule Risk Action

The general principle is to take action against risks on a planned basis. The phases and the iterations within phases provide the mechanism for scheduling risk action. For example, plan to deal with risks that affect the ability to build the system in the iteration(s) in the inception phase. That is, you retire them, if possible, or at least have a contingency plan.

The alternative, no risk schedule, has not worked very well in our experience. In the absence of a conscious effort to act on risks early, they usually manifest themselves late in the schedule while performing integration test and system test. At that point, resolving any serious problems, which may require extensive modifications to the system, can delay delivery by weeks or more. In the iterative approach, the construction of prototypes, builds, and artifacts from the first phase onward uncovers risks while there is still time to alleviate them.

We appreciate that it is hard to identify and describe some kinds of risks. For many reasons, some risks may be "obscure"—usually because people did not look for them hard enough. Another reason risks may go unnoticed is that some of the people involved are taken in by the hype that overstates what can actually be accomplished at the contemplated price in the desired time. If some risks slide through the identification screens, then the project cannot plan them into iterations and mitigate them in some kind of order.

Whatever the reason, on some projects some risks will be overlooked until late in the schedule, especially when a project team has little experience in risk management. With practice and experience, teams will improve their capacity to sequence risks in an order that permits the project to proceed along a logical path. In the construction phase, for instance, the risks that could throw the second iteration off schedule should be mitigated no later than the first iteration in that phase. The goal is to have each iteration in the construction phase proceed uneventfully and according to plan. That is not likely to happen if the project runs into an unexpected risk that cannot be quickly resolved.

## 12.6  Use-Case Prioritization

In this section we discuss the selection of use cases to use as drivers within a single iteration. Recall that every iteration in the Unified Process is driven by a set of use cases. Actually, it is more exact to say that an iteration is driven by a set of scenarios through use cases. It is more exact because in the early iterations we don't necessarily take whole use cases. We take only the scenarios or paths through them that are pertinent to the task at hand. Sometimes when we say that we select use cases, we mean that we are selecting the scenarios that are pertinent to the iteration.

The work that results in this selection is called *prioritize the use case* (see Section 7.4.2). The use cases are prioritized in the order in which they—or scenarios of them—should be dealt with in iterations. They are ranked over several iterations. In early iterations some use cases (or scenarios of them) are ranked, but many are not yet identified and thus are not ranked. All use cases that are identified are also ranked. The ranking results in a use-case ranking list.

Controlling this ranking is risk. We rank the use cases in the order of the risk that they embody. Here, we use the term *risk* in a broad sense. For example, having to change the architecture of the system in later phases is a risk that we want to avoid. To not build the right system is a risk that we want to mitigate early by finding the true requirements. The selection process is thus risk-driven. We place the risks we identify on a risk list, as discussed in section 12.5.1 and we translate each risk into a use case that when implemented mitigates the risk. That use case will then be inserted at a position in the use-case ranking list that corresponds to its level of risk.

In early iterations we devote the prioritize use cases activity to risks related to the scope of the system and the architecture. In later iterations, we select new use cases to fill in the architecture already selected with more functionality. We put more muscles on the skeleton. The later use cases are added in some logical order. That logical order corresponds to ranks in the use-case ranking list. For example, use cases that need other use cases in order to function are ranked lower and thus are developed after the others. See Section 5.3 for a discussion of the iterative approach as a risk-driven endeavor. In the next three sections we deal with the three risk categories: specific risks, architectural risks, and requirements risks.

### 12.6.1 Risks Specific to a Particular Product

This is the kind of risk—the technical risks—that we discussed in Section 5.3.1. We translate them to use cases that, when realized properly, mitigate the risk. Each risk is mapped to a use case that, when implemented, mitigates it. We have to identify these risks one by one, because dealing with them is not formally built into the process. What we mean by "formally built into the process" is that the process provides a specific place in which to deal with a certain type of risk. For example, certain architectural risks are considered in the inception phase, others in the elaboration phase, as discussed in Section 12.6.2. Risks that are not formally built into the process need to be managed one by one and mitigated before their presence would affect the progress of development.

### 12.6.2 Risk of Not Getting the Architecture Right

One of the most serious risks is that of not building a system that can evolve gracefully over the coming phases or during its lifetime, that is, not establishing a resilient architecture. This risk is dealt with explicitly during the inception and elaboration phases, when we make sure that we have the right architecture and can freeze it (except for minor changes in the construction phase). That is what we meant in the previous paragraph when we said that finding and dealing with certain kinds of risks is built into the Unified Process. In this case, for instance, the inception and elaboration phases deal explicitly with architecture.

How do we determine which use cases are most important to getting the architecture right? How do we mitigate the risk of not getting a stable architecture? Well, we seek the architecturally significant use cases. They are the ones that cover the main tasks or functions the system is to accomplish. You ask yourself the question, why do we build this system?

The answer is found in the *critical* use cases—those that are most important to the users of the system. In addition, the use cases that have important nonfunctional requirements, such as performance, response times, and so on, fall into this category.

These use cases usually help find the skeleton of the system on top of which we add the rest of the functions required (See Section 7.2.4).

Other categories of use cases are

- *Secondary.* These use cases support the critical ones. They involve secondary functions, such as supervision and compilation of operating statistics. For the most part, this category of use cases has only a modest impact on the architecture, although they may still need to be developed early if, for example, a stakeholder has a keen interest in seeing some data output, such as the transaction fee described in the example in Section 12.6.3. Then it would be ranked higher because we want to mitigate the risk of not getting requirements right.
- *Ancillary* (nice to have). These use cases are not key to the architecture or to critical risks. This level of use cases seldom comes into play during the iterations in the inception and elaboration phase. If it does, it is only incidental to filling out the critical or important use cases.
- *Optional.* A few use cases may be critical or important, even though they may not always be present. We may need to work on them because they affect the architecture when they are present.

Moreover, we want to be sure that we have been through all the use cases that could possibly impact the architecture. We don't want to leave any functionality in the shadow so that we discover too late that we don't have a stable architecture. We need high coverage of the use cases that might affect the architecture. High coverage is important, not just for finding the architecture but for making sure that we can accurately predict the costs of developing the product in the first cycle. We must avoid the risk of finding out too late that we cannot accommodate a newly discovered functionality.

That is why we need to cover about 80% of the use cases in the elaboration phase. By "cover," we mean that we understand the use cases and the impact they may have on the system. In practice, on the average we identify around 80% of the use cases and include them in the use-case model, but usually we do not find it necessary to describe in detail all of them. In a typical project we may find it necessary to describe only parts of the use cases. Some of these descriptions may be brief, only a few lines, if that is enough to clarify what we need to know in this phase. In relatively simple projects we may detail a minor fraction of the use cases when working on requirements. In larger projects with high risks we may find it advisable to describe in detail 80% or more of the use cases.

## 12.6.3  Risk of Not Getting Requirements Right

Another serious risk is not getting a system that does what the users really want it to do. The means for dealing with this risk is also built into the process. By the end of the elaboration phase we want to be certain that we are building the right system. This finding cannot be deferred because in the construction phase money begins to flow in larger amounts. Which use cases are required to make sure that we are developing the system that is right for its users? Which use cases assure that the system can evolve in the other phases in such a way that we will be able to add all the requirements needed for the first release? We cannot leave any functionality in the shadow. We need to know that what we build can grow.

The first part of the answer, of course, is to do the requirements workflow right. We might create a business model (or in some cases, a more limited domain model). The second part of the answer is, through early iterations and prototyping, to build the system that users require and get feedback on it as early as possible. It is only through real use that we can be sure that we have built the right system.

---

**Example** | **Billing and Payment System**

In the Billing and Payment system we could assume that the bank would decide that it is very important to them to make money on its services. Maybe it wants to charge a small fee for each transaction. Incorporating this fee would be an addition of new functions to the core use cases Order Goods and Services, Confirm Order, Invoice Buyer, and Pay Invoice. From the standpoint of the architect, however, the charging function may not be very important in getting the architecture right. Charging can be dealt with as an extension to other use cases; it can be combined with a few use cases that cover charging. As far as the developers are concerned, the charging function is quite routine; they have done it before. Yet, from the customer's view, it is extremely important that the charging use cases are correctly implemented before delivery. For that reason, it is categorized as a high risk, so it becomes important.

In consequence, when the project manager considers the order of iterations, he or she has to weigh the importance of the charging function. On the one hand, if he finds that charging in the case at hand is a simple function that poses no real challenges to developers, he might decide that developers do not need to deal with it during the elaboration phase, and he might safely defer it to the construction phase. On the other hand, if he finds that charging presents a number of intricate internal problems (separate from other use cases), he should plan to deal with charging as part of an iteration during the elaboration phase. One of these "intricate problems," might be the customer's need to see charging resolved at an early point.

---

## 12.7  Resources Needed

You may feel that the iterative plan of phase-based software development possesses considerable merit, but several questions may be nagging you:

- How much are the inception and elaboration phases going to cost, both in terms of effort and in terms of staff qualifications needed?

- Where is the money to pay for these phases to come from?
- How much time are these two phases going to take?
- By how many months will the early phases delay what many people regard as the real business of software development, that is, construction?

### 12.7.1 Projects Differ Widely

It is no secret, of course, that proposed software systems differ widely in their readiness to enter development. Let us list four examples:

1. A totally new or unprecedented product in an unexplored domain—a green field. No one knows much about what is to be done or even if it is possible to do it. There is little experience to go on. We will have to depend on experienced people to make some informed guesses. Under these circumstances whoever wants this system is in some sense responsible for financing the inception and elaboration phases. The phases have to be financed almost as if they were research, that is, on some kind of cost-plus basis. Not enough is known to hold the project in the inception or elaboration phases to a fixed budget or schedule. In this kind of situation, defining the scope, finding a candidate architecture, identifying the critical risks, and making the business case are time-consuming tasks for the inception phase. Similarly, reaching the objectives of the elaboration phase, that is, getting the project to the point at which you can plan the construction phase, takes more time.

2. A product of a type that has been done before in a field in which earlier products provide examples but no reusable components. These earlier products provide a guide to the candidate architecture, but it may take a few days to make certain that the earlier architecture does indeed fit. Under these circumstances, the inception phase will probably be brief (a few weeks). It may require only one or two experienced people full time, but it will likely draw upon the knowledge of other experienced people that the small project team needs to consult. Because this kind of product has been done before, major risks are unlikely, but it may be necessary to spend a few days establishing that fact.

3. A legacy product exists, but it is to be converted to an up-to-date form, such as going from mainframe to client/server. To some extent, parts of the legacy code can be encapsulated and used in the new system. The inception team has to find a candidate architecture. Since other organizations have reused legacy products, the team knows it can be done. If the organization proposing to do the work has not done it before, however, cost and schedule information may not be known. It will have to devise an architectural baseline. It will have to identify an interface between the new and the old system starting from use cases and finding subsystems—one of the subsystems being an encapsulation of the parts of the legacy system that need not be changed.

4. Components exist, either in the commercial marketplace or in-house. The software organization expects that a considerable percentage of the new

system, perhaps 50% to 90%, can be put together from these components, but there will be gaps that require new code. The project will need to identify and specify the interfaces between both the reusable components and the new components, as well as between external systems and users. Developing from components does take time and effort, and the team may run into risks. On the whole, however, component-based development is faster and less expensive than developing from scratch.

These examples are not intended to define distinct categories. Rather, they represent overlapping positions. Thus we have to think in terms of starting states. How much experience does our organization have in the application area? How large a base of reusable components can we draw upon? Is this proposal more than a new release of an existing product? Will it push the state of the art? Is it a distributed system (where we have done only single-platform work)?

### 12.7.2 A Typical Project Looks Like This

In spite of the uncertainties that different starting states introduce, the initial development cycle of a medium-sized project might distribute effort and schedule approximately as shown in Figure 12.4. In general, to lay out the architecture and to mitigate the risks, phase-based development moves work to the front part of the cycle, as compared to development based on the waterfall approach.

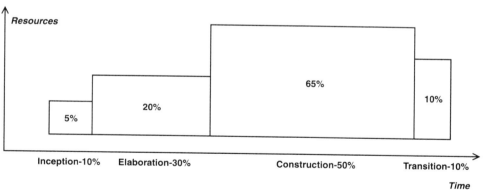

**FIGURE 12.4**  The largest block of effort and schedule time remains in the construction phase, but the other three phases require significant amounts of time and effort.

### 12.7.3 Complex Projects Have Greater Needs

What is the effect if we hypothesize a larger, more complex project—one with new functionality, distributed architecture, or, for example, severe real-time operation—that is also using new underlying technology? We will probably have to do a larger number of iterations. We will have to put more time and effort into the inception and elaboration phases. As a result, these two phases may grow as shown in Figure 12.5.

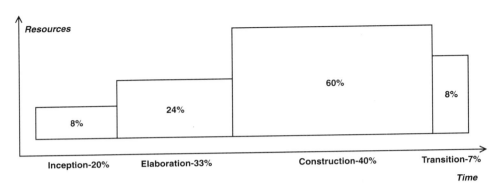

**FIGURE 12.5** Under the conditions imposed by a still more difficult project, more work is done in the early phases relative to the later phases. Primarily more calendar time is spent in the early phases.

We hasten to emphasize that the percentages shown in these figures are hypothetical. They should not be applied arbitrarily to real projects. They are intended to demonstrate the point that the more unknowns a project presents, the more time and effort will have to be spent in the inception and elaboration phases. For instance, in the example we spend more time in inception and elaboration than on the other two phases. However, the effort does not have the same impact, so we don't need to increase the resources in the same proportion, even if they also increase. At the same time, effort and time for the project as a whole increases.

The use of frameworks shortens construction dramatically but has less effect on the earlier phases. The inception and elaboration phases will be longer if reuse must be considered, but functions that are already available as frameworks don't need to be analyzed and designed, so overall, less time and effort are required by the project.

### 12.7.4 New Product Line Calls for Experience

In most cases, certainly for novel or difficult systems, the team has to acquire information beyond what it possesses itself. The natural source of this information is persons knowledgeable in the field of the proposed system. Even when detailed requirements are available, the team needs these interviews in order to find the architecture and to focus on the risks. Finding knowledgeable people is half the battle. Ordinary users may know only their piece of the entire process; they may not know what computer systems are capable of doing.

A common failing when beginning work on a new product line is to try to do so without *reusing knowledge*. Since most knowledge of the way the company actually works resides in the minds of people, rather than in documents (which are often unread anyway), reusing knowledge basically comes down to "reusing" experienced people. This failing expresses itself in the assignment of new people to the initial project team, rather than reassigning people experienced in the company's ways of doing things, if not in the new product line itself.

When a company plans to develop a new line of products, it knows in one part of its collective mind that this work will require its most competent and experienced people. At the same time, however, in another part of its collective mind, it is thinking that people of this caliber are highly important to keeping the current business going. They have to satisfy existing customers. The company has to keep the existing money stream flowing.

There is no easy answer to this dilemma. The executives for whom these experienced people are now working are torn between these two objectives—obviously, both the current product line and the new product line are important. In practice, many of the senior executives have been attached to the current line for many years. They are psychologically wedded to it. Often, most of them are reluctant to risk current business by giving away their key people to the new project. Consequently, the new team will have only a few people with experience, and they may not be the strongest leaders—managerial or technical. They may be the people that the executives were willing to let go. These new leaders then have to fill out their teams with a large number of new people, often directly from college.

In addition to their inexperience, the new people will bring a particular cultural attitude with them. They tend to view everything old—what the company has been doing—as outmoded. Only the new is good. The newcomers fail to appreciate the importance of subjects they did not learn at school, such as production methods and life cycle management.

We have observed that companies often fail to staff the development of a new product line with the talent needed to develop it fully in time for the market window. Deficiencies are usually not corrected until the second generation of the product. In essence, the first generation turned out to be just a field trial, although that may not have been the company's original intention.

### 12.7.5 Paying the Cost of the Resources Used

Supporting the team working with the first two phases, small as it may be, still takes funds. In fact, the difficulty of obtaining funds to support these two phases has been one of the forces leading software organizations to undertake the construction phase prematurely, sometimes resulting in well-publicized failures. Where are these funds to come from?

- In the case of a software organization producing a product to be sold, the funds come from "overhead" and, as such, are under the control of management. In the longer perspective, however, they originated with clients or customers. In other words, the software organization has to set current prices high enough to cover the cost of developing future products.
- In the case of a software organization producing a product for an in-house client, the cost of the first two phases comes either from its own overhead, from funds transferred to it from the client, or from funds allocated to it by

higher management. What the latter two methods of financing come down to is that management outside of the software organization has to understand the value of the early phases and allocate funds to support them.

- In the case of a software organization producing a product for a separate corporate client, the cost of the first two phases may come from its own overhead. It has this overhead to spend, however, only if it built this expense into past bids. If the next project fits within the software organization's normal business, this source of funds may be sufficient. If the proposed project looks to be risky beyond these normal bounds, there is a case that the client should contribute to the costs of the first two phases.

The reality is that important work is accomplished in the first two phases, and accomplishing it takes time and money. Moreover, in addition to funds, accomplishing it takes cooperation from the client. That cooperation—providing people from whom the software organization draws the information it needs—also costs money (although it may not be formally entered into the accounts).

## 12.8 Assess the Iterations and Phases

If the benefits of the iterative way of working are to be realized fully, the project must assess what it has accomplished at the end of each iteration and phase. The project manager is responsible for this assessment. It is done not only to assess the iteration itself but to promote two further goals:

- To replan the next iteration in light of what the team has learned in doing this one and to make any necessary changes.
- To modify the process, adapt the tools, extend training, and take other steps as suggested by the experience of the assessed iteration.

The first objective of an assessment is to examine what has been accomplished in terms of the preset evaluation criteria. The second is to review progress against the iteration or project plan:

- Is work proceeding within budget and on schedule?
- Is it meeting quality requirements, as revealed by tests or by observation of prototype, component, build, or increment operation by the stakeholders concerned?

Ideally, the project will meet the criteria. The project manager distributes the assessment results to the stakeholders concerned and files the document. It is not updated, as he reports the next assessment in a new document.

### 12.8.1  Criteria Not Achieved

Assessments rarely go that smoothly. Frequently, an iteration did not sufficiently achieve the criteria. The project may have to carry this work over to the next iteration (or the appropriate later iteration). This work may involve

- Modifying or extending the use-case model.
- Modifying or extending the architecture.
- Modifying or extending the subsystems being developed thus far.
- Searching for further risks.
- Adding certain skills or backgrounds to the team.

Or, simply, more time may need to be allocated to carry out the existing plan. If this is the case, the project might extend the schedule of the first iteration. In that event, it should specify a firm completion date.

### 12.8.2  The Criteria Themselves

One point to consider, however, is the evaluation criteria themselves. The team might have established the criteria at a time when it did not yet have available all the relevant information. In the course of the iteration it might have discovered additional needs or found that needs it initially listed had proved unnecessary. Hence the evaluators might have to change the criteria, not just check to see if they have been achieved.

### 12.8.3  The Next Iteration

A **major milestone** (Appendix C) marks the completion of a phase, the point at which not only the project team but the stakeholders, particularly the funding authorities and representatives of the users, concur that the project has achieved the milestone criteria and that passage to the next phase is justified.

On the basis of the assessment, the project manager (assisted by some of the people who worked on the iteration or phase, amplified by some of the people scheduled for the next iteration) does the following:

- Determines that the work is ready to advance to the next iteration.
- If rework is needed, allocates in which of the following iterations it should be accomplished.
- Plans the next iteration in detail.
- Updates the plan, in less detail, for iterations beyond the next one.
- Updates risk list and project plan.
- Compares the iteration's actual cost and schedule against those planned.

We note that, in component-based development, the metric (i.e., lines of code completed) is not a reliable indicator of progress. To the extent that a developer can reuse already designed building blocks (subsystems, classes, and components), good progress can be made while yet little new code is written.

### 12.8.4 Evolution of the Model Set

A key characteristic of phased, iterative development is the evolution of the model set. This evolution contrasts with the waterfall model, in which we imagine that, first, the requirements are completed, then the analysis, and so on. In iterative development, the models grow together, as an accord, through the phases. In earlier iterations some models are ahead of others. For example, the use-case model is ahead of the implementation model. Instead of one model evolving rather independently of the next model, we think in terms of one state of the entire system evolving into a more advanced state of the entire system, as we diagrammed in Figure 5.7. Each iteration—perhaps each build within an iteration—represents an advance in state of the entire system. This advance is reflected in the gradual movement toward completion of the model set. The degree to which this evolution has progressed at each assessment is an important indicator for the assessment group to consider.

In the next chapter we return to project beginnings and consider the inception phase on its own merits.

# *Chapter 13*

## Inception Launches the Project

T he overall intent of the inception phase is to launch the project. Before inception, you may have just a worthy idea floating around. The idea may be stimulating if it is totally new in a new field. It may be quite sedate if it is a new release of an existing product. Inception can be as simple as one person putting together a vision statement, sketching an architecture using various diagrams, and making a reasonable business case. It may be as complex as a whole research project. The point is, we don't stereotype inception into just one mode. After inception, even if the system is new, you have bounded the problem you are trying to solve and done enough to give yourself a level of confidence that it is both possible and desirable to develop a system.

Of course, this confidence is not yours alone. The work done during the inception phase provides the client (or its representatives), the development organization, and other stakeholders with the assurance that the architect and developers will be able to mitigate critical risks, formulate a candidate architecture, and make the initial business case.

## 13.1 The Inception Phase in Brief

The goal in the inception phase is to make the business case to the extent necessary to justify launching the project. To make that case, we first have to delimit the scope of the proposed system. We need to know the scope in order to discern what it is we are to cover in the development project. We need this scope to understand what the architecture has to cover. We need it to define the limits within which we will prospect for critical risks. We need it to provide the boundaries for cost, schedule, and return-on-investment estimates—the ingredients of the business case.

We are trying to get just enough of an architecture to assure ourselves that there is an architecture that can support the system scope. That is what we mean by "candidate architecture."

We are also trying to forestall a fiasco. Many difficult projects have floundered because they encountered critical risks, perhaps as late as system integration and testing, that they could not mitigate within the budget and schedule time still available. Uncertainty, or risk, is there, like it or not. Our only recourse is to mitigate the risks early or reduce scope or increase time and resources (i.e., costs) to avoid unmitigatable risks.

We are trying to make the initial business case—to view the envisioned system in economic terms, that is, early estimates of cost, schedule, and return on investment. We are asking:

- Will the gains accruing from the use or sale of the software product more than offset the cost of developing it?
- Will it reach the market (or internal application) in time to obtain these gains?

We are trying to support the project team with a development environment—process and tools. Of course, a software organization's development environment is the product of years of effort, much of it occurring before a given project is initiated. However, we tailor the Unified Process to the type of system being developed and the competence level of the development organization that is to do the work. These are the kinds of issues the inception phase is intended to address.

## 13.2  Early in the Inception Phase

Start to *plan;* expand the system *vision,* and begin to put your *evaluation criteria* together.

### 13.2.1  Before the Inception Phase Begins

Even before the inception phase began, you had some knowledge of what you were going to do. Someone—a client organization, your own marketing people, or even someone from your own development organization—had an idea and justified it to the extent of getting something underway. The extent of work done before the inception phase begins varies widely. Although this extent covers a spectrum, we may distinguish three points along this spectrum:

- Software organizations that produce products for general sale. The amount of information you have to start with may be quite substantial. The marketing and management people have probably given considerable study to the next product and have had some of the development people do exploratory studies. In other words, they have actually done some of the inception phase work.

■ Software organizations that produce systems for other units of the same company, that is, the typical in-house development organization. We encounter, broadly speaking, two situations. In the first, a department feels the need for a software system and asks the software organization to produce it. The requesting department provides a description of what it has in mind but may have little grasp of the software ramifications. In other words, the software organization has little information as the inception phase gets under way. In the second, general management has felt a need for a companywide system and has had a business-engineering group working on what it should support. In such a case, the inception phase may begin with a good understanding of the requirements.

■ Software organizations that produce systems for clients. The initial request for proposal often contains considerable detail, perhaps many pages of requirements. In other, less formal client relationships, the client may have had only a brief vision of his needs.

If the product were being evolved from an earlier release, much of the work of planning the first iteration of the new project would have been done in the last iteration of the previous cycle. In the case of a largely new project, however, the originators would like to see their concept further developed. They may have made a rough estimate of how much work would be required, obtained funds to cover the inception phase, and established a schedule.

## 13.2.2 Planning the Inception Phase

At the beginning of a project, you run into a dilemma. Well-meaning people advise you to plan, but you don't have much information on which to base a plan. You recognize what has to be planned by knowing what needs to be done. That, we cover later in Sections 13.3 and 13.4. In the meantime, you can get started by taking these steps:

■ Get together the information that people gathered before the project began.
■ Get it organized so that it is usable.
■ Get together a few people who know how to use it.
■ Figure out what is missing, not in terms of all four phases, but in terms of the highly limited objectives of the inception phase.

In other words, limit this work to what you need to accomplish the key objectives of this phase, which we summarize in Section 13.1. Then, make a tentative plan to clarify the requirements that bear upon these initial goals and to detail them in the corresponding use cases. Plan to create a candidate architecture. You plan to carry this architecture only far enough to establish that the project is feasible, usually just to sketches of the architectural views. As soon as you can, try to establish that you will need one iteration, or in some cases two.

Keep in mind that the initial plan is *tentative*. As you gather more information, you modify the plan to accommodate what you find out. You try, of course, to complete the inception phase within the limits of schedule and cost that management (or the client) initially set. Because management perforce had to set these figures on the basis of limited knowledge, keep management (and stakeholders) informed of progress during the phase. It may prove necessary to change these figures.

### 13.2.3 Expanding the System Vision

At the beginning of the life cycle, the team may have available little more than a one-page vision statement. It contains a feature list (see Section 6.3), little performance information, scant knowledge of the risks that the developers may encounter, perhaps a vague reference to a possible architecture (maybe just the phrase "client/server" or the like), and a round number guess at the economics involved (such as 10 million dollars and two years).

This initial team may include the project manager, the architect, an experienced developer or two, a test engineer (particularly if test problems loom large), and probably representatives of the client or users. The first step is to expand the vision statement to the degree necessary to guide the inception phase.

Now, it is easy to state this point, but it is hard to carry it out. That is why there should be representatives of the interests involved. That is why they should be people with experience. That is why they should integrate differing views, not just compromise on a midpoint. That is why it takes a little time to think through this very difficult task. Bear in mind that we are not seeking consensus; we are seeking the best answer. Right answers come from a leader, from the person responsible for managing the money being put into this work, but also a leader informed by knowledgeable specialists.

In the case of a product that is similar to one done before, they may merely have to establish this similarity, and doing so may take only a few days. Some inception phases are just a day long, (e.g., a second cycle for an existing simple product). A green-field project may take several months.

In the case of highly original systems, the inception phase may be lengthy and costly.

### 13.2.4 Setting the Evaluation Criteria

When the project manager has enough information to set forth the fine-grained plan for the first iteration, he also sets forth the evaluation criteria that indicate the iteration has reached its objectives. The "fine-grained" plan for the first iteration may be rather coarse because of the sparsity of information. If that is the case, the evaluation criteria may be rather general. As the iteration proceeds and more becomes known, the project manager will be able to refine the criteria. However, for the four objectives of the inception phase, we offer some general evaluation criteria:

***Resolve system scope***    The initial vision no doubt provided some idea of the system scope, but it did not precisely define it. In the inception phase the project draws a line around exactly what is to be within the proposed system and what is without. Then it identifies the external actors, which may be other systems or people, with which the system is to interact. It specifies at a high level the nature of this interaction. The issues include:

- Is what is to be within the system clear?
- Are all the actors identified?
- Is the general nature of the interfaces (user interfaces and communication protocols) to the actors set forth?
- Can what is within the scope stand by itself as a functioning system?

***Resolve ambiguities in the requirements needed in this phase***    The "requirements" at the beginning of the inception phase may range from a broad vision to many pages of textual description. However, these initial requirements are likely to contain ambiguities. The issues for evaluation are:

- Has the limited number of use-case requirements (functional as well as non-functional) needed to reach the objectives of this phase been identified and detailed?
- Have requirements been identified and detailed in the Supplementary Requirements (see Section 6.7)?

***Establish a candidate architecture***    As a matter of experience, the people in the inception phase can focus rather quickly on the functions that are new or require unprecedented performance. Among these, they have to select the few that might imperil the development of the whole system. For these few functions, they develop at least one workable architecture. The evaluation criteria are:

- Does it meet users' needs?
- Is it likely to work? (Consider this criterion in the light of the extent to which the candidate architecture has been carried. Since a prototype was not prepared, for instance, the candidate-architecture description is judged on its "promise" to work.)

To answer this question, we must consider several issues. Can it appropriately employ the technology (databases, network, etc.) it will be built upon ? Can it be efficient? Can it exploit resources? Can it be reliable and fault tolerant? Will it be robust and resilient? Will it evolve smoothly as requirements are added?

***Mitigate the critical risks***    Critical risks are those that, unmitigated, would imperil the success of the project. Issues to evaluate include:

- Have all the critical risks been identified?
- Have the identified risks been mitigated or is there a plan for mitigating them?

"Mitigated" does not necessarily mean that a critical risk has been entirely eliminated in this phase. It might mean that the client is willing to modify the related requirements, rather than face the likelihood of project failure. It might mean that the project team perceives a path around the risk, though it will not work out the details until a later phase. In other cases, it might mean that the project team sees a way to reduce the risk's probability or to minimize its severity if it does occur. It might mean drawing up a contingency plan to deal with its occurrence. None of these issues yields to a simple, mechanical judgment, at least in marginal situations. The major objective of the inception phase is to provide a point in the software development process at which the project manager, senior executives, and the financially responsible stakeholders (including customers) can exercise business judgment.

***Judge the worth of the initial business case***    The issue for evaluation is: Is the initial business case good enough to justify going ahead with the project?

The initial business case covers another project area calling for fine judgment on the part of the responsible executives. In a familiar area, you would probably have good business-case numbers by the end of the inception phase. In a novel, difficult area, however, you might have only a wide range of numbers on which to base judgment.

## 13.3  The Archetypal Inception Iteration Workflow

In inception we carry on three sets of activities. One is planning the iterations, as described in Sections 12.4–12.7 and Section 13.2.3; the second is the five core workflows, discussed briefly in Section 13.3.1 and extensively in Section 13.4; and the third is the selection of the development environment appropriate for the project, as described in Section 13.3.2. In addition, Section 13.5 describes the initial business case, and Section 13.6, assessments in this phase.

### 13.3.1  Introduction to the Five Core Workflows

The principal objective of the inception phase is to establish the business case—the case from a business standpoint of going ahead with the project. To establish this objective, we need to work out the scope of the proposed system, sketch out an architecture, identify the risks critical to project success, and outline a plan to mitigate them. If we are proposing a new type of system, we may have to demonstrate it and its use by building a prototype—a proof-of-concept (usually throwaway) prototype. Prototypes can also be used selectively to manage and mitigate risk: identify high-risk areas and prototype key parts of the system with tricky functionality or known performance or reliability problems. For instance, in a fault-tolerant financial trading system you may want to prototype a failover mechanism very early on.

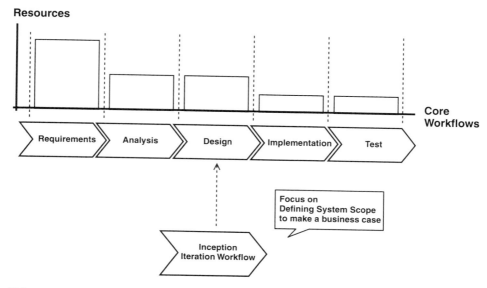

**FIGURE 13.1** The work of an iteration in the inception phase proceeds through the five core workflows. The relative sizes of the rectangles only indicates which workflows will require the most attention and the least attention.

Most of the work of the inception phase is accomplished in the first workflow, requirements, as shown in Figure 13.1, with some work following in the analysis and design workflows. There is little work in the final workflows, implementation and test. In this phase it is our concern to demonstrate new concepts, not to assure that the exploratory prototypes, if any, operate correctly in every detail.

The system analyst identifies the use cases and actors that define the scope of the system. The architect prioritizes these use cases, selecting those that are relevant for the candidate architecture. He or she prepares an initial architecture description for the candidate architecture. The use-case specifiers detail some paths through the identified use cases. The use cases described in detail are those relevant to understanding the system scope and the candidate architecture, to understanding the critical risks, that is, those relevant to making the initial business case. One result of this work is the first use-case model, if the project is a green-field development, or a new version of the use-case model, if an existing system is being further developed. We may also prepare a use-case ranking list, as discussed in Chapter 12.

In the analysis workflow we create an initial analysis model for most of the use cases or scenarios of use cases that we deal with in inception. The analysis model is important to understand the use cases clearly. It is also important to understand what underlies our first cut at the architecture.

If the system is new or unprecedented, the team in the inception phase may prepare an exploratory prototype by quickly putting together something to demonstrate the key ideas. Such a prototype is aimed at demonstrating the concepts involved, not at evolving into the eventual implementation. In other words, it is likely to be a throwaway. In some instance, establishing that there is an algorithm to carry out a new computation may be sufficient, providing the team can see that component engineers will have no problem implementing the algorithm in components capable of the needed performance.

The iteration may be ended in the form of the "candidate-architecture description," including outlines of the views of the models, as soon as the project manager determines that the candidate architecture appears to be able to function and the risk is either less than critical or mitigatable. That would be the case when the architecture is well established in the past experience of the project and the stakeholders.

### 13.3.2  Fitting the Project into the Development Environment

The development environment consists of a process, the tools to carry out that process, and services for the projects. It includes process configuration and improvement; tool selection, acquisition of tools, and toolsmithing; technical services; training; and mentoring.

Tools include those for supporting the core workflows: requirements, analysis, design, implementation, and test, as well as administrative tools for project management (planning, estimating, tracking), configuration and change management, document generation, and process on-line tools. In addition to these tools, which are often general purpose and obtained from tool vendors, a project may develop special tools, either within the project or within the company, to support its unusual needs. Services refer to system administration, data backup, and telecommunications.

In the inception phase, work on bringing the software organization's development environment into a supporting relationship with the project begins. It continues into the elaboration phase as the project encounters a greater need for tool support and other services. The project organization procures its development environment in parallel with the other work going on in this phase.

### 13.3.3  Finding Critical Risks

In Chapter 12, we devoted Sections 12.5 and 12.6 to identifying and mitigating the risks that affect development. In the inception phase, it is the *critical* risks that it is our task to identify and mitigate or plan to mitigate. A critical risk is one that would make the project infeasible. In Section 13.2.4 we discussed what it means to mitigate a critical risk. It is of the utmost importance to find risks of this magnitude during the inception phase. If we find such a risk and cannot see a way to mitigate it or a contingency plan to contain it, we must consider abandoning the project.

## 13.4  Execute the Core Workflows, Requirements to Test

In this section of the chapter we describe the things we need to do in this phase in more detail. The description covers the work in the inception phase for a green-field

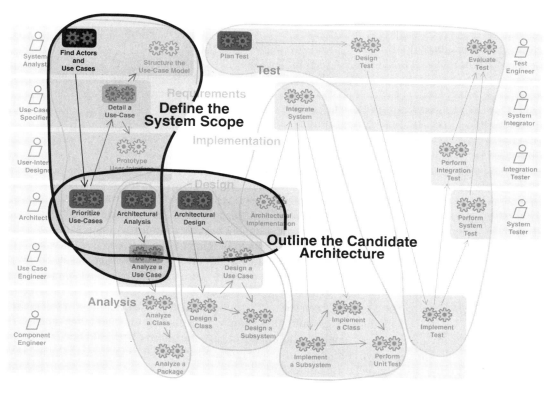

**FIGURE 13.2** The enclosures focus on the primary activities of the inception phase: defining the system scope and outlining the candidate architecture. Despite the apparent detail of this figure, it is only a schematic of the workers and artifacts described in Chapters 6–11.

product, that is, a new product, starting from a clean slate. Further developing an existing product would usually be much simpler.

Each iteration is a miniwaterfall, passing through all five core workflows from requirements to test. In Part II we devoted a chapter to each of the core workflows—two chapters to the first one, requirements. In this section we are going to devote a subsection to each of the five workflows, but we are going to consider them integrated within the context of the inception phase. To show where the emphasis is, we have drawn a couple of free-hand enclosures on Figure 13.2. One encloses the activities concerned with finding the system scope, and the other, with understanding the candidate architecture.

The worker titles shown on this figure represent roles that people take during development. In this phase, however, since the team is small, its members take on the roles of many workers.

### 13.4.1 Capture the Requirements

In the inception phase the emphasis is primarily on the first core workflow, the requirements workflow. This workflow includes identifying and detailing the use cases pertinent to this phase. It includes the following subjects, described in Chapter 6:

1. List requirements that are candidates for the system feature list.
2. Understand system context.
3. Capture the pertinent functional requirements as use cases.
4. Capture the related nonfunctional requirements.

***List candidate requirements***    Features often originate in the experience that customers or users have with predecessor systems or similar systems. In the case of products with large distributions, new features arise from demands in the marketplace. In addition, workers in the development organization itself conceive many feature possibilities. Some features originate in interactions between the software organization and the users; some originate in marketing. Features from all of these sources become candidate requirements on the feature list, described in Chapter 6.

***Understand the system context***    If the client has a business model (or a domain model), the people in the inception phase can work with it. If the client does not presently have such a model, we should encourage the client to develop one, even though doing so usually requires time and resources far exceeding those at the disposal of a single project. Be aggressive.

You should identify the use cases for business or technical systems that tell you what process you support. You should identify the workers and the core work products (work units and business entities). In all, you should have done 50% to 70% of the work of the business model before you proceed to the detail of modeling the relevant use cases. You can't develop software without knowing the process it is to support.

***Capture functional requirements***    The functional requirements are represented as use cases, as discussed in Chapter 7 and in Section 13.4.1.1.

***Capture nonfunctional requirements***    The nonfunctional requirements that are use-case specific are also attached to the use case to which they apply (Sections 6.3 and 7.2.3.2). Those that are specific for an object in the business or domain model go to a term in the glossary attached to the use-case model (Section 6.3); those that are more general, which are much fewer in number, go to the supplementary requirements (Section 6.7). Some of the latter are very important to select the platform, the systemware and middleware architecture, and will be very important in this phase (see Section 4.3, "Use Cases and Architecture").

### 13.4.1.1 Capture Requirements as Use Cases

Now we return to Figure 13.2 and discuss the activities there. In this section we go through how we capture requirements as use cases in terms of the activities shown in Figure 13.2.

**Find Actors and Use Cases** (see Section 7.4.1)   "Complete" requirements, or the completion of the use-case model, is beyond the resources of the inception phase. The workers in this phase have to, first, sort out the fraction of the use cases needed to accomplish the work of this phase and, second, detail them, as set forth in Chapter 7. Finding these use cases is outlined in Section 12.6.

The problem in the inception phase, again, is to restrict the volume of work mainly to detailing those use cases that affect the objectives of the phase. Ignore branches or paths through a use case and use cases themselves that are unimportant to the system scope, the candidate architecture, pose no critical risk, or have little effect on the initial business case.

To sort out the use cases to be worked with in the inception phase, the project manager works with the system analyst and the architect. The system analyst cares about being able to set the scope of the system. The architect will have to give some thought to all use cases in order to rule out those that don't need to be considered further. The architect must deal with critical and significant risks and identify those use cases that are needed to plan the architecture work, work that primarily is done in the next phase. The amount of effort required might be very slight in parts of the system where the architect has been through the use cases in prior systems and knows there is nothing of importance to the objectives of this phase there. The architect has to look at all the use cases at least to the extent of ruling them out of consideration at this point.

**Prioritize Use Cases** (see Section 7.4.2)   Next, the architect considers the use-case model and gives input to the project manager creating the project plan/iteration plan. This work goes on in parallel with the core workflow activities in each phase; that is, you can plan future iterations at the same time as you detail already found use cases. The iteration plan is the end result manifesting the prioritization of the use cases associated with the objectives of this phase.

**Detail a Use Case** (see Section 7.4.3)   At the same time that we accept the reality of this restriction of work, however, we reiterate the importance of completing all the pertinent branches in the use cases dealing with in the inception phase, that is, the use cases needed to set the system scope, plan the mitigation of the critical risks, and plan the work on the architectural baseline. In all too many cases, people believe that they understand the requirements needed, but actually they have overlooked some key ones. They have a tendency to believe that the benefits from detailing the needed use cases are not worth the cost. On the contrary, it is worth the cost, always providing the detailing is truly necessary.

To know where you are going is the objective. It does not mean, however, that you worked through a vast numbers of use cases. Usually, since you don't need to make an architectural prototype in this phase, you don't need to work through implementation and test at all. However, if you want to demonstrate the core ideas with a throwaway prototype, you will have to consider a small percentage of the **use-case mass** (Appendix C), to be explained next, for this prototype. You may have to detail something like 10% of the use-case mass in the use-case model.

What this statement means is that, while we may look at many use cases, we detail only a fraction of them. We go into more detail with the ones that are pertinent. For instance, if we select 50% of the eventual total of use cases as potentially pertinent to this phase and then find that only 20% of the scenarios of each one, on the average, need to be detailed further, we have worked out in detail only 10% of the entire use-case mass. The point is that we are trying to hold the cost and schedule of the inception phase down. Exactly what these percentages are on individual projects depends on how difficult or unusual they are.

All the functional requirements needed in this phase are represented as use cases, as discussed in Chapter 7.

**Prototype User Interface** (See Section 7.4.4)    Not of interest in this phase.

**Structure the Use-Case Model** (See Section 7.4.5)    This activity is not in focus here.

### 13.4.2 Analysis

The goals of the analysis workflow in general are to analyze the requirements, to refine them and to structure them in an object model that works as a first cut of the design model. The result in this phase is an initial analysis model. We use this analysis model to define the use cases precisely and to help guide us to the candidate architecture—the more fully worked out baseline architecture is a matter for the elaboration phase. That means, of course, that very little of the analysis model is completed in the inception phase (say 5%). In fact, we might characterize the analysis model in the inception phase as a first rough cut; it is just a first step to the architectural view of the analysis model.

**Architectural Analysis** (See Section 8.6.1)    The task in the inception phase is to sort out the use cases or scenarios that we need to look at carefully for the purposes of this phase—primarily understanding and refining them. Given this initial set of use cases and scenarios, the architect builds a first simple version of the analysis model for those parts of the system. It need not be extensive, and it need not be perfect. The project need not expect to simply build on it in the next phase. They may, in fact, discard it, except for its guidance value.

**Analyze a Use Case** (See Section 8.6.2)    In some situations considering use cases one by one is not sufficient. The use-case model deals with only one use case at a time. In reality, use cases share resources, such as databases, computational resources, and so on, within the system. The analysis model reveals these shared resources. Therefore, we often have to carry analysis far enough to resolve these conflicts.

In this iteration workflow you may analyze and thus refine some of the use cases (the 10% of the use case mass) that you detailed in Section 13.4.1.1. You may detail half of them, that is about 5% of the use case mass.

***Analyze a Class and Analyze a Package***    If they are done at all in this phase, they are done minimally.

### 13.4.3  Design

The primary goal of the design workflow in this phase is to sketch on a design model for the candidate architecture to include in the preliminary architecture description.

If we need to develop a demonstration prototype, we do that by using prefabricated modules, 4GLs, or any fast development technique that just demonstrates the idea. Demonstrating unfamiliar user interfaces and algorithms makes it believable to all the stakeholders that the project is worth pursuing further. We demonstrate this prototype to representative users to ensure that it meets their needs and, if necessary, to make changes to meet their needs better.

***Architectural Design*** (see Section 9.4.1)    The intent in the design workflow is to develop an initial or first outline of the design model, a first step to the architectural view of the design model realizing the use cases (we identified in the requirements workflow earlier) as collaborations among subsystems/classes. We are keen on identifying interfaces (and at most defining some of their operations) between the subsystems/classes even if this is just an outline of the design. These interfaces are important because they are the core of the architecture. Moreover we need to identify the generic design mechanisms that we need as the underlying layers of the subsystems that will realize the use cases that we have identified. We select the system software and the frameworks to be used in the middleware layer (see Section 9.5.1). We should do this initial design model even though it will be sketchy since in this phase we are going just to the extent of a candidate-architecture description.

The design model realizes not only the functional requirements represented by the designated use cases, but the nonfunctional requirements, such as performance, that may be at risk.

If the proposed system is to be deployed over nodes, the architect will design a small-scale version of the deployment model, limited, for instance, to performance-challenged nodes or connections between nodes. At this point the project manager might ask a use-case engineer to model parts of two nodes and the interaction between them where the challenge lies.

***Design a Use Case*** (See Section 9.4.2)    In inception the work on designing use cases is minimal.

***Design a Class and Design a Subsystem***     Again, if they are done at all in this phase, they are done minimally.

***13.4.4 Implementation***     The extent of activity in this workflow depends upon decisions the project manager made earlier. Should he or she halt the inception phase at the point of a candidate-architecture description?

On the one hand, some contend that you cannot be sure that the candidate architecture functions until you (and the stakeholders) observe a prototype working. You cannot be sure that you have retired a risk until the part of the prototype addressed to it actually works. On the other hand, to hold staff and time in the inception phase to a minimum, we halt the workflows in inception as soon as we have an architecture description that seems likely to work. Deciding just how far to develop the candidate architecture is a responsibility of the project manager.

In the normal event he or she halts with the candidate-architecture description, in which case following the implementation workflow is not needed.

However, a demonstration prototype (a throwaway prototype) may be needed. In that event the project will follow an implementation workflow, although it may be small.

### 13.4.5 Test

In parallel with the activities in analysis, design, and implementation, as Figure 13.2 shows, the test engineers are acquainting themselves with the general nature of the proposed system, considering what testing it will require, and developing some tentative test plans. However, no substantial amount of testing occurs during inception, as illustrated by Figures 11.2 and 13.1, because the exploratory demonstration prototype is generally illustrative rather than ongoing. Still, the project manager may find a small amount of testing helpful.

## 13.5  Make the Initial Business Case

When we have found out, late in the inception phase, that the project has a candidate architecture and can overcome the critical risks, it is time to transform the vision into economic terms by considering the project's resource requirements, investment costs, revenue projections, and market (or internal) acceptance. One side of the business case is the business bid; the other side is the economic gains accruing from eventual use of the product.

### 13.5.1  Outline Business Bid

Estimating formulas, which underlie the business bid, usually depend upon the "size" of the eventual product. At the end of the inception phase, however, this size (remember that only a small percentage of the use-case mass has been worked out) may differ from the final size by a substantial percentage, say 50%. The estimate at this point, then, may differ from the actual cost at the end of the project by that same 50%.

For example, take use cases as a measure of size for estimating purposes. The span of person-hours to design, implement, and test a use case ranges from a hundred hours to several thousand hours. Where a given use case falls within this range depends upon several factors:

- *Style.* If the developers bring more features within the bounds of a single use case, it will be more powerful than an average use case, but it may cost more person-hours.
- *Complexity of the proposed system.* The more complex the system, the more costly it is likely to be (at a given size). Find out if you can simplify the system by reducing its functionality.
- *Size.* A use case of a small system is usually easier to realize than a use case of a large system. This system-size factor may have an impact of as much as 10 times on the person-hours per use case.
- *Type of application.* Severe real-time systems in a distributed environment, fault tolerant/high availability systems, for example, have a significant impact on the cost per use case by a factor 3 to 5, compared to MIS applications on a client/server platform.

This list is not exhaustive. Development organizations and stakeholders can narrow the estimating variables by building their own base of experience. In the absence of an experience basis, we suggest that you make estimates as you traditionally have. Then add estimates of the cost and time of learning a new approach, using new tools, and adopting the other new features of the Unified Process. After one or two experiences with the Unified Process, organizations find their costs have dropped drastically, time-to-market has greatly improved, and system quality and reliability have increased.

Project teams are not normally in a position to make the final business case at the end of the inception phase. Not enough facts have been put together yet. For one thing, the Unified Process does not call for the "firm bid" until the end of the elaboration phase. That is why we are calling the business case in the inception phase the *initial* business case. This initial case has only to be good enough—in fact, very rough—to justify moving into the elaboration phase. For instance, at the current state of the personal computer marketplace, you would not have to do an inception phase to find out that there is no business case for putting another routine word processor on the market. In the case of projects that companies actually contemplate, however, the business case is always an issue; it always takes a lot of investigation.

The staff requirements and schedule of the early iterations themselves have to be supported financially. The need project managers of early iterations have for data on which to base the effort and schedule of future projects is often little appreciated. Therefore, organizations should keep track of appropriate metrics for the inception phase. These numbers would give them a base for estimating what the numbers for iterations in the inception phase of the next project might be. Past numbers could be modified in accordance with informed judgment as to whether the next project is going to be more complex or less complex than the base projects.

### 13.5.2 Estimate Return on Investment

This business estimate provides one side of the business case. For the other side, there is no neat formula for computing the gains the software will provide. In the case of marketable software, the number of units sold, the price at which the product will sell, and the period over which sales will endure—all are matters for marketing to consider and executives to judge. In the case of software for internal use, ask the affected departments to estimate the savings they expect. The margin of error is usually large, but at least the estimate provides a basis for weighing the gains against the costs.

For a commercial software product, the business case should include a set of assumptions about the project and the order of magnitude return-on-investment if those assumptions are true. To assure that the business case will be reasonably certain to pay off, management often sets a large return-on-investment hurdle ratio.

At this point you can make a business case in general; that is, it looks as if it would be profitable or worthwhile to proceed with the project. It looks as if the project will pay off. What we need as we conclude the inception phase is not exact numbers but the knowledge that the system is within the economic reach of the development organization and its client(s). At this point, you don't yet have the detailed information necessary to complete the business case in financial terms. To do that, you have to get to the stage of having a reasonably firm and accurate bid and schedule. You check these assumptions again at the end of the elaboration phase when you have defined the project more precisely.

## 13.6  Assess the Iteration(s) in the Inception Phase

Near the beginning of the inception phase, as soon as adequate information became available, the project manager set criteria with which to evaluate the completion of the first iteration and the whole phase, as detailed in Section 13.2.4. As the inception phase draws to a close, the project manager also appoints a group (which may be just a couple of people) to evaluate it. The assessment group usually includes a representative of the customer or users. For a project of some magnitude, it may be necessary to include representatives for all the affected stakeholders. Some of the criteria may turn out not to be achievable within the original plan. Examples of these criteria include

- Extension of the use-case model to the point needed by this phase.
- Bringing a proof-of-concept exploratory prototype to the point of demonstration.
- Suspicion that all the critical risks have not been found.
- The fact that critical risks already listed have not been adequately mitigated or sufficiently covered by a contingency plan.

The project manager carries the criteria not yet fulfilled over to later iterations and modifies the plans and schedules of the affected iterations accordingly. For example, that additional workers with certain skills or backgrounds may need to join the team in the later iteration.

A crucial result of the assessment of the inception phase is the major decision of whether to go ahead or cancel. You examine the objectives of this phase—scope, critical risks, candidate architecture—and decide either to proceed with it or to cancel it. You may have to wait for this first major milestone before deciding to go forward. You should cancel as soon as you have the facts to justify doing so—there is no use spending additional effort. However, this decision is not an arbitrary one. To go forward or to halt requires the concurrence of the stakeholders, particularly the funding authorities and representatives of the users. After all, in the case of a possible cancellation, the customer may devise a way around the obstacle.

## 13.7  Planning the Elaboration Phase

Toward the end of the inception phase, as we become concerned with the cost and schedule of the elaboration phase, we begin to plan it. We want to elaborate about 80% of all the requirements; we want to leave nothing of importance to the architecture in the shadow. We need to do this both to be able to make a closer bid than the limited data in inception permitted and to be able to use this to select our architecture. Eighty percent of the use-case mass is the approximate proportion we usually need to make the business bid. Within that 80%, we may need to analyze 50% of it to understand the requirements well.

To get to the architecture baseline, we may need as much as 80% to be sure that we have not left anything of importance out. From this 80% we select the significant part of the entire use-case mass upon which we will base the design of the architectural baseline. These significant use cases are a still smaller percentage of the entire use-case mass than the 80% we have looked at, say, 40% of the use cases and 20% of each one as an average. The product of those two percentages is a use-case mass of only 8%. In other words, less than 10% of the use-case mass usually illuminates all that we need to know at this point about the significant use cases. We use this fraction to drive the work on the architecture baseline, which includes an architecture description and versions of all the models.

In this way we work our way to the iterations needed in the elaboration phase—if more than one is needed. We can assume one iteration, but there may be more in complex cases. We decide what is suitable to do in each iteration, which requirements to implement and test, and thereby which risks to mitigate.

Experience indicates that much of the design and implementation developed in the inception phase, such as the exploratory proof-of-concept prototypes, will not be suitable for building on in the next phase.

By now you may be having some difficulty keeping track of all these percentages. Therefore, we have brought them together in Table 13.1 for easy reference.

**TABLE 13.1** Working with use cases.

| | Business model completed | Use cases identified | Use-case mass described | Use-case mass analyzed | Use-case mass designed, implemented, and tested |
|---|---|---|---|---|---|
| Inception phase | 50%–70% | 50% | 10% | 5% | A small percentage for a proof-of-concept prototype |
| Elaboration phase | Almost 100% | 80% or more | 40%–80% | 20%–40% | Less than 10% |
| Construction phase | 100% | 100% | 100% | 100% if maintained | 100% |
| Transition phase | | | | | |

Note: The numbers in the table are just rough indicators. We distinguish between identifying and saying a few words about a use case and describe them more fully, which is done in the Detail a Use Case activity (Section 7.4.3). Analyzing use cases is done in the Analyze a Use Case activity (Section 8.4.2). The column to the right indicates how much of the use case mass is in the baseline at the end of the phases.

## 13.8 The Deliverables for the Inception Phase

The inception phase produces the following:

■ A feature list.
■ A first version of a business (or domain) model that describes the context of the system.
■ A first cut of the models representing a first version of the use-case model, the analysis model, the design model. Of the implementation model and test model, there may be something rudimentary. There is also a first version of the supplementary requirements.
■ A first draft of a candidate architecture description with outlines of views of the use case, analysis, design, and implementation models.
■ Possibly a proof-of-concept exploratory prototype, demonstrating the use of the new system.
■ An initial risk list and a use-case ranking list.
■ The beginnings of a plan for the entire project, including a general plan for the phases.
■ A first draft of the business case, which includes: business context and success criteria (revenue projection, market recognition, project estimate).

The stakeholders should now have a fairly good understanding of the vision and feasibility of the project. An order of priority among use cases has been established. The information is now in hand to enable the project manager to plan the next phase in detail. The results achieved in this phase are refined in the elaboration phase, to which we turn in Chapter 14.

# Chapter 14

## The Elaboration Phase Makes the Architectural Baseline

As we enter the elaboration phase, we pass a major milestone signaling three accomplishments:

- We have formulated an initial architecture—the candidate architecture—signifying that we know how to build for the proposed system an architecture that will encompass its novel and difficult parts.
- We have identified the most serious risks—the critical risks—and explored them to the degree that we are confident that building the system will be feasible.
- We have established an initial business case with enough detail to move into this second phase and have obtained the assent of the stakeholders, in particular, the ones who are funding the venture.

### 14.1 The Elaboration Phase in Brief

Our principal objectives are:

- To capture most of the remaining requirements, formulating the functional requirements as use cases.

- To establish a sound architectural foundation—the architectural baseline—to guide the work of the construction and transition phases and to extend guidance to future generations.
- To continue to monitor the remaining critical risks and to identify the significant risks to the point at which we can estimate their impact on the business case and particularly the bid.
- To fill in further details of the project plan.

To accomplish these objectives, we take a "mile wide and inch deep" view of the system. In some cases where technical risks predominate or are the most significant risks, we may need to go deeper to establish a sound architecture. In a large project we may thus concurrently need to take an "inch wide and mile deep" view of the system's hot spots. System architects need to identify the hairiest parts of the system as early as possible and initiate prototype/pilot "pathfinders" to identify and manage risk.

We make architectural decisions on the basis of an understanding of the *whole* system: its scope and its functional and nonfunctional requirements, such as performance. Moreover, in making these decisions, we have to balance the requirements, as expressed in use cases and the use-case model, against the architecture. The two develop in conjunction with each other, and they influence each other (see Section 4.3).

The primary focus in the elaboration phase is formulating the architecture baseline. This focus involves fleshing out about 80% of the use cases and addressing the risks that interfere with this objective. In this phase we add to the development environment, not only to carry out the activities of this phase but to get ready for the construction phase. Toward the end of this phase we will have accumulated the information necessary to plan the construction phase. Also, by this time we will have enough information to make a reliable business case, work that we initiated in inception.

## 14.2 Early in the Elaboration Phase

At the beginning of the elaboration phase we receive from the inception phase a plan for the elaboration phase, a partially filled out use-case model, and a candidate-architecture description. We may have the beginnings of an analysis model and a design model. However, we cannot count on reusing these models, although they may provide some guidance. One task of the elaboration phase, in fact, is to fill out these models, again not completely but to the extent necessary to reach the architectural baseline.

We may also have a proof-of-concept prototype to demonstrate the use of the system. However, we cannot expect to build on this prototype. It is usually prepared in the quickest available way to establish feasibility, not to provide a base on which to build in the next phase.

### 14.2.1 Planning the Elaboration Phase

The planning of this phase conducted at the end of the inception phase may not have been complete. Often, the resources that will be available in the elaboration phase are not known in full until the phase has begun. In some cases, there is a time lapse between the end of the inception phase and the beginning of the elaboration phase. With more up-to-date knowledge of the resources, the schedule, and the people available, the project manager modifies the previous iteration plan and phase plan.

### 14.2.2 Building the Team

Not everything the team working in the inception phase uncovered was recorded. Therefore, the project manager carries over as much of the team as needed into elaboration. They serve, in part, as "team memory." Moreover, additional capabilities come to the fore in elaboration. For instance, people who have a working knowledge of the reusable building blocks that may be appropriate for this project will be needed. Also, the elaboration team is usually a little larger than the inception team. New people will come on board. The project manager should select some of these people so that they can carry over into the construction phase, perhaps to become leaders of design teams.

### 14.2.3 Modifying the Development Environment

In the light of developments in the inception phase and expected in the elaboration phase, the project manager continues to implement changes in the development environment, first discussed in Section 13.3.2.

### 14.2.4 Setting Evaluation Criteria

The specific criteria to be attained by an iteration or the elaboration phase as a whole are unique to each project, but we may consider the results in terms of the objectives of this phase.

#### 14.2.4.1 Extend the Requirements    The evaluation criteria are:

- Have the requirements, actors, and use cases needed to design the architectural baseline, identify the significant risks, and support the business case and bid been identified?
- Have they been detailed sufficiently to carry out the objectives of this phase?

#### 14.2.4.2 Establish Baseline Architecture    The evaluation criteria are:

- Does the executable architectural baseline meet not only the requirements formally captured so far, but also the needs felt by the stakeholders as they view a working baseline?

- Does the architectural baseline appear to be robust enough to withstand the construction phase and the addition of features that later releases may require?

### 14.2.4.3 Mitigate the Significant Risks    The evaluation criteria are:

- Have the critical risks been adequately mitigated, that is, either eliminated or buffered by a contingency plan?
- Have all the significant risks been identified? (See significant risks in Sections 12.2.2 and 12.5)
- Have the significant risks been investigated to the point of being biddable?
- Are the risks still on the risk list susceptible to routine disposal in the construction phase?

### 14.2.4.4 Judge the Worth of the Business Case    The evaluation criteria are:

- Is the project sufficiently well defined to bid price, schedule, and quality?
- Is the business case likely to provide the return on investment or meet the investment hurdle rate that the business prescribes?
- In short, are we ready for a fixed-price contract (or the equivalent in in-house development)?

## 14.3 The Archetypal Elaboration Iteration Workflow

The archetypal iteration consists of the five workflows, illustrated in Figure 14.1. The workflows were described in Part II, but in this chapter we are concerned only with the part they play in elaboration. Again, we carry on four sets of activities partly in parallel. One set is the core workflows; the second is planning the iterations, as described in Sections 12.4–12.7 and in Section 14.2.1; the third is the assessment, described in Sections 12.8 and 14.6; and the fourth is further preparation of the development environment, first discussed in Section 13.5. In this section we provide only an overview of the core workflows and their role in elaboration. In Section 14.4 we back it up with detail.

During "architectural design" we capture, analyze, design, implement, and test only architecturally relevant requirements. We pay little attention to details that are not architecturally significant. We defer these details to the construction phase. The architectural baseline resulting from these efforts will be just a skeletal system. By itself, it will not do much, except for the parts that we have to implement in sufficient detail to verify that the architecture as a whole will work. We develop the baseline architecture in one, two, or, in extreme cases, several iterations, depending on the scope of the system, risks, degree of novelty, complexity of technical solution, and developer's experience.

The intent of risk investigation in this phase is not to eliminate risk altogether but to reduce it to a level acceptable for the construction phase. Another way to put this is to say that the elaboration phase addresses the technical risks that are architectural—

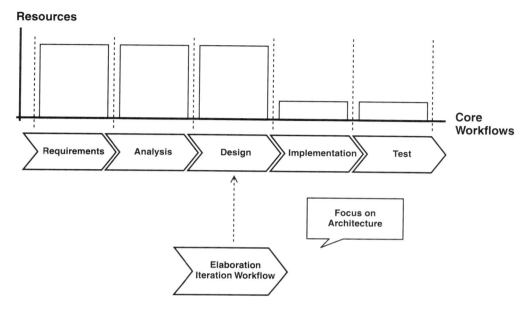

**FIGURE 14.1** The work of an iteration in the elaboration phase proceeds through the five core workflows. Most of the work is done during requirements capture, analysis, and design; we need to understand most of the requirements and to design the system. By comparison, implementation and testing require fewer resources.

by implementing the architecture! What do we mean by "level of risk acceptable in the construction phase"? We mean that the risk has been explored to the point at which we can visualize the way in which it can be mitigated and can estimate the amount of effort and time that this mitigation will take. The risk will not actually be eliminated until the use cases that bracket the risk are implemented, sometimes in the elaboration phase, usually in the construction phase, and occasionally not until the transition phase.

### 14.3.1 Capture and Refine Most of the Requirements

What does capturing "most of the requirements" mean here? We opened the discussion of this issue in Section 13.7 when we began to plan the elaboration phase. There we said we should aim at having identified about 80% of the use cases. We may describe in detail 40%–80% of the use case mass. We don't need to identify all use cases, and we don't need to describe the ones we identify in detail because we know from previous experience that certain subsystems can be readily designed (architecturally), contain no unexpected risks, and can be accurately bid. See also Chapters 6 and 7.

Of the use case mass that we describe in detail, we select perhaps half to examine very carefully through analysis. Of that half we may find it necessary to consider only a fraction of the scenarios to design, implement, and test to get to the architecture and to mitigate the risks. See Table 13.1. The aim is to capture the requirements to the degree necessary to achieve the objectives of this phase.

### 14.3.2 Develop the Architectural Baseline

The architect prioritizes the use cases and carries out analysis, design, and implementation activities—on the architectural level, as detailed in Chapters 8, 9, and 10. Other workers perform analysis and design activities, as described in Chapters 8 and 9; that is, they analyze classes and packages (see Chapter 8) and design classes and subsystems (see Chapter 9).

The test engineers focus on building the test environment and testing the components and the whole baseline that implement the architecturally significant use cases.

### 14.3.3 Iterate While the Team Is Small

While the team is still small, as it is in elaboration, it is time to iterate and try out different solutions (technologies, frameworks, structures, etc.). If the project is challenging, you may need three or four iterations before you get a stable architecture. Later on in the construction phase, when you may have scores of people on the team and hundreds of thousands of lines of code to keep track of, you need to work from the stable architecture and grow the system incrementally.

A single iteration may be sufficient if the system is small and simple, but it may be only the first step if the system is large and difficult. Additional iterations depend on considerations such as the complexity of the system and the architectural baseline needed to guide it, and the seriousness of the risks.

Iterations continue until the architecture reaches a stable level, that is, it represents the system acceptably and it has reached the point where few changes are likely.

## 14.4 Execute the Core Workflows—Requirements to Test

In the elaboration phase we build on the work of the inception phase. However, in inception we only had to make it believable that we could, in a later phase, build an architecture. Now, in elaboration, we will actually do it. We will revisit what we did before, but probably find little that we can actually reuse. We are now looking not just for use cases that represent critical risks, but for use cases that are architecturally significant. Second, we need a much larger coverage of the use cases to support a high-fidelity bid. Moreover, we face the task of ending the phase with an executable architectural baseline, a stable baseline to which we can add in the construction phase. Therefore, we must build with more attention to quality and extensibility than the inception phase called for.

At the beginning of this iteration, we go through the risks and identify the use cases, as described in Chapter 12. We need to cover about 80% of the requirements to find the architecturally significant ones, as well as to gather enough information to

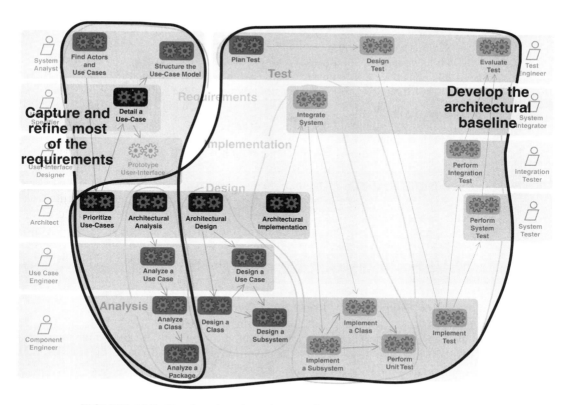

**FIGURE 14.2** The free-hand enclosures focus on the primary activities of the elaboration phase.

make a bid. It usually takes about that proportion of the use cases to find the 10% that are relevant to developing the architectural baseline.

In the following hypothetical project, we assume a moderately difficult system that can reach the architectural baseline in one iteration. We assume green-field development. As we have already indicated, the project manager has the beginnings of a project plan and an iteration plan for this first iteration in some detail, carried over from the inception phase. The first step is to add detail to the iteration plan in collaboration with the architect and senior developers.

The following account is arranged in terms of the five workflows. This sequencing of the workflows might lead you to think that we perform them sequentially, but the work within the workflows may go on concurrently, as shown in Figure 14.2.

## 14.4.1  Capture the Requirements

In this section we find, prioritize, detail, and structure the use cases (see Chapters 6 and 7 for a detailed discussion of requirements).

### 14.4.1.1 *Find Use Cases and Actors*    The system analyst identifies additional use cases and actors, beyond those identified in the inception phase (see Section 7.4.1). While we need to *understand* about 80% of the use cases to achieve the objectives of this phase, we don't have to *detail* that many. We may identify nearly all (the 80%), we describe only a fraction of them, and we analyze only parts of those that we describe. By "understand" we mean "to comprehend what is architecturally significant" and to be sure that we have not left anything in the shadows that can have an impact on the architecture or the bid.

How much we capture is also dependent on how much fidelity we need to have. If we are about to bid a fixed price, for instance, we may have to detail more of the use cases, maybe up to 80% of them. For some complex systems, we may have to identify nearly all the use cases and detail up to 80% of them. If we are financing the project ourselves, we may stop at a lower percentage. Stopping there would increase the risk, of course. It would be a management trade-off to accept greater risk in return for less time and effort in the elaboration phase. It would be "pound wise and penny foolish" perhaps unknowingly to face a substantial later risk for the sake of a trifling immediate gain.

### 14.4.1.2 *Prototype User-Interfaces*    Another activity that occurs during requirements capture is identifying the user interfaces (see Section 7.4.4).

We care about user interfaces during elaboration only if they are architecturally interesting. However, this is seldom the case—only in a few cases are the user interfaces unique in some way. If they are, we may have to create our own user-interface framework of some kind. One example is when the system that we are developing is, itself, a user-interface framework. Another example is a system with unique communication protocols that are important to the architecture in terms of performance or response time.

There is one more reason to do a user interface even if it is not significant from an architectural point of view. That is to learn from real users that it works. However, we should go to this extreme only if we have not been able to demonstrate the value of the system during inception. As a general rule, it is not necessary to prototype user interfaces during elaboration.

### 14.4.1.3 *Prioritize Use Cases*    Building on the partial use-case model prepared in the inception phase, we pursue two threads: to fill in more of the use cases and to work with the architectural baseline (see Section 7.4.2). At first we spend time on finding more of the use cases and then we move over to the architecture. However, we must coordinate these two threads. Our decisions are influenced by the priorities attached to the perceived risks and by the order in which we decide to pursue development. See Chapter 7, Section 7.4.2, "Prioritize Use Cases," and Chapter 12, Section 12.6, "Use Case Prioritization." From the use-case model, the architect produces a view of it that is included in the architecture description.

### 14.4.1.4 *Detail a Use Case*    Use-case specifiers fill in the details of the use cases that are necessary to understand the requirements thoroughly and that we need to

create the architectural baseline. See Chapter 7, Section 7.4.3, "Detail a Use Case" for the use-case specifier. In this phase we confine our efforts to preliminary descriptions of the architecturally significant and the complex use cases. Within the use cases we select for detailing, we do not usually detail all parts of them but instead confine our detailing to the scenarios we need in this phase. We avoid describing any more than is necessary. However, as we said earlier, in some complex cases it may be necessary to detail almost all of the scenarios and use cases, that is, nearly 100% of the use-case mass.

### 14.4.1.5 *Structure the Use-Case Model*    The system analyst reviews what he or she has done and looks for similarities, simplifications, and opportunities to improve the structure of the use-case model. The analyst employs mechanisms such as extends and generalizations (see Section 7.4.5) to get a more well-structured, easy-to-understand model. The model may get easier to modify and extend and maintain, since we, for example, reduce redundancy. However, sometimes the analyst does not discover the better structure at this point. It may have to wait until he or she is further along in the iteration, sometimes not until the use cases have been subjected to the analysis and design workflows.

---

**Example**    Structuring the Use-Case Model

---

As the developers work with the use-case model, they discover that several use cases have similar realizations. For example, the use cases Order Goods or Services, Confirm Order, Invoice Buyer, and Send Reminders all involve sending Trade objects between Buyers and Sellers. A reusable use case for this common behavior is Submit Trade Objects, which is introduced by restructuring the use-case model. As the developers proceed to realize the use cases, they will reuse the realization of Submit Trade Objects. The trade objects involved in this set, such as Invoice, Order, and Order Confirmation, change state in a similar way, support similar operations, and get sent between Buyers and Sellers. The fact that these similarities exist means that they can all be built from one abstract class: Trade Object.

---

## 14.4.2 Analysis

We started a draft of the analysis model in inception (see Chapter 8 for a detailed discussion of analysis). We build on that now, but we may find that we have to throw away substantial pieces of it. In the elaboration phase we need to work with the use cases that are architecturally significant and with the complex ones that we need to refine to better understand the underpinnings of the bid.

In this section we cover the activities architectural analysis, analyze a use case, analyze a class, and analyze a package. We need to take care of the use cases in analysis that are architecturally significant. This proportion is usually less than 10% of the use-case mass. We also analyze the use cases to understand them more

## *Adapt Requirements to Architecture*

As we capture further requirements—fill out additional use cases—we use our expanding knowledge of the developing architecture to do this work more skillfully (see Section 4.3). When we evaluate the value and cost of each suggested new requirement or use case, we do so in the light of the architecture baseline that we already have. The architecture tells us that some requirements will be easy to implement while others will be difficult.

After studying the situation a new requirement would create, we might find, for example, that a change to the requirements—a change that would have little or no semantic impact—could make the implementation work more simply. It would work more simply because the change in requirements would lead to a design more compatible with the existing architecture. We negotiate this change in requirements with the customer.

As we proceed to analyze, design, implement, and test the system, we need to align any changes in the design with the architecture already in place in the existing design model. Effecting this alignment means that we must take into account the subsystems, components, interfaces, use-case realizations, active classes, and so on that already exist. In this way, we can create a new design cost-effectively from what is already there.

---

**Example**    **Renegotiating Requirements**

Imagine that we are a company that sells a software package called Portfolio-Plus, which analyzes stock portfolios, to private customers. Three years ago customers were happy to enter changes of the stock prices manually. With the explosion of the World Wide Web, customers have become much more demanding. They can get the quotes effortlessly, for free and almost in real time. To stay competitive, we need to allow PortfolioPlus to receive stock quotes at the same pace.

Due to the architecture of PortfolioPlus, changing it "to tune in and listen to quote tickers" directly would be a lot of work. A less expensive alternative could use the API we had developed earlier for receiving input from an Excel spreadsheet. A simple and cost-effective solution would implement a macro in PortfolioPlus that not only loads an Excel spreadsheet but requests a new version of it from our Web site, with the quotes the user needs. Our job then boils down to three tasks:

- Generating the spreadsheet on our Web site when PortfolioPlus customers request it.
- Enabling the Web site to accommodate PortfolioPlus users in the expected volume.
- Writing the macro that fetches the spreadsheet.

**Example**   Real Life

This example demonstrates reuse in a real sense and shows the impact negotiations may have on a project.

By negotiating the requirements with the customer in the light of an available architecture, companies have been able to build systems of lower cost and higher quality. A typical example involving a telecom company illustrates this improvement.

The customer had prepared a thorough list of requirements in a form similar to use cases. As it estimated the cost of developing this system, it found out that building it on a custom basis would take about 25 person-years. The software supplier showed the telecom company that, by modifying its requirements to align with an existing architecture, it could get something similar, though not exactly the same. By patterning after this existing architecture, it was possible to cut the development cost by 90%!

The telecom company decided to go with this architecture. It got a system that was a standard product, slightly changed to accommodate its special needs. It saved more than 20 person-years of development effort. On top of that, it did not face the ongoing expense of maintaining custom software and hardware and could instead rely on the much less expensive maintenance that came with the standard product.

The difference between what the customer initially wanted and what it finally agreed to buy was the result of how the vendor had architected the use cases. Slight alterations to the user interfaces, different ways to supervise the main processes, different ways to measure and present traffic flow, and so on accounted for that dramatic 90% cost reduction. In addition, the customer got more functionality than it had requested. It received at a low price what earlier customers had, in effect, already largely paid for. The software vendor could keep the price for these additional functions low since it had already implemented and tested them.

precisely and to discern their interference with one another. In total we may need to look at 50% of the mass of use cases that we describe in detail.

### 14.4.2.1 Architectural Analysis

In the inception phase we carried architectural analysis only to the point necessary to establish that a feasible architecture does exist (see Section 8.6.1). That usually was not very far. Now, in the elaboration phase, we have to extend architectural analysis to the point at which it can support a full-fledged architecture, that is, an executable architectural baseline.

For this purpose the architect does an initial (high-level) partitioning of the system into analysis packages, working from the architectural view of the use-case model, the related requirements, the glossary, and the domain knowledge available in the form of a business model (or a simplified domain model). He may employ a layered architecture. He identifies application-specific and application-general packages; these are the most important packages from a problem perspective. While looking at the "driver" use cases in the architectural view of the use-case model, the architect may identify obvious and architecturally significant service packages and analysis classes.

Also, while working from the collective needs of the use cases, the architect is looking for the underlying mechanisms needed to support the implementation of the use cases. He identifies the generic analysis mechanisms (see Section 8.6.1.3) that are needed. These mechanisms include both generic collaborations (see Chapter 3) and generic packages. Generic collaborations include such features as error recovery and transaction processing. Generic packages refer to features such as persistency, graphic user interfaces, and object distribution.

The architect is now in a position to improve the view of the analysis model.

### 14.4.2.2 Analyze a Use Case

Many use cases, as described in the use-case model only, will not be clearly understood (see Section 8.6.2). The use cases have to be refined in terms of analysis classes that exist in the requirements world but are not necessarily directly implemented. This need for refinement is particularly acute for complex use cases and those that are assumed to have impact on one another, that is, use cases that are dependent on one another. For instance, for a use case to be able to access information, some other use cases must have provided the information.

Thus, the architecturally interesting use cases and the use cases that are important to understand are refined in terms of these analysis classes. The other use cases, the ones that are not interesting from the perspective of architecture or understanding the requirements, are not refined or analyzed. For these use cases, the use-case engineers just need to get an understanding of what they are and the fact that they will have no impact. They will know how to deal with them when it is time to realize them—during construction.

The significant or complex use cases need not be described in much detail, only to the level the analysts need to understand the job the use cases are outlining, that is, the architectural baseline and the business case. If we looked at 80% of the use cases for the purpose of understanding their role in the system, and described less than 40%

of the use-case mass, then we can usually take care of somewhat less in analysis, because some of those use cases will not have any impact on the business case. (See Table 13.1 regarding these percentages.)

Then the use-case engineers start to find analysis classes that realize the use cases. They use the architecturally significant classes that were identified by the architect as input. They allocate responsibilities to these classes. Much of the work in analyzing a use case is to go through each use case in the use-case model and specify it in more detail in terms of classes and their responsibilities. They also show their relationships (between classes) and their (the classes') attributes.

---

**Example**    Class Responsibilities

As the developers work with the Pay Invoice use case in the first iteration, they suggest a class for scheduling and effecting payments—the Payment Scheduler—with the following responsibilities:

- Create a payment request.
- Initiate the transferal of money on the due date.

In a later iteration the developers may find that more responsibilities are required. Adding them should not require restructuring the classes. In a good analysis model, we should be able to add new responsibilities without having to throw away what already was there or, even worse, in later iterations to have to restructure the classes already found. Later, when developers expand the scope of their work, say, during a second elaboration iteration they may discover that the class will have more responsibilities, which they should be able to accommodate without restructuring. These responsibilities might include

- Track the payments that have been scheduled.
- Notify an Invoice when it has been Scheduled for payment and when it has been paid (Closed).

---

On the basis of this use-case analysis work, the architect selects the classes that are significant architecturally. These classes become the basis for the architectural view of the analysis model.

***14.4.2.3 Analyze a Class***    Component engineers refine the classes identified in the preceding steps. They merge the responsibilities that have been allocated to them from different use cases. They identify the available analysis mechanisms and find out how they are used by each class. (See Section 8.6.3.)

*14.4.2.4 Analyze a Package*    As we noted in architectural analysis above, the architect considers the services of the system and the grouping of the classes into service packages. This is done in the architectural analysis activity; given this grouping into service packages, the component engineers take over the responsibility for the packages and refine and maintain them. (See Section 8.6.4.)

### 14.4.3  Design

In this phase we typically design and implement less than 10% of the use-case mass. This small percentage is only a fraction of the use-case mass we identified in this phase. In the elaboration phase we design at the architectural level. That means we design the architecturally significant use cases, classes, and subsystems. Packages in analysis and subsystems in design are critical for defining architectural views. Whereas various classifiers may or may not be architecturally significant, packages and subsystems typically are. (See Chapter 9.)

*14.4.3.1 Architectural Design*    The architect is responsible for the design of the architecturally significant aspects of the system as described in the architectural view of the design model (see Section 9.3.6). The architectural view of the design model includes subsystems, classes, interfaces, and realizations of the architecturally significant use cases, included in the view of the use-case model. Other aspects of design fall to the use-case engineer and the component engineer.

The architect identifies the layered architecture (including generic design mechanisms), subsystems and their interfaces, architecturally significant design classes, and node configurations, discussed in the following sections:

**Identify the layered architecture**    The architect continues the work started in inception and designs the layered architecture. He revisits the system software layer and the middleware layer discussed in (see Section 9.5.1.2.2) and selects the final products to be used. The architect may incorporate existing legacies developed by his own organization in which cases he or she identifies what parts can be reused and the interfaces to those parts. The architect selects the products in the lower layers as implementations of the design mechanisms that correspond to the analysis mechanisms found in earlier steps (see Section 14.4.2.1). Recall that by "design mechanisms" we mean mechanisms in the operating system on which the proposed system is to operate, programming languages, database systems, object request brokers, and so on. The implementation environment limits the design mechanisms that can be employed by the product. They are obtained either by building them or by buying products that implement them. They are often the subsystems of the middleware and system software of a layered architecture. They can be built or selected in parallel with the analysis workflow. The component engineers will design in terms of them.

| Example | Java RMI for object distribution |
| --- | --- |

The Java RMI is used for object distribution, that is, the java.rmi package will be used in the elaboration iteration to implement the Submit Trade Object use case.

**Identify subsystems and their interfaces**   The architect then goes on and works with the higher layers of the architecture, close to the application layers. Thus, based on the packages in the analysis model, he identifies corresponding subsystems that are to be included in the design model. Usually he attempts to make each service package in the analysis model a service subsystem in the design; higher-level analysis packages become design subsystems in the design model.

This approach works well in some cases, but in other cases the impedance between analysis and design comes into play. In some situations an analysis package does not map to a design subsystem but to a legacy system (or part thereof). It may not be a simple one-to-one mapping. Rather, the legacy system may realize several analysis packages or parts of them, or an analysis package may map to several different legacy systems, that is, it is a many-to-many relationship.

In other situations the architect may select reusable building blocks such as frameworks, either developed in-house or provided by external vendors. These blocks may not exactly match the package structure that the analysis model presents as a proposal, so the architect may have to select a subsystem structure for the architectural design that is somewhat different from the one chosen in the architectural analysis work.

**Identify architecturally significant design classes**   The architect "translates" the architecturally significant analysis classes to design classes. As more design classes are identified, he selects those that are architecturally interesting, such as active classes, and describes them in the architecture description.

**If it is a distributed aystem, identify nodes and their network configurations**   The architect considers the concurrency and distribution required by the system by studying the threads and processes required and the physical network of processors and other devices. The use cases already designed, particularly as shown in interaction diagrams, are an important input to this effort. The architect allocates the objects used in the interaction diagrams to active classes, and these, in turn, are assigned to the processors and other devices. This step distributes functionality in both a logical and physical sense.

The architect prepares a new version of the architectural view of the design model and a new version of the view of the deployment model, both of which are included in the architecture description.

### 14.4.3.2 Design a Use Case   The architecturally significant use cases are now designed in terms of design subsystems, service subsystems, or design classes (see Section 9.5.2.) (The other use cases that were identified, detailed, and analyzed are

not carried through design in this phase.) This activity is similar to what we did in analysis (the activity Analyze a Use Case), with a few important distinctions. In analysis we wanted to analyze and refine the use cases and to get a specification that would be robust, resilient to future changes, and reusable. That specification would work as a first cut on design. We worked to find the responsibilities of the identified analysis classes.

In design, we go into much more detail. Moving from analysis to design, the component engineers have to adapt the analysis model to get a workable design model because the latter is constrained by the design mechanisms. However, the analysis packages and classes do give us a direct way to find subsystems and design classes. Once these are found we describe not only what responsibilities these design elements need to have but the detailed interactions between them.

In analysis, we described how the focus moved from one element to the next in performing a use case. We used different kinds of interaction diagrams to show this movement. In design, we also specify the operations used for the communication. In design, we need to take into account which reusable subsystems, frameworks, or legacy system to reuse and then which operations they have provided. If they are difficult to understand, the design will be hard to understand.

The result of this activity is a set of use-case realizations—design, one such artifact for each architecturally significant use case.

*14.4.3.3 Design a Class*    We design the classes that participated in the use-case realizations in the previous step. Note that the classes are usually not yet completed; they will participate in more use-case realizations worked out in later iterations. The component engineers integrate the different roles of each class into a consistent class, as described in Section 10.3.

*14.4.3.4 Design a Subsystem*    The component engineers design the subsystems resulting from the architectural design. During these steps the architect updates the architectural view of the design model as necessary.

## 14.4.4 Implementation

This workflow implements and tests the architecturally significant components, working from the architecturally significant design elements. The result is the architectural baseline, implemented usually from less than 10% of the use-case mass. In this section we cover the activities architectural implementation, implement a class, and implement a subsystem, and integrate system. (See Chapter 10.)

*14.4.4.1 Architectural Implementation*    Based on the architectural view of the design model and the architectural view of the deployment model, the components required to implement the service subsystems are identified. The executable components are mapped to the nodes in the computer network on which they will be executed. The architect then illustrates this in the architectural view of the implementation model. (See Section 10.5.1.)

### 14.4.4.2 Implement a Class and Implement a Subsystem    In the design
workflow, component engineers designed a number of classes relevant to the creation
of the architectural baseline. This baseline is to be an executable early version of the
system we are about to build. In this workflow the component engineers implement
these classes in terms of file components (there is usually one or more components
implementing a service subsystem from the design model). The activity Perform Unit
Test assures that each component works as a unit. (See Sections 10.5.3 and 10.5.4.)

### 14.4.4.3 Integrate System    On the basis of the small percentage of use cases
that are to be implemented in this iteration, the system integrator works out the integration sequence in an integration build plan and then incrementally integrates the
subsystems and their corresponding components into the executable architectural
baseline. (See Section 10.5.2).

---

**Example**   **Three Builds**

The system integrator suggests three initial builds. See Figure 14.3.

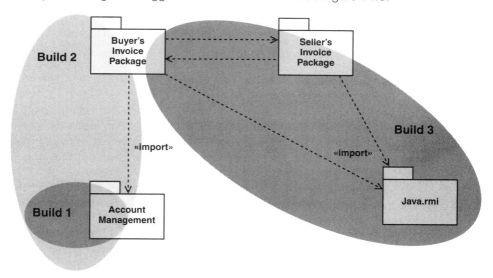

**FIGURE 14.3** The first iteration consists of three builds. Note that Build 2 includes
also the results from Build 1.

The example shown in Figure 14.3 consists of three builds, each of which is
subject to the activity Perform Integration Test:

1. The classes of the Account Management subsystem that wraps the legacy
   banking system.

2. The classes of the Buyer's Invoice Package that are involved in the Pay Invoice use case, plus the first build.
3. The classes of the Seller's Invoice Package and the Buyer's Invoice Package that are involved in the Invoice Buyer use case. These subsystems initially harbor the generic classes for the Submit Trade Object abstract use case. Later these generic classes are moved to a subsystem that is reusable in several other subsystems. This build has to integrate with the Java RMI package.

---

While we could manage to work (with some pain) without tools in the inception phase, in the elaboration phase it is clearly impractical to work without tools. For example, we now begin to have versions to manage, so we need configuration management tools. We need to stand on top of what we have been doing. It is possible for people to work with paper and pen until they get to elaboration, but they shouldn't finish this phase without having the architectural baseline under tool control.

For another example, workers will have been able to use the "production" language, say, Java, and tool set, and that usage will provide the advantage of trying out the development environment and familiarizing the workers with new tools and methods. In such a case, the first increment is more likely to use the infrastructure of the ultimate system, that is, the middleware and system software. The prototype is more likely to evolve into the real system.

### 14.4.5  Test

The focus here is to ascertain that the subsystems with their interfaces on all levels (service subsystems as well as design subsystems) and all layers (from systemware to application-specific layers) work; see Chapter 11. Of course, we can test only the executable components. If they work, we have some assurance that other things (in other models) will also work.

Starting from the lower architectural layers, it means testing object distribution, object storing, and retrieving (persistence) and concurrent objects and other mechanisms in the lower layers of the system. It includes not just testing for functionality but for acceptable performance. Many of the layers need not be tested per se; what we need to test is how the upper layers make use of the lower ones.

In the application-specific and application-general layers the tests consider how well the system scales when new subsystems are incorporated using interfaces already supported.

***14.4.5.1  Plan Test***    A test engineer selects goals that evaluate the architecture baseline. A goal, for example, could be to execute a use-case scenario within a given response time up to a specified level of load. (See Section 11.5.1)

***14.4.5.2 Design Test***   On the basis of these goals, the test engineer identifies the test cases that will be needed and prepares test procedures to test subsequent subsystem integrations and later the whole baseline. (See Section 11.5.2.)

***14.4.5.3 Perform Integration Test***   As components are tested, they become available for integration tests. The integration testers test each build. (See Section 11.5.4.)

***14.4.5.4 Perform System Test***   When the system, as defined by the use cases that are architecturally significant, has been integrated, the system tester tests it. This system (which is a version of the ultimate system) is the architecture baseline. The tester feeds back flaws to the component engineers or architect for correction. (See Section 11.5.5.)

The test engineers review system test results to verify that they accomplish the original goals or to determine how the test cases must be modified to achieve those goals.

---

**Example**   **Inconsistent Transfers Pose Major Risk**

---

System tests establish that most of the functionality seems to meet the expected quality goals, with one exception: When the testers execute the Pay Invoice use case, some of the results are incorrect. The legacy wrapper in the Account Management subsystem does not yield a predictable result for some transfers of noninteger amounts of the dollar, such as $134.65. Other transfers do work well, such as for $124.54. The testers call attention to this problem, and the architect labels it a major risk. The project manager appoints a task force to address it immediately.

---

## 14.5  Make the Business Case

The underlying reason for mitigating risks and baselining the architecture is to bring the project to the point in development at which the team can enter the construction phase with full confidence that it can build the product within business limits. Essentially, there are two business limits. One is the estimate—schedule, effort, and cost for a given quality. The other is the return on investment (or some comparable metric) indicating that the proposed system will be economically successful.

At the end of the inception phase, the software organization could judge the merits of the business case only within a very broad range—at least in the case of novel, large, or difficult projects. By the end of the elaboration phase, it has advanced its knowledge of the project to the point where it has greatly narrowed these limits. It can prepare a bid and make the business case within the much narrower limits of business practice.

### 14.5.1  Prepare the Business Bid

The development team is expected to carry out the construction phase on a business-like basis, whether the business arrangement is a contract with an external client, a relationship with another department within the same company, or the development of a product for sale to many customers.

We observe that software estimating is often based on the size of the project and the productivity of the project organization. The organization's productivity is derived from experience on past projects, but the size estimate is based on what it has learned in the elaboration phase. To make a realistic estimate, it has to pursue the elaboration phase to the point where it has a good grasp of the work to be done in the construction phase. That, the architectural baseline provides. Second, if the project presents risks of some magnitude, it has to investigate them to the extent of being able to estimate how much time and effort overcoming them will take.

### 14.5.2  Update Return on Investment

The business case, reduced to its essentials, is this: Will the gains accruing from the use or sale of the software product more than offset the cost of developing it? Will it reach the market (or internal application) in time to obtain these gains?

The software organization now has available an estimate of the cost of the construction and transition phases in the form of the business bid. This bid provides one side of the business case. For the other side, there is no neat formula for computing the gains the software will provide.

In the case of marketable software, the number of units sold, the price at which the product will sell, and the period over which sales will endure are all matters for marketing to consider and executives to judge. In the case of software for internal use, the project can ask the affected departments to estimate the savings they expect. The margin of error in estimating the potential gains is usually large, but at least the exercise provides a basis for weighing the gains against the costs.

## 14.6  Assess the Iterations in the Elaboration Phase

Each iteration is assessed at its conclusion against the criteria set in the iteration plan prepared before it started, as outlined in Section 14.2.5. The assessment team reviews the results of each iteration to verify that the baseline does indeed represent an architecture that will carry out the original goals and mitigate the risks.

If there are to be several iterations, the result of the initial one may be only a first cut at the architecture. That cut may be fairly well-described architectural views of the different models: use case, analysis, design, deployment, and implementation. The result of the second iteration is the second cut at the architecture. The final iteration provides the architectural baseline. At the conclusion of each iteration, the project manager, usually in conjunction with an assessment group, evaluates what was actually accomplished against the preset criteria. If the project is not achieving these criteria, the project manager reorients it, as outlined in Chapter 12. During the elaboration phase, that may mean carrying over unfinished activities to the next iteration.

Because the project manager has brought in the client and other stakeholders to concur in the achievement of each minor milestone, they typically find the major milestone (end of phase) less traumatic. The project team will have developed a closer relationship with the client than the one it often obtains in relationships growing out of the waterfall model. The client will have had opportunities to feed back improvements to the developing models along the way.

Now, at the end of the elaboration phase, the assessment convinces stakeholders that the elaboration phase has mitigated the serious risks and has built a stable architectural baseline. It convinces them that the system can be constructed according to the project plan and the bid for the construction phase.

## 14.7 Planning the Construction Phase

Toward the end of the elaboration phase, the project manager begins to plan the first construction iteration in detail and to lay out the remainder in more general terms. The number of iterations required depends upon the size and complexity of the project. Project managers usually plan two or three, sometimes four or more in the case of a large and complex undertaking. Within each iteration they outline a number of builds, each adding a relatively small piece to what has already been done.

Project management is still carrying many risks on the risk list. The project manager plans the order of investigating the remaining risks in order to mitigate each one before it turns up in the build or iteration sequence. The operative principle remains the same: Reduce risks before they interrupt the build sequence.

The elaboration phase will have filled out only percentages of each of the models. The project manager considers the order in which to work on the remaining use cases and scenarios and to complete the filling in of the models. This consideration leads to the sequencing of the builds and iterations. In large projects, to reduce overall schedule time by utilizing more people, the project manager sorts out work that the workers can accomplish along parallel tracks. Developing large, industrial-strength systems means that the project team has to find parallel paths through the work because such projects face a time constraint. The team is looking for a way to deploy a large number of people, often in the scores.

This way is based on the subsystems established in the architectural baseline. In the design workflow (inspired by analysis packages) we find subsystems on different levels. Subsystems have interfaces, and one higher-level objective was to identify and define these interfaces. The interfaces are the core of the architecture. With the subsystems and interfaces identified and specified, we are very well equipped to work in parallel.

One individual is responsible for a service subsystem within a design subsystem. A group is responsible for a design subsystem.

If the individuals or small groups are to work with a reasonable degree of independence, the interfaces that bound their areas of activity must be solid. To emphasize the importance of these interface specifications, they are sometimes called *contracts.* A contract commits the current developers and those in subsequent cycles to this interface. It is the fact that an interface is firmly established that makes pluggable architecture possible. Later, developers can substitute another subsystem, as long as they do not break the interface contract. Building subsystems that interconnect through an interface contract (or the equivalent) is much the same in principle as building systems of systems, which we discussed in the sidebar in Section 7.2.3, "Modeling Large Systems."

## 14.8  The Key Deliverables

The deliverables are

- Preferably a complete business (or domain) model which describes the context of the system.
- A new version of all models: use cases, analysis, design, deployment, and implementation. (At the end of the elaboration phase these models will be complete to less than 10% apart from the use case and analysis model that may include more (in some cases up to 80%) use cases to ascertain that the requirements have been understood. The majority of all use cases have been understood to make sure that no architecturally important use cases are left aside and that we can estimate the costs of introducing them.)
- An executable architectural baseline.
- An architecture description, including views of the use case, analysis, design, deployment, and implementation models.
- Updated risk list.
- Project plan for the construction and transition phases.
- A preliminary user manual (optional).
- Completed business case, including business bid.

*Chapter 15*

# Construction Leads to Initial Operational Capability

The overriding purpose of this phase is to produce a software product ready for initial operational release, sometimes called a "beta release." The product should be of quality appropriate to the application and in keeping with the requirements. The construction should take place within the limits of the business plan.

At the end of the elaboration phase, we brought the proposed system up to the level of an executable architectural baseline. The previous phases have reduced the critical and significant risks to routine levels that are manageable within the construction plan. During the elaboration phase the project team laid the foundation for the architecturally significant model elements of the design and the deployment models. This foundation included the subsystems, classes (the active ones), and components and the interfaces between them. It also included the realizations of the significant use cases. It accomplished this partitioning on the basis of detailing as little as 10% of the use case mass. Recall that almost all requirements (typically about 80%) were captured but did not have to be detailed completely to satisfy the objectives of the elaboration phase. That is where we are going in the construction phase.

## 15.1  The Construction Phase in Brief

The team working in the construction phase, starting from an executable architecture baseline and working through a series of iterations and increments, develops a software product ready for initial operation in the user environment, often called beta testing. It details the remaining use cases and scenarios, modifies the architectural description, if necessary, and continues the workflows through additional iterations, filling out the balance of the analysis, design, and implementation models. It integrates the subsystems and tests them; it integrates the entire system and tests it.

As the project passes from the elaboration phase into the construction phase, a change of emphasis occurs. Where the inception and elaboration phases might be compared to research, the construction phase is analogous to development. The emphasis shifts from the accumulation of the knowledge base needed to build the project to the actual construction of a system or product within parameters of cost, effort, and schedule.

During the construction phase the project manager, architect, and senior developers ensure that the use cases are prioritized, grouped into builds and iterations, and developed in an order that avoids backtracking.

They keep the risk list current by constantly refining it so that it reflects the project's current real risks. Their objective is to end this phase with all risks mitigated (except those that arise in operation and are dealt with in the transition phase). The architect keeps watch that the construction adheres to the architecture and, when necessary, modifies the architecture to incorporate changes that arise in the construction work.

## 15.2  Early in the Construction Phase

The project manager planned the construction phase at the end of the elaboration phase. When he or she receives authorization from the funding authority to proceed, he may have to modify the plan for the construction phase to the degree that circumstances have changed. In particular, we may cite two circumstances that often occur.

One is the possible gap in time between the elaboration and construction phases. The funding authorities may immediately authorize the construction phase, enabling the project manager and the project team to carry over without interruption and to maintain their detailed knowledge of the project. Unfortunately, there may be a gap of months between the submission of the proposal and bid and the actual award of the contract or other authorization to proceed. In the meantime, the project manager and the team disperse to other work and may not be completely reassembled when the go-ahead is received. In the worst circumstance, a new project manager and mostly new people take over the construction phase.

The second circumstance is that the funding and schedule are less than those planned by the project in the elaboration phase. The scope may have been reduced to match the funding and schedule or perhaps not. The point we are leading up to is that at the beginning of the construction phase, the circumstances may differ—a little or a lot—from those on which the planning at the end of the elaboration phase was based. Like it or not—and we usually do not—the project manager will have to replan to some degree. In almost every case he will have to adapt the project plan from the elaboration phase to fit the available staff resources and the schedule the stakeholders have set.

### 15.2.1  Staffing the Phase

In the construction phase, the work spreads beyond the architecture (i.e., the model elements that are architecturally significant). The service subsystems the architect identified in the elaboration phase were not complete—they implemented the core use cases and their core scenarios only. The project manager assigns additional people to this work.

The architectural baseline with its representation of subsystems and interfaces is the source from which the project manager draws to split up the work. Each subsystem becomes the responsibility of a developer acting as a component engineer. Normally, as we said in Chapter 9, the developer responsible for a subsystem is also responsible for the classes in that subsystem. It is unusual for a developer to be responsible for only a single class; that is too fine-grained a division of the work.

The construction phase staffs the following positions for the major work of the phase: use-case engineer, component engineer, test engineer, system integrator, integration tester, and system tester. Compared to the elaboration phase, the number of people acting as workers increases greatly, on the order of double, as shown in Section 12.7. Table 13.1 suggests the approximate amount of work left for the construction phase in each workflow—60% in analysis and 90% in design, implementation, and testing.

In addition to the workers listed earlier, the architect continues to be available, though the time he or she devotes to this phase is usually less. Moreover, because some 20% of the requirements remains to be captured, the system analyst and the use-case specifier continue to work.

### 15.2.2  Setting the Evaluation Criteria

The specific criteria to be attained by an iteration or the construction phase as a whole are unique to each project. They have been set, in effect, in the course of developing the use cases. As we have noted in earlier chapters, the use cases themselves correspond to functional requirements. They also have nonfunctional requirements, such as performance, attached to them. They are used to mitigate risks. Each build or iteration implements a set of use cases. The evaluation criteria for this set of use cases are then based on the functional and nonfunctional requirements related to that set of use cases.

These evaluation criteria, related to the use cases, enable the developers themselves to see clearly when they have completed a particular build or iteration.

Furthermore, additional material is prepared during the construction phase for which evaluation criteria are needed. For example,

*User material*    A first cut of the written material to support end users, such as user guides, help text, release notes, user manuals, and operator manuals, are prepared in the construction phase. The evaluation criterion is: are they sufficient to support the users in the transition phase.

*Course products*    A first draft of the course material to support end users, such as slides, notes, examples, and tutorials, are initially prepared in this phase. Are they sufficient to support the users in the transition phase?

For the construction phase as a whole, the evaluation criterion is whether the initial operational capability is sufficiently mature and stable to put beta releases in the user community without exposing the software organization or the user community to unacceptable risks.

## 15.3  The Archetypal Construction Iteration Workflow

The archetypal iteration consists of the five workflows, illustrated in Figure 15.1. The workflows are described in detail in Part II, but in this chapter we are concerned only

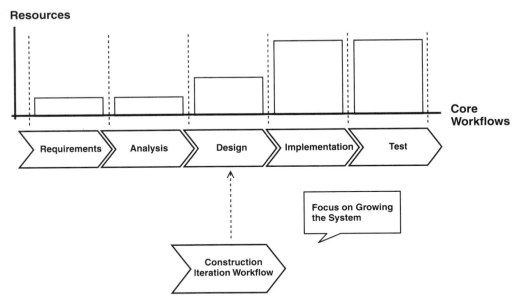

**FIGURE 15.1**  The work of an iteration in the construction phase proceeds through the five workflows—requirements, analysis, design, implementation, and test. The remaining requirements are detailed and analyzed, but the workload in those two workflows is relatively light. Most of this work was done in the two previous phases. Design plays an important role, and it is in this phase that most of the work in the implementation and test workflows takes place. (The size of the bars is illustrative only and will change on different projects.)

with the part they play in construction. Again, we carry on four sets of activities partly in parallel. The first is the five core workflows; the second is planning the iterations, as described in Sections 12.4–12.7 and in Section 15.2; the third is the business case, described in Sections 13.5 and 15.5; and the fourth is the assessment, described in Sections 12.8 and 15.6. In this section we provide an overview of the five core workflows. In the next section we back it up with detail.

In the early iterations of the construction phase the initial workflows receive more emphasis; the later ones, less emphasis. This emphasis shifts throughout the construction iterations. For example, if we were to draw a bell-shaped curve illustrating these successive workloads, the peak of the curve would shift from left to right, as each successive iteration brings more focus on the implementation workflow.

***Building the system***    By now requirements and architecture are stable. The emphasis is on completing use-case realization for all the use cases, designing the required subsystems and classes, implementing them as components, and testing them both individually and in builds. In each build the developers take a set of use cases, as laid out by the project manager and the system integrator, and realize them.

Use-case–driven, architecture-centric, iterative development builds software in relatively small increments and adds each increment to the previous accumulation of increments in such a way as always to maintain an executable build. It orders the sequence of increments progressively so that the builders never have to go back several increments and do them over.

Building the software in relatively small increments makes a project more manageable. It reduces the scope of the analysis, design, implementation, and test workflows to the lesser number of issues and problems found within a single increment. It largely isolates risks, defects, and fixes within the small compass of a single build, making them easier to find and deal with.

The earlier phases have investigated and mitigated critical and significant risks, but project management is still carrying many risks on the risk list. In addition, new risks may appear as the developers pursue builds and iterations and as users try out increments. For example, most programming languages have been around for a long time and a project may quite understandably assume that the compiler it plans to use will function satisfactorily. However, languages do grow and compilers are reissued, and a reissued compiler can contain defects. In one 80,000 source-lines-of-code project, the project manager eventually discovered that repetitive faults in successive tests were being caused by the compiler. Then a further delay ensued until the compiler manufacturer found the subtle defect and corrected it.

## 15.4 Execute the Core Workflows—Requirements to Testing

In the preceding section we outlined the general intent of the construction phase. In this section we present these activities in more detail, using Figure 15.2 as our guide. As in earlier chapters, this section is arranged in terms of the five workflows. Also, as

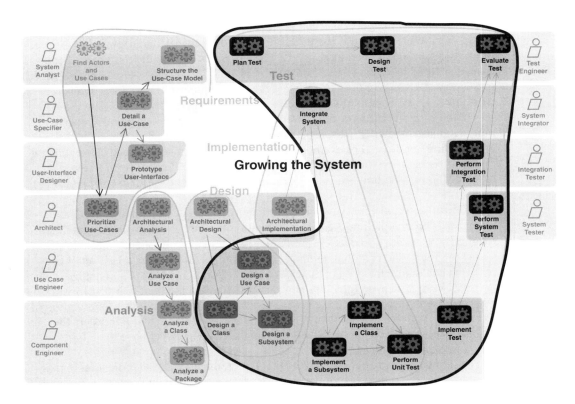

**FIGURE 15.2** The free-hand enclosure focuses on the primary activities of the construction phase.

before, while the arrangement is sequential, work within the workflows goes on concurrently, as shown in the figure.

In the course of this work, the workers participate in the workflows as outlined in Part II. They build on all the artifacts in the architectural baseline or in later iterations.

In the elaboration phase the project may have designed and implemented less than 10% of the use-case mass—just enough to provide the architecture baseline. Now in the construction phase the project faces the task of adding muscle to this architectural skeleton. In effect, it is going to fill in the models illustrated in Chapters 4 and 5. In particular, see Figure 5.7, showing the models filling in during the progress of the four phases. Each build and each iteration add more use-case realizations, classes, subsystems, and components to the evolving model structure.

In the following subsections of this section we describe the workflows sequentially, as diagrammed in Figure 15.2, but the workers do not actually do the work in this sequence. For example, we do test planning early in each iteration to trigger the test work required within the iteration. This test planning can be done before detailing use-cases, analysis, design, and implementation. This parallel work is not reflected in the following text. It bears repeating to note that all five workflows are repeated in each iteration.

### 15.4.1 Requirements

With this introduction to the construction phase, we turn next to finding use cases and actors, prototyping the user interfaces, detailing the use cases, and structuring the use cases. In the elaboration phase we identified all the use cases and actors; we *understood* about 80% of the mass, but we described in detail something on the order of 20%—from this number we were able to pick the small number (less than 10% that we needed to implement at that time) because we needed only enough detail to establish the architectural baseline. In the construction phase, of course, we are going all the way to the initial operational system, so we have to carry requirements capture all the way (i.e., identify and detail all 100% of them).

*Find Actors and Use Cases*     Usually only a minor fraction of the use cases and the actors remains to be identified in the construction phase (less than 20%). The system analyst updates the use cases and actors in the use case model, if necessary.

*Prototype User Interface*     In the inception and elaboration phase we did not, as a general rule, carry user interfaces to prototypes only if we had a new type of interface or needed one for demonstration purposes. However, the user interfaces must now be designed. How much we do here depends on the kind of system we are building.

For some systems—especially those in which some use cases require a very complex user interface—the user interface is hard to grasp without building a prototype. So we build a prototype (or several if needed) and have users try it out. Based on feedback, we massage the prototype until it satisfies the needs of users. Designing the user interface is part of the requirements workflow and not design (even if the name suggests so) and needs to be done before moving to the succeeding workflows. The prototype then becomes the user-interface specification (see Chapter 7 for details).

For systems that are expected to sell in quantity, we build a user-interface prototype, even if it is not very complex. The cost of replacing an unsatisfactory interface in the field would be too great.

*Prioritize Use Cases*     In the elaboration phase, we ranked the use cases needed for the development of the architectural baseline. In this phase, as we identify the use cases, we add them to the ranking list in order of priority (see Sections 12.6 and 7.4.2).

*Detail a Use Case*     Use-case specifiers complete detailing, working in the order of importance on all remaining use cases and scenarios of use cases.

***Structure the Use-Case Model***    The system analyst may want to improve the structure of the use-case model. However, since the system has a stable architecture at this stage, any changes must primarily concern use cases not yet worked with. Each changed use case requires a corresponding use-case realization in analysis and design models.

### 15.4.2 Analysis

In this subsection we again consider the activities architectural analysis, analyze a use case, analyze a class, and analyze a package initiated in the elaboration phase. In that phase we needed to take care only of those use cases that were architecturally significant or needed to support the business bid. To give the reader some feeling for where we are at this point, we may have analyzed 40% of the use-case mass in the elaboration phase. That is about half of the use-case mass, about 80%, that we typically need to support the bid. Please do not take these percentages literally. We reiterate that they vary somewhat with the circumstances of each project. Now, in the construction phase we are concerned with all the use cases, but we may not necessarily extend the analysis model with them.

As discussed in Chapter 8 (see Section 8.3), there are cases when the analysis model will not be maintained after the first elaboration phase for a new product. However, in other cases the project manager may continue using the analysis model in the construction phase and, indeed, all the way to the end of the project and beyond for the life of the product. Since the latter case is the more complex, we will in the following assume this case. The essential difference between the elaboration phase and the construction phase is that in construction we now complete the analysis model. The analysis model that we had at the end of the elaboration phase was the architectural view—it was to a large extent about architecture. Now the architectural view of the analysis model will be only part of the entire analysis model. At the end of construction the whole analysis model is in place. The architectural view is only a small subset of it.

***Architectural Analysis***    The architect has prepared the architectural view of the analysis model by the end of the elaboration phase. Consequently, he has little in this set of activities to do in the construction phase, aside from updates made necessary by changes that affect the architecture.

***Analyze a Use Case***    In the elaboration phase the architect used only those use cases that were architecturally significant and applied them to the architectural view of the analysis model. In each iteration in the construction phase we extend the analysis model with those use cases that are included in the iteration.

***Analyze a Class***    Component engineers continue the work they began in the elaboration phase.

***Analyze a Package***     The architect identified the packages in the elaboration phase and refined them in the construction phase to the extent made necessary by the new use cases. The component engineer maintains the packages in construction.

## 15.4.3  Design

In this phase we typically design and implement the remaining 90% of the use cases—those that were not employed to develop the architecture baseline. We emphasize again, as we consider the design workflow, that it and the other workflows are repeated in each new iteration.

***Architectural Design***     In the construction phase the architect will not, as a general rule, be adding design subsystems and service subsystems. These elements already exist, in skeleton form to be sure, in the architectural baseline.

The architect may add subsystems if they are similar, maybe alternatives, to the ones that already are in place. For instance, if there is a subsystem for a communication protocol and he adds another communication protocol that does not require new interfaces, then it is agreeable to add a new subsystem for that communication protocol.

The behavior of a service subsystem can usually be derived from parts of a single use case or a set of related use cases. Another way to say this is that a service subsystem plays one dominant role to help realize one single use case. Between 40% and 60% of the responsibilities of a service subsystem comes from one such use case. When the percentage is high, say 80%, the project manager evaluates whether the project should complete the remaining 20% of the service subsystem in the same build or let it go to a later build. It may be a good idea to authorize its completion at this time even if the other parts of the subsystem come from use cases with lower rank than the dominant use case. Even though these remaining use cases have a lower priority and could be deferred, it may be more efficient to complete the entire package while it is in play.

On the one hand, working the lower priority use cases at this time enables the component engineer to develop the entire subsystem at one time. He is more likely to get it structurally right by virtue of having examined the entire subsystem at the same time. If he, or some one else, has to come back to the subsystem in a later build to work on the remaining low-priority use cases, he may find discrepancies that necessitate a change of the entire design. He may have to rewrite code because it does not work well with the added code derived from lower-priority use cases. Therefore, it is good to include parts based on use cases to be designed later if—and this is important—the impact they will have is quite clear. The reason is that it is better to do a piece of work as a whole at one time than to scatter bits of it over several iterations.

On the other hand, doing the lower-priority use cases in an early build conflicts with our general intention to examine the high-priority use cases first. The general rule is if it is convenient and not unduly time-consuming to pick up a few low-priority use cases along with the high-priority ones, then do so. Even so, however, the intention is to get the design right, not to implement and test all the low-priority use cases we pick up. The project manager should defer those tasks (design, implementation, and testing of lower-priority use cases) to a later build where their priority places them.

The architect improves the architectural view of the design and deployment model to reflect the experience of the construction phase. However, in general, he completed the architecture at the end of the elaboration phase, so what he does at this time is update it. For an account of the other activities of this workflow (use case, class, and subsystem design), refer to Chapter 9. Suffice it to say here that the design is a principal focus of the construction phase (and implementation even more so), as Figure 15.1 indicates. Its outcome is the design model and the deployment model. Both are maintained throughout the development cycle and carried over to future cycles. The design model is the "blueprint" for the implementation model and the implementation itself.

## 15.4.4 Implementation

This workflow implements and performs unit tests of all the components, working primarily from the design model. The result, after some number of iterations, plus system integration and testing, is the initial operational release, representing 100% of the use-case mass. In this subsection we cover the activities architectural implementation, implement a class and implement a subsystem, perform unit test, and integrate system.

It is in this workflow that the project accomplishes most of the work of the construction phase, building the components, as described in Chapter 10. The project fills each component with more and more code, build after build, iteration after iteration, until at the end of the construction phase, all the components are "filled."

*Architectural Implementation*    By this time the architecture is firmly established. The architect's role, other than continued surveillance, is only to update it, if necessary.

*Implement a Class and Implement a Subsystem*    Component engineers implement the classes and subsystems in the implementation model. They implement the stubbed classes required to make builds.

*Perform Unit Testing*    The component engineer is responsible for performing a unit test of the component he produces. He corrects the design and implementation of the component, if necessary.

*Integrate System*    The system integrator creates an integration build plan that outlines the sequence of builds. This plan sets forth the use cases or scenarios within the use case that the build is to implement. These use cases and scenarios lead to the subsystems and components.

System integrators generally find it advisable to begin building in the lower layers of a layered-architecture hierarchy, such as the system-software layer or the middleware layer (illustrated in Figure 4.5). Subsequent builds expand upward into the application-general and application-specific layers. It is hard to put a build together without having the supporting functions provided by the lower layers in place.

For example, the software organization in one chemical company planned to do an increment, on the average, every two weeks. Projects at Microsoft Corporation are said to do a build each day—after a project gets to the point of having a code build. Each build is subjected to testing—testing of new additions and regression testing of the added code with what was already there—assuring that the developing code is workable. This daily build process verifies each day that the code units checked in since the previous day are compatible. This practice pressures the developers not to "break the build." At the same time, however, it reduces the long-term pressure on the project organization, since integration issues are uncovered during testing, usually each night, and resolved soon after. Doing a build each day might sound like it puts considerable time pressure on a project, but it need not. Developers check in their code when they think it is ready. There is little point to checking in code that is not ready—it will likely break the build. However, individual developers are under time pressure to check in their code in time to meet the build integration plan.

The length of each build period is certainly a matter for consideration in each organization. The guiding principle is to build frequently enough to obtain the advantages that frequent builds bring with them.

To keep each build small, the system integrator often requires a stub or driver to represent a component that is not yet built. A stub is a very simple element that simply provides a response to a stimulus—or all the stimuli that the component can receive from other (not yet completed) components in the build. Similarly, a driver provides a stimulus to the other components that are part of a build under test. Because they are simple, stubs and drivers are unlikely to introduce additional complications.

Thus, the system integrator takes into account the order in which to put together the components in order to form a functional, testable configuration. He documents his findings in the integration build plan, showing when each build is needed to meet integration and test schedules. The system integrator brings together completed and stubbed classes into an executable build, in accordance with the plan for construction. He makes the successively larger builds, and the integration testers test and regression-test them. In the final step of each iteration and ultimately of the phase itself, the system integrator links the entire system, and the system testers test and regression-test it.

This planning sequences the order of the builds in each iteration and the order of the iterations in the construction phase. Because there are often compilation dependencies from the upper layers of a layered architecture on the lower layers, system integrators may have to plan compilation from the bottom up.

### 15.4.5 Test

The efforts of the test engineers to discover what can be tested effectively and to devise test cases and test procedures to do so, as described in Chapter 11, come to fruition in the construction phase. It is a principal activity of this phase, as Figure 15.1 shows. While perform unit test is the responsibility of the component engineers, the test engineers are available for technical assistance. However, the component engineers and their associates, the integration tester and the system tester, are responsible for the test of builds, i.e., increments at the end of iterations, and ultimately the final build, that is the entire released system.

*Plan Test*    The test engineers select goals that test the successive builds and finally the system itself.

*Design Test*    The test engineers find out how to test the requirements in the build set in order to verify the testable requirements. They prepare test cases and procedures for this purpose. From the test cases and procedures from preceding builds, they select those still pertinent and modify them for use in regression testing of the successive builds. The test engineers verify the components that are to be tested together, as originally established in test planning. The purpose of these integration tests is to verify the interfaces between the components being tested and the fact that the components work together.

*Perform Integration test*    Integration testers execute the test cases, following the test procedures. When the build passes, the system integrator adds additional builds, as they become available, and the integration tester continues testing them. When the integration tests find faults, the testers log them and notify the project manager. The project manager (or his designee) determines the next step. This designee may be the system integrator, who possesses the pertinent technical knowledge. The next step might be, for example, further work within the same build, deferral of the fix to the next build, or, particularly in the case of an especially serious failure, assignment to people especially qualified to investigate it.

*Perform System test*    By the time the successive builds reach the end of an iteration, they have attained the status of a partial system and enter the jurisdiction of the system tester. The system tester executes the system test cases, following the system test procedures. When these tests find faults, the system tester logs them and reports them to the project manager or his designee for resolution.

At the end of the last iteration of the construction phase, the system tester tests the initial operational release. Again he feeds back failures to the project manager for assignment to the responsible component engineer for fixing.

*Evaluate Test*    As integration and system testing proceed, the test engineers review the test results at the end of each build in light of the goals originally established in the test plan (possibly modified by subsequent iterations). The purpose of evaluating a test is to assure that the test achieves its goals. If a test does not meet its objectives, the test cases and procedures need to be modified to achieve the test goals (see Section 11.5.6).

## 15.5  Controlling the Business Case

One purpose of the business bid, prepared at the end of the elaboration phase, is to serve as a guide for the project manager and stakeholders in executing the construction phase. To that end, the project manager compares the actual progress at the end of each iteration against the planned schedule, effort, and cost. He reviews data on project productivity, quantity of code prepared, size of the database, and other metrics.

The number of lines of code completed is seldom a good measure of progress in component-based development. Since one of its goals is to reuse classes and components, a component engineer and other workers can make good progress with builds and iterations and yet write little new code. A more pertinent measure of work accomplished, in these circumstances, is the completion of builds and iterations according to the plan.

Discrepancies of more than a few percent, especially in the negative direction, lead the project manager to corrective action. Similarly, more sizable discrepancies lead to review meetings with the stakeholders.

As the project manager learns more about the product's cost and capabilities during the construction phase, he may find it necessary to update the business case and communicate the new case to the stakeholders.

## 15.6  Assess the Iterations and the Construction Phase

On the basis of a review of the test results and other evaluation criteria, including that outlined in Section 15.2.2, the project manager and an assessment group

- Review what was accomplished in an iteration against what was planned.
- Plan in which of the following iterations work not completed is to be accomplished.
- Determine that the build is ready to advance to the next iteration.
- Update the risk list.
- Fill in the plan for the next iteration.
- Update the plan for iterations beyond the next one.
- At the end of the final iteration of this phase, determine that the product has passed system test and has reached initial operational capability.
- Authorize entry into the transition phase.
- Update the project plan.

## 15.7  Planning the Transition Phase

The project team cannot expect to plan its transition phase in as much detail in advance as it did for the earlier phases. The members know, of course, that they are going to get beta releases (or the equivalent) out to selected users for evaluation. This part of the transition phase, selecting the beta testers, reproducing the operating code, preparing test instructions, and so on—they can plan in some detail.

The feedback they receive—risks, problems, failures, suggestions—can hardly be known in advance. If a team has had some experience with beta testing, it will have an idea of what to expect. It will be able to estimate the approximate number of experienced people it will need to cope with the problems the beta testers uncover.

## 15.8  The Key Deliverables

The deliverables are

- Project plan for the transition phase.
- The executable software itself—the initial-operational-capability release. This is the final build from construction.
- All artifacts, including models of the system.
- Maintained and minimally updated architecture description.
- Preliminary user manual in enough detail to guide beta users.
- Business case, reflecting situation at end of phase.

The intention is that the deliverables labeled "complete" will actually be so. Operation of the software in the user community in the transition phase may find that some of them are not actually correct. They will then be modified to be correct.

*Chapter 16*

---

# Transition Completes Product Release

**A**s the project enters the transition phase, the system has reached initial operational capability.

The project manager has deemed it sufficiently trustworthy for the system to operate in the user environment, although it need not be perfect. For example, some problems, risks, and defects that did not become evident in system testing at the end of the construction phase may show up in the user environment. There may be features that users belatedly discover a need for. If they are very important and consistent with the existing product, the project manager may agree to add them. However, the changes must be so small that they can be introduced without severely impacting the project plan. If a proposed feature does impact the schedule, the need for it must be acute. In most cases, we believe it is better to add them to the feature list and carry them over to the next development cycle, that is, to the development of the next version of the system.

The basic intentions of this phase are to

- Meet the requirements, as established in the earlier phases, to the *satisfaction* of the stakeholders.
- Handle all the issues needed for operation in the user environment, including the correction of flaws reported back by beta users or acceptance testers.

Acceptance testing is a responsibility of the customer, although some customers contract it to a specialized acceptance test organization.

## 16.1 The Transition Phase in Brief

This phase focuses on establishing the product in the operational environment. The way in which the project makes this focus varies with the nature of the product's relation to its market. For instance, if a product is going to market, the project team distributes a beta release to typical users located at representative "beta customers" sites. If a product is going to a single client (or perhaps a number of sites within a large organization), the team installs the product at a single site.[1]

The project monitors feedback from the operating sites to

- Find out whether the system really does what the businesses and its users request.
- Discover unanticipated risks.
- Note unresolved problems.
- Find failures.
- Fix ambiguities and gaps in the user documentation.
- Focus on areas in which users appear to be deficient and in need of information or training.

On the basis of feedback of this sort, the team modifies the system or its related artifacts. The team prepares for product production, packaging, deployment, and system rollout in general.

In this phase, it is not seeking to reformulate the product. The project team and the client should have incorporated significant changes in the requirements in earlier phases. Rather, the team is seeking minor deficiencies that were overlooked in the construction phase that it can correct within the existing product baseline.

In a client relationship the team may also provide assistance in setting up an environment suitable for the product and in training the client organization to use the product effectively. It may assist these users in carrying on parallel operation of the new system with the legacy system it replaces. It may aid in the conversion of old databases to the new configuration.

---

1. We may mention two other possibilities: alpha testing and third-party validation. The alpha test is similar to the beta test except that it is conducted within the company developing the software but outside of the development organization itself. The people performing the alpha test are actual users. In third-party validation, a company specializing in testing conducts acceptance testing under contract to the customer.

In the case of products going to many users (the "shrink-wrap marketplace"), these services are built into the installation program that is part of the product, supplemented by help desk assistance.

The transition phase ends with product release.

## 16.2 Early in the Transition Phase

Software is produced under a number of business arrangements. Without going into great detail, we can subsume these arrangements under two patterns:

***Production by a software vendor for sale in a marketplace to many customers***    Sometimes this marketplace is very large, as in the personal computer market. Other times it is smaller, as in the production of reusable components for software producers or of prefabricated programs that can be adapted to each installation. In these marketplaces, although the size may vary, there is a one-to-many relationship (vendor to many customers) that influences the work of the transition phase.

***Production by a software house under a contract to a single customer***
This pattern has several variations, such as:

- The software organization working for a single client with a single site.
- The software organization working for a client with many suborganizations and sites.
- The outsourcing software company, such as EDS, Computer Science or Andersen Consulting, sometimes developing software in the initial instance for a single site or client but later adapting it to other sites or clients.
- The in-house software organization developing software for other departments of the same company under company-specified accounting arrangements.

The relationship between the organization of the transition phase and the user or customer varies under these different patterns. Under these patterns the transition phase begins with an initial operational release that has passed in-house system testing and major milestone assessment at the end of the construction phase. However, the project team in the transition phase prepares additional artifacts, such as installation scripts, data-conversion programs, or data-migration programs, or modifies those produced in the construction phase to ready this executable program for release beyond its own boundaries.

### 16.2.1 Planning the Transition Phase

A project can hardly expect to plan its transition phase in as much detail in advance as it did the construction phase. On the one hand, the project manager knows that this phase is going to get beta releases (or the equivalent), developed in the construction phase, out to selected users for test. This knowledge provides the basis for early planning of the transition phase. There is a known amount of work involved in producing the beta release, preparing beta-test documentation, selecting beta users, and so on. On the other hand, there will be an unknown amount of work resulting from the beta-test feedback. The project manager will want to have some people standing by. He may assign them to work on other projects but have them available for stints on transition problems.

In planning the transition phase, the project manager expects that the initial operational release from the construction phase will require little rework as a result of beta-user feedback. In fact, if the project has been carried out on an iterative basis, that should be the case. This development process allows developers to experiment in early iterations and find their errors of conception in tests of early increments and observation of their operation. Similarly, plain mistakes should be caught and corrected build-by-build as work proceeds. In short, early rework is *good*. In the transition phase, in the wake of iterative development, it should be less than 5%. However, project managers should count on it to be more than zero. At least a few omissions and errors will pass through all the screens. A tendency for a project to deprecate the possibility of rework may be the effect of

- Too much schedule pressure, leading to the "haste makes waste" syndrome.
- Absence of adequate system test and assessment at the end of the construction phase.
- Failure to focus on the considerable work still remaining in the transition phase.
- The feeling that even contemplating the need for rework will make that need materialize.
- The disposition to regard rework as "bad," as an admission of project incompetence.

The issue of "good enough" software may arise in the planning of the transition phase. It is a fact of life that no software product is perfect. For example, products are delivered with some percentage of remaining defects, with some requirements deferred to a later release, or with some needs discovered by beta users that the transition phase lacks the resources to accommodate. There are three "answers" to the "good enough" issue.

First, the phases and iterations of the Unified Process are intended to identify risks, capture accurate requirements, and plan the project accordingly. In the Unified Process, the project team executes these efforts in conjunction with the users and customers. In consequence, the initial operational release, or beta release, should come close to what both the project and the stakeholders expect.

Second, since neither the project nor the stakeholders expect the initial operational release to be without flaws, they have allowed some schedule and resources for the transition phase.

Third, since the project reached the first two "answers" in cooperation with the stakeholders, a result may be an extension of the phase or a deferral of the unexpected work to the next development cycle.

### 16.2.2 Staffing the Transition Phase

Since the emphasis in this phase is getting a release out to users, first to beta test or acceptance test the product, and then to use it, staff requirements are much the same as those of the construction phase, although the emphasis may be a little different.

Analyzing feedback from beta or acceptance testing and responding to it may require people who are more service-oriented than development-oriented. Considering the merits of even a minor enhancement may require experts on not only large parts of the system but on the nature of the application to which it is being applied. Also, where testing merely finds the defect, tracing it to its origin often requires considerable insight into the entire system, or at least into that part of it in which the fault appears to originate. Moreover, user and course material, though initiated in the construction phase, usually needs to be rewritten by a technical writer before the product is delivered to ordinary customers. During this phase the architect is on call, but primarily to assure and maintain architectural integrity, and sometimes (although seldom) to consider minor architectural changes.

### 16.2.3 Setting the Evaluation Criteria

At the end of the construction phase, following system test, the product was believed to meet initial operational capability, or, in other words, to meet the terms of the requirements specification. For the transition phase, it is necessary to evaluate only the issues that arise in that phase. Basically, there are five issues:

1. Did the beta users cover the key functions, for example, those represented by all the use cases, involved in the successful operation of the product in the field?
2. Similarly, did the product pass acceptance tests conducted by the customer? The test criteria are set by the contract, which has been agreed to by both the development organization and the client. In addition, acceptance testing usually runs the software in production mode for an agreed-upon period of time.
3. Is the user material of acceptable quality?
4. Is required course material (including teacher instructions, if any) ready to use?
5. Finally, do customers and users appear to be satisfied with the product? We comment on this issue further in Section 16.4.6.

## 16.3 The Core Workflows Play a Small Role in this Phase

Activity in all five workflows is low in this phase, as shown in Figure 16.1. Because nearly all the work was done in construction, the level of activity in this phase is low, just enough to correct the problems found in test in the using environment. However, that is not to say there is not a lot of work in this phase (see Section 16.4 for details). There should be almost no work in the requirements, analysis, and design workflows. Design activities typically recede during the transition phase, and in any case they generally consist of little more than small design improvements necessary to correct problems or defects or to effect last-minute (and usually minor) enhancements. The focus shifts toward fixing defects to eliminate the failures that occur during early usage, to assuring that the fixes themselves are correct, and to regression testing to assure that the fixes did not introduce new defects.

The archetypal iteration consists of the five workflows that we discussed in earlier chapters. In this chapter we are concerned only with the part they play in transition. More broadly, we carry on four sets of activities partly in parallel. One is the five

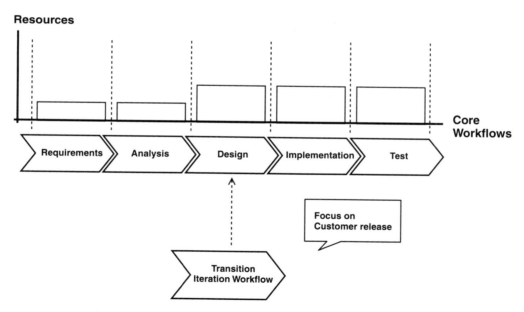

**FIGURE 16.1** The work of an iteration in the transition phase proceeds through the same five workflows as in earlier phases. (The size of the bars is illustrative only and will change on different projects.) The implementation and test workflows have the most focus in this phase. It is here that defects found in beta and acceptance testing are found, identified, fixed, and retested. In a few cases redesign may be needed to fix defects, leading to a small buildup of the design workflow. Requirements is little affected.

core workflows in the iteration(s); the second is planning the iterations, as described in Sections 12.4–12.7; the third is further consideration of the business case, as discussed in Section 16.5, and the fourth is assessment, described in Sections 12.8 and 16.6. In this section we provide only an overview of the transition phase. In the next section we add detail.

## 16.4  What We Do in the Transition Phase

A project carries out transition activities along the following lines:

- Preparing the actual beta (or acceptance test) release from the (initial operational capability) release produced by the construction phase.
- Installing (or arranging to install) this release at the site, plus activities at the site, such as migrating data from the previous system.
- Acting on the feedback from the test sites.
- Adapting the now corrected product to user circumstances.
- Completing the project artifacts.
- Determining when the project ends.

This sequence of activities will vary in detail depending on whether the project is producing software for the market or for a client. In the first case, there will be many potential users, and the selection and guidance of beta users will be a considerable task. Moreover, as real users, they do not follow a prescribed test schedule. They use the product as they want and report back what they find.

In the second case, the client probably selects a site for the initial installation and the acceptance test there will follow a formal, agreed-upon, systematic procedure. The results reported are primarily deviations from the formal specifications. If problems turn up that are beyond the scope of the existing contractual arrangement, the parties agree upon a follow-up arrangement.

The scheme of activities will also vary, depending on whether the software product is originating from a "green field" or is an enhancement of an existing or similar product. Again, it is an opportunity for software organizations to specialize the process to the circumstances they face, as we discussed in Chapter 2.

### 16.4.1  Getting the Beta Release Out

Most of the initial set of users for beta (or acceptance) test will be experienced. The transition organization expects them to work from relatively preliminary documentation, but it also provides them with specific instructions on how to feed back the findings of their tests and observations. Early in the transition phase the project team pulls together the previously prepared documentation the beta users or acceptance testers need. They supplement this documentation with specific beta instructions. They select beta users and distribute the beta release and accompanying materials to them.

### 16.4.2  Installing the Beta Release

Activities at the test site(s) vary between beta test and acceptance test. There are normally a large number of beta sites, and the transition staff are not present at them. They must issue specific instructions as to how to install the test software, how to operate it, what problems/issues beta customers and users should focus on, and how to report faults or other problems found. If the release is an upgrade or a replacement of previous software, the transition staff has to provide instructions as to how the beta users migrate data or convert databases to the new release. The instructions may have to provide for parallel operation of the beta release and the previous software for a period of time.

In contrast, in acceptance testing, pertinent members of the project staff will probably be present. There will be a formal acceptance-test document, but it will be supplemented by informal communication. Faults and problems will be fixed on the spot when possible or carried back to the project members with appropriate qualifications when necessary.

### 16.4.3  Responding to the Test Results

The project collects and analyzes the test results for the purpose of taking action. The results are likely to fall into two classes: relatively minor code faults that simply have to be run down and corrected (although that may be difficult in some cases) and more important problems that may ramify more widely, even extending to the possibility of a change in the architecture.

***Failures***    A failure results in the first instance from a component defect, but that defect may have to be traced back to a flaw at the design, analysis, or even earlier models. If the tracing turns out to be difficult, the transition people may have to seek assistance from the component engineer or other staff who did the original work in the area. At any rate, a competent person fixes the defect and the testing staff test and regression test it. In addition, the project considers questions such as

- Is this defect likely to be related to other defects not yet discovered?
- Can it be corrected without affecting architecture or design?
- Has it been corrected without introducing new defects?

***Broader problems***    Some of the difficulties found in beta testing may require more extended consideration than a "failure fix." For example, they may extend to the degree of calling for an additional iteration following test. They may suggest changes, improvements, or features that should be handled formally, such as through the machinery of a Change Control Board. In this connection, as changes are implemented, we emphasize the importance of maintaining configuration control. As we have stated before, substantial changes that would exceed resources, delay delivery, or change the architecture should, if at all possible, be deferred to the next development cycle.

It remains important to maintain the architectural integrity of the system while correcting problems and defects. To this end the architect follows the progress of the transition work. He works in a "follow-up mode" to make sure that problem and defect fixes follow the architecture. He (or the architectural team) makes sure that problems are not fixed for the sake of expediency in a way that damages the architecture. Achieving this goal sometimes requires a little architectural fine-tuning. If activities in the phase do affect the architecture, the architect updates its description.

Of course, few software organizations deliver products that are perfect. On this account the project manager has to weigh the cost and time delay of particular items of rework as aspects of the business case.

### 16.4.4 Adapting the Product to Varied User Environments

As we noted earlier, software organizations provide product in two broad relationships to the market: the marketplace products (one to many) and the single-client relationship (one to one). In either relationship, there may be the further task of migrating data or converting a database from an old system to the new one.

*Marketplace relationship*    The marketplace may be a highly diversified set of destinations for which the team has to prepare different versions of the executable program. Some of the variants include country, language, currency units, and other measurement units. If the product is to run on different operating nodes in a network, it may have to be modified for each different node.

The users of the first general release are likely to be less experienced than the beta users, so the team amplifies the preliminary beta-test documentation to meet the needs of ordinary users.

Market-distributed products are usually installed by the user or by a system administrator in a company. In other instances, a local vendor makes the installation. The team prepares procedures for the installer to employ and a script for the help line. These procedures may be quite complex, for example, in cases where the product is being installed on a number of personal computers or workstations linked by an intranet. The procedures are still more complex where parts of the product are installed on different nodes and the nodes have to be brought up in a prescribed manner. Different types of nodes may require different installation procedures.

*Single-client relationship*    Transition of a system to a single client under a contractual arrangement follows much the same pattern as the one just enumerated. However, there are a few differences:

- The client's representatives have probably been participating in the earlier phases, providing feedback to increments.
- They have observed final system tests on the premises of the software contractor.
- They may have participated in some of the assessment sessions marking the passing of the construction milestone.

- The software organization probably assisted in installing the system in the client's initial site. In the case of large, complex systems it may have performed the bulk of the installation.
- Representatives of the contractor observed acceptance testing and may have made on-the-spot fixes when these were feasible. In the case of more difficult problems, they carried the details back to their own organization to obtain expert assistance in making changes or fixes.
- Acceptance testing concludes when the client and the contractor find that the system meets the requirements they previously agreed upon. Of course, they may encounter additional needs or changes in needs, leading to a follow-on contract.

***Data migration or conversion***   There is usually an existing system that is being replaced, leading to the need for procedures to migrate data or convert databases. The old data may have been in a product developed by the same software house, and it can be very simple to move to the new product. However, if it is in a product developed by another vendor, possibly a competitor, it may be more difficult to transfer the data. The responsibilities may include:

- Replacing the older system with the new one, either with complete takeover of the existing tasks by the new system or sometimes with parallel operation of both systems until the user is satisfied that the new system is operating properly.
- Transferring data from the old system to the new one, sometimes with a change of data formats.
- In addition to providing instructions for these transfers, the documentation may contain tests to enable users to verify that the installation has been done successfully.
- The team may add further explanatory information to the help line, especially information needed to assist users with installations that go awry.

### 16.4.5  Completing the Artifacts

The transition phase does not close until the project has completed all artifacts, including models and architecture description. We emphasize, in particular, that the model set should be complete at the end of construction, not suddenly filled out toward the end of the transition phase. Rather, it evolves through all the iterations and all the phases, as we described in Section 12.8.4. It is corrected, if necessary, in the transition phase. At the end of transition we have verified through actual use that all the artifacts are consistent with one another.

### 16.4.6  When Does the Project End?

The transition phase ends, not only when all the work and artifacts are completed, but when the customer is "satisfied." Just when are the users satisfied? That determination depends upon the marketplace relationship.

In the case of products for the marketplace, the project manager concludes that the vast mass of customers will be satisfied when the project has acted upon the feedback from the beta tests. At that point, it issues a general release. In most cases, of course, the environment and the product continue to evolve, but the software organization responds to that evolution in later releases or, in the case of major change, another development cycle. Since successful products and custom systems are typically extended via minor, then major revisions, in a very real sense the "project" never ends. The transition phase terminates when the project transfers responsibility for continued maintenance to a support organization.

In the case of products contracted for a client, the project manager concludes that the customer is satisfied when the system passes acceptance testing. That point, of course, depends upon the interpretation of requirements spelled out in the original contract (signed at the end of elaboration), as modified by additions during the later phases. The customer might contract certain kinds of maintenance support to the software vendor. Alternatively, the customer might handle its own maintenance or contract it to a third party. The details may differ, but the point is, the transition phase, as such, has ended.

## 16.5  Completing the Business Case

The costs and schedule of the transition phase were covered in the business bid at the end of the elaboration phase. By the end of the transition phase, further information on which to judge the merit of the business case has become available.

### 16.5.1  Controlling Progress

The project manager compares actual progress in the phase against the schedule, effort, and cost planned for the phase.

At the end of the transition phase, which is also the end of the project in budgetary terms, the project manager convenes a group to review actual schedule time, person-hours, cost, defect rates, and such other metrics as the company may employ, in relation to the planned numbers for the entire project to

- See if the project attained the planned goals.
- Ascertain reasons why it did not (if that is the case).
- Add the project's metrics to the company's metrics database for future use.

### 16.5.2  Review of the Business Plan

This plan forecasts whether the project would be successful economically. Again, there are two patterns: production on a contract and production for the market. In the first case, success is easy to define: Did the contracted price cover the project's costs? Of course, this relatively simple issue may be complicated by related considerations such as whether the company successfully opened a new business area or whether some of the components or subsystems produced on this contract can lead to reduced costs on future contracts.

In the second case, the business plan is more complicated. Success is measured by whether the product will achieve such goals as the company's hurdle rate on the capital invested in the development. At the end of the transition phase and the project, all the data, such as the level of future sales, is not yet in, but at this point the company knows what it has expended and has a better sense of future prospects than it had when the project began. The responsible executive arranges to have the available data pulled together and convenes a group to review it.

## 16.6  Assess the Transition Phase

The project manager assembles a small group to assess the transition phase (see also Section 12.8) and to conduct a postmortem of the development cycle as a whole. This assessment differs from those at the completion of the previous phases for two reasons. First, it is the last phase; there is no subsequent phase to which to pass work not yet completed. However, in a system of some size, there will be a product group to which useful ideas can be passed. Second, although it is the last phase of the current development cycle, there will likely be future development cycles. The assessment group should record findings that will be of use to them.

These findings will fall into two categories, as discussed in the following subsections.

### 16.6.1  Assess the Iterations and the Phase

On the one hand, if the project organization has carried out the first three phases effectively, the transition phase should run smoothly and complete within the schedule and budget allocated. Beta testing finds only routine failures that the team readily corrects. The assessment group finds little of note that will be of value to the product group or the project dealing with the next life cycle.

On the other hand, if the project organization failed to identify all the important risks, failed to devise an architecture that accommodates the requirements, or failed to implement a design that provides the needed system, deficiencies of this kind will become painfully evident in the transition phase. As a result of these deficiencies, the project manager may have to extend the transition phase just to reach a minimally satisfactory system. He may have to push a "good enough" system into the user community. He may have to defer features originally specified in the requirements to a later release.

These deficiencies, of course, become fodder for the final assessment group. They are, in effect, assessing the entire project—all four phases. They are recording an unsatisfactory project experience. From a process point of view, the purpose of assessment is to enable the project working on the next release to do better. In particular, assessment, as such, should not be the basis for negative personnel actions. These actions should be based on other evidence. If the assessment group feels that findings may be misused, they may pull their punches. Getting the facts in full is important to the future success of the organization.

### 16.6.2  Postmortem of the Project

In contrast to the assessment, the postmortem is largely devoted to analyzing what was done right and what was done wrong by the project organization. The intent is to provide a record that will enable later projects to organize more effectively and to carry out the development process more successfully; for example,

- Points pertinent to the system that was developed should be recorded for use by maintainers and by the team on the next release. For instance, while reasons for selecting the design that was used are often recorded, reasons for rejecting other possible designs may also be useful to later teams.
- Points pertinent to the development process itself should be thought through. For example,
  - Is further general training needed?
  - What areas require specialized training?
  - Should mentoring be continued?
  - Does this project's experience with specialized aspects of the Unified Process (see Chapter 2) provide insights that would benefit future projects?

## 16.7  Planning the Next Release or Generation

Industry's experience over the software decades demonstrates that few software products endure unchanged for long. The hardware and operating systems on which they run develop further. The business or governmental environment changes. Greater and greater parts of the commercial, industrial, governmental, and personal worlds are brought within the reach of software. Nearly every software system enters a new development cycle almost immediately. The new cycle repeats the inception, elaboration, construction, and transition phases.

## 16.8  The Key Deliverables

The deliverables for this phase are very similar to those listed for the construction phase (see Chapter 15), but they have been corrected and are now complete:

- The executable software itself, including installation software.
- Legal documents such as contracts, license documents, waivers, and warranties.
- Completed and corrected product release baseline including all models of the system.
- Completed and updated architecture description.
- Final user, operator, and system administrator manuals and training materials.
- Customer support references and web references on where to find more information, to report defects, and to find information on fixes and upgrades.

*Chapter 17*

---

# Making the Unified Process Work

The development of software at the mission-critical systems level remains exceedingly complex as the preceding chapters of this book have made clear. In this final chapter, we once again, as a review, pull together the many interlocking strands. It is our intent to show, more briefly than in the preceding chapters, how these strands are related and how they work together.

In addition, we extend this chapter to two new areas. First, if the software process itself is complex, it follows that the management of this process is also complex. Second, the transition from no process or an ad hoc predecessor process to the Unified Process will not be a simple affair.

## 17.1 The Unified Process Helps You Deal with Complexity

First of all, there are the four phases: inception, elaboration, construction, and transition. Beyond the phases of the initial cycle, since major software systems go on and on, come further releases and, for major overhauls, later generations. Within these phases are the interlocking workflows, architecture, risk management, iterations, and increments, such as

- Software development driven by the use cases through the workflows: requirements, analysis, design, implementation, and test.

- Development guided by architecture—the skeleton of structural and behavioral elements that allow the system to evolve gracefully.
- Development using building blocks and components, supporting extensive reuse.
- Development carried out through iterations and builds within the iterations, resulting in incremental growth of the product.
- Development controlled with risks.
- Development visualized and recorded in the Unified Modeling Language (UML).
- Development assessed at milestones.

Four milestones anchor the process: life cycle objectives, life cycle architecture, initial operational capability, and product release. [1]

### 17.1.1  The Life Cycle Objectives

The first milestone clarifies the objectives of the product life cycle by raising questions such as

- Have you made the system scope clear? Have you established what is to be within the system and what is outside of it?
- Have you reached agreement with the stakeholders on the key requirements of the system?
- Is there an architecture that implements these features in sight?
- Have you identified risks critical to the successful execution of the project? Do you see a way to mitigate them?
- Will the product in use generate values justifying the investment to build it?
- Is it feasible for your organization to proceed with the project?
- Do the stakeholders concur in the objectives?

Answering these questions is the business of the *inception phase*.

### 17.1.2  The Life Cycle Architecture

The second milestone clarifies the architecture for the product life cycle through questions such as

- Have you created an executable architectural baseline? Is it resilient and robust? Can it evolve over the life of the product?
- Have you identified and mitigated the major risks to the point of assuring that they will not upset the project plan?
- Have you developed a project plan to the level necessary to support a realistic bid covering schedule, cost, and quality?

- Will the project, as now planned and bid, provide an adequate return on investment?
- Have you obtained stakeholder concurrence?

Answering these questions is the business of the *elaboration phase.*

### 17.1.3 Initial Operational Capability

The third milestone establishes that the product has attained initial operational capability: Have you reached a level of product capability suitable for initial operation in the user environment, particularly for beta testing?

That is the key question at the third milestone. As we begin the approach to this milestone, we have a baseline architecture, we have investigated the risks, we have a project plan, and we have resources. So here we build the product. If we have settled on the life cycle objectives and the life cycle architecture, building proceeds smoothly. An important task in this phase is sequencing the builds and iterations. A good sequence means that the prerequisites for each new iteration are in place. A good sequence avoids having to go back and redo an earlier iteration because of something learned later.

Still, in spite of our efforts to avoid problems, some still arise. Surmounting these work-a-day problems is what we do here. Building the system is the business of the *construction phase.*

### 17.1.4 Product Release

The fourth milestone establishes that the product is ready for unrestricted release to the user community: Can the product operate successfully in typical user environments?

There is work to be done after we reach initial operational capability, namely, beta testing, acceptance testing, and correction of problems and defects arising from operation in the working environment. When we have something users are satisfied with, we deliver the product.

These tasks are the business of the *transition phase.*

## 17.2 The Major Themes

Running through the four major milestones and tying them together are themes, such as requirements, architecture, component-based development, the Unified Modeling Language, iteration, and risk management. (The order in which we list the themes does not reflect their order of importance. All are important. They all have to work together.)

***Get the requirements right***    Get them right through use-case modeling, analysis, opportunities for feedback, and so on. The best beginning of the Unified Process is use-case driven.

*Get the architecture right*    Projects of any considerable size have to be architecture-centric. Architecture enables a system to be partitioned and have the partitions collaborate. Architecture solidifies the interfaces between the partitions, enabling teams to work independently on either side of the interface, *and keep it right*. Architectural surveillance keeps the project on technical track.

*Use components*    The firm interfaces of the architecture (as well as the standard interfaces of standard groups) are one of the elements that make component-based development possible. Reusable building blocks reduce development cost, get products to market faster, and improve quality.

*Think and communicate in UML*    Software development is more than writing code. UML (along with the other features of the Unified Process) makes software development into an engineering discipline. It is a drawing language in which software people can think, visualize, analyze, communicate, and record.

Without a standard communication means like UML people would have great difficulty comprehending what other people and teams are doing. They have difficulty passing information lengthwise through the phases and on to later releases and generations.

*Iterate*    Iterations and builds provide advantages: small chunks of work, small work groups, a tie to risk management, frequent check points, and frequent feedback points.

*Manage risks*    Identify risks—critical, significant, routine—put them on a risk list, and mitigate them before the point at which they come up in the development process.

## 17.3 Management Leads Conversion to Unified Process

Beyond the task of managing and controlling an ongoing process is that of converting a company or public enterprise from old ways to the new way. At present the world of business and government has many organizations with little in the way of software process. Of course, they are developing software, so they are doing it somehow, but they are not doing it in an organized, repeatable way. Also, there are many others who have some kind of software process but are, perhaps vaguely, dissatisfied with it. They, too, are developing software, sometimes with considerable success, but they feel there must be some better way. Indeed there is. How do these companies get started on the road to the better way?

A single professional down in the ranks is not in a position to carry out this transition. He may be the one to act as the champion of the new way, once the organization has decided to go for it. No, it is clearly a responsibility of the executive at the top of the software engineering business. It is his to lead because it affects his entire organization. He has to get the idea that there is such a thing as a better way and that it is a good thing to have. He has to feel that competition is making it imperative to do something soon. Perhaps he gets the germ of this idea from a fellow executive whose organization is already moving in the software-process area.

### 17.3.1  The Case for Action

Because the new way will carry over to other parts of the software development organization and to the entire company, the first executive needs to seek the support of the other executives. He can do this through a case-for-action statement. Basically, this statement makes the case that the way we are doing things is no longer good enough. It costs too much. The quality is low, and, probably most important, "time to market" is too long. Even if we are using our software in-house, we are not getting the competitive benefits of better software soon enough. Year-to-year gains of five percent are no longer good enough. Big gains in these three areas—cost, schedule, and quality—are now possible, because other companies have demonstrated them.

The case for action statement leads into what that action might be. Software development organizations, as a general rule, are not in the business of developing methods, tools, building blocks, or components. There are other organizations doing these things. For instance, there are organizations producing and selling components. There are organizations like SAP providing prefabricated systems that can be adapted to your business. (A prefabricated system is a large framework in which the customer, with the assistance of the vendor, makes minor adaptations to fit the specifics of his business.) There are organizations like Rational Software Corporation, which backs up the Unified Process. The software executive's task is to find out where he can get the help his organization needs.

Given that the options are not many, there is for most software organizations just one way forward. That is component-based development. Whether we try to do a lot ourselves, as in banking, insurance, defense, telecom, and other, or whether we try to find a prefabricate, building on top of reusable building blocks is an issue for the software executive to work out in terms of his own situation. In most cases there will still be some—or much—software development to do in-house. Someone has to acquire the building blocks; someone has to fit them to the company specifics. That takes a software process. In many cases software executives will find that the Unified Process is the answer to that part of their needs.

### 17.3.2  The Reengineering Directive Persuades

The initiating executive explains carefully, at length, and without hype in the reengineering directive why the company is moving to an improved software process. The directive covers

- The current business situation and the fact that it is changing.
- What customers now expect.
- The competition the company is up against.
- The challenges the company faces.

- The diagnosis that these challenges lead to.
- The risks that not changing will bring on.
- What the company has to do about software process in particular [2].[1]

***Assurance of support***    Project managers have to feel confident of continuing financial support. Among other things, this assurance covers initial training, mentoring as project managers oversee initial applications of the new process, and continued training as needs shift. Don't try to transition to the new process without having someone who has done it before. The mentors must know how to do it. They can be external or internal. Starting a new project with a new process depends upon full integration of four supports: process, tools, training, and mentors.

***Continuance of existing projects***    In a company of some size with many projects underway, the current projects and most of those coming up in the near future will have to continue on the present process. Not everyone can be trained at once. Not every project can afford the possible turmoil of considerable change.

At the same time the reengineering directive should make clear that project managers and staff, who are continuing on existing projects, are not being shunted aside. They will, in their turn, be trained and assigned to projects working under the Unified Process. The transition takes time. The company must necessarily continue its existing business as part of the price of being here for the future. It trains these others so they can participate in discussions of what will come. They must not feel like outsiders. If they do, they can damage the transition effort severely.

***Confidence in own future***    The people involved in this transition are software professionals. The field has changed drastically in its lifetime, short by historic standards. Some have had difficulty keeping up. Middle managers, preoccupied as they are by administrative duties, especially feel this burden. It helps the transition if they feel reasonably confident of their own futures. Companies with a historic record of taking care of their own have an advantage here, but all should be mindful of its importance.

### 17.3.3 Implementing the Transition

The software executive faces implementation issues.

***The champion***    The first issue is an organization through which to implement the transition. Since the software executive himself is likely to be already fully occupied, he needs a technically qualified engineer to champion the change day by day, that is, to supervise the changeover. This champion needs to understand the Unified Process and, to gain that understanding, he takes some training and one-on-one consultation.

---

1. In [2], the content of the reengineering directive, as it applies to reuse, was described. The psychology underlying this directive is equally applicable to the software process.

The champion is probably a project manager who is technically competent. He or she might be an architect with project-manager skills. He has studied the Unified Process, is convinced that it can help the company, and is willing to stand on the barricades for it. At the same time, however, he also has the confidence of both the executives who are sponsoring him and the people participating in the project. He knows how to work both with managers and with technical people. He or she is a person who is good at convincing other people. He is usually interested in methods and process, but at the same time he is mature enough not to try to start all over again with his own unique method. Rather, he adapts the Unified Process to the particular needs of the first project.

The champion need not have been through a project with the Unified Process before. In fact, he is not likely to have had this opportunity since he has been working within the organization for some time. He just has to understand what it means to do it. He just has to be willing to stand up and do it—with help, of course, from the project manager and the mentor, discussed next.

**The manager of the first project**    In addition to this champion (by the way, if you can't find this exceptional man or woman that we have been describing, take the best one you have and give him every support), the responsible software executive also needs an exceptionally capable project manager. He needs one who feels in his bones that it is important both to adopt the new process and to carry it through. The project still has to run successfully in the face of the perplexities that may attend the adoption of the new process.

**The mentor**    Training is not everything. In particular, it is not hands-on experience with the new way. So, the champion and the project manager need to be backed by a consultant (internal or external) who has been through projects using the Unified Process. The mentor does not need managerial experience, although it is not bad to have it. He does need two special talents. One is the ability to anticipate problems in the project. This ability, of course, is founded on his having been through a project adopting the Unified Process before. Second, he has to be able to work well with the varied people he will encounter, particularly the champion, but also the project manager, the people on the project, and the sponsoring executive.

**Where to start**    The first project should be a real one where the results count. Our experience with artificial pilot projects has not been encouraging. They tend to become a backwater. Their results, whatever they are, do not make much of an impression. This first project should be mission-critical, but the schedule should not be overly time-critical. Aha, you say, all important projects always have short time schedules.

We know. Actually, work under the Unified Process proceeds more rapidly than under older ways. We look for risks early, we get architecture worked out early, so construction actually proceeds faster. Moreover, the first project will be guided by mentors. They are mentors because they have been through the process before. They make it work.

Going for the full approach on a real project is actually safer, although that does not mean doing too many new things at the same time. Process, yes. The tools that go with the process, yes—they go together if the tools are well integrated. But a new operating system, a new database technology, a new programming language, a new distributed system platform, probably no—don't pile on too many new things at the same time, particularly a technology not closely integrated with another technology. Depending on circumstances, you might be able to accommodate one more new technology. Don't take on a big system as the first one.

*Further considerations*    Our experience tells us a few more things:

- The approach we present here is not always the way it is done, but it is the systematic way of adopting the Unified Process.
- A more gradual, more stepwise approach may fall into the opposite trap. Because progress is almost invisible, support gradually evaporates and the transition fails.
- Sometimes, it is true, people eventually succeed in reengineering the software process in some piecemeal way, but you cannot count on it, it takes a long time, and it often fails.
- In any case it is best to have the transition under effective management control and to see it through. Failures resulting from lack of control are difficult to repair.

## 17.4 Specializing the Unified Process

The Unified Process, as presented in this book, is not the only word on this subject. Indeed, there are two other highly important things to say about it. First, it is a framework. It has to be tailored to a number of variables: the size of the system in work, the domain in which that system is to function, the complexity of the system, and the experience, skill, or process level of the project organization and its people. Second, this book, detailed as it may have appeared to you, is just an overview of the working process. Actually, to apply it, you need considerable further information. We discuss these two specializations of the Unified Process in the next two subsections.

### 17.4.1 Tailoring the Process

Software systems and products and the organizations that build them remain as diverse as ever. Consequently, while there are certain constants in the Unified Process, like the four phases and the five workflows, there are also numerous factors that vary. For instance, what should the relative length of the phases be? How many iterations are appropriate in each phase under different circumstances? At what point is the candidate architecture (or critical risk mitigation, baseline architecture, business case, and so on) sufficiently established?

The answer to questions such as these depends upon the size of the system, the nature of the application, the extent of the project organization's domain experience, the complexity of the system, the experience of the project team, the level of capability of software management, even the degree to which the stakeholders can work together effectively.

To take one example—if the system is relatively small, if the project team is experienced in the domain (has done earlier releases or similar products)—the inception phase may be very brief. The team (and probably the stakeholders, as well) knows that there are no critical risks standing in the way of successful development. They know that a previously used architecture can be used again. The result is that a few days confirming the scope of the system and assuring that no new risks have appeared within the scope may suffice to complete the inception phase.

To take another example—if the system is large, complex, and new to the project team, we can expect that the inception phase, as well as the elaboration phase, will be much longer and go through more iterations.

The number of variations of these themes is as large as the number of systems to be built. That is where experience comes in. That is where the project manager is well advised to bring in the experience of other software people, as well as the knowledge of the stakeholders. You can "tailor the process" to fit your circumstances [3].

### 17.4.2 Filling in the Process Framework

The Unified Process presented in this book is only an overview to the process you need to manage a team of people working in concert. The book aims at providing practitioners and managers with an understanding of the process. It does not provide for team members the detailed guidelines that they need to guide their daily work. It names some of the artifacts the process creates/uses; there are others. It does not provide document templates. It does not identify all the different types of workers; there are more. It refers from time to time to the fact that tools can be a great help in carrying out the process. Indeed, much of the routine work involved in implementing the process can be carried by tools, and carried more quickly and accurately than by unassisted people. The book, however, does not detail what the tools are, which ones are used for what, and how to use them. Essentially, the book covers the basic ideas. It describes some workflows, some artifacts, some workers and some of their activities, and the uses of the Unified Modeling Language.

There is much more. For this highly developed version, you need the Rational Unified Process. This process product is an on-line searchable knowledge base amounting to about 1800 pages of material. It enhances team productivity by providing each team member with productivity-enhancing guidelines, templates, and tool assistance for critical development activities. The process is integrated with Rational's tools. In fact, the tools and the process were developed together. The content is continuously updated. It is supported by a comprehensive set of courses. It is the basis from which mentors provide personal guidance.

The Rational Unified Process is a further development of the long-standing Rational Objectory Process. If you have been employing the latter, you can easily upgrade to the new Rational Unified Process.

## 17.5  Relate to the Broader Community

In addition to providing a more effective working environment within the project and more effective relations with users and stakeholders, the Unified Process provides a more satisfactory interface to the broader community:

- *The educational community*   Educators and trainers can focus their courses on what students need to know to work in the Unified Process and to think and visualize in the Unified Modeling Language.
- *The software community*   Architects, developers, and others can transfer between projects, and even companies, without a long period of adjusting to the new company's unique practices.
- *The reuse community*   Projects can reuse subsystems and components more easily, because they are represented in the UML.
- *The tools community*   Projects will be supported by more effective tools, because the larger market for the Unified Process provides better financial support for tool development.

## 17.6  Get the Benefits of the Unified Process

Firm up requirements early by evolving use cases in concert with actual users and process-engineering people; move from requirements to the later workflows (analysis, design, and so on) more effectively—because the Unified Process is **use-case driven** (Appendix C).

Solidify what the project is to do; guide the project in the doing; provide a guide to future generations of the product. All this through a life cycle architecture that is understandable, resilient, robust, and evolvable for years to come—because the Unified Process is *architecture-centric.*

Learn from the experience of successive builds and iterations, both developers and stakeholders—because the Unified Process is **iterative** (Appendix C) and *incremental.*

Minimize the possibility that critical risks will imperil the success of the project or that significant risks will jeopardize its budget or schedule—because the Unified Process is **risk-driven** (Appendix C).

Improve the speed of the development process, reduce its cost, and enhance the quality of the product through the reuse of building blocks—because the Unified Process is *component-based.*

Enable every member of the project team, as well as the stakeholders, to work in concert—because the Unified Process is more than a guide for individual developers, it is an *engineered process.*

Having this process framework of phases, iterations, milestones, and assessments provides a number of points at which stakeholders can latch onto the development and find out what is going on. Knowing what is going on and informed by their knowledge of the application, stakeholders can feed back suggestions for system improvement. Most important, because the early phases consider key aspects such as architecture and risks, they can input their ideas while the project still has time to make good use of them.

Based on 30 years of practical work, the Unified Process brings together the experience of several thought-leaders and experienced organizations. It is unified over many applications and techniques, such as

- *"Visualize-able"*   The visual models and artifacts employed in the Unified Process are expressed in the Unified Modeling Language, leading to its many advantages, such as extensive software reuse and blueprints of the software.
- *"Tool-able"*   The fact of a unified process and a standard language provides the financial support for more extensive tooling that, in turn, makes the process more effective.
- *Tailorable*   It is a process framework, not a rigid process. It is specializable to different application areas and organizational needs.
- *Extensible*   The Unified Process does not limit its users to a single way of carrying out an activity, for instance, risk analysis. Users may draw on other sources for guidance. What the Unified Process does is provide logical places in the process at which the activity, in this case, risk analysis, is to take place, basically "early" rather than "late."

The Unified Process enables organizations in many ways. The most important is that it provides the way within which the project team can work together. Moreover, it provides the way within which the project team can work with users and with stakeholders.

## 17.7 References

[1] Barry Boehm, "Anchoring the software process," *IEEE Software,* July 1996, pp. 73–82.

[2] Ivar Jacobson, Martin Griss, Patrik Jonsson, *Software Reuse: Architecture, Process and Organization for Business Success,* Reading, MA: Addison-Wesley, 1997.

[3] Walker Royce, *Software Project Management: A Unified Framework,* Reading, MA: Addison-Wesley, 1998.

# Appendix A

## Overview of the UML

### A.1 Introduction

The older branches of engineering have long found it useful to represent designs in drawings. From the early days of software, programmers have embodied their concepts in various kinds of drawings or, more broadly, in models. The software community needs a means of communicating its models, not only among project members but outward to stakeholders and across time to the developers of later generations. It needs a language, not only to communicate with others but to provide a setting in which individual developers can themselves think and analyze. Moreover, they can't keep it all in their heads for months and years. They have to record it on paper or electronically. The Unified Modeling Language (UML) is a standard modeling language for software—a language for visualizing, specifying, constructing, and documenting the artifacts of a software-intensive system. Basically, the UML enables the developers to visualize their work products in standardized blueprints or diagrams. For example, the characteristic symbols or icons used to capture requirements are an ellipse to represent a use case and a straw man to represent a user using the use case. Similarly, the central icon used in design is a rectangle to represent a class. These icons are just a graphical notation, that is, a syntax. In Section A.2, we give an overview of the graphical notation of the UML. Refer to [2] for an extensive reference and [3] for a user's guide. However, behind this graphical notation, the UML also specifies a meaning, that is, semantics. We give a brief overview of this semantics by providing short definitions of the central UML terms in Section A.3. For a treatment of the UML semantics we refer to [2] and [3] again. Another reference that treats both the notation and the semantics of the UML is its public documentation set [1], although it is more formal in nature. Other general references on the UML are [4] and [5].

### A.1.1 Vocabulary

The UML provides the developers with a vocabulary that includes three categories: things, relationships, and diagrams. We will mention them here simply to give you a feeling for the basic structure of the language.

There are four kinds of things: structural, behavioral, grouping, and annotational. There are seven primary kinds of *structural things:* use cases, classes, active classes, interfaces, components, collaborations, and nodes. There are two kinds of *behavioral things:* interactions and state machines. There are four kinds of *groupings:* packages, models, subsystems, and frameworks. And there is one primary kind of *annotational things:* note.

Within the second category, relationships, we find three further classifications: dependency, association, and generalization.

And in the third category, diagrams, UML provides nine types: use case, class, object, sequence, collaboration, statechart, activity, component, and deployment diagrams.

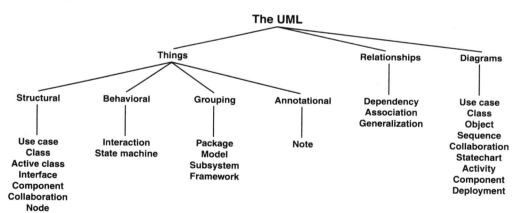

**Figure A.1.**  The vocabulary of the UML.

### A.1.2 Extensibility Mechanisms

The UML provides *extensibility mechanisms,* which enable its users to refine its syntax and semantics. The UML can thereby be tailored to a specific system, project, or development process if necessary. For an example of such a tailoring, refer to Appendix B.

The extensibility mechanisms include stereotypes, tagged values, and constraints. Stereotypes provide a means of defining new elements by extending and refining the semantics of already existing elements such as things and relationships (see Section A.1.1). Tagged values provide a means of defining new properties of already existing elements. Finally, constraints provide a means of imposing rules (such as consistency rules or business rules) on elements and their properties.

## A.2 Graphical Notation

The remaining figures in this appendix are from *The Unified Modeling Language User Guide* by Grady Booch, James Rumbaugh, and Ivar Jacobson [3].

### A.2.1 Structural Things

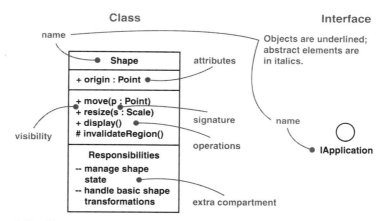

**Figure A.2.** Classes and interfaces.

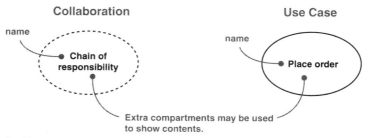

**Figure A.3.** Use cases and collaborations. (Note that names of, for example, use cases may be put outside the symbol if appropriate.)

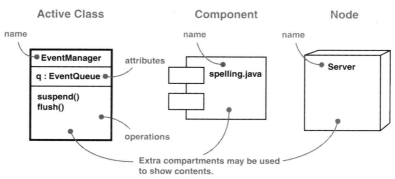

**Figure A.4.**  Active classes, components, and nodes.

## A.2.2  Behavioral Things

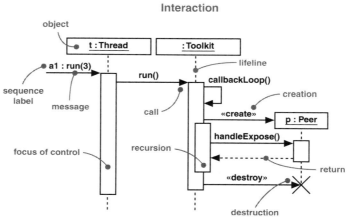

**Figure A.5.**  Interactions.

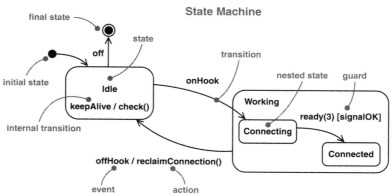

**Figure A.6.**  State machines.

### A.2.3 Grouping Things

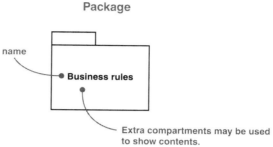

**Figure A.7.** Packages.

### A.2.4 Annotational Things

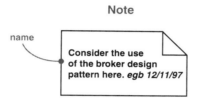

**Figure A.8.** Notes.

### A.2.5 Dependency Relationships

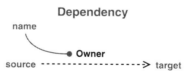

**Figure A.9.** Dependency relationships.

### A.2.6 Association Relationships

**Figure A.10.** Association relationships.

### A.2.7  Generalization Relationships

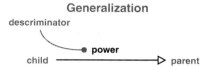

**Figure A.11.**  Generalization relationships.

### A.2.8  Extensibility Mechanisms

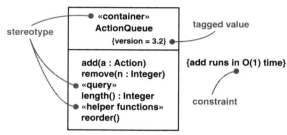

**Figure A.12.**  Extensibility mechanisms.

## A.3  Glossary of Terms

**abstract class**  A class that cannot be directly instantiated.

**action**  The specification of an executable statement that forms an abstraction of a computational procedure. An action results in a change in state and is realized by sending a message to an object or modifying a value in an attribute.

**action state**  A state that represents the execution of an atomic action, typically the invocation of an operation.

**activation**  The execution of an action.

**active class**  A class whose instances are active objects. See *process, task, thread.*

**active object**  An object that owns a process or thread and can initiate control activity.

**activity**  The state of exhibiting some behavior.

**activity diagram**  A diagram that shows the flow from activity to activity; activity diagrams address the dynamic view of a system. A special case of a state diagram in which all or most of the states are action states and in which all or most of the transitions are triggered by completion of actions in the source states.

**actor**  A coherent set of roles that users of use cases play when interacting with these use cases.

**adornment**  Detail from an element's specification added to its basic graphical notation.

**aggregate**  A class that represents the "whole" in an aggregation relationship.

**aggregation**  A special form of association that specifies a whole-part relationship between the aggregate (the whole) and a component part (the part).

**association**  A structural relationship that describes a set of links, where a link is a connection among objects; the semantic relationship between two or more classifiers that involves the connections among their instances.

**association class**  A modeling element that has both association and class properties. An association class can be seen as an association that also has class properties, or as a class that also has association properties.

**association end**  The endpoint of an association, which connects that association to a classifier.

**asynchronous action**  A request where the sending object does not pause to wait for results.

**attribute**  A named property of a classifier that describes a range of values that instances of the property may hold.

**binary association**  An association between two classes.

**binding**  The creation of an element from a template by supplying arguments for the parameters of the template.

**cardinality**  The number of elements in a set.

**class**  A description of a set of objects that share the same attributes, operations, relationships, and semantics.

**class diagram**  A diagram that shows a set of classes, interfaces, and collaborations and their relationships; class diagrams address the static design view of a system; a diagram that shows a collection of declarative (static) elements.

**classifier**  A mechanism that describes structural and behavioral features. Classifiers include interfaces, classes, datatypes, components, and nodes.

**client**  A classifier that requests service from another classifier.

**collaboration**  A society of classes, interfaces, and other elements that work together to provide some cooperative behavior that's bigger than the sum of all the elements; the specification of how an element, such as a use case or an operation, is realized by a set of classifiers and associations playing specific roles used in a specific way.

**collaboration diagram**  An interaction diagram that emphasizes the structural organization of the objects that send and receive messages; a diagram that shows interactions organized around instances and their links to each other.

**comment**  An annotation attached to an element or a collection of elements.

**component**  A physical and replaceable part of a system that conforms to and provides the realization of a set of interfaces.

**component diagram**  A diagram that shows a set of components and their relationships; component diagrams address the static component view of a system.

**composite**  A class that is related to one or more classes by a composition relationship.

**composition**  A form of aggregation with strong ownership and coincident lifetime as part of the whole; parts with nonfixed multiplicity may be created after the composite itself, but once created they live with it; such parts can also be explicitly removed before the death of the composite.

**concrete class**  A class that can be directly instantiated.

**concurrency**  The occurrence of two or more activities during the same time interval. Concurrency can be achieved by interleaving or simultaneously executing two or more threads.

**constraint**  An extension of the semantics of a UML element, allowing you to add new rules or modify existing ones.

**container**  An object that exists to contain other objects, and that provides operations to access or iterate over its contents.

**containment hierarchy**  A namespace hierarchy consisting of elements and the containment relationships that exist between them.

**context**  A set of related elements for a particular purpose, such as specifying an operation.

**datatype**  A type whose values have no identity. Datatypes include primitive built-in types (such as numbers and strings) as well as enumeration types (such as boolean).

**delegation**  The ability of an object to issue a message to another object in response to a message.

**dependency**  A semantic relationship between two things, in which a change to one thing (the independent thing) may affect the semantics of the other thing (the dependent thing).

**deployment diagram**  A diagram that shows a set of nodes and their relationships; a deployment diagram addresses the static deployment view of a system.

**diagram**  The graphical presentation of a set of elements, most often rendered as a connected graph of vertices (things) and arcs (relationships).

**distribution unit**  A set of objects or components that are allocated to a task or a processor as a group.

**element**  An atomic constituent of a model.

**event**  The specification of a significant occurrence that has a location in time and space; in the context of state machines, an event is an occurrence of a stimulus that can trigger a state transition.

**executable**  A program that may be run on a node.

**export**  In the context of packages, to make an element visible outside its enclosing namespace.

**extensibility mechanism**  One of three mechanisms (stereotypes, tagged values, and constraints) that can be used to extend the UML in controlled ways.

**façade**  A façade is a stereotyped package containing nothing but references to model elements owned by another package. It is used to provide a "public" view of some of the contents of a package.

**fire**  To execute a state transition.

**focus of control**  A symbol on a sequence diagram that shows the period of time during which an object is performing an action, either directly or through a subordinate operation.

**framework**  An architectural pattern that provides an extensible template for applications within a specific domain.

**generalization**  A specialization/generalization relationship, such that objects of the specialized element (the subtype) are substitutable for objects of the generalized element (the supertype).

**guard condition**  A condition that must be satisfied in order to enable an associated transition to fire.

**import**  In the context of packages, a dependency that shows the package whose classes may be referenced within given packages (including packages recursively embedded within it).

**inheritance**  The mechanism by which more specific elements incorporate the structure and behavior of more general elements.

**instance**  A concrete manifestation of an abstraction; an entity to which a set of operations can be applied and which has a state that stores the effects of the operations; a synonym for object.

**interaction**  A behavior that comprises a set of messages exchanged among a set of objects within a particular context to accomplish a specific purpose.

**interaction diagram**  A diagram that shows an interaction, consisting of a set of objects and their relationships, including the messages that may be dispatched among them; interaction diagrams address the dynamic view of a system; a generic term that applies to several types of diagrams that emphasize object interactions, including collaboration diagrams, sequence diagrams, and activity diagrams.

**interface**  A collection of operations that are used to specify a service of a class or a component.

**interface inheritance**  The inheritance of the interface of a more specific element; does not include inheritance of the implementation.

**lifeline**  See *object lifeline.*

**link**  A semantic connection among objects; an instance of an association.

**link end**  An instance of an association end.

**location**  The placement of a component on a node.

**message**  A specification of a communication between objects that conveys information with the expectation that activity will ensue; the receipt of a message instance is normally considered an instance of an event.

**metaclass**  A class whose instances are classes.

**method**  The implementation of an operation.

**model**  A semantically closed abstraction of a system.

**multiple classification**  A semantic variation of generalization in which an object may belong directly to more than one class.

**multiple inheritance**  A semantic variation of generalization in which a type may have more than one supertype.

**multiplicity**  A specification of the range of allowable cardinalities that a set may assume.

**n-ary association**  An association among *n* classes. When *n* equals two, the association is binary. See *binary association*.

**name**  What you call a thing, relationship, or diagram; a string used to identify an element.

**namespace**  A part of the model in which the names may be defined and used; within a namespace, each name has a unique meaning.

**node**  A physical element that exists at run time and that represents a computational resource, generally having at least some memory and often times processing capability.

**note**  A comment attached to an element or a collection of elements.

**object**  See *instance*.

**object constraint language (OCL)**  A formal language used to express side effect-free constraints.

**object diagram**  A diagram that shows a set of objects and their relationships at a point in time; object diagrams address the static design view or static process view of a system.

**object lifeline**  A line in a sequence diagram that represents the existence of an object over a period of time.

**operation**  The implementation of a service that can be requested from any object of the class so as to effect behavior.

**package**  A general purpose mechanism for organizing elements into groups.

**parameter**  The specification of a variable that can be changed, passed, or returned.

**persistent object**  An object that exists after the process or thread that created it has ceased to exist.

**postcondition**  A constraint that must be true at the completion of an operation.

**precondition**  A constraint that must be true when an operation is invoked.

**primitive type**  A predefined basic type, such as an integer or a string.

**process**  A heavy-weight flow of control that can execute concurrently with other processes.

**property**  A named value denoting a characteristic of an element.

**realization**  A semantic relationship between classifiers, wherein one classifier specifies a contract that another classifier guarantees to carry out.

**receive**  The handling of a message instance passed from a sender object.

**receiver**  The object handling a message instance passed from a sender object.

**relationship**  A semantic connection among elements.

**responsibility**  A contract or obligation of a type or class.

**role**  The specific behavior of an entity participating in a particular context.

**scenario**  A specific sequence of actions that illustrates behavior.

**scope**  The context that gives specific meaning to a name.

**send**  The passing of a message instance from a sender object to a receiver object.

**sender**  The object passing a message instance to a receiver object.

**sequence diagram**  An interaction diagram that emphasizes the time ordering of messages.

**signal**  The specification of an asynchronous stimulus communicated among instances.

**signature**  The name and parameters of a behavioral feature.

**single inheritance**  A semantic variation of generalization in which a type may have only one supertype.

**specification**  A textual statement of the syntax and semantics of a specific building block; a declarative description of what something is or does.

**state**  A condition or situation during the life of an object during which it satisfies some condition, performs some activity, or waits for some event.

**statechart diagram**  A diagram that shows a state machine; statechart diagrams address the dynamic view of a system.

**state machine**  A behavior that specifies the sequences of states an object goes through during its lifetime in response to events, together with its responses to those events.

**stereotype**  An extension of the vocabulary of the UML, allowing you to create new kinds of building blocks that are derived from existing ones but that are specific to your particular problem.

**stimulus**  An operation or a signal.

**subsystem**  A grouping of elements, of which some constitute a specification of the behavior offered by the other contained elements.

**subtype** In a generalization relationship, the specialization of another type, the supertype.

**supertype** In a generalization relationship, the generalization of another type, the subtype.

**supplier** A type, class, or component that provides services that can be invoked by others.

**swim lane** A partition on an activity diagram for organizing responsibilities for actions.

**synchronous action** A request where the sending object pauses to wait for results.

**system** A collection of subsystems organized to accomplish a specific purpose and described by a set of models, possibly from different viewpoints.

**tagged value** An extension of the properties of a UML element, allowing you to create new information in that element's specification.

**task** A single path of execution through a program, a dynamic model, or some other representation of control flow; a thread or a process.

**template** A parameterized element.

**thread** A light-weight flow of control that can execute concurrently with other threads in the same process.

**trace** A dependency that indicates a historical or process relationship between two elements that represent the same concept without specific rules for deriving one from the other.

**transient object** An object that exists only during the execution of the thread or process that created it.

**transition** A relationship between two states indicating that an object in the first state will perform certain specified actions and enter the second state when a specified event occurs and specified conditions are satisfied.

**type** A stereotype of class used to specify a domain of objects together with the operations (but not methods) applicable to the objects.

**usage** A dependency in which one element (the client) requires the presence of another element (the supplier) for its correct functioning or implementation.

**use case** A description of a set of sequence of actions, including variants, that a system performs that yields an observable result of value to a particular actor.

**use-case diagram** A diagram that shows a set of use cases and actors and their relationships; use case diagrams address the static use-case view of a system.

**view** A projection of a model, which is seen from a given perspective or vantage point and omits entities that are not relevant to this perspective.

**visibility** How a name can be seen and used by others.

## A.4 References

[1] OMG Unified Modeling Language Specification. Object Management Group, Framingham, MA, 1998. Internet: www.omg.org.

[2] James Rumbaugh, Ivar Jacobson, and Grady Booch, *The Unified Modeling Language Reference Manual,* Reading, MA: Addison-Wesley, 1998.

[3] Grady Booch, Jim Rumbaugh, and Ivar Jacobson, *The Unified Modeling Language User Guide,* Reading, MA: Addison-Wesley, 1998.

[4] Martin Fowler, *UML Distilled,* Reading, MA: Addison-Wesley, 1997.

[5] Hans-Erik Eriksson, Magnus Penker, *UML Toolkit,* New York: John Wiley & Sons, 1998.

# *Appendix B*

# The Unified Process-Specific Extensions of the UML

## B.1  Introduction

This appendix describes the extensions of the UML as required by the Unified Process. These extensions are described in terms of stereotypes and tagged values, that is, in terms of extension mechanisms provided by the UML, together with the graphical notation used to depict some of the stereotypes. The stereotypes that are not part of or differ from the standard extensions of the UML [1] and [2] are marked with an asterisk (*).

For an overview of the UML, refer to Appendix A.

## B.2  Stereotypes

| Stereotype | Applies to | Brief description |
|---|---|---|
| use-case model | model | A model containing actors and use cases and their relationships; a model describing what the system should do for its users and under what constraints. |
| use-case system | top-level package | The top-level package of the use-case model. («use-case system» is a subtype of «topLevelPackage») |

*continued*

| Stereotype | Applies to | Brief description |
|---|---|---|
| analysis model | model | An object model the purposes of which are (1) to describe the requirements precisely; (2) to structure them in a way that facilitates understanding them, preparing them, changing them, and, in general, maintaining them; and (3) to work as an essential input for shaping the system in design and implementation—including its architecture. |
| analysis system | top-level package | The top-level package of the analysis model. («analysis system» is a subtype of «topLevelPackage») |
| control class | class | A class within the analysis model that represents coordination, sequencing, and control of other objects, and that often is used to encapsulate control related to a specific use case. |
| entity class | class | A class within the analysis model used to model information that is long-lived and often persistent. |
| boundary class | class | A class within the analysis model used to model interaction between the system and its actors, that is, users and external systems. |
| use-case realization— analysis* | collaboration | A collaboration within the analysis model that describes how a specific use case is realized and performed, in terms of analysis classes (i.e., control, entity, and boundary classes) and their interacting analysis objects. |
| analysis package* | package | A package providing a means of organizing the artifacts of the analysis model in manageable pieces. An analysis package can consist of analysis classes (i.e., control, entity, and boundary classes), use-case realizations—analysis, and other analysis packages (recursively). |
| service package* | package | A variant of an analysis package that is used at a lower level of the analysis package hierarchy (in the analysis model) to structure the system according to the services it provides. |
| design model | model | An object model that describes the physical realization of use cases and focuses on how functional and non-functional requirements together with other constraints related to the implementation environment impacts the system under consideration. |

| Stereotype | Applies to | Brief description |
|---|---|---|
| design system | top-level subsystem | The top-level subsystem of the design model. («design system» is a subtype of «topLevelPackage») |
| design class* | class | A design class represents a "seamless abstraction" of a class or similar construct in the system's implementation. |
| use-case realization—design* | collaboration | A collaboration within the design model that describes how a specific use case is realized and performed, in terms of design subsystems and design classes and their objects. |
| design subsystem | subsystem | A subsystem providing a means of organizing the artifacts of the design model in manageable pieces. A design subsystem can consist of design classes, use-case realizations—design, interfaces, and other design subsystems (recursively). |
| service subsystem* | subsystem | A variant of a design subsystem that is used at a lower level of the design subsystem hierarchy (in the design model) to structure the system according to the services it provides. |
| deployment model* | model | An object model describing the physical distribution of the system in terms of how functionality is distributed among computational nodes. |
| implementation model | model | A model describing how elements in the design model, such as design classes, are implemented in terms of components such as source code files and executables. |
| implementation system | top-level subsystem | The top-level subsystem of the implementation model. («implementation system» is a subtype of «topLevelPackage») |
| implementation subsystem | subsystem | A subsystem providing a means of organizing the artifacts of the implementation model in manageable pieces. An implementation subsystem can consist of components, interfaces, and other implementation subsystems (recursively). |
| test model* | model | A model primarily describing how executable components (such as builds) in the implementation model are tested by integration and system tests. |
| test system* | top-level package | The top-level package of the test model. («test system» is a subtype of «topLevelPackage») |
| test component* | component | A component automating one or several test procedures or parts of them. |

## B.3 Tagged Values

| Tagged value | Applies to | Brief description |
|---|---|---|
| survey description | use-case model | A textual description intended to explain the use-case model as a whole. |
| flow of events | use case | A textual description of the sequence of actions of the use case. |
| special requirements | use case | A textual description that collects all requirements (e.g., nonfunctional requirements) on a use case that is not captured in its flow of events. |
| special requirements | analysis class (i.e., control, entity, and boundary class) | A textual description that collects nonfunctional requirements on an analysis class. Those are requirements that are specified in analysis but are better handled in design and implementation. |
| flow of events—analysis | use-case realization—analysis | A textual description that explains and complements the diagrams (and their labels) defining the use-case realization. |
| special requirements | use-case realization—analysis | A textual description that collects requirements, such as nonfunctional requirements, on a use-case realization. Those are requirements that are specified in analysis but are better handled in design and implementation. |
| implementation requirements | design class | A textual description that collects requirements, such as nonfunctional requirements, on a design class. Those are requirements that are specified in design but are better handled in implementation. |
| flow of events—design | use-case realization—design | A textual description that explains and complements the diagrams (and their labels) defining the use-case realization. |
| implementation requirements | use-case realization—design | A textual description that collects requirements, such as nonfunctional requirements, on a use-case realization. Those are requirements that are specified in design but are better handled in implementation. |

## B.4 Graphical Notation

Most of the stereotypes presented in Section B.2 do not impose any new graphical symbols of their own, and can instead be depicted by showing the stereotype key-words within guillemets (« and ») in the symbol that the stereotypes apply to.

However, the control, entity, and boundary classes impose new symbols that can be depicted as shown in Figure B.1.

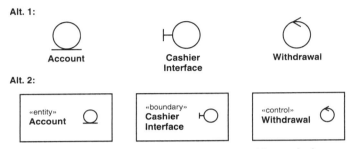

**Figure B.1** The three standard class stereotypes used in analysis.

## B.5 References

[1] OMG Unified Modeling Language Specification. Object Management Group, Framingham, MA, 1998. Internet: www.omg.org.

[2] James Rumbaugh, Ivar Jacobson, and Grady Booch, *Unified Modeling Language Reference Manual,* Reading, MA: Addison-Wesley, 1998.

# *Appendix C*

## General Glossary

### C.1 Introduction

This appendix collects and defines the general terms used to describe the Unified Process, except terms related to the UML, or terms related to the Unified Process-specific extensions of the UML. For brief definitions of these terms, refer instead to Appendix A, "Overview of the UML," and Appendix B, "The Unified Process-Specific Extensions of the UML."

### C.2 Terms

**abstraction** The essential characteristics of an entity that distinguish it from all other kinds of entities. An abstraction defines a boundary relative to the perspective of the viewer.

**activity** A tangible unit of work performed by a worker in a workflow that (1) implies a well-defined responsibility for the worker, (2) yields a well-defined result (a set of artifacts) based on a well-defined input (another set of artifacts), and (3) represents a unit of work with crisply defined boundaries that is likely to be referred to in a project plan when tasks are assigned to individuals. Can also be seen as the execution of an operation for a worker. See *artifact, worker.*

**analysis (workflow)**  A core workflow whose primary purpose is to analyze the requirements as described in requirements capture by refining and structuring them. The purpose of doing this is (1) to achieve a more precise understanding of the requirements, and (2) to achieve a description of the requirements that is easy to maintain and that help us give structure to the system as a whole—including its architecture.

**application system**  A system that offers a coherent set of use cases to an end user.

**application system suite**  A set of different application systems that are intended to work together to add value to some actors. See *application system*.

**application-general layer**  The part (the packages or subsystems) of a system that is reusable within a business or domain. This layer is used by the application-specific layer. See *application-specific layer*.

**application-specific layer**  The part (the packages or subsystems) of a system that is application-specific and not shared by other parts (subsystems). This layer uses the application-general layer. See *application-general layer*.

**architectural baseline**  The baseline released at the end of the elaboration phase, focusing on the system's architecture. See *elaboration, architecture, baseline*.

**architectural pattern**  A pattern that defines a certain structure or behavior, usually for the architectural view of a specific model. Examples are the *Layer, Client-Server, Three-Tier,* and the *Peer-to-Peer* patterns, each of which defines a certain structure to the deployment model and also suggests how components (functionality) should be allocated to its nodes. See *pattern, architectural view*.

**architectural prototype**  Primarily an executable prototype with a focus on the architectural view of the implementation model and the components manifesting the prototype. If an architectural prototype is evolutionary, it is likely to be baselined and manifested by a more complete but prototypical (or sketchy) architecture description (including all its architectural views). See *evolutionary prototype, baseline, architecture description, architectural view*.

**architectural style**  Systems that share a similar high-level structure and key mechanisms are said to have a similar architectural style.

**architectural view**  A projection into the structure and behavior of a specific model of a system, focusing on the architecturally significant aspects of that model.

**architectural view of the analysis model**  The view of a system's architecture encompassing the analysis classes, packages, and use-case realizations; a view that primarily addresses the refinement and structuring of the system requirements. The structure in this view is preserved as much as possible when we design and implement the system's architecture. See *architectural view of the design model, architectural view of the implementation model*.

**architectural view of the deployment model**  The view of a system's architecture encompassing the nodes that form the system's hardware topology upon which the system executes; a view that addresses the distribution, delivery, and installation of the parts that make up the physical system.

**architectural view of the design model**  The view of a system's architecture encompassing the design classes, subsystems, interfaces, and use-case realizations that form the vocabulary of the system's solution domain; a view that also encompasses the threads and processes that form the system's concurrency and synchronization mechanisms; a view that addresses the nonfunctional requirements, including the performance, scalability, and throughput requirements of a system.

**architectural view of the implementation model**  The view of a system's architecture encompassing the components that are used to assemble and release the physical system; a view that addresses the configuration management of the system's releases, made up of somewhat independent components that can be assembled in various ways to produce a running system.

**architectural view of the use-case model**  The view of a system's architecture encompassing the architecturally significant use cases.

**architecture**  The set of significant decisions about the organization of a software system, the selection of the structural elements and their interfaces by which the system is composed, together with their behavior as specified in the collaborations among those elements, the composition of these structural and behavioral elements into progressively larger subsystems, and the architectural style that guides this organization: these elements and their interfaces, their collaborations, and their composition. Software architecture is concerned not only with structure and behavior but with usage, functionality, performance, resilience, reuse, comprehensibility, economic and technology constraints and trade-offs, and aesthetic concerns.

**architecture description**  A description of the system's architecture that includes the architectural views of models. See *architectural view, architectural view of the use-case model, architectural view of the analysis model, architectural view of the design model, architectural view of the deployment model, architectural view of the implementation model.*

**architecture-centric**  In the context of the software life cycle, meaning that a system's architecture is used as a primary artifact for conceptualizing, constructing, managing, and evolving the system under development.

**artifact**  A tangible piece of information that (1) is created, changed, and used by workers when performing activities, (2) represents an area of responsibility, and (3) is likely to be put under separate version control. An artifact can be a model, a model element, or a document. See *worker, activity.*

**baseline**  A set of reviewed and approved artifacts that (1) represents an agreed basis for further evolution and development, and (2) can be changed only through a formal procedure such as configuration and change management. See *architectural baseline, configuration management.*

**build**  An executable version of the system, usually for a specific part of the system. Development proceeds through a succession of builds.

**business process**  The total set of activities needed to produce a result of perceived and measurable value to an individual customer of a business.

**cohesive**  The capability of an entity (such as a system, subsystem, or package) of holding its parts together.

**component-based development (CBD)**  The creation and deployment of software-intensive systems assembled from components, as well as the development and harvesting of such components.

**concurrency**  Occurs when several more or less independent jobs (threads, processes) share a single hardware device (processor) simultaneously.

**configuration management**  The task of defining and maintaining configurations and versions of artifacts. This includes baselining, version control, release control, status control, and storage control of the artifacts. See *artifact, baseline*.

**construction phase**  The third phase of the software life cycle, where the software is brought from an executable architectural baseline to the point where it is ready to be transitioned to the user community.

**contingency plan**  A plan describing how to act if certain risks materialize. See *risk*.

**core workflow**  One of the requirements, analysis, design, implementation, or test workflows. See *workflow, requirements*, *analysis*, *design*, *implementation*, *test*.

**customer**  The person, organization, or group of people that orders a system to be built, either from scratch or refined in successive versions. *Client* is a synonym.

**defect**  A system anomaly, such as a symptom of a software fault discovered during testing, or a problem discovered in a review meeting. See *test*.

**design (workflow)**  A core workflow whose primary purpose is to formulate models that focus on nonfunctional requirements and the solution domain, and that prepares for the implementation and test of the system.

**design mechanism**  A number of design classes, collaborations, or even subsystems in the design model that realize common requirements such as requirements on persistency, distribution, and performance.

**developer**  A worker participating in a core workflow such as a use-case engineer, component engineer, and so on. See *core workflow*.

**distribution**  Occurs when several more or less independent jobs (threads, processes) are distributed among different hardware devices (processors).

**domain area**  An area of knowledge or activity characterized by a set of concepts and terminology understood by practitioners in that area.

**elaboration phase**  The second phase of the software life cycle, where the architecture is defined.

**engineering artifact**  An artifact created in the core workflows. See *core workflow*.

**evolutionary prototype**  A prototype that is evolved and refined eventually to become a part of the system under development. A prototype that is likely to be subject to configuration management. See *configuration management.*

**exploratory prototype**  A prototype that is used only for exploratory purposes and that is thrown away when those purposes are fulfilled. A prototype that is not likely to be subject to configuration management. See *configuration management.*

**external release**  A release exposed to customers and users, external to the project and its members. See *release.*

**forward engineering**  In the context of software development, the transforming of a model into code through a mapping to a specific implementation language. See *reverse engineering.*

**framework**  A microarchitecture that provides an incomplete template for systems within a specific domain. Can, for example, be a subsystem built to be extended and/or reused.

**functional requirement**  A requirement that specifies an action that a system must be able to perform, without considering physical constraints; a requirement that specifies input/output behavior of a system. See *requirement.*

**green-field project**  An unprecedented project. See *project.*

**implementation (workflow)**  A core workflow whose essential purpose is to implement the system in terms of components, that is, source code, scripts, binaries, executables, and the like.

**inception phase**  The first phase of the software life cycle, where the seed idea for the development is brought up to the point of being sufficiently well founded to warrant entering into the elaboration phase.

**increment**  A small and manageable part of the system, usually the delta or difference between two successive builds. Each iteration will result in at least one (new) build and will thus add an increment to the system. However, a sequence of builds may be created within an iteration, each one adding a small increment to the system. Thus an iteration will add a larger increment to the system, possibly accumulated over several builds. See *build, iteration.*

**incremental integration**  In the context of the software life cycle, a process that involves the continuous integration of the system's architecture to produce releases, with each new release embodying incremental improvements over the other.

**integration**  See *system integration.*

**internal release**  A release not exposed to customers and users, but internally only to the project and its members. See *release.*

**iteration**  A distinct set of activities conducted according to a devoted (iteration) plan and evaluation criteria that results in a release, either internal or external. See *release, internal release, external release.*

**iteration plan**  A fine-grained plan for an iteration. A plan that states the expected cost in terms of time and resources, and the expected output in terms of artifacts, for the iteration. A plan that states who should do what within the iteration and in what order. This is done by allocating individuals to workers and by describing a detailed iteration workflow for the iteration. See *iteration, artifact, worker, iteration workflow.*

**iteration workflow**  A workflow representing an integration of the core workflows: requirements capture, analysis, design, implementation, and test. A description of an iteration that includes participating workers, the activities they perform, and the artifacts they produce. See *workflow.*

**iterative**  In the context of the software life cycle, a process that involves managing a stream of executable releases.

**layer**  A well-defined part of a system, defined by packages or subsystems. See *application-specific layer, application-general layer, middleware layer, system-software layer.*

**legacy system**  An existing system "inherited" by a project. Usually an old system that is created using more or less obsolete implementation technologies, but that nevertheless must be incorporated or reused—either as a whole or part—when a new system is built by the project. See *project.*

**life cycle**  See *software life cycle.*

**major milestone**  Milestone where management makes important business decisions. Each phase ends with a major milestone at which managers make crucial go/no-go decisions and decide on schedule, budget, and requirements on the project. We can think of the major milestones as synchronization points where a well-defined set of objectives is met, artifacts are completed, decisions are made to move or not into the next phase, and where the managerial and the technical realm conjuncts. See *phase, project, artifact.*

**management artifact**  An artifact that is not an engineering artifact, such as a project plan created by the project manager. See *engineering artifact.*

**mechanism**  A common solution to a common problem or requirement. Examples are design mechanisms providing persistency or distribution facilities in the design model.

**middleware layer**  A layer offering reusable building blocks (packages or subsystems) for utility frameworks and platform-independent services for things like distributed object computing and interoperability in heterogeneous environments. Examples are object request brokers, platform-neutral frameworks for creating graphical user interfaces, or, in general, products that realize generic design mechanisms. See *system-software layer, object request broker, user interface, design mechanism.*

**milestone**  See *major milestone, minor milestone.*

**minor milestone**  An intermediate milestone between two major milestones. Can, for example, be when an iteration ends, or when a build within an iteration is finalized. See *major milestone, iteration, build.*

**model-driven**  In the context of the software life cycle, meaning that the system developed is organized in terms of different models with specific purposes and whose elements relate (trace) to each other.

**nonfunctional requirement**  A requirement that specifies system properties, such as environmental and implementation constraints, performance, platform dependencies, maintainability, extensibility, and reliability. A requirement that specifies physical constraints on a functional requirement. See *requirement, performance requirement, reliability, functional requirement.*

**nontechnical risk**  A risk related to management artifacts and to aspects such as available resources (individuals), their competencies, or delivery dates. See *management artifact, risk, technical risk.*

**object request broker**  A mechanism for transparently marshaling and forwarding messages to objects distributed in heterogeneous environments. See *distribution.*

**pattern**  A common solution to a common problem in a given context.

**performance requirement**  A requirement that imposes behavioral conditions on functional requirements, such as the speed, throughput, response time, and memory usage. See *functional requirement, requirement.*

**phase**  The span of time between two major milestones of a development process. See *major milestone, inception, elaboration, construction, transition.*

**portability**  The degree to which a system, as running in a specific execution environment, easily can be changed to a system running in another execution environment.

**problem domain**  A domain area in which a problem is defined—usually a problem that is to be "solved" by a system. The problem domain is usually understood by the customer of the system. See *domain area, customer.*

**process**  See *business process, software development process, Unified Process.*

**project**  A development effort taking a system through a life cycle. See *software life cycle.*

**project plan**  A plan that outlines an overall "road map" for a project, covering the schedule, major milestone dates and criteria, and the breakdown of the phases into iterations. See *project, major milestone.*

**prototype**  See *user-interface prototype, architectural prototype, evolutionary prototype, exploratory prototype.*

**regression test**  The retesting of (parts of) a build that was previously tested in previous builds. Regression tests are primarily done to verify that "old functionality" in "old builds" still works when "new functionality" is added in "a new build." See *test, build.*

**release**  A relatively complete and consistent set of artifacts—possibly including a build—delivered to an internal or external user; the delivery of such a set. See *artifact, build.*

**reliability**  The ability of a system to behave correctly in its actual execution environment. Can, for example, be measured in terms of system availability, accuracy, mean time between failures, defects per 1,000 lines of code (KLOC), and defects per class.

**requirement**  A condition or capability to which a system must conform.

**requirements (workflow)**  A core workflow whose essential purpose is to aim development toward the right system. This is achieved by describing the system requirements well enough so that an agreement can be reached between the customer (including the users) and the system developers on what the system should and should not do. See *requirement, customer, developer.*

**reverse engineering**  In the context of software development, the transforming of code into a model through a mapping from a specific implementation language. See *forward engineering.*

**risk**  A project variable that endangers or eliminates success for a project. Risks can be that a project will experience undesirable events, such as schedule delays, cost overruns, or outright cancellation. See *technical risk, nontechnical risk.*

**risk-driven**  In the context of the software life cycle, meaning that each new release is focused on attacking and reducing the most significant risks to the success of the project.

**robustness**  An entity's, usually a system's, resilience to change.

**software development process**  A business process (or business use case) of a software development business. The total set of activities needed to transform a customer's requirements into a consistent set of artifacts representing a software product and—at a later point in time—to transform changes in those requirements into new versions of the software product. See *business process, Unified Process.*

**software life cycle**  A cycle over four phases in the following order: inception, elaboration, construction, transition. See *inception, elaboration, construction,* and *transition.*

**solution domain**  A domain area in which a solution (of a problem) is defined—usually a solution manifesting the design and implementation of a system. The solution domain is usually understood by the developers of the system. See *domain area, developer.*

**supplementary requirement** A generic requirement that cannot be connected to a particular use case or to a particular real-world class such as a domain or business entity class. See *requirement.*

**system integration** To compile and link part of a system's components together into one or more executables (which also are components).

**system-software layer** A layer containing the software for the computing and networking infrastructure, such as operating systems, database management systems, interface to specific hardware, and so on. This is the bottom layer in the hierarchy of layers. See *middleware layer.*

**systemware** See *system-software layer.*

**technical risk** A risk related to engineering artifacts and to aspects such as implementation technologies, architecture, or performance. See *engineering artifact, architecture, performance requirement, nontechnical risk.*

**test (workflow)** A core workflow whose essential purpose is to verify the result from implementation by testing each build, including both internal and intermediate builds, as well as final versions of the system to be released to external parties. See *implementation, build, internal release, external release.*

**test case** A specification of one case to test the system, including what to test with which input, result, and under which conditions.

**test evaluation** An evaluation of the results of the testing efforts such as test-case coverage, code coverage, and the status of defects. See *test, test case, defect.*

**test plan** A plan that describes the testing strategies, resources, and schedule.

**test procedure** A specification of how to perform one or several test cases or parts of them. See *test case.*

**transition phase** The fourth phase of the software life cycle, where the software is turned into the hands of the user community.

**Unified Modeling Language** A standard modeling language for software—a language for visualizing, specifying, constructing, and documenting the artifacts of a software-intensive system. A language used by the unified process. A language that enables developers to visualize their work products (artifacts) in standardized blueprints or diagrams. See *artifact, Unified Process, developer.*

**Unified Process** A software development process based on the unified modeling language that is iterative, architecture-centric, use-case driven, and risk-driven. A process that is organized around the four phases: inception, elaboration, construction, and transition, and that is further organized around the five core workflows: requirements capture, analysis, design, implementation, and test. A process that is described in terms of a business model, which in turn is structured in terms of three primitive building blocks: workers, activities, and artifacts. See *software development process, Unified Modeling Language, iterative, architecture-centric, use-case driven, risk-driven, phase, inception, elaboration,* *construction, transition, core workflow, requirements, analysis, design, imple-mentation, test, worker, activity, and artifact.*

**use-case driven**  In the context of the software life cycle, meaning that use cases are used as a primary artifact for establishing the desired behavior of the system and for communicating this behavior among the stakeholders of the system. Also meaning that use cases are the primary input to the analysis, design, imple-mentation, and test of the system, including the creation, verification, and vali-dation of the system's architecture. See *analysis, design, implementation, test, architecture.*

**use-case mass**  The complete set of actions of all use cases in a use-case model.

**user**  A human interacting with a system.

**user interface**  The interface through which a user interacts with a system.

**user-interface prototype**  Primarily an executable prototype of a user interface, but may at early stages of development consist of only paper drawings, screen bitmaps, and the like.

**view**  A projection of a model, which is seen from a given perspective or vantage point and omits entities that are not relevant to this perspective.

**visual modeling**  To visualize work products (artifacts) in standardized blueprints or diagrams. See *artifact.*

**waterfall approach**  A system development approach in which the development is arranged as a linear sequence of work in, for instance, the following order: requirements capture, analysis, design, implementation, and test. See *require-ments, analysis, design, implementation, test.*

**worker**  A position that can be assigned to a person or a team, requiring responsibili-ties and abilities such as performing certain activities and developing certain artifacts. See *activity, artifact.*

**workflow**  A realization of (a part of) a business use case. Can be described in terms of activity diagrams that include participating workers, the activities they per-form, and the artifacts they produce. See *core workflow, iteration workflow.*

# Index

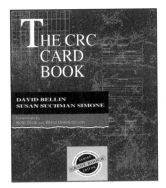

## The CRC Card Book

David Bellin and Susan Suchman Simone
Forewords by Kent Beck and Ward Cunningham
Addison-Wesley Object Technology Series

CRC Cards help project teams "act out" the various parts of a problem domain. The application developer can use these cards to define the Classes, the Relationships between classes, and the Collaboration between these classes (CRC) prior to beginning the object-oriented design of the application program. The case studies in this book are presented in the engaging style of a novella to demonstrate how personalities and organizational culture come into play when using the CRC technique. C++, Java, and Smalltalk experts provide implementation examples in each language.

0-201-89535-8 • Paperback • 320 Pages • ©1997

## Object Solutions

*Managing the Object-Oriented Project*
Grady Booch
Addison-Wesley Object Technology Series

*Object Solutions* is a direct outgrowth of Grady Booch's experience with object-oriented projects in development around the world. This book focuses on the development process, and is the perfect resource for developers and managers who want to implement object technologies for the first time or refine their existing object-oriented development practice. Drawing upon his knowledge of strategies used in both successful and unsuccessful projects, the author offers pragmatic advice for applying object technologies and controlling projects effectively.

0-8053-0594-7 • Paperback • 336 pages • ©1996

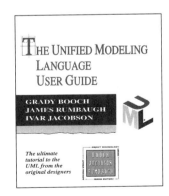

## The Unified Modeling Language User Guide

Grady Booch, Ivar Jacobson, and James Rumbaugh
Addison-Wesley Object Technology Series

*The Unified Modeling Language User Guide* is a two-color introduction to the core eighty percent of the Unified Modeling Language, approaching it in a layered fashion and showing the application of the UML to modeling problems across a wide variety of application domains. This landmark book is suitable for developers unfamiliar with the UML or modeling in general, and will also be useful to experienced developers who wish to learn how to apply the UML to advanced problems.

0-201-57168-4 • Hardcover • 512 pages • ©1999

### Surviving Object-Oriented Projects
*A Manager's Guide*
Alistair Cockburn
Addison-Wesley Object Technology Series

This book allows you to survive and ultimately succeed with an object-oriented project. Alistair Cockburn draws on his personal experience and extensive knowledge to provide the information that managers need to combat the unforeseen challenges that await them during project implementation. Independent of language or programming environment, the book supports its key points through short case studies taken from real object-oriented projects, and an appendix collects these guidelines and solutions into brief "crib sheets"—ideal for handy reference.

0-201-49834-0 • Paperback • 272 pages • ©1998

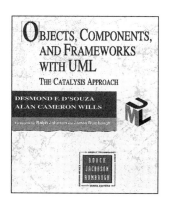

### Objects, Components, and Frameworks with UML
*The Catalysis^SM Approach*
Desmond Francis D'Souza and Alan Cameron Wills
Addison-Wesley Object Technology Series

Catalysis is a rapidly emerging UML-based method for component and framework-based development with objects. The authors describe a unique UML-based approach to precise specification of component interfaces using a type model, enabling precise external description of behavior without constraining implementations. This approach provides application developers and system architects with well-defined and reusable techniques that help them build open distributed object systems from components and frameworks.

0-201-31012-0 • Paperback • 816 pages • ©1999

### Real-Time UML
*Developing Efficient Objects for Embedded Systems*
Bruce Powel Douglass
Addison-Wesley Object Technology Series

The Unified Modeling Language is particularly suited to modeling real-time and embedded systems. *Real-Time UML* is the introduction that developers of real-time systems need to make the transition to object-oriented analysis and design with UML. The book covers the important features of the UML, and shows how to effectively use these features to model real-time systems. Special in-depth discussions of finite state machines, object identification strategies, and real-time design patterns are also included to help beginning and experienced developers alike.

0-201-32579-9 • Paperback • 400 pages • ©1998

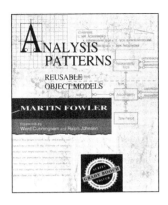

### Analysis Patterns
*Reusable Object Models*
Martin Fowler
Addison-Wesley Object Technology Series

Martin Fowler shares with you his wealth of object modeling experience and his keen eye for solving repeating problems and transforming the solutions into reusable models. *Analysis Patterns* provides a catalog of patterns that have emerged in a wide range of domains, including trading, measurement, accounting, and organizational relationships.

0-201-89542-0 • Hardcover • 384 pages • ©1997

### UML Distilled
*Applying the Standard Object Modeling Language*
Martin Fowler with Kendall Scott
Foreword by Grady Booch, Ivar Jacobson, and James Rumbaugh
Addison-Wesley Object Technology Series

Recipient of *Software Development* magazine's 1997 Productivity Award, this concise overview introduces you to the Unified Modeling Language, highlighting the key elements of its notation, semantics, and processes. Included is a brief explanation of UML's history, development, and rationale, as well as discussions on how UML can be integrated into the object-oriented development process. The book also profiles various modeling techniques associated with UML—use cases, CRC cards, design by contract, dynamic classification, interfaces, and abstract classes.

0-201-32563-2 • Paperback • 208 pages • ©1997

### Software Reuse
*Architecture, Process, and Organization for Business Success*
Ivar Jacobson, Martin Griss, and Patrik Jonsson
Addison-Wesley Object Technology Series

This book brings software engineers, designers, programmers, and their managers a giant step closer to a future in which object-oriented component-based software engineering is the norm. Jacobson, Griss, and Jonsson develop a coherent model and set of guidelines for ensuring success with large-scale, systematic, object-oriented reuse. Their framework, referred to as "Reuse-Driven Software Engineering Business" (Reuse Business) deals systematically with the key business process, architecture, and organization issues that hinder success with reuse.

0-201-92476-5 • Hardcover • 560 pages • ©1997

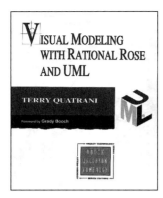

### Visual Modeling with Rational Rose and UML

Terry Quatrani
Addison-Wesley Object Technology Series

Terry Quatrani, the Rose Evangelist for Rational Software Corporation, teaches you visual modeling and the UML, enabling you to apply an iterative and incremental process to analysis and design. With the practical direction offered in this book, you will be able to specify, visualize, document, and create software solutions. Highlights of this book include an examination of system behavior from a use case approach; a discussion of the concepts and notations used for finding objects and classes; an introduction to the notation needed to create and document a system's architecture; and a review of the iteration planning process.

0-201-31016-3 • Paperback • 240 pages • ©1998

### Software Project Management

*A Unified Framework*
Walker Royce
Foreword by Barry Boehm
Addison-Wesley Object Technology Series

This book presents a new management framework uniquely suited to the complexities of modern software development. Walker Royce's pragmatic perspective exposes the shortcomings of many well-accepted management priorities and equips software professionals with state-of-the-art knowledge derived from his twenty years of successful from-the-trenches management experience. In short, the book provides the software industry with field-proven benchmarks for making tactical decisions and strategic choices that will enhance an organization's probability of success.

0-201-30958-0 • Hardcover • 448 pages • ©1998

### The Unified Modeling Language Reference Manual

James Rumbaugh, Ivar Jacobson, and Grady Booch
Addison-Wesley Object Technology Series

James Rumbaugh, Ivar Jacobson, and Grady Booch have created the definitive reference to the UML. This two-color book covers every aspect and detail of the UML and presents the modeling language in a useful reference format that serious software architects or programmers should have on their bookshelf. The book is organized by topic and designed for quick access. The authors also provide the necessary information to enable existing OMT, Booch, and OOSE notation users to make the transition to UML. The book provides an overview of the semantic foundation of the UML through a concise appendix.

0-201-30998-X • Hardcover with CD-ROM • 576 pages • ©1999

### Applying Use Cases
*A Practical Guide*
Geri Schneider and Jason P. Winters
Addison-Wesley Object Technology Series

*Applying Use Cases* provides a practical and clear introduction to developing use cases, demonstrating their use via a continuing case study. Using the Unified Software Development Process as a framework and the Unified Modeling Language as a notation, the authors lead the reader through applying use cases in the different phases of the process, focusing on where and how use cases are best applied. The book also offers insight into the common mistakes and pitfalls that can plague an object-oriented project.

0-201-30981-5 • Paperback • 208 pages • ©1998

### Enterprise Computing with Objects
*From Client/Server Environments to the Internet*
Yen-Ping Shan and Ralph H. Earle
Addison-Wesley Object Technology Series

This book helps you place rapidly evolving technologies—such as the Internet, the World Wide Web, distributed computing, object technology, and client/server systems—in their appropriate contexts when preparing for the development, deployment, and maintenance of information systems. The authors distinguish what is essential from what is incidental, while imparting a clear understanding of how the underlying technologies fit together. The book examines essential topics, including data persistence, security, performance, scalability, and development tools.

0-201-32566-7 • Paperback • 448 pages • ©1998

### The Object Constraint Language
*Precise Modeling with UML*
Jos Warmer and Anneke Kleppe
Addison-Wesley Object Technology Series

The Object Constraint Language is a new notational language, a subset of the Unified Modeling Language, that allows software developers to express a set of rules that govern very specific aspects of an object in object-oriented applications. With the OCL, developers are able to more easily express unique limitations and write the fine print that is often necessary in complex software designs. The authors' pragmatic approach and illustrative use of examples will help application developers to quickly get up to speed.

0-201-37940-6 • Paperback • 144 pages • ©1999

# Addison-Wesley Computer and Engineering Publishing Group

## Free
## Object Technology
## Poster

### Register this Book

Visit: **http://www.awl.com/cseng/register**

Register your book by entering this code: **csng-evwe-jzvj-mava**, and we will mail you a copy of this useful poster, highlighting key elements of UML Notation and key figures from this book—a handsome display to be referred to again and again. Offer available while poster supplies last.

### Contact Us via Email

**cepubprof@awl.com**
Ask general questions about our books.
Sign up for our electronic mailing lists.
Submit corrections for our web site.

**bexpress@awl.com**
Request an Addison-Wesley catalog.
Get answers to questions regarding
your order or our products.

**innovations@awl.com**
Request a current Innovations Newsletter.

**webmaster@awl.com**
Send comments about our web site.

**jcs@awl.com**
Submit a book proposal.
Send errata for an Addison-Wesley book.

**cepubpublicity@awl.com**
Request a review copy for a member of the media
interested in reviewing new Addison-Wesley titles.

We encourage you to patronize the many fine retailers
who stock Addison-Wesley titles. Visit our online directory
to find stores near you or visit our online store:
**http://store.awl.com/** or call **800-824-7799**.

**Addison Wesley Longman**
**Computer and Engineering Publishing Group**
**One Jacob Way, Reading, Massachusetts 01867 USA**
**TEL 781-944-3700 • FAX 781-942-3076**